Society
Old Testament Study

BOOK LIST 2000

edited by
Lester L. Grabbe

Sheffield Academic Press

Copyright © 2000 The Society for Old Testament Study

Published by Sheffield Academic Press Ltd
Mansion House
19 Kingfield Road
Sheffield S11 9AS
England

Printed on acid-free paper in Great Britain
by The Cromwell Press
Trowbridge, Wiltshire

British Library Cataloguing in Publication Data

A catalogue record for this book is available
from the British Library

ISBN 1-84127-161-6

Contents

One copy of the *Book List* is supplied free to all members of the Society.

Copies of this *Book List* may be obtained from Sheffield Academic Press, Mansion House, 19 Kingfield Road, Sheffield S11 9AS, England. Back Numbers of the *Book List* are also available from the address. The price of a single copy is £17.00 including postage. Payment should be made by cheque in sterling payable to Sheffield Academic Press, or by bank transfer to HSBC plc, 251 Fulwood Road, Broomhill, Sheffield, S10 3BE, Sort Code 40-41-18, Account No. 11090860 (please quote SWIFTCODE MIDLGB22 if ordering from overseas).
Customers in the USA should order from Scholars Press.

Review copies of books for the *Book List* should be sent to the Editor:

Professor George J. Brooke
Department of Religions and Theology
University of Manchester
Manchester M13 9PL
England

PREFACE

This is my eighth and last issue as editor of the *Book List*. It is appropriate that some account be given of my stewardship over this duty and privilege conferred by the Society for Old Testament Study. For the most significant innovation during my term of office, I can claim no credit (except that I supported the change when it was proposed): in 1998 the *Book List* became an annual issue of the *Journal for the Study of the Old Testament*. This not only saved the Society thousands of pounds in printing costs each year but more than doubled the circulation list at a stroke; it is also likely that the actual readership went up far more than just double, because of the superior distribution of *JSOT*. Other innovations have been the addition of two new indexes—an Index of Periodicals and Series (beginning in 1993) and an Index of Publishers (beginning in 1999)—and the inclusion of all names of authors/editors (where available) and not just their initials (1994).

When I became editor, the former editor (and my predecessor at Hull University) the late Professor R.N. Whybray wrote me a letter, pointing out in his forthright way that, when he was editor, about 400 books a year were being reviewed and suggesting that I should be seeking to emulate that good example. This did not happen my first year, but every year after that well over 400 books were reviewed; indeed, in two issues, more than 500 books were reviewed, not to mention almost 500 in the present issue. A total of more than 3650 volumes have been reviewed during these past eight years (an average of just under 460 per year). As always, this work of reviewing has fallen on the approximately one hundred volunteer reviewers of the Society who make the *Book List* possible. In addition, every year many reviewers have agreed to take books at short notice in order to keep the list as up to date as possible as we go to press. Without their help and generosity of spirit, the *Book List* would be impossible, and I am very grateful to every reviewer for the support they have given during my term of office.

In addition, a number of reviewers have kindly gone on to make book suggestions to me or to provide extra reviews or otherwise help in the editorial process. This year this number includes Professor A.G. Auld, Professor K.A. Kitchen, Professor M.A. Knibb, Professor W.G. Lambert, Professor A.R. Millard, Professor S.C. Reif, Dr W.G.E. Watson, and Dr N. Wyatt. Professor G.L. Prato kindly provided a list of books published in Italy.

It has become more and more difficult to get the *Book List* done the past few years because of other commitments. Thus, it is with a good deal of relief that I turn the task over to my successor, but I confess there is also a certain amount of sadness. I wish the new editor, Professor George J. Brooke of Manchester University, every success in the post.

The following abbreviations and symbols are employed in addition to those on the basic *JSOT* list:

Bible Bibliog.	=	*Bible Bibliography 1967–1973: Old Testament* (1974)
B.L.	=	*Book List*
Decade	=	*A Decade of Bible Bibliography 1957–66* (1967)
Eleven Years	=	*Eleven Years of Bible Bibliography 1946–56* (1957)
LXX	=	Septuagint/Old Greek Version
MT	=	Masoretic Text

Lester L. Grabbe
University of Hull

Dedicated to the memory of
Professor Robert P. Carroll
(1941–2000)

President 1999

1. GENERAL

ALEXANDER, PATRICK, H., *et al.* (eds.), *The SBL Handbook of Style: For Ancient Near Eastern, Biblical and Early Christian Studies* (Peabody, MA; Hendrickson, 1999), pp. xiv + 280. $24.95. ISBN 1-56563-487-X.

This gives the standard usage for much publication in biblical scholarship in North America. The SBL style is also used by journals other than the *Journal of Biblical Literature* and also by a number of publishing houses. Although it does not cover every question about language usage and the like (the *Chicago Manual of Style* is widely used for this), this is the most comprehensive set of guidelines yet issued for SBL publications. One can only wish that a greater convergence between publishers in the English-speaking world could be encouraged.

ED.

AWERS, J.-M. and A. WÉNIN (eds.), *Lectures et relectures de la Bible: Festschrift P.-M. Bogaert* (BETL, 144; Leuven: Peeters/University Press, 1999), pp. xlii + 482. BEF 3000. ISBN (Peeters) 90-429-0745-2; (University) 90-6186-957-9.

There is much of interest in this largely francophone tribute to Professor Pierre-Maurice Bogaert on the occasion of his 65th birthday and retirement in September 1999. In the first section (Old Testament: Hebrew Bible), M. Vervenne writes (in English) on Exod. 14.20 MT–LXX, asking whether the variation is textual or literary; F. Goncalvès returns to the discussion of the priority of 2 Kgs 18.13–20.19 and Isaiah 36–39; J. Vermeylen discusses the literary and B. Renaud the textual history of Jer. 31.3-34; and J. Lust (in English) defines the meaning of 'exile' and 'diaspora' with particular reference to Ezekiel. In the next and longest section (Old Testament: Greek and Latin Bible), A. Schenker explores the LXX choice of *diathēkē* for *bryt* in the light of both Ptolemaic law and the book of Genesis; J.W. Wevers writes (in English) on the Balaam narrative according to the LXX and R. Hanhart (in German) on the Greek and Old Latin textual history of 1 and 2 Ezra in their relation to each other: J.-Cl. Heilewyck discusses the Latin version of Esther in the first Bible of Alcalá, M. Gilbert the Greek and Latin additions to Ecclesiasticus 24, and M. Harl Zeph. 3.7b-13 according to the LXX and in early Christian tradition, while A. Wénin asks, following a recent book by Kabasele Mukenge, 'Is there a "Book of Baruch"?' 'Intertestament et Nouveau Testament' are represented by E. Tov (in English) on the papyrus fragments found in the Judaean desert, J.-M. van Cangh on the evolution of the tradition of the Last Supper (Mk 14.22-26 and parallels), C. Focant on the ultimate 'why?' prayer: the re-reading of Psalm 22 (21) in Mark's passion narrative, and J.-M. Sevrin on 'what the eye has not seen': 1 Cor. 2.9 as word of Jesus. The final section on the reception of the biblical text is made up of S. Brock (in English) on the *Ruaḥ Elohim* of Gen. 1.2 and its reception history in the Syriac tradition; G. Dorival on Origen, witness to the texts of the OT; F. Dolbeau on a middle Latin poem on the OT: *Liber prefigurationum Christi et ecclesiae*; J-.P. Delville on OT citations in the Vita of Julienne de Cornillon; and A. Kabasele Mukenge on the re-reading of Gen. 4.1-16 in the African context.

A.G. AULD

BALL, EDWARD (ed.), *In Search of True Wisdom: Essays in Old Testament Interpretation in Honour of Ronald E. Clements* (JSOTSup, 300; Sheffield: Sheffield Academic Press, 1999), pp. 292. £50.00/$85.00. ISBN 1-84127-071-7; ISSN 0309-0787.

The articles in this *Festschrift* for a long-serving member and past president of the Society are the following: history-interpretation-theology: issues in biblical religion (A.G. Auld), canon and OT interpretation (J. Barton), literary criticism in the service of OT interpretation (W.H. Bellinger, Jr), the role of OT theology in OT interpretation (W. Brueggemann), hermeneutical reflections on C. Vitringa, eighteenth-century interpreter of Isaiah (B.S. Childs), the concept of *imitatio Dei* in the OT (E.W. Davies), frontiers and borders in the OT (J.W. Rogerson), God's covenant partners—Noah, Abraham, Moses (R. Rendtorff), the theology of Exodus (G.I. Davies), the wisdom of characters and readers in 2 Samuel and 1 Kings (I.W. Provan), themes and theology in Isaiah (H.G.M. Williamson), the centre of the Book of the Twelve (K. Jeppesen), interpreting Nahum as Christian Scripture (Ball), wisdom, suffering and the freedom of God in Job (R.N. Whybray), reading Lamentations without primary reference to its original historical setting (P.M. Joyce), theology and hermeneutics in Chronicles (R.J. Coggins). There is an introductory appreciation of the honoree by R. Mason, but no bibliography of publications (but see his *Old Testament Prophecy*, pp. 265-70 [*B.L.* 1997, pp. 88-89]).

ED.

BEGG, CHRISTOPHER T. (ed.), *Old Testament Abstracts*, vol. 22 (Washington, DC: Catholic Biblical Association of America, 1999), pp. iv + 600. $26.00 p.a. ISSN 0364-8591.

OTA, unchanged from previous years, needs no description here. It continues to provide a very valuable resource for scholars.

M.A. KNIBB

BETZ, HANS DIETER, DON S. BROWNING, BERND JANOWSKI and EBERHARD JÜNGEL (eds.), *Religion in Geschichte und Gegenwart: Handwörterbuch für Theologie und Religionswissenschaft*, Band 2. C-E (4th completely revised edn; Tübingen: J.C.B. Mohr [Paul Siebeck], 1999), pp. lx + 1850 cols. DM 398. ISBN 3-16-146942–9.

Major entries of potential interest include the following: *Calvin; Cambridge*

Universität; Canonical Approach, I. *Altes Testament* (C.R. Seitz); *Cargokulte; Chaldäa/Chaldäer; Chaos*, II. *Biblisch* (B. Janowski); *Charisma* (nothing on the OT); *Chronikbücher* (S. Japhet); *Chronologie*, II. *Altes Testament and antikes Judentum* (H. Lichtenberger); *Creatio ex nihilo*, I. *Biblisch* (W. Gross); *Dalman* (S. Timm), *Damaskus; Damaskusschrift* (H. Lichtenberger); *Dämonen/Geister; Dan* (M.M. Niemann); *Daniel/Danielbuch* (J.J. Collins); *Daniel-Zusätze* (K. Koch); *David*, I. *Biblisch*, II. *Altes Testament* (W. Dietrich), III. *Judentum* (M. Jacobs, J. Dan); *Debora/ Deboralied; Dekalog*, I. *Altes Testament* (E. Otto), *II. Judentum* (G. Reeg); *Dekonstruktion/Dekonstruktivismus*; *Delitzsch, Franz; Demetrios (Fragmente); Demut*, II. *Altes Testament*, III. *Judentum: Deuterojesaja* (H.-J. Hermisson); *Deuteronomistisches Geschichtswerk* (W. Dietrich); *Deuteronomium* (E. Otto), *Deutscher Verein zur Erforschung Palästinas* (U. Hübner); *Deutsches Evangelisches Institut für Altertumswissenschaft des Heiligen Landes* (U. Hübner); *Devarim Rabba; Diaspora*, I. *Religionsgeschichtlich*, II. *Jüdische Diaspora* (T. Rajak, J. Dan); *Diaspora-Aufstände; Disputation*, I. *Judentum; Divination/Mantik; Dor* (E. Noort); *Dothan; Dura-Europos; Durkheim; Ebal; Ebla* (A. Archi); *Edom* (W. Dietrich); *Ehe*, II. *Altes Testament* (E. Otto); *Ehescheidung*, I. *Altes Testament und Judentum* (B. Jackson); *Eichhorn; Eichrodt; Eid*, II. *Altes Testament*, III. *Judentum; Eigenschaften Gottes*, II. *Biblisch*, IV. *Judentum; Eigentum*, II. *Altes Testament* (F.S. Frick); *Eissfeldt; Ekha Rabba(ti); Ekron, Ekstase* (I.M. Lewis); *El* (P. Xella); *Elephantine; Elephantine-Urkunden* (B. Lang); *Eli/Eliden; Elia; Elia-Apokalypse; Elias Levita; Elisa; Engedi; Engel*, II. *Altes Testament* (M. Görg), IX, *Judentum; Enthusiasmus*, II. *Biblisch* (J.D.G. Dunn); *Epigraphik*, I. *Semitische Inschriften* (J. Renz); *Epiphanie*, III. *Altes Testament; Erlassjahr/Jobeljahr; Erlösung/Soteriologie*, IV. *Altes Testament* (H. Spieckermann); *Erstlinge; Erwählung*, I. *Altes Testament* (K. Seybold); II. *Biblisch; Erziehung*, IV. *Biblisch*, 1. *Altes Testament* (M.V. Fox); *Erzväter/ Erzväter-/Erzelternüberliegerung; Eschatologie*, II. *Altes Testament* (H.P. Müller), VIII. *Judentum; Esra/Esrabücher; Essener/Therapeuten* (H. Lichtenberger); *Ester Rabba; Esther/Estherbuch* (A. Meinhold); *Esther-Zusätze; Ethik*. III, *Biblisch*, 1. *Altes Testament* (E. Otto), IV. *Judentum; Ethnologie (Völkerkunde)*, III. *Altes Testament* (B. Lang); *Euhemerismus; Eupolemos; Evans-Pritchard; Ewiges Leben*, III. *Altes Testament* (B. Janowski), VII. *Judentum; Exegese*, IV. *Biblisch*, 1. *Altes Testament* (T. Seidl), VII. *Biblische Szenen in der Kunst*, VIII. *Judentum; Exile*, II. *Judentum* (J. Dan); *Exkommunikation*, IV. *Judentum* (A. Oppenheimer); *Exodus* (M. Görg); *Exodusüberlieferung* (E. Zenger), *Ezechiel, (Tragiker); Ezechiel, Apokryphon; Ezechiel/Ezechielbuch* (F.-L. Hossfeld), *Eziongeber* (E.A. Knauf).

L.L. GRABBE

BIRD, PHYLLIS A., *Missing Persons and Mistaken Identities: Women and Gender in Ancient Israel* (Minneapolis: Fortress Press, 1997), pp. xi + 291. $20.00. ISBN 0-8008-3128-5.

B. was one of the first of the feminist interpreters of the Bible to emerge in the wave of feminist interpretation that began just over twenty years ago. Feminist scholarship has moved a great distance since she first began writing, and B. has moved only part of the way along the paths taken by some of her successors. In that sense she may be classed among the more conservative feminist biblical interpreters. Her work reflects her training in traditional methods of interpretation. This collection of essays spans a long period and covers many subjects. Some of them are clearly aimed at readers from church-based backgrounds, while others are in a more scholarly mould. Specific texts and narratives are dealt with, as well as more general questions, such as biblical authority. The content is thoughtful and for the most part well argued. The collection also provides illustrations of how B.'s thinking has moved on, for example, in the inclusion of three essays on the key text, Genesis 1–3, and her later emphasis on gender as well as feminist issues. There have been many developments in feminist biblical scholarship generally since B. started writing, and her comments on these developments are also well worth reading.

C. SMITH

BRIEND, JACQUES and MICHEL QUESNEL (eds.), *Supplément au Dictionnaire de la Bible*, vol. 13, fasc. 72 (*Sophonie-Sumer*) (Paris: Letouzey & Ané, 1999), cols. 1-256. FF 341. ISBN (series) 2-7063-0161-9; (vol. 13) 2-7063-0214-3.

This fascicle has the following articles: *Sophonie* (J. Asurmende), *Succession de David* (Cl. Wiéner), *Sukkot* (R. Martin-Achard on the OT); however, about 70 per cent of this fascicle is taken up with the entry *Sumer*, and a good deal of the entry (on literature, religion, and Sumer and the Semites) remains for the next fascicle. Of particular interest will be the sections on Sumerian laws (R. Westbrook) and schools and education (D. Charpin).

L.L. GRABBE

CHAZAN, ROBERT, WILLIAM W. HALLO and LAWRENCE H. SCHIFFMAN (eds.), *Ki Baruch Hu; Ancient Near Eastern, Biblical and Judaic Studies in Honor of Baruch A. Levine* (Winona Lake, IN: Eisenbrauns, 1999), pp. xxxiv + 675 (Eng.) + 52* (Heb). $59.50. ISBN 1-57506-030-2.

The honoree, editor of *Israel Exploration Journal* and professor at New York University is blessed by not only seven articles on the section on 'Ancient Near East', twenty under 'Bible', and nine under 'Judaica'—these in English apart from one in French—plus five articles in Hebrew (three on ancient history, one on Dead Sea Scrolls, one on rabbinica), but also by a 'brief biography', an 'appreciation' and a 'personal reflection' by the editors, and a bibliography of his writings. No-one who knows him would begrudge this erudite and gracious man a fulsome *Festschrift*, reflecting his wide interests, notably in epigraphy and biblical literature, and of which a decent percentage (higher than in many *Festschriften*) is worthy of his own standards. It also contains a nice balance of eminent and less eminent scholars (and as usual, eminence is not the index of quality!). There are indexes, and abstracts of the Hebrew essays.

P.R. DAVIES

DEMPSTER, MURRAY W., BYRON D. KLAUS and DOUGLAS PETERSEN, *The Globalization of Pentecostalism: A Religion Made to Travel* (foreword by Russell P. Spittler; Carlisle: Paternoster; Oxford: Regnum, 1999), pp. xvii + 406. £14.99. ISBN 0-870345-29-0.

This collection of articles attempts to map contemporary Pentecostalism in its various aspects. This includes an article on biblical studies in the Pentecostal tradition and its changing approaches, such as the embracing of critical methods (at least in certain forms and by certain practitioners). A Pentecostal anthropologist discusses 're-historicizing' Pentecostal experiences. In this context, G.T. Sheppard looks at postmodern hermeneutics and its implications for the politics of scriptural interpretation.

ED.

DYK, J.W., P.J. VAN MIDDEN, K. SPRONK and G.J. VENEMA (eds.), *Amsterdamse cahiers voor exegese van de Bijbel en zijn tradities 17: Hosea* (Maastricht: Shaker Publishing, 1999), pp. viii + 130. ISBN 90-423-0077-9.

The 'new look' and partly new title of the *Amsterdamse cahiers* mark a change of editors and a move to a regular thematic focus (usually on a biblical book), as well as a greater emphasis on the history of the interpretation and influence of the Bible. This issue contains the following articles (all in Dutch): E. Bons and E. Eynikel, 'Hosea in Recent Exegetical Publications' (since 1990); K. Spronk, 'Hosea as Part of the Book of the Twelve Prophets' (a survey of research since K. Budde); R. Abma, 'Neglect the Torah, Leave the Land! Concepts of Biblical Theology in the Book of Hosea' (with a special study of 8.1-7); K.A. Deurloo, 'Solidarity and Compassion' (on 2.21 as the climax of a message of judgment and restoration); J.W. Dyk, 'Exile or Forgiveness? Hosea 1.6 in the Light of Verbal Valency Patterns' (a linguistic case for translating the final phrase 'But I shall surely forgive them' [cf. Ps. 99.8]); C. den Hartog, 'The Divine Name in Hosea 1.9—A Commentary on Exodus 3.14?' (The rendering 'I shall not be for you' is preferred); J. Siebert-Hommes, '"For Otherwise—I Shall Strip her Naked": The Use of the Marriage Metaphor in the Book of Hosea' (it is no longer acceptable as it stands: the metaphoric woman must be given back her voice); and D. Monschouwer, 'Hosea in the Liturgy' (on readings selected for Christian and Jewish worship). There are also English summaries of the articles and (another new feature) an index of biblical passages.

G.I. DAVIES

EXUM, J. CHERYL (ed.), *Biblical Interpretation: A Journal of Contemporary Approaches*, vol. 7 (Leiden: E.J. Brill, 1999), pp. vi + 468. Nlg 164.00/$94.00 p.a. ISSN 0927-2569.

Volume 7.1 consists of K.L. Noll, 'Looking on the Bright Side of Israel's History: Is There a Pedagogical Value in a Theological Presentation of History?', Thomas R. Hatina, 'Intertextuality and Historical Criticism in New Testament Studies: Is There a Relationship', Judith E. McKinlay, 'Rahab: A Hero/ine?', Francis

Landy, 'Strategies of Concentration and Diffusion in Isaiah 6', Ehud Ben Zvi, 'Wrongdoers, Wrongdoing and Righting Wrongs in Micah 2', and James W. Watts, 'Reader Identification and Alienation in the Legal Rhetoric of the Pentateuch'. Volume 7.2 contains S. Brent Plate and Edna M. Rodríguez Mangual, 'The Gift that Stops Giving. Hélène Cixous's "Gift" and the Shunammite Woman', F. Scott Spencer, 'Out of Mind, Out of Voice: Slave-Girls and Prophetic Daughters in Luke–Acts', Archie C.C. Lee, 'Returning to China: Biblical Interpretation in Postcolonial Hong Kong', with a series of responses to Lee's article by Philip Chia, 'Postcolonization and Recolonization: A Response to Archie Lee's "Biblical Interpretation in Postcolonial Hong Kong" ', Kwok Pui-Lan, 'Response to Archie Lee's Paper on "Biblical Interpretation in Postcolonial Hong Kong"', Katharine Doob Sakenfeld, 'Social Location in the Hebrew Bible and Hong Kong' and Fernando F. Segovia, 'Postcolonialism and Comparative Analysis in Biblical Studies', with a final response from Archie Lee, 'Identity, Reading Strategy and Doing Theology'; there are also some book reviews. Volume 7.3 is made up of four pieces: F.W. Dobbs-Allsopp, 'Rethinking Historical Criticism', Barbara Green, 'Great Trek and Long Walk: Readings of a Biblical Symbol'; André LaCocque, 'The Different Versions of Esther', and Tom Thatcher, 'Early Christianities and the Synoptic Eclipse: Problems in Situating the Gospel of Thomas'. When I first read volume 7.3 I thought the Dobbs-Allsopp and Green papers were among the finest pieces I had read so far in the short history of *Biblical Interpretation*. I still think so and hope that they get anthologized in due course when the first decade of the journal's existence is celebrated in a Reader. Volume 7.4 consists of Walter Houston, 'The King's Preferential Option for the Poor: Rhetoric, Ideology and Ethics in Psalm 72', Siegfried Risse, '"Wir Sind die jungen Raben!" Zur Auslegungsgeschichte von Ps 137, 9b', Mark K. George, 'Constructing Identity in 1 Samuel 17', and Deryn Guest, 'Hiding behind the Naked Women in Lamentations: A Recriminative Response'. There are also twenty pages of reviews. I think *Biblical Interpretation* has now fully established itself as the outstanding journal creation of the 1990s in Biblical Studies. Well done, Brill and Exum.

R.P. CARROLL

FRADES, EDUARDO (ed.), *ITER: Revista de Teología*, Vol. 9.2 (= issue 18) (Caracas: Publicaciones del Instituto de Teología para Religiosos, 1998), pp. 168. Bs 5000/$14.00 p.a. ISSN 0798-1236.

FRADES, EDUARDO (ed.), *ITER: Revista de Teologia*, vol. 10.1 (= issue 19) (Caracas: Publicaciones del Instituto de Teología para Religiosos, 1999), pp. 143. Bs 5000/$14.00 p.a. ISSN 0798-1236.

This is a semi-annual Spanish-language journal of the Instituto de Teología para Religiosos of Venezuela. Both issues have a 'turn of the millennium' aim, with specific themes. Issue 18 consists of 'words to the (Plenary) Council (of Venezuela)', with two articles on theology and exegesis and one on evangelizing the contemporary city. The article on 'exegesis and theology' by F. is wide-ranging and refers a good deal to works of European and North American biblical scholarship. Issue 19 is devoted to the theme of 'God the Father', with articles on the question of 'what shall we do with God in the 21st century?', images of God in the OT and NT (creator, liberator, lawgiver, father/mother), 'woman created in God's image and likeness', and several articles relating to the NT.

ED.

GILLINGHAM, SUSAN E., *One Bible, Many Voices: Different Approaches to Biblical Studies* (Grand Rapids, MI: Eerdmans, 1999 [1998]), pp. xx + 280. $19.00. ISBN 0-8028-4661-0.

This is the American edition of the book reviewed in *B.L.* 1999 (p. 12).

ED.

GÖRG, MANFRED (ed.), *Biblische Notizen: Beiträge zur exegetischen Diskussion*, vol. 98 (Munich: Institut für Biblische Exegese, 1999), pp. 99. DM 7.00. ISSN 0178-2967.

The 'Notizen' related to the OT are by M. Gerhards on 2 Kings 30, M. Görg on ancient Egyptian religion in the West, B. Gosse on Genesis 3, H.-G. von Mutius on a non-masoretic edition of Genesis 1–3, A.L.H.M. van Wieringen on Isaiah 36–37 and W. Zwickel on Hebrew plant names as place names. Also, P. Guillaume shows how the NT miracles seem to repeat those by Elijah and Elisha. The 'Abhandlungen' are by J. Becker on the 'I am' formula, B.R. Knipping on the formula '(A) land flowing with milk and honey', C. Spaller on current hermeneutics and B.M. Zapff on the twelve prophets. The contributions are in English, French and German, printed in whatever font the authors submitted on diskette.

W.G.E. WATSON

GROSS, WALTER, *Studien zur Priesterschrift und zu alttestamentlichen Gottesbildern* (Stuttgarter Biblische Aufsatzbände [SBAB], 30; Stuttgart: Katholisches Bibelwerk, 1999), pp. 336. EUR 40.39/DM 79.00/AS 577/SwF 75.00. ISBN 3-460-06301-7.

The fifteen studies included in this volume have all been published previously and are here reproduced in their original form. Five of them are devoted to major theological themes of the Priestly Document: two examine the idea of the image of God in humankind and another the concept of *creatio ex nihilo*. The study of the pillar of fire and cloud in Exodus 13–14 engages with the most recent Pentateuchal source criticism as also does that arguing that P looks forward to the restoration of an Israelite state with a restored monarchy. Six studies consider negative aspects of the biblical experience of God: the prophet's commission to harden the heart of Israel (Isa. 6), God's role in creating darkness and woe (Isa. 45.7), God as the enemy of the individual (Ps. 88) and the all-encompassing presence of God (Ps. 139). Biblical assertions concerning the hiddenness of God's presence are reviewed against contemporary theological dilemmas as also is biblical language concerning God's anger. The four concluding studies address wider issues: the contrast between transient laws and an unchanging decalogue, the dangers of establishing a false contrast between prophet and institution, the idea of the people of God in Isaiah and Yahweh and the religion of non-Israelite peoples. The centrality of many of these topics will undoubtedly ensure a welcome for their wider availability.

R.E. CLEMENTS

HARLAND, P.J. and C.T.R. HAYWARD (eds.), *New Heaven and New Earth: Prophecy and the Millennium: Essays in Honour of Anthony Gelston* (VTSup, 77; Leiden–Boston–Cologne: E.J. Brill, 1999), pp. xii + 332. Nlg 160.00/$89.00. ISBN 90-04-10841-6; ISSN 0083-5889.

This is a worthy tribute to a long-time member and former president of the Society. The subjects are learning to be a true prophet—the story of Balaam (R.W.L. Moberly), Balaam's prophecies as interpreted by Philo and the Pentateuchal targums (Hayward), the future in Chronicles (P.B. Dirksen), Job 19.25-27 (J. Gibson), the question of an eschatalogical dimension in the Psalter (M.A. Vincent), reading Isa. 11.6-9 today (R.E. Clements), Isa. 51.6 reconsidered (H.G.M. Williamson), the value of human life in Ezekiel (Harland), three Christian commentators on Hosea (G.I. Davies), Qohelet, Hosea and attribution in biblical literature (S. Weeks), social background of Malachi (J.W. Rogerson), apocalyptic, revelation and early Jewish wisdom literature (J.K. Aitken), Judith, Tobit, Ahiqar and history (A.R. Millard), Canaanite Mot in prophecy and apocalypse (J.F. Healey), the vision in Revelation 4–5 (M. Barker), apocalyptic material in Aphrahat and Šubḥalmaran (D.J. Lane), the 'Demonstration on Love' by Aphrahat translated (L. Stuckenbruck), Cotton Mather's obsession with Jewish conversion (L. Munk), George Stanley Faber and anti-pope prophecy (S.W. Gilley). There is an appreciation of the honoree (by A. Loads) and a bibliography of his writings.

ED.

HAYES, JOHN H. (ed.), *Dictionary of Biblical Interpretation* (Nashville: Abingdon Press, 1999), pp. (vol. 1) xlix + 653; (vol. 2) xxxii + 675. $195.00. ISBN 0-687-05531-8.

This is one of the best dictionaries of biblical interpretation I have had the pleasure of coming across, and since I received it for review in June (1999) I have almost daily dipped into it for general reading and regularly this semester (October–January) have consulted it for assistance in writing some new lecture notes. It is a most user-friendly publication and a first-rate hermeneutical tool for the active biblical scholar. I could imagine it also becoming an invaluable *vade mecum* for students, thinking ministers of religion and interested parties desperately seeking information on either a topic or a name in the long, complex and convoluted history of biblical interpretation. So, at the outset of this review, I would like to congratulate and thank the general editor, John Hayes, for overseeing, contributing to and editing a magnificent two-volume work.

By way of general description of the *Dictionary*'s shape, format, intention and performance I can do no better than cite from H.'s incredibly brief one-page Preface

(p. xlix): 'The *Dictionary of Biblical Interpretation* is intended as an aid and guide to the lengthy and complex history of biblical interpretation. Three types of articles appear in the work. (1) The history of the interpretation of all the canonical and deuterocanonical books as well as some other ancient non-biblical books is covered in one category of articles. In these essays emphasis has been placed on the last two centuries of interpretation. (2) The biographies and contributions of numerous interpreters are discussed in a second category of articles. In this area, no work can be exhaustive and difference of opinion would result in varying lists of entries. As the work goes to press, the editor could even suggest some modifications in the present entry list. The primary principles of selection were the importance of the person's contributions and the representative character of his or her work. A few living and still active persons born before 1930 have been included; here obviously the greatest uneasiness about selection exists. (3) A third category of articles includes review and discussion of various methods and movements that have influenced and informed the reading and study of Scripture.' I share the editor's 'greatest uneasiness' at exactly the same point and would, for instance, have included the work of Joseph Blenkinsopp (currently President of this illustrious Society) in the *Dictionary*. If there are other more glaring omissions in the volumes then I must admit to having missed them completely myself. Otherwise, from Abbo of Fleury to Zwingli this is a magnificently comprehensive pair of volumes embracing the huge landscape of the history of biblical interpretation and I am unwilling to nit-pick about its imagined weaknesses.

Space does not permit a close analysis of its many strengths, but I will admit to being very impressed by the contents of its wide range of articles especially on such topics as 'Afrocentric Biblical Interpretation', 'Armenian Biblical Interpretation', 'Art, The Bible and', 'Asian Biblical Interpretation', 'Hermeneutics', 'Ideological Criticism', 'Jeremiah', 'Liberation Theologies', 'Poetry, Hebrew Bible', 'Post-Colonial Biblical Interpretations', 'Prophecy and Prophets, Hebrew Bible', 'Qohelet', 'Quadriga', 'Quranic and Islamic Interpretation of Biblical Materials', 'Religionsgeschichtliche Schule', 'Septuagint', 'Sociology and Hebrew Bible Studies', 'Structuralism and Deconstruction' and other articles far too numerous to list here. A very impressive collection of material indeed. Although it lacks an entry for 'Fundamentalism' it is arguable that such a topic is incorporated into the piece on 'Evangelical Biblical Interpretation', in which case that article ought to have been much longer. But I am quibbling now. A magnificent piece of work and I recommend it most highly.

R.P. CARROLL

HERRMANN, WOLFRAM, *Von Gott und den Göttern: Gesammelte Aufsätze zum Alten Testament* (BZAW, 259; Berlin and New York: de Gruyter, 1999), pp. vii + 236, including 5 plates. DM 168.00. ISBN 3-11-015115-4; ISSN 0934-2575.

The opportunity to produce a volume of collected essays has enabled the author to publish German versions of essays that appeared in English in the *Dictionary of Deities and Demons in the Bible* and also to publish corrected versions of essays that were subjected to censorship when they appeared in the former East Germany. In other cases, articles have been revised in the light of critical reviews. Two main interests are apparent in the essays. First, many deal with *religionsgeschichtlich* matters, drawing upon Egyptian, Ugaritic and Phoenician sources. Noteworthy here are the articles on Ashtarte, the royal inscriptions from Byblos, Baal Zebub, and El and Baal. Several deal with specific texts, including Eccl. 3.14, Lev. 19.18 and Ps. 68.5. The other interest centres upon hermeneutical and practical problems of biblical interpretation, including articles on the problem of death in ancient Israel, the estimation of women in the OT and early Jewish literature, and the question of how the OT can be interpreted and preached given the vast difference between the contemporary and the biblical situations.

J.W. ROGERSON

HUPPER, WILLIAM G. (ed), *An Index to English Periodical Literature on the Old Testament and Ancient Near Eastern Studies*, VIII (American Theological Library Association, 21; Lanham, MD: Scarecrow Press; Folkestone, Kent: Shelwing, 1999), pp. xix + 484. $65.00/£61.75. ISBN 0-8108-3645-9.

Two additional journals have been added to those covered in vol. VII (*B.L.* 1999, p. 14): *Irish Church Quarterly* and *Zeitschrift für Religions- und Geistesgeschichte* (of which only the English language articles are, of course, drawn). The division and subdivision of the contents into about 200 categories (e.g. 'Studies on Hell'; 'Studies on the Old Testament in Music'; 'Studies on Hebrew Phrases in the Qumran Literature') can be extremely useful: a forthcoming author and subject index (to the entire set) will certainly enhance the value of this collection.

P.R. DAVIES

IZRE'EL, SHLOMO (gen. ed.), *Israel Oriental Studies*; RUBIN, URI and DAVID J. WASSERSTEIN (eds.), *Israel Oriental Studies. XVII. Dhimmis and Others: Jews and Christians and the World of Classical Islam* (Winona Lake, IN: Eisenbrauns, 1997), pp. 256. $49.50. ISBN 1-57506-026-4; ISSN 0334-4401.

IZRE'EL, SHLOMO (gen. ed.), *Israel Oriental Studies*; IZRE'EL, SHLOMO, ITAMAR SINGER and RAN ZADOK (eds.), *Israel Oriental Studies. XVIII. Past Links: Studies in the Languages and Cultures of the Ancient Near East* (Winona Lake, IN: Eisenbrauns, 1998), pp. 459. $59.50. ISBN 1-57506-035-3; ISSN 0334-4401.

Vol. 17 mainly concerns Jews in the Islamic world. Two articles in particular should be noted: one in French is on three falsehoods about Abraham in the Islamic interpretative tradition; the second is a study of the section of Shahrastani's *Book of Religions and Sects* on the Maġariyya, whose identity is still debated but who may tell us much about the author's working methods. Vol. 18 is dedicated to Anson Rainey and is divided into three sections. The section on linguistics and philology includes articles on the history of the alphabet in the second millennium BCE (W. Röllig), the use of the *qtl* and *yqtl* forms in Ugaritic, new readings from the Kirta Epic, books in the Late Bronze age in the Levant (A. Millard), mood and

modality in Classical Hebrew, notes on Hebrew etymology, a Ramasses topograph-
ical list, and a number of articles on aspects of Akkadian (including the Amarna
letters). The section on geography, history, culture has articles on Borsippa, Mari,
place names in the Sinuhe narrative, a diviner family in the Emar texts, the Ugaritic
references to Amuru, Yaman and the Aegean isles, references to 'Canaan' in Late
Bronze archives (R.S. Hess), Ashtaroth in the Amarna period, and Abdi-Ashirta in
the Amarna letters. A final section gives reviews on Sivan's Ugaritic grammar (*B.L.*
1999, pp. 202-203), *Dictionary of Northwest Semitic* (*B.L.* 1995, pp. 176-77), *Egyptian Evidence for the Semitic Languages* (*B.L.* 1995, p. 176), and the *Dictionary of
Deities and Demons* (*B.L.* 1996, pp. 21-22; 1999, p. 19).

L.L. GRABBE

JEEVES, MALCOLM A. and R.J. BERRY, *Science, Life, and Christian Belief: A Sur-
vey of Contemporary Issues* (Leicester: Inter-Varsity; Grand Rapids, MI: Baker
Book House, 1998), pp. 305. £16.99/$19.99. ISBN (Inter-Varsity) 0-85-111-459-8;
(Baker) 0-8010-2226-6.

Those readers who think they can predict the conclusions of this book may be in
for a surprise. Granted, the overall conclusions are predictable: true science is in har-
mony with 'biblical' (i.e., a particular Christian interpretation of the Bible) truth. A
somewhat apologetic attempt to distance 'scientific Creationism' from biblical fundamentalism is unconvincing (though the authors are right that the Scopes trial represented more than just religious concerns but also a good deal of political and social
Angst). What may be shocking to many of the intended readership (especially considering the publishers) is that the authors accept and argue for evolution as a scientific fact: 'Our unease with the way that God has chosen to work is no scientific
ground for criticizing evolution… There are proper scientific debates about the evolutionary process, but…they are not about whether or not evolution has occurred at
all' (p. 128).

ED.

KILIAN, RUDOLF, *Studien zu alttestamentlichen Texten und Situationen* (ed. Wolf-
gang Werner and Jürgen Werlitz; Stuttgarter Biblische Aufsatzbände [SBAB], 28;
Stuttgart: Katholisches Bibelwerk, 1999), pp. 299. EUR 40.39/DM 79.00/AS 577/
SwF 68.00. ISBN 3-460-06281-9.

This collection in honour of K.'s 65th birthday includes essays (all previously
published, all in German) on the following subjects: apodictic and casuistic law in
light of Egyptian analogies, Gen. 1.2 and the primaeval gods of Hermopolis, prophetic call reports, Psalm 22 and the priestly oracle of salvation, the birth of Im-
manuel from the virgin, Isaiah's commission to harden the hearts, the human in the
ethical decalogue, reflections on OT eschatology, reflections on Isa. 40.3-5, reflections on Israel's critique of myth, the sacrifice of Isaac in light of historical-critical
exegesis, notes on the Yahwist in the Abraham narrative, observations on the meaning of *mišpāṭ* in the first Servant Song, a re-reading of Psalm 110, God in history—

history and the divine image—reflections on the OT experience of God. The volume
concludes with a select bibliography of the honoree.

ED.

KORSMEYER, JERRY D., *Evolution and Eden: Balancing Original Sin and Contemporary Science* (New York and Mahwah, NJ: Paulist Press, 1999), pp. iv + 170.
$14.95. ISBN 0-8091-3815-8.

K. reconsiders Genesis 1–11 and the Catholic doctrine of original sin in light of
the scientific paradigm of human evolution and glibly suggests that the problem is
'a sin of origin'. The First Adam was not to blame nor was Eve framed, since the
account of the fall in the opening chapters of the Bible is mythological and ahistorical. A literal interpretation of creation is set aside in favour of a theory that proposes human evolution from bacteria over several billion years. Oddly maintaining
the idea of sin in the guise of 'alienation'—that is the self-conscious defiance of the
divine call of individuals to transcend natural instincts and cultural formation—K.
maintains that love and creativity are consistent with the gospels and clues from the
universe. A work that covers such a large interdisciplinary topic in so few pages
inevitably glosses over nuances and even whole topics. How, for example, would
K. work into his scheme the neo-Darwinian theory of the selfish gene as expounded
above all by Richard Dawkins? The use of official Catholic pronouncements on
original sin is tactical, but just as post-Vatican II interpretations represent a range of
views, so also there is no single evolutionary theory.

T.H. LIM

LANGE, ARMIN, HERMANN LICHTENBERGER and DIETHARD RÖMHELD (eds.),
*Mythos im Alten Testament und seiner Umwelt: Festschrift für Hans-Peter Müller
zum 65. Geburtstag* (BZAW, 278; Berlin–New York: de Gruyter, 1999), pp. viii +
309. DM 178.00. ISBN 3-11-014653-3; ISSN 0934-2575.

Under the section on the Ancient Orient are the motive for the flood in the Atra-
ḥasis myth (R. Albertz), poetology and the tense system in Babylonian ritual texts
(M. Dietrich), astral Molek (K. Koch), some passages in KTU 1.19 I 2-19 (J. Hoftijzer). Under OT: demythologizing or re-vision of myth as a challenge to religious
language instruction in OT teaching (D. Baltzer), the myth 'Reed Sea' (H.-J. Fabry),
epistemical modalities in the book of Proverbs (E. Jenni), the inter-relationship between charisma and institution (B. Kedar-Kopfstein), conflict between new year
festival and exodus in Psalm 81 (O. Loretz), the 'welfare' of the land in Jer. 29.5-7
(K.-F. Pohlmann), poetry and arithmetic in Psalms 29 and 137 (S. Segert, in English), Babel and the confusion of tongues in Gen. 11.1-9 (P. Swiggers, in English),
Gen. 1.2 as the key to an older version of the priestly creation narrative (P. Weimar),
the classification of myths (C. Westermann), the mythical in Psalms 84–85 (E. Zenger). Under Early Judaism is just one essay: *R⁽ᵉ⁾šāfîm*: from gods to birds of prey
(E. Lipiński, in English). Under Philosophical-Hermeneutical Implications is one

essay: authority, personality and myth: approaches with examples from theology and literature (J.V. Sandberger). There is a bibliography of the honoree's publications.

ED.

LEVINE, BARUCH A., PHILIP J. KING, JOSEPH NAVEH and EPHRAIM STERN (eds.), *Frank Moore Cross Volume* (Eretz Israel, 26; Jerusalem: Israel Exploration Society, 1999), pp. ‎יב‎ + 191 (Heb.); xxiv + 235 (Eng., Fr., Ger.). $90.00. ISBN 965-221-037-4.

Fifty-six essays honour Cross, ranging over his interests. Several treat early documents: P.K. McCarter (two inscribed arrowheads), A. Lemaire (18 Hebrew seals and 4 sealings), Y. Shoham (the hoard of bullae from the City of David), R. Younker (an Ammonite seal), W. Röllig (seventh-century Aramaic handwriting), A. Millard (owners and users of Hebrew seals). Early texts are studied by Z. Begin and A. Gruschka (Lachish Letter 4), W.G. Dever (Khirbet el-Qôm and Asherah), E. Lipiński (Early Aramaic land ownership deeds), J. Naveh (Dan and Ekron inscriptions), A. Kloner and H. Eshel (a seventh-century ostracon from Mareshah). A.F. Rainey (the Taanach Letters). J. Strugnell argues for an originally long version of Ahiqar. The Dead Sea Scrolls naturally feature: M. Broshi explains 4Q247 'A Commentary on the Apocalypse of Weeks'; S.W. Crawford contrasts Jubilees' authoritative status at Qumran with the positions of the Temple Scroll and the Rewritten Pentateuch; E. Puech re-examines 4Q246, the 'Son of God' fragment: E. Qimron offers various improved readings; L.H. Schiffman discusses 'The House of the Laver in the Temple Scroll'; J.C. VanderKam relates the number of David's songs in 11QPs to the solar calendar. J.A. Fitzmyer demonstrates 'The So-called Aramaic Divorce Text from Wadi Seiyal' is rather a statement by a divorced wife renouncing claims on her former husband. Other essays include I. Finkelstein on 'The Beginning of the State in Israel and Judah', J. Huehnergard's case for *nabî'* as a passive form and J. Hoftijzer's for 'your throne belongs to God' or 'your mighty throne' in Ps. 45.7; D.N. Freedman and J.R. Lindbom give examples to show that LXX Jeremiah is often shorter than MT by haplography and E. Tov characterizes the additional passages in the long version. H. Tadmor examines the careers of the Assyrian officers of 2 Kgs 18.17; B. Halpern identifies *yad derek* (1 Sam. 4.13) with the protecting wall outside some Iron Age city gates; M. Haran and M. Cogan separately consider the 'books of the chronicles of the Kings of Israel and Judah'; A. Mazar describes Beth-Shean's Iron Age II chronology and meagre ostraca, while L.E. Stager links the Garden of Eden with gardens in Jerusalem and iconography in the Dome of the Rock, and D.E. Fleming equates ancient bull figurines with senior gods, calves with junior gods. As usual, *Eretz Israel* offers a rich menu.

A.R. MILLARD

LANG, BERNHARD, *et al.* (eds.), *Internationale Zeitschriftenschau für Bibelwissenschaft und Grenzgebiete*, vol. 44 (Düsseldorf: Patmos, 1997–98 [1999]), pp. xv + 475. DM 158.00. ISBN 3-491-66044-0; ISSN 0074-9745.

Bernhard Lang and his more than 30 associates have assembled notes on 2754 articles and books from 1997–98 in familiar format, among them an endorsement of the new larger format of the *Book List*. With L.'s move to Scotland, St Andrews University has joined Paderborn as sponsor of this far-reaching 'international review'.

A.G. AULD

LOADER, JAMES ALFRED and HANS VOLKER KIEWELER (eds.), *Vielseitigkeit des Alten Testaments: Festschrift für Georg Sauer zum 70. Geburtstag* (Wiener alttestamentliche Studien, 1; Frankfurt–Bern–New York: Lang, 1999), pp. 475. SwF 43.00. ISBN 3-631-32557-6; ISSN 1435-9618.

The first two sections of this collection are on the 'thematic circles of a Viennese Old Testament scholar'. Except as noted, the essays are in German. The first thematic circle is on language, literature and religion: the introduction of formal and familiar speech in the OT by *'mr 'l-* and *'mr l-* (J. Ernst), Jacob's 'way' to his brother's countenance (G. Fischer), the lightening of the burden motif in Exod. 18.13-27 and the model of 'management by concentration and delegation' (G. Harkam), the succession of Solomon (H.J. Stoebe), the question of acrostics in Deutero-Isaiah (K. Seybold), the contribution of Psalm 47 to the theme of Israel and the nations (J. Hausmann), the OT understanding of punishment (R.P. Knierim), the characteristics and meaning of OT wisdom literature (J. Marböck), aspects of religious critique in the OT (W. Schmidt), Naomi and Job, Schubert and Mahler—reflections on an OT contribution in Vienna (Loader). The second thematic circle covers archaeology, history and environment: method and theory in biblical archaeology (C. Scheepers [Eng.]), Mount Gerizim (H.V. Kieweler), Canaanites in early Israel (V. Fritz), Rachel's tomb (Z. Kallai [Eng.]). Naamah the Ammonite, wife of Solomon (A. Malamat [Heb.]), ecological and natural background conditions for the origin of agriculture as the basis of cultural development in the Near East (R. Albert, M. Kohler-Schneider, M. Watzka), Pharaonic population movements under Ramesses II (H. Goedicke [Eng.]), Babylonian and Assyrian edicts of economic redress and their impact on the OT (H. Olivier [Eng.]), on the Edomite mountain fastnesses in south Jordan (M. Lindner, J. Zangenberg). The final section is on theology and preaching and includes articles on Pseudo-Cyprian, the ethic of the law according to Luther, Luther and Johannes Eck on the Jews, the OT in the reformation programme of illustrations, speaking about God in an age of nihilism. A bibliography of the honoree is given, but there are no indexes.

ED.

MACARTHUR, JOHN (author and general editor), *The MacArthur Topical Bible* (Nashville: Word Publishing, 1999), pp. vii + 1592. $34.99. ISBN 0-8499-1572-4.

This dictionary of subjects from Bible and life is based, like *The MacArthur Study Bible* (1997, but not noted in the *B.L.*), on the New King James Version. Each subject is illustrated by relevant biblical material: most often a relevant verse cited in full; but occasionally a whole passage, such as Gen. 32.3-23 to illustrate Prudence. The subjects which conclude G are Grace, Grass, Greed and Grief; and so the user is left without Guidance. The first sub-section on Amos is Prophesied of Israel's salvation, and cites Amos 9.11-15 in full; and the remainder cite only 1.1 and the visions; the fourth and fifth of these encompass all of 8.1-14 and 9.1-10. Users of the *B.L.* will do well to stay loyal to their existing concordances and dictionaries.

A.G. AULD

MIES, FRANÇOISE (ed.), *Bible et littérature: L'homme et Dieu mis en intrigue* (Le Livre et le rouleau, 6; Brussels: Editions Lessius, 1999; distributed by Cerf, Paris), pp. 175. N.P. ISBN 2-87299-083-8.

The first in a series of volumes generated by conferences held at the University of Notre Dame de la Paix of Namur, this collection of papers aims at a selective exploration of the literary character of the Bible. Under the title 'Is there a narrator in the Bible?', J.-P. Sonnet contrasts the omniscient narrator behind the scenes in Genesis with the subjective and perspectival narrative modes in the modern novel (Flaubert, James, Proust *et al.*). A consideration of Thomas Mann's *Joseph und seine Brüder* then leads back to the biblical story of Joseph who, by virtue of his extraordinary knowledge (dreams, clairvoyance, prophetic powers) ends by expressing the point of view of the super-narrator in the last chapter of Genesis (Gen. 50.19). The last of the five papers, by André Wénin, reflects on Mann's imaginative retelling of the drama of Joseph and Potiphar's wife (Gen. 39.7-20) compared with the treatment of the episode in the midrash. He notes how Mann humanizes the anonymous wife, tied to a eunuch in a loveless marriage. Maurice Gilbert takes us through the 22 quatrains of Victor Hugo's poem *Booz endormi* line by line noting the remarkable transformation which the book of Ruth undergoes at the poet's hands. Then, after a summary of the book of Job, the editor writes on Elie Wiesel's reading of the book in the light of rabbinic commentary and the Holocaust. Surprisingly, Wiesel did not read the biblical book until after the war, but then went on to publish two commentaries. The author ends with a discussion of Wiesel's cantata *ani maamin* 'I believe' featuring the trial of God *d'après* the book of Job.

J. BLENKINSOPP

MIES, FRANÇOISE (ed.), *Toute la sagesse du monde: Hommage à Maurice Gilbert, SJ* (Le livre et le rouleau, 7; Brussels: Editions Lessius, 1999; distributed by Cerf, Paris), pp. 767. N.P. ISBN 2-87299-083-6.

This *Festschrift* has 33 contributions (all in French), covering many aspects of wisdom, ancient and modern. Only those more relevant to the OT will be noted here. The first section (Wisdom, Man and God) has an essay on the epilogue of Job (J. Lévêque) and one on the partnership of God and Abraham from a midrashic perspective (A. Singer). In Wisdom, the Individual and Society are essays on education in ethics according to Proverbs (J. Trublet), wisdom and bioethics (J. Duchêne), the management of time in Judaism (A. Guigui), the idealized story of Solomon (P. Gibert), Father Lagrange—an exegete in quest of God (B. Montagnes), 1 Kgs 3.16-28 (J.-N. Aletti), the brevity of human life in Psalm 90 (B. Costacurta), the art of living in hope—a dialogue with the First Testament (A. Wénin), is it wise to hope in God?—the enigma of Job (Mies). The section on Wisdom, Intelligence and Love has an article on Hebrew and Greek thought (N. Rigaux), and Wisdom, Words and the Future of Words has a poem on the Song of Songs ('How to Voice Desire': X. Dijon). There are also articles on wisdom and the Holy Spirit in Luke–Acts, wisdom as the meeting place between Christianity and Chinese religion, wisdom and human rights, wisdom and the judge, the lame wisdom of Kirkegaard, science and wisdom, readings of John 3, 4, 9, between style and argument in 1 Cor. 1.18-31, Hesiod at the origins of Greek wisdom, the books of wisdom in the work of Olivier Messiaen. The honoree gives a final address entitled, 'Do not interrupt the music' (a quotation from Ben Sira 32.2). There is a bibliography of his works and an index of biblical passages.

ED.

MORELAND, J.P. and JOHN MARK REYNOLDS (eds.), *Three Views on Creation and Evolution* (Counterpoints; Grand Rapids, MI: Zondervan, 1999), pp. 296. $17.00. ISBN 0-310-22017-3.

This forms an inner-evangelical debate about creation and how it is to be related to contemporary scientific views. The views expressed are (1) 'young earth creationism', (2) 'progressive (old earth) creationism', and (3) 'fully gifted creation' (theistic evolution). Each position statement is responded to, and a final postscript gives some concluding reflections. In many ways, this may seem like—and is—a very parochial discussion, yet the fact that evangelicals are seriously willing to tolerate and even argue for theistic evolution is an encouraging sign.

L.L. GRABBE

MÜLLER, GERHARD (ed.), *Theologische Realenzyklopädie (TRE): Band 29: Religionspsychologie—Samaritaner* (Berlin and New York: de Gruyter, 1998), pp. 798. DM 394.00. ISBN 3-11-016127-3.

MÜLLER, GERHARD (ed.), *Theologische Realenzyklopädie (TRE): Band 30: Samuel —Seele* (Berlin and New York: de Gruyter, 1999), pp. 913. DM 394.00. ISBN 3-11-016243-1.

Articles of potential interest in vol. 29 include *Religionsvergehen, II. AT und Judentum, Reuchlin, Reue, I. Biblisch* (Jörg Jeremias), *Richterbuch* (U. Becker), *Ritualmord* (including the Aqedah), *Ritus, II. Judentum* (including the OT), *Rosenstock-Huessy, Rosenzweig, Rowley* (P.W. Coxon), *Ruth* (A. Meinhold), *Saadja Gaon, Sabbat, Sabbatai Zwi, Sacharja/Sacharjabuch* (I. Willi-Plein), *Sadduzäer, Saint Andrews Universität, Salbung, II. Altes Testament, Salomo/Salomoschriften, Salomo ben Isaak (Raschi), Samaria, Samaritaner* (F. Dexinger). Vol. 30 has the following: *Samuel, Samuel- und Königsbücher* (W. Dietrich), *Sanhedrin/Synhedrium, Sartre, Saul, Schamanismus, Schicksal, II. Altes Testament und Judentum, Schöpfer/Schöpfung* (R.G. Kratz/H. Spieckermann on OT and ancient Near East), *Scholem* (J. Dan), *Schrift, Heilige* (Kratz on OT and NT, G. Stemberger on Judaism), *Schrift und Schreiber* (V. Fritz), *Schriftauslegung, I. Judentum* (G. Stemberger),

Schriftgelehrte, I. Judentum, Schriftlesung, II. Judentum (Stemberger), *Schürer, Seele.* Each volume has complete indexes.

L.L. GRABBE

NETHÖFEL, WOLFGANG and PAUL TIEDEMANN, *Internet für Theologen: Eine praxisorientierte Einführung* (Darmstadt: Primus Verlag, 1999), pp. xiii + 152. DM 34.00/SwF 31.50/AS 248. ISBN 3-89678-109-X.

KAUFMANN, DIETER and PAUL TIDEMANN, *Internet für Althistoriker und Altphilologen: Eine Praxisorientierte Einführung* (Darmstadt: Primus Verlag, 1999), pp. xii + 186. DM 34.00/SwF 31.50/AS 248. ISBN 3-89678-110-3.

OHRMUND, ANDREAS and PAUL TIEDEMANN, *Internet für Historiker: Eine praxisorientierte Einführung* (Darmstadt: Primus Verlag, 1999), pp. xii + 142. DM 34.00/SwF 31.50/AS 248. ISBN 3-89678-111-1.

The Internet resources for various branches of scholarship are expanding rapidly. These three volumes bring together a good deal of material of potential interest to many readers. Each has a similar format and they actually share a good deal of text. The first part in each book gives the same introduction to the Internet, explaining such things as what the World Wide Web is and the meaning of terms like FTP. Each also has a third part on publishing on the Internet and an appendix with further publications to consult (all in German) and a glossary of terms. It is the second section that is different in each of the volumes, being devoted to the various addresses and websites of relevance for the subject in question in each case: theology, historians and ancient (classical) historians and philologists. These can be added to the Scholars Press volume noticed in *B.L.* 1999 (p. 9).

L.L. GRABBE

NEUSNER, JACOB and WILLIAM SCOTT GREEN (eds.), *Dictionary of Judaism in the Biblical Period* (Peabody, MA: Hendrickson, 1999), pp. xxvi + 693. $59.95. ISBN 1-56563-458-6.

This is a large collection of short articles on Judaism and aspects of early Christianity and Graeco-Roman culture. The 'biblical period' of the title 'refers...to the era during which the sacred writings of both Judaism and Christianity were formulated and canonized, in other words, from about 450 BCE, when the Pentateuch as we know it was formulated, to the closure of the Babylonian Talmud around 600 CE' (p. vii). In practice, the scope is even broader, including for example, the fourteenth-century Samaritan author Abul Fath. The criterion for including items appears to be whether students of ancient Judaism would benefit from knowing something about it. The standard of accuracy in the considerable number of articles sampled by the reviewer is very high, and there has been a genuine attempt to avoid ideological bias. The shortness of most articles, and the lack of attribution and bibliography means, however, that this well-produced dictionary is likely to be more helpful to students in American colleges than to people working in British universities.

P.M. CASEY

SEITZ, CHRISTOPHER and KATHRYN GREENE-MCCREIGHT (eds.), *Theological Exegesis: Essays in Honor of Brevard S. Childs* (Grand Rapids, MI: Eerdmans, 1999; distributed in the UK by Alban Books, Bristol), pp. viii + 396. $38.00/£23.99. ISBN 0-8028-4198-8.

This *Festschrift* for Brevard Childs's 75th birthday consists of 19 essays divided among three sections: I Canonical method, II Canonical Readings and the OT, III Canonical Readings and the NT. In Section I, Roy A. Harrisville reviews Childs's project in 'What I Believe my Old Schoolmate is Up To', George Lindbeck discusses 'Postcritical Canonical Interpretation: Three Modes of Retrieval' and Paul McGlasson outlines 'The Significance of Context in Theology: A Canonical Approach'. In the OT section, Corrine Paton's essay on 'Canon and Tradition: The Limits of the Old Testament in Scholastic Discussion' looks at the particular features of Catholic biblical criticism; Gary A. Anderson's 'Is Eve the Problem?' finds patristic traditions favouring Romans 5 over 1 Tim. 2.14; R.W.L. Moberly in 'Toward an Interpretation of the Shema' argues that *herem* is already a metaphor in Deuteronomy; Christopher Seitz's 'The Call of Moses and the "Revelation" of the Divine Name' claims that different levels of tradition in the Pentateuch actually agree over the revelation of the name YHWH; Leslie Brisman finds an ironizing canonical context for divinely inspired slaughter in 'Sacred Butcher: Exodus 32.25-29'; Mark Smith's 'Matters of Space and Time in Exodus and Numbers' explores the influence of festival liturgy on the shaping of the Pentateuch; Larry Lyke in 'The Song of Songs, Proverbs and the Theology of Love' argues that the metaphors are both divine and human; Ellen F. Davis's '"And Pharaoh Will Change His Mind..."' discusses the nature of revelatory language in Ezekiel; and Claire Matthew McGinnis offers 'Swimming with the Divine Tide: An Ignatian Reading of 1 Samuel'. The NT essays are: Kathryn Greene-McCreight 'Dogs at the Foot of the Cross and the Jesus who never Tires of Meeting Us'; Peter R. Rodgers 'The Text of John 1.34'; Rowan A. Greer 'The Good Shepherd: Canonical Interpretations in the Early Church?'; Stephen Fowl 'Learning to Narrate Our Lives in Christ'; and Ephraim Radner 'The Absence of the Comforter: Scripture and the Divided Church'. In general, the essays follow Childs's example in offering painstaking and wide-ranging scholarship in the service of a rather soothing view of the tensions between biblical texts and in the history of interpretation.

H.S. PYPER

SEKINE, SEIZO, *et al.* (eds.), *Annual of the Japanese Biblical Institute*, vol. 24 (Tokyo: Japanese Biblical Institute, 1998), pp. 116. ISBN 4-947668-37-7; ISSN 0912-9243.

The first article in this volume, David C. Hymes, 'Numbers 12: Of Priests, Prophets, or "None of the Above"' (pp. 3-32), shows that the chapter in question is more unified than commonly thought and includes references to Ugaritic, Mesopotamian and Egyptian material. The other three articles (one in German) are on the NT.

W.G.E. WATSON

Society of Biblical Literature 1999 Seminar Papers (SBLSP, 38; Atlanta: Scholars Press, 1999), pp. 642. $35.00. ISBN 0-88414-010-5; ISSN 0145-2711.

Quite a few of the essays in this volume relate to the OT or Jewish literature: Seleucid royal ideology (E.S. Gruen), social construction of Judaea in the Greek period (M.R. Kurtz), Ben Sira and the problem of foreign rule (B.G. Wright, III), the responses of 1 and 2 Maccabees to Seleucid hegemony (R. Doran), creation in Ezekiel (three articles: S.L. Cook, J. Galambush, D.L. Petersen), Enoch as scientist, sage and prophet (G.W.E. Nickelsburg), non-linear time in apocalyptic texts (F.F. Daily), rearrangement of biblical material in Josephus's *Antiquities*, book I (L.H. Feldman), new resources for the study of Josephus (J. Sievers), Israel and 'the nations' in Deutero-Isaiah (C. Franke), the *Book of Elchasai* as a Jewish apocalyptic writing (G.P. Luttikhuizen), Ezekiel, the exile and the torah (R.L. Kohn), the ideology of rule in Daniel 1–6 (2 articles: M. Henze, D.J. Harrington), the prophetic marriage metaphor in the Book of the Twelve and the major prophets (G. Baumann), the place and function of Joel in the Twelve (M.A. Sweeney), the nations in Micah as an example of context-oriented exegesis in the Twelve (B.M. Zapff), the day(s) of Yhwh in the Twelve (J.D. Nogalski). There are also articles on the Matthean controversy stories, 'prophetic' and 'apocalyptic' eschatology in Mark 13, canonical versus non-canonical portrayals of apostolic witnesses, Romans (four essays), *Acts of Peter*, Stoic philosophy and Jewish Scripture in the argument about law in Romans, Matthean journeys of Jesus.

ED.

SOUTHGATE, CHRISTOPHER (ed.), *God, Humanity and the Cosmos: A Textbook in Science and Religion* (Edinburgh: T. & T. Clark; Harrisburg, PA: Trinity Press International, 1999), pp. xxviii + 449. £17.50/$35.00. ISBN (Clark) 0-567-08679-8; (Trinity) 1-56338-228-1.

Although this book really has very little to say about the Bible, except in passing, it is in actuality a rather good textbook in science and religion which would admirably suit the needs of intelligent students in the schools. Most of the contributors are theologians of one sort or another, but some of them also are, or have been, scientists, so the main thrust of the book aspires toward an integration of science, technology, religion and ethics. That is not an unworthy aspiration, but there were times when I longed to hear a sceptical or Humean voice offering different and dissenting readings of the relationship between science and religion because such dissident voices too are part of the contemporary debate. But that criticism apart, this is a rewarding volume which might be read with profit by every member of SOTS, especially those in the educational institutions.

R.P. CARROLL

SWEENEY, MARVIN A. (ed.), *Review of Biblical Literature*, vol. 1 (Atlanta: Society of Biblical Literature, 1999), pp. v + 442. $35.00 ($25.00 for SBL members). ISSN 1099-0046.

As it abolishes Scholars Press, the Society of Biblical Literature is launching a new on-line collection of book reviews that will be of interest to all biblical scholars. This is the print version of the new reviews going into the electronic database (http://www.bookreviews.org) which apparently already has more than 600 reviews (from the *Journal of Biblical Literature*) available. New reviews go immediately into the database and are available for consultation via the worldwide web. Most of the volume is taken up with reviews of books on the OT and NT and related subjects, organized by subject category. There is also a 72-page section on 'major reviews', with several reviews of Brueggemman's *Theology of the Old Testament* (*B.L.* 1998, pp. 142-43) plus a reply by the author; a review of several books on the Minor Prophets (E. Bosshard-Nepustil [*B.L.* 1998, p. 701], B.M. Zapff, and A. Schart) by the editor; and a NT book.

ED.

VANDERKAM, JAMES C., *From Revelation to Canon: Studies in the Hebrew Bible and Second Temple Literature* (Supplements to Journal for the Study of Judaism, 62; Leiden–Boston–Cologne: E.J. Brill, 2000), pp. xi + 604. Nlg 265.00/$156.00. ISBN 90-04-11557-9; ISSN 1384-2161

This publishes V.'s non-Qumran articles over several decades. Most of the essays have been published before; however, the introductory essay (on revealed literature in the Second Temple period) is an exception. Also the article, 'Studies in the Chronology of the Book of Jubilees' appears in English for the first time (originally published in German). The main sections are Hebrew Bible (Davidic complicity in the deaths of Abner and Eshbaal; *bhl* in Ps. 2.5; Ezra–Nehemiah or Ezra and Nehemiah); Calendar and Festivals (on Jaubert's hypothesis; 2 Macc. 6.7a and calendrical change; Hanukkah; Jn 10 and the Feast of Dedication); High Priesthood (Joshua and Zech. 3; Jewish high priests of the Persian period; high priesthood in early Maccabaean times; Simon the Just); Apocalyptic Studies (the prophetic-sapiential origins of apocalyptic thought; prophecy and apocalyptic in the ancient Near East) and Studies in *1 Enoch* and *Jubilees*. In almost all cases the essays appear here unrevised, with only minor corrections of errors. It is good to have these available, since I noticed several I had not come across before. But there is the conundrum of buying such an expensive volume when one has already read many of the essays.

ED.

WEAVER, JOHN, *Earthshaping Earthkeeping: A Doctrine of Creation* (London: Lynx, 1999; distributed by SPCK, London), pp. xix + 712. £12.99. ISBN 1-901443-11-6.

A lifelong Christian, W. is a geologist who has also studied theology, and he is now Director of Pastoral Training at Regent's Park College, Oxford. In this book, he seeks to describe and then integrate the biblical accounts of creation and modern scientific insights to produce a 'theology for earthkeeping'. While W. is attempting an important task, I fear he may have ended up pleasing nobody: the OT scholarship is not very up to date, and is unlikely to be comprehensible to non-specialists (how many geologists would understand J, E, P and D without explanation?); and, similarly, non-geologists (like me) will probably find the scientific discussions difficult to follow—all of which is a pity, as we need to be reminded that biblical studies cannot be conducted in isolation, cut off from other disciplines or from very real contemporary concerns.

C.H. KNIGHTS

WEDDERBURN, ALEXANDER J.M. and DAVID E. ORTON (ed.), *Review of Theological Literature*, vol. 1/1 (Leiderdorp: Deo, 1999; international distributors, T. & T. Clark, Edinburgh), pp. 128. £49.50/EUR 72.50/$79.50 p.a. (4 issues). ISSN 1389-0972.

The *Review of Theological Literature* is a quarterly selection of articles and reviews from the *Theologische Literaturzeitung* translated into English. (Reviews which originally appear in English in the *ThLZ*, and most of its reviews of English-language publications, are not selected.) One's instant reaction is to ask whether this periodical is really necessary, since most theologians serious enough to want to consult these reviews will already have a reading knowledge of German. But on reflection, this could well be a shrewd publishing venture. Most English-speaking scholars will find it easier to browse through the *RTL* than the *ThLZ*, not only for the obvious linguistic reason but also because it is laid out much more readably, in pages not columns. And Orton, who translated nearly all the reviews in this first volume (six OT, nine NT including the leading article, ten systematics, ten historical theology-cum-religious studies), deserves applause not only for the encyclopaedic knowledge of theology this task requires, but also for capturing so precisely the different registers of the contributions. These range from the sniffy (the review of Lüdemann's Nag Hammadi translations) to the diplomatic (Pannenberg on Ratzinger) to the chatty (the account of a book on the wives—and in two instances the mistresses—of the great theologians). On the strength of this first issue, *RTL* deserves to become an important tool for established scholars and advanced undergraduates alike.

D.V.N. BAGCHI

WILLIAMS. JAY G., *The Times and Life of Edward Robinson: Connecticut Yankee in King Solomon's Court* (SBL Biblical Scholarship in North America, 19; Atlanta: Scholars Press, 1999), pp. x + 384. $39.00. ISBN 0-88414-012-1.

Edward Robinson (1794–1863), the first professor of biblical studies at Union Theological Seminary, New York, and one of the first Americans to mediate German scholarship, particularly lexicographical, to the English-speaking world, is important especially for his detailed exploration of the Holy Land in 1838 and

1852, when he made many identifications of biblical sites which are still accepted. This new biography makes use of recently discovered papers which illuminate the first half of his life, especially his stay in Germany in 1826–30, when he studied with Gesenius at Halle. It is a fascinating but rather odd book; the title accurately indicates the contents. W., properly wishes to set Robinson against the background of his times, but fails to discriminate between what illuminates Robinson's life, such as the New England Calvinism which defined his beliefs, and what does not, such as the social history of New York in the 1840s. However, everyone interested in the history of biblical scholarship will enjoy this book. There are bibliographies of travel writing about Palestine before Robinson, of Robinson's own works, and of sources. The number of misprints in the German does no honour to the accomplished linguist whom the book commemorates.

W.J. HOUSTON

WILLIAMS, PRESCOTT H., JR and THEODORE HIEBERT (eds.), *Realia Dei: Essays in Archaeology and Biblical Interpretation in Honor of Edward F. Campbell, Jr at his Retirement* (Scholars Press Homage Series, 23; Atlanta: Scholars Press, 1999), pp. xii + 270. $49.95. ISBN 0-7885-0610-2.

The articles include the 'prodigal sons' of Hosea 11 (R.G. Boling, posthumous re-publication of an article from 1965), Abrahamic covenant traditions in the ethics of Matthew (R.L. Brawley); the association of literacy and the writing of biblical literature (about the eighth century, as literacy began to spread—M.D. Coogan); a bulla of Hezekiah (F.M. Cross) and one of Nathan-Melech (P.K. McCarter), both from the private collection of S. Moussaieff and thus without clear provenance; Exod. 15.1-18, 21 (D.N. Freedman); the musical tradition of Israel (P.J. King); an argument for dating Jonah to the sixth century BCE (G.M. Landes, expanding a paper from 1981); Iron II tomb pottery from Tekoa (N.L. Lapp); women's guilds and groups in Israel (C. Meyers); Deuteronomy texts relating other gods to Yhwh (P.D. Miller); translation of Theodoret's commentary on Ruth (M.M. Mitchell); economic survival and Ruth, based on conversations about the book with Asian women (K. Doob Sakenfeld); the fortess-temple at Shechem and its relationship to the biblical text (L.E. Stager, arguing against G.E. Wright's identification); ethics and archaeology (H.O. Thompson). There is also an appreciation of the honoree (by Williams) and a bibliography of his works (by E. and E. Hilgert).

ED.

2. ARCHAEOLOGY AND EPIGRAPHY

ARNOULD, CAROLINE, *Les arcs romains de Jérusalem: Architecture, décor et urbanisme* (NTOA, 35; Freiburg: Universitätsverlag; Göttingen: Vandenhoeck & Ruprecht, 1997), pp. 319 + 23 plates. SwF 98.00. ISBN (Universitätsverlag) 3-7278-1141-2; (Vandenhoeck & Ruprecht) 3-525-53910-X.

This study concentrates on two archways in Roman Jerusalem: the 'ecce homo' arch and the one underneath the present Damascus gate. Two main sections give in detail the history of discovery and research, a physical description, the context, and a technical and sylistic comparison of each arch, and then make suggestions about their dating and construction. The section on the 'ecce homo' arch places it in the later second century CE, while the arch under the Damascus gate, though earlier, is still from the reign of Hadrian. A third section discusses Aelia Capitolina and the relationship of the arches to it in the context of history and urbanism.

ED.

BAUMGARTEN, JOSEPH, TORLEIF ELGVIN, ESTHER ESHEL, ERIK LARSON, MANFRED R. LEHMANN, STEPHEN PFANN and LAWRENCE H. SCHIFFMAN (eds.), based in part on earlier transcriptions by JÓSEF T. MILIK, *Discoveries in the Judaean Desert XXV: Qumran Cave 4: XXV Halakhic Texts* (Oxford: Clarendon Press, 1999), pp. xi + 173 and 12 plates. £50.00. ISBN 0-19-827006-2.

This volume contains an important and interesting collection of texts that deserve to be read, as Tov indicates in his preface, alongside such texts as 4QMMT, the Temple Scroll, the Damascus Document, and the Rule of the Community, for the light that they cast on one another. Baumgarten has been responsible for a substantial part of the volume, including editions of the work now known as 4QMiscellaneous Rules (4Q265) and of 4QTohorot A–C (4Q274–278). The former work, originally known as 4QSerekh Damascus because of apparent connections both with the Damascus Document and the Rule of the Community, has very diverse contents, including 'halakhic' and communal rules, and narrative that was probably intended as support for the rules. B. argues that the closest analogy is provided by 4QOrdinances (4Q159), and the title 'Miscellaneous Rules' best reflects its contents. For the latter, B. provides a valuable introduction that also takes into account the purification liturgies (4Q284, 4Q414, 4Q512). Editions of the first two of these, the first by B. himself, the second by E. Eshel, are included in the present volume. B. is also responsible in this volume for the edition of 4QHarvesting (4Q284a, formerly known as 4QLeqet), which is likewise concerned with issues of purity. In addition to the above, the volume contains editions of three other halakhic text: 4QHalakha A (4Q251) by E. Larson, the late M.R. Lehmann, and L. Schiffman; 4QHalakha B (4Q264a), by B.; and 4QHalakha C (4Q472a, a single fragment, extremely difficult to read), by T. Elgvin. Finally, the volume begins with an edition by Pfann of the fragments of the text known as 4Qpap cryptA Midrash Sefer Moshe (4Q249), which is written, as its title indicates, in the esoteric script named 'Cryptic A'. The extant fragments deal chiefly with leprosy of houses, and the text apparently reflects the outcome of the study of the Torah by the community, as embodied in legal decisions.

M.A. KNIBB

BECKMAN, GARY, *Hittite Diplomatic Texts* (ed. Harry A. Hoffner, Jr; SBL Writings from the Ancient World, 7; Atlanta: Scholars Press, 2nd edn, 1999), pp. xx + 224. $14.95. ISBN 0-7885-0551-3.

This is the second edition of a volume noted in *B.L.* 1997 (p. 20). Additions to the original collection are Treaty §1A (Arnuwanda of Hatti and the men of Ismerika), Letter §23A (from a Hittite king to another Anatolian ruler), and §27A (Indictment of Mita of Pahhuwa and an intra-Anatolian treaty).

N. WYATT

CARMEL, ALEX and EJAL JAKOB EISLER *Der Kaiser reist in Heilige Land: Die Palästinareise Wilhelms II. 1898* (Abhandlungen des Gottlieb-Schumacher-Instituts, Universität Haifa; Stuttgart–Berlin–Cologne: Kohlhammer, 1999), pp. 187 (Eng.) + ‫א‬ (Heb.), including 151 illustrations. EUR 40.39/DM 73.83/AS 577/SwF 72.00. ISBN 3-17-015820-8.

The journey of Kaiser Wilhelm II to Haifa, Jaffa and Jerusalem in October–November 1898 is commonly understood as a device of German foreign policy to secure a strategic position in the Middle East as the Ottoman Empire declined. The authors, who have built up their narrative and its pictorial framework with material from the Kaiser's descendants as well as official records, dispute this view. They argue that the visit had much more limited aims, chiefly religious, and they relate it to earlier European, especially German, involvement in a 'peaceful Crusade' to the Holy Land. This probably isolates the time spent in Palestine too much from the rest of the Kaiser's grand tour. Although it has no direct relevance to OT studies, this book will be of value to those who are interested in the broader historical context of modern study and exploration of the Holy Land: according to Gustaf Dalman it was a speech addressed to the Kaiser in Jerusalem (curiously not referred to here) that led eventually to the foundation of the Deutsche Evangelische Institut für Altertumswissenschaft des Heiligen Landes, over which Dalman himself and in later years Albrecht Alt and Martin Noth presided with such distinction.

G.I. DAVIES

CHARLESWORTH, JAMES H. and CAROL A. NEWSOM (eds.), *The Dead Sea Scrolls: Hebrew, Aramaic, and Greek Texts with English Translations. Volume 4B. Angelic Liturgy: Songs of the Sabbath Sacrifice* (The Princeton Theological Seminary Dead Sea Scrolls Project; Tübingen: J.C.B. Mohr; Louisville, KY: Westminster/John Knox Press, 1999), pp. xxiii + 196. DM 148.00/$99.00. ISBN (Mohr) 3-16-146914-3; (Westminster) 0-664-2126-2.

This edition is that of Carol Newsom, published in 1985, with assistance by B.A. Strawn for the apparatus and by Strawn and H.W.L. Reitz in the construction of the composite texts. (Charlesworth's contribution is unspecified.) After an excellent introduction covering the language and theology of the text and its relation to Hebrew Bible, other Qumran texts, NT and other ancient Jewish literature, the first part of the edition itself presents the texts of the eight Cave 4 fragmentary manuscripts (4Q400-7), the fragments of the single manuscript of the work from Cave 11 (11Q17) and the fragment from Masada (Mas1k). In the second part of the volume, a composite text of each of the 13 songs is offered and it is here that Newsom's reconstructions, curtailed in the first part, are introduced, according to the principles followed in earlier volumes for the *Serekh ha-Yahad* and the *War Scroll* (see *B.L.* 1995, p. 25; 1996, p. 24). While the composite texts (the novelty in this edition) are not intended as a reconstruction of any 'original' manuscript or form of the work, they do enable the shape of the liturgical cycle to be more easily comprehended. They also demonstrate how much of the text of the cycle is still lost. Apart from the minor blemish of an impossibly precise dating of the manuscripts, this is a very fine resource for one of the most significant of texts from Qumran, which, as Newsom argues, is probably of pre-sectarian origin and with strong links to later Jewish and Christian traditions.

P.R. DAVIES

CURRID, JOHN D., *Doing Archaeology in the Land of the Bible: A Basic Guide* (Grand Rapids, MI: Baker Book House, 1999), pp. 128. $14.99. ISBN 0-8010-2213-4.

This guide was prompted by C.'s experience of teaching archaeology to those whose primary interest is in the Bible, and his belief that there was need for a book 'that would explain the fundamentals of archaeology to people who know little or nothing about the subject' (p. 11). The book gives a brief account of the story of Palestinian archaeology, then considers various aspects of archaeology, for example, the nature of a tell, site identification, excavation techniques, and different types of find from potsherd to public building. Useful definitions of technical terms are scattered throughout the text, and there are several line drawings and colour plates. The final chapter offers a very brief 'case study', showing how the topics treated earlier in the work were relevant to the identification and excavation of et-Tell/Bethsaida. (It is unfortunate that C. was not able to include mention of the proposed sanctuary, and its iconic stele, from the gate-area as examples of archaeological discoveries requiring careful interpretation). This will be a useful addition to reading lists for introductory courses on archaeology and the Bible.

A.H.W. CURTIS

The Dead Sea Scrolls Electronic Reference Library 2, including the Dead Sea Scrolls Database (Non-Biblical Texts) edited by Emanuel Tov (prepared by the Foundation for Ancient Research and Mormon Studies and its Center for the Preservation of Ancient Religious Texts at Brigham Young University, Provo, Utah; Leiden–Boston–Cologne: E.J. Brill; Oxford: Oxford University Press, 1999), 1 booklet (32 pp.) + 1 CD-ROM. Nlg 464.98/EUR 211.00/$259.00. ISBN 90-04-10891-2.

The first volume (CD-ROM) published the facsimiles of the Qumran scrolls. This now presents the texts in printed form, along with a translation, and bibliography. It should be stressed that these are mainly the texts from Qumran, because some other important texts are omitted. For example, the Cairo *Damascus Document*, which many wish to use alongside the material from Cave 4, is absent (even though it is found in the recent Brill study edition of García Martínez and Tigchelaar [*B.L.* 1998, p. 26; 1999, p. 29]). Some of the texts from Murabba'at and Naḥal Ḥever are included, but all those from Masada, Wadi Daliyeh, and most of the other sites in the Judean Desert are omitted. Some of the Qumran texts from Cave 4 are also omitted, though a later version will include them. The translation used is that of García Martínez as found in his 1994 edition (translated from the Spanish by W.G.E. Watson: *B.L.* 1996, p. 26; cf. 1998, p. 26). The CD-ROM also contains the text of the Hebrew Bible, the LXX (Rahlfs' edition), the Vulgate, and the Authorized Version. This, together with the first CD-ROM, makes a formidable tool for studying the Qumran texts. The ability to search these texts, call up a photograph of the manuscript, zoom in on particular sections, and compile comparative examples and passages with the same word or phrase will be invaluable. We can only look forward to the day when all the texts from the Judean Desert are available.

L.L. GRABBE

DEUTSCH, ROBERT, *Messages from the Past: Hebrew Bullae from the Time of Isaiah through the Destruction of the First Temple. Shlomo Mousaieff Collection and an up to Date Corpus* (Tel Aviv: Archaeological Center Publications, 1999), pp. 205. $80.00. ISBN 965-90240-3-7.

This is the English edition of the Hebrew work noticed in *B.L.* 1999 (p. 26). With its clear photographs and drawings of the bullae belonging to S. Mousaieff and its comprehensive lists of personal names, this is an important addition to knowledge of Hebrew glyptic and onomastics in the late eighth and seventh centuries BC. The number of known bullae, over 510 are listed here, is striking evidence for the use of seals and especially of sealing papyrus documents.

A.R. MILLARD

ELAYI, J. and M.R. HAYKAL, *Nouvelles découvertes sur les usages funéraires des Phéniciens d'Arwad* (Supplément no. 4 à Transeuphratène; Paris: Gabalda, 1996), pp. 175 + 38 plates. FF 250.00. ISBN 2-85021-094-3; ISSN 0996-5904.

The accidental discovery of Persian period tombs in the area of Amrit and Tartous on the mainland facing Arvad stimulated this monograph. After an introductory survey of the region, chapter 1 summarizes earlier reports and excavations, notably E. Renan's, and all known stone sarcophagi found there are listed. Chapter 2 describes a necropolis of seven tombs south of Tartous. Three stone anthropoid sarcophagi were recovered and their presentation leads to a discussion of Phoenician terms for 'tomb', 'coffin', etc. and of the origins of this type of sarcophagus. The famous coffin of Eshmun'azor, thought to be booty from Egypt, is assigned to the sixth century; local forms dated from the fifth century onwards. Other anthropoid sarcophagi from various tombs are the subject of chapter 3. One tomb opened at Amrit in 1996 produced five terracotta anthropoid sarcophagi, described in chapter 4. The heads were made from moulds, four in Greek style, one in Egyptian. Two of the coffins had been broken and mended in antiquity. A survey of anthropoid sarcophagi in terracotta embraces Egyptian and 'Philistine' examples, as well as these later Phoenician ones (pp. 105-14), and the meagre evidence for funerary practices is considered (pp. 114-17). An analysis of two skeletons forms an appendix. All the tombs were bereft of grave goods, but this comprehensive account of the coffins advances knowledge of Phoenician burial customs and craftsmanship under Achaemenid rule.

                                                                    A.R. MILLARD

FRANKEL, RAFAEL, *Wine and Oil Production in Antiquity in Israel and Other Mediterranean Countries* (JSOT/ASOR Monograph Series, 10; Sheffield: Sheffield Academic Press, 1999), pp. 230 + CD-ROM. £80.00/$135.00. ISBN 1-85075-519-1.

The core of this monograph is a detailed and comprehensive classification, for the first time, of archaeological evidence for different ways of producing wine and (olive) oil, supported by textual and pictorial evidence and surviving examples from more recent time. The simplest techniques involved mere rock-cuttings, which usually cannot be dated, but the datable evidence shows that already in pre-exilic times more sophisticated equipment involving a beam and weights was in use, with significant regional variations. Evidence from the Hellenistic, Roman and Byzantine periods is also included in the complex classification system. A simpler account of the main conclusions has been provided in R. Frankel, S. Avitsur and E. Ayalon, *History and Technology of Olive Oil in the Holy Land* (Arlington VA, 1994), but it is useful to have this detailed analysis in print as well (and on the accompanying CD-ROM, which contains another 450 pages of data!). Also valuable are the 'preamble' summarizing current knowledge about the cultivation of vines and olives, production processes and the varied uses of olive oil in antiquity, the two appendices on biblical and mishnaic vocabulary for the production of wine and oil and their different varieties, and the extensive bibliography.

G.I. DAVIES

GIBSON, E. LEIGH, *The Jewish Manumission Inscriptions of the Bosporus Kingdom* (Texte und Studien zum Antiken Judentum, 75; Tübingen: J.C.B. Mohr [Paul Siebeck], 1999), pp. x + 201. DM 128.00. ISBN 3-16-147041-0; ISSN 0721-8753.

The Bosporan inscriptions, which refer to emancipation of slaves in the *proseuche*, and ascribe a role of guardianship to the community (*synagoge*) of the Jews, are potentially of great importance for our understanding of Judaism in the Bosporan Kingdom. Based on a Princeton PhD (1997), this book surveys the inscriptions in the wider context of Bosporan history and Greek and Jewish traditions of manumission of slaves. An appendix reproduces the Greek text of the inscriptions discussed, together with an English translation, and there is a fifteen-page bibliography. It is surprising that the author, working in a subject dominated by Russian scholarship, is apparently unable to read Russian.

N.R.M. DE LANGE

HACHLILI, RACHEL, *Ancient Jewish Art and Archaeology in the Diaspora* (Handbuch der Orientalistik: Erste Abteilung, Der Nahe und Mittlere Osten, 35; Leiden–Boston–Cologne: E.J. Brill, 1998), pp. xxxiii + 499 + many figures and plates. Nlg 401.08/$223.00. ISBN 90-04-10878-5; ISSN 0169-9423.

As one might expect, a good portion of this book is devoted to art and architecture as they relate to the synagogues of late antiquity, including studies of symbols, motifs and inscriptions. However, burial and funeral practices are also investigated. One chapter relates Jewish, Christian, and pagan art. Some of the burials in Alexandria and Leontopolis belong to the first and second centuries BCE. However, most of the material is from post-70 times, often centuries later, including now apparently the data from the Roman catacombs which were once thought to date from the first century CE or earlier. The question of dating needs to be taken into account in any attempt to use this highly interesting material to elucidate Second Temple Judaism.

ED.

LAUGHLIN, JOHN C.H., *Archaeology and the Bible* (Approaching the Ancient World; London and New York: Routledge, 2000), pp. x + 196. £11.95/$18.99. ISBN 0-415-15994-6.

The purpose of this book is to provide for the interested and serious student a brief overview of the history, methods and implications of archaeological discoveries and research, and seeks how to interrelate the resulting data with the world and text of the Hebrew Bible. There is a brief survey of archaeological pioneers through to the 'new archaeology', which provides 'explanations' rather than mere 'descriptions'. There is a chapter on fieldwork, what it includes, and the importance of recording finds. Successive chapters deal with the archaeological periods from the Neolithic to Iron II, with relevant archaeological data being inter-related with problem areas of Israelite history as told in the biblical text. The author states that archaeology is the 'one discipline that can provide us with contemporary evidence of the culture out of which the Bible came…and can illuminate the context in which the stories were placed by their authors and give a different perspective from that preserved in the text' (p. 155). The author gives a balanced view in this general introduction to the subject, which includes minimal notes, but a useful comprehensive bibliography.

J.R. DUCKWORTH

LEFKOVITS, JUDAH K., *The Copper Scroll (3Q15): A Re-evaluation: A New Reading, Translation, and Commentary* (STDJ, 25; Leiden–Boston–Cologne: E.J. Brill, 2000), pp. xx + 592. Nlg 315.13/$176.00. ISBN 90-04-10685-5; ISSN 9169-9962.

As the title indicates, this is a textual reconstruction and detailed commentary on the *Copper Scroll*, with translation and an introduction that covers the main data about the finding and opening, as well as the various theories about the meaning of the document. There is a 'discussion' chapter that attempts to synthesize some of the main findings from the detailed analysis. L. concludes that the Scroll 'lists the hidden treasure of the Jerusalem Temple'. Some of his discussion is marred by the uncritical appropriation of rabbinic literature to describe pre-70 history.

ED.

NEVETT, LISA C., *Houses and Society in the Ancient Greek World* (New Studies in Archaeology; Cambridge: Cambridge University Press, 1999), pp. xi + 220. £40.00/ $64.95. ISBN 0-521-64349-X.

This is a commendable attempt to combine archaeology with textual and iconographic evidence to determine an aspect of ancient society. The advantages are that the archaeology does not have the gender and social biases of the written evidence. For example, the internal divisions of the household between the sexes seem to have been more to keep male outsiders from contact with female household members than for separation of the sexes within the household. This study well illustrates the importance of archaeology to control and correct the written records; on the other hand, the written records are an important part of the evidence and not to be rejected or neglected.

ED.

POTTS, D.T., *The Archaeology of Elam: Formation and Transformation of an Ancient Iranian State* (Cambridge: Cambridge University Press, 1999), pp. xxix + 490. £60.00/$85.00; paper £22.95/$37.95. ISBN 0-521-56358-5; paper 0-521-56496-4.

This substantial volume deals with ancient Elam from the latter part of the fifth millennium BC until the early Islamic period, with numerous maps, plans, drawings (some of rather poor quality), photographs, and useful data in tabular form, including chronological summaries for each period, and a full bibliography. There is brief reference to biblical citations (pp. 3, 6-8) in the preliminary section, but the most relevant part for OT study is chapter 9 (pp. 309-53) which deals with Elam in the Achaemenian period. In this the public buildings at Susa are discussed (pp. 325-37) with occasional reference to the Book of Esther, Ahasuerus (= Xerxes I; p. 334), and 'Shushan the Palace' (p. 352). In general the book is well informed with frequent reference to published texts.

T.C. MITCHELL

ROLLE, RENATE and KARIN SCHMIDT, in co-operation with ROALD F. DOCTER (eds.), *Archäologische Studien in Kontaktzonen der antiken Welt* (Veröffentlichung der Joachim Jungius-Gesellschaft der Wissenschaften Hamburg, 87; Göttingen: Vandenhoeck & Ruprecht, 1998), pp. 886. DM 240.00. ISBN 3-525-86278-4; ISSN 1435-9596.

Produced by the Archaeological Institute of Hamburg University to span some of its concerns and research interests, this volume is divided mainly by geographical area: Orient, Egypt, Cyprus (articles on the excavations at Elephantine, Astarte at Kition); Greece, Ionia and the Aegean; Greeks and Phoenicians in the Tyrrhenian region (articles on trade, ceramic objects, amphorae and tombs); Carthage and North Africa (elements for a study of Punic mentality, the Punic world between the Levant and the Maghrib [E. Lipiński], Carthage and the Greeks); Mediterranean contacts with the Iberian Peninsula (Phoenician colonization in Portugal and the orientalization of the Iberian Peninsula, Phoenician colonization in Spain, the Iberian Peninsula and Cyprus before 218 BCE, the Phocaeans in the west, archaeological news on Punic Carteia); the Iberian Peninsula under the Romans (Nero's golden house in Rome as a possible oriental discovery, a relief of the goddess Cybele, the self-representation of Roman provincial settlements in a wall painting, an over-stamped coin as possible opposition to Claudius's taking of power); Middle Europe and the Black Sea Area.

ED.

SCHÄFER, PETER and SHAUL SHAKED (eds.) with the assistance of R. Leicht, B. Rebiger and I. Wandrey, *Magische Texte aus der Kairoer Genize, Band III* (Texte und Studien zum Antiken Judentum, 72; Tübingen: J.C.B. Mohr [Paul Siebeck], 1999), pp. xi + 501, including facsimiles 55-84. DM 238.00. ISBN 3-16-147141-5; ISSN 0721-8753.

This continues the publication of the magical texts from the Cairo Genizah. Volumes 1 and 2 were reviewed in *B.L.* 1995 (p. 35) and 1998 (p. 37). This volume includes incantation prayers, exorcism amulets, spells for finding lost objects, love charms, protective spells, healing magic, and spells to harm one's enemy. There are a number containing a magical use of the psalms (*Shimmush Tehillim*) and a theoretical discourse.

ED.

STRUGNELL, JOHN, DANIEL HARRINGTON and TORLEIF ELGVIN (eds.), in consultation with JOSEPH A. FITZMYER, *Discoveries in the Judaean Desert XXXIV: Qumran Cave 4. XXIV Sapiential Texts, Part 2 4QInstruction (Mûsār lᵉMēvîn): 4Q425ff., with a Re-edition of 1Q26* (Oxford: Clarendon Press, 1999), pp. xvi + 584 and 31 plates. £95.00. ISBN 0-19-826982-X.

This second and final volume of wisdom texts from Qumran's cave 4 contains the principal editions of what the editors claim to be seven copies of a work they designate in English as 'Instruction' and in Hebrew more fully as *Mûsār lᵉMēvîn*. This title now replaces the provisional working title, Sapiential Work A. Harrington and Strugnell provide the editions of 4Q415, 416, 417, 418, 418a, together with 1Q26; Elgvin provides the edition of 4Q423. There are also editions of 4Q418b, entitled hesitantly 'Text with Quotation from Psalm 107?', and of 4Q418c which might be yet another copy of 'Instruction'. The length of this volume results from the exhaustive consideration of every possibility for each partial reading in these fragmentary manuscripts. Since, for example, just over 300 fragments, some of them very small, are provisionally assigned to 4Q418, the discussion of possibilities for suitable readings is almost endless. It is fortunate, therefore, that in addition to the comprehensive editions of the manuscripts, there is a 40-page general introduction in which the overlaps between the various manuscripts are listed and the principal ethical, admonitory, cosmological and eschatological contents of the ten largest extant fragments of the work are outlined. The editors remain justifiably indecisive about the technical phrase 'the mystery that is to come' (*rz nhyh*); it may refer to a written book, to an oral tradition or to creation itself. Despite the possibility that three of the nine or more uses of *yaḥad* could be translated as 'community', the editors characterize the work as pre-sectarian, belonging to the line of tradition between Proverbs and Sirach, and they suggest that it was subsequently of considerable authority at Qumran, possibly being quoted (4Q418 55 10) in 1QHª 10.27-28. All the manuscripts are dated palaeographically as early, middle or late Herodian. The whole work is only understandable as an instruction to a male student alone, if the feminine verbal forms and pronominal suffixes in 4Q415 2 ii 1-9 are viewed as teaching given to the student in the correct form to pass on directly to a woman.

G.J. BROOKE

TALMON, SHEMARYAHU and YIGAEL YADIN (eds.), *Masada VI: Yigael Yadin Excavations 1963–1965, Final Reports* (Jerusalem: Israel Exploration Society, 1999), pp. 252, including 20 illustrations. $80.00. ISBN 965-221-034-X.

This beautifully produced volume publishes together all the Hebrew and Aramaic scroll fragments found at Masada during the 1963–65 excavations. The book is in two parts. In the first Talmon publishes the principal editions of fourteen fragmentary scrolls. Seven of them are biblical: MasGen (Gen. 46.7-11), MasLevª (Lev. 4.3-9), MasLevᵇ (Lev. 8.31–11.40), MasDeut (Deut. 33.17–34.6), MasEzek (Ezek. 35.11–38.14), MasPsª (Pss. 81.2–85.6), and MasPsᵇ (Ps.150.1-6). The form of the text in all of these manuscripts is akin to that of the MT, though there are a few significant variants in MasGen, MasEzek and MasPsª; this overall textual uniformity in a group of manuscripts from the turn of the era is a significant witness to the emerging authority of the proto-MT text type. Three manuscripts are Bible-related compositions: MasapocrGen (A Hebrew Apocryphon of part of the Joseph cycle), MasJub or MaspsJub (Jubilees or Pseudo-Jubilees because of the presence of the 'prince of Mastema'), and MasapocrJosh (an Apocryphon on the closing chapters of Joshua which Talmon associates closely with 4Q378 and 4Q379). Three are fragments of other compositions: MasShirShabb (Songs of the Sabbath Sacrifice, edited by C. Newsom and Y. Yadin himself), an unidentified Qumran-type fragment, and an unclassified (Aramaic?) fragment. The remaining fragment is a piece of papyrus inscribed in Palaeo-Hebrew which Talmon identifies as a text of Samaritan origin since it contains the name *hrgryz[ym]* written as one word as is customary in Samaritan tradition. Most of these fragments seem to have been written 50–100 years before the fall of Masada and so were almost certainly brought there from elsewhere. Talmon is keen to suggest that three or more could have come from Qumran, though he does not identify the Qumran covenanters as Essene. The second part of the volume is a reproduction of Yadin's 1965 edition of the Ben Sira fragments, together with five pages of notes for improved readings collected by E. Qimron and a 20-page bibliography compiled by F. García Martínez of studies on Ben Sira which have been published between 1965 and 1977.

G.J. BROOKE

VANDERKAM, JAMES C. and MONICA BRADY (eds.), *Discoveries in the Judaean Desert XXIX: Qumran Cave 4: XX Poetical and Liturgical Texts, Part 2* (Oxford: Clarendon Press, 1999), pp. xiii + 478 + 28 plates and 3 foldout plates. £90.00. ISBN 0-19-827005-4.

This is the second and final volume containing poetical and liturgical texts from Qumran cave 4. The book contains the principal editions of the following texts: Curses (4Q280; B. Nitzan), Works Containing Prayers A-C (4Q291-293; B. Nitzan), Works of God (4Q392; D. Falk), Communal Confession (4Q393; D. Falk), Liturgical Work A (4Q409; E. Qimron), Hodayot[a-f] (4Q427-432) and Hodayot-like Texts A-C (4Q433-433a, 440; E. Schuller), Barkhi Nafshi[a-e] (4Q434-438; M. Weinfeld and D. Seely), Lament by a Leader (4Q439; M. Weinfeld and D. Seely), Prayers, including Individual Thanksgiving A-B, a Personal Prayer, and an Incantation (4Q441-444; E. Chazon), Poetic Fragments (4Q445-447; E. Tigchelaar), more Prayers of various kinds (4Q449-457b; E. Chazon), the Self-Glorification Hymn and a Prayer Concerning God and Israel (4Q471b-c; E. Eshel), and Liturgical Work B-C (4Q476-476a; T. Elgvin). The evident difficulties which the editors have had in naming these fragmentary compositions should not undermine the significance of these materials for the better understanding of many aspects of prayer in the late Second Temple period. Nearly half the volume is taken up with the Hodayot manuscripts. 4QH[b] is most like 1QH[a]. Although the other manuscripts do not provide evidence of major recensional activity, Schuller highlights the differences between them in the order of the psalms and even in content, and suggests that there were various distinct collections of thanksgiving psalms being copied at approximately the same time in the mid-first century BCE. Most intriguingly the extant remains of 4QHᵉ contain only Hymns of the Teacher, perhaps suggesting they were collected together independently at some time. The Barkhi Nafshi manuscripts are also a substantial part of this book; the editors align their contents closely with Qumran sectarian literature but stress the particular interest of several poems in describing the 'hidden among the gentiles'. Other important sets of fragments, such as 4Q409 and 4Q471b, have been made known already in detailed preliminary publications. Overall there is a wealth of carefully presented material here which will repay years of study.

G.J. BROOKE

3. HISTORY, GEOGRAPHY AND SOCIOLOGY

AMIT, YAIRAH, *History and Ideology: An Introduction to Historiography in the Hebrew Bible* (trans. Yael Lotan; The Biblical Seminar, 60; Sheffield: Sheffield Academic Press, 1999), pp. 127. £12.95/$19.95. ISBN 1-85705-928-6.

This book originated as a series of broadcast lectures given on the Israeli Defence Forces Radio. It is very much an introduction to the subject, with some notes and bibliography offering the opportunity of further exploration. Having discussed the centrality of history to the Hebrew Bible, the author dates its beginnings to the end of the eighth century, the impulse to its origin being the downfall of the northern kingdom. Judges and Samuel, in distinction from Deuteronomy, Joshua and Kings, are held to be pre-deuteronomistic. Genesis–Numbers is a post-deuteronomistic priestly account, while Chronicles makes use of the deuteronomistic history and other sources to create a new presentation in order to counter tendencies of the Chronicler's own age. A brief and very superficial discussion of the relationship of ideology and history concludes that neither Kings nor Chronicles is purely ideological or purely historical.

A.D.H. MAYES

ASH, PAUL S., *David, Solomon and Egypt: A Reassessment* (JSOTSup, 297; Sheffield: Sheffield Academic Press, 1999), pp. 157. £29.95/$46.50. ISBN 1-84127-021-0; ISSN 0309-0787.

This began life as a PhD thesis under J. Maxwell Miller and aims to investigate Israelite contacts with Egypt under David and Solomon. It has three main chapters, covering epigraphic evidence, archaeological evidence and biblical evidence. The book seems a bit thin to cover so much ground; nevertheless, it packs in a remarkable amount of information and covers most of the main issues, including such questions as whether Egyptian princesses married foreign rulers, Shoshenq's campaign, trade in horses with Egypt, and the queen of Sheba. None of the epigraphic texts cited to show close contacts is in fact decisive, and generally there is little evidence at all. Similarly, the archaeology shows strong Egyptian involvement with Palestine to about 1050, then rapid decreasing indications to about 900; increase in evidence for contacts is found only in the later Iron age. The generally negative conclusions of this study will not be welcomed in all quarters. Many of the points raised will inevitably be controversial, but A.'s interpretations generally have a good deal of support and show much careful, thoughtful work.

L.L. GRABBE

BLOIS, LUKAS DE and ROBARTUS J. VAN DER SPEK, *An Introduction to the Ancient World* (London and New York: Routledge, 1999 [1997]), pp. xx + 321. Paper £16.99/$25.99. ISBN 0-415-12773-4; (paper) 0-415-12774-2.

In three unequal parts the reader is introduced to the ancient Near East and Egypt (Part I, pp. 3-65), Greece (Part II, pp. 70-148) and Rome (Part III, pp.151-295). The historical sketches in Part I are very brief, e.g. the Middle Kingdom in Egypt is covered in about one page, the Hittite Empire in less, leading to rather uninformative generalizations. Separate chapters describe religion, economy, and society and government. Such matters are incorporated within the historical sections of Parts II and III, with much more discussion of the influences and pressures at work (e.g. the stability of the Athenian democracy; criticism of the Athenian Democracy, pp. 117-18). The chapter devoted to the Hellenistic era (pp. 129-49) is clear and helpful, with attention to the non-Hellenistic aspects. The roles of Near Eastern powers and cultural elements are noted in the later chapters of the Roman part, too. There are 34 sketch maps, 42 line drawings and 96 black and white photographs, over three-quarters of them for the Greece and Rome parts. This is a basic introduction suitable for students with no previous knowledge, competent, but too brief and, for *B.L.* readers, too heavily weighted to the Classical World. However, within those limits, adequate accounts are given of Israel and Judah, their religion and developments, and of early Christianity.

A.R. MILLARD

BRANDT, AXEL, *Moralische Werte in den* Res Gestae *des Ammianus Marcellinus* (Hypomnemata, 122; Göttingen: Vandenhoeck & Ruprecht, 1999), pp. 447. DM 130.00. ISBN 3-525-25219-6.

Because he is a late writer, Ammianus is not often quoted alongside Thucydides and Polybius as a model of ancient historiography, but many would so evaluate him. In his history (*Res gestae*) he deals with a number of Roman rulers, several of whom presided over military disasters. This study examines Ammanianus's judgments about particular moral qualities (positive and negative) in those about whom he wrote, illustrating that questions of personal and moral character were an important element to the structure and evaluation of historiography in some ancient historians.

ED.

BRAYBROOKE, MARCUS, JAMES HARPUR and FELICITY COBBING, *The Essential Atlas of the Bible* (London: SPCK, 1999), pp. 144. £20.00. ISBN 0-281-05275-1.

This is not a work that OT specialists will need or want to consult. It consists of about 67 two-page spreads, of which 35 are devoted to the OT. Topics treated include 'the creation of the world', 'the call of Noah', 'Jacob's journey' and 'the fall of Jericho'. Each spread summarizes the biblical account and illustrates it with reproductions of cities, artefacts, landscapes, archaeological sites and maps. The latter are reproductions of three-dimensional representations of the areas illustrated, and have the merit of indicating the physical features of the landscapes. Whether their presence justifies designating the work as an 'atlas' is a fine point. There is almost no engagement with biblical scholarship at the level of literary and historical matter. Some of the captions are puzzling. For example, that accompanying the Black Obelisk of Shalmaneser III, which shows, but fails to mention, the 'tribute of Jehu'. On pp. 74-75 the sixth-century CE mosaic from the nave of the synagogue at Bethshean is used to illustrate Judaism in the period immediately after Alexander the Great. Elsewhere, the mirror image of an excerpt from Codex Sinaiticus is reproduced, and a coin from the second Jewish Revolt is upside down. While an adult readership is presumably envisaged, the book would be more suitable for use with children.

J.W. ROGERSON

BROSIUS, MARIA and AMÉLIE KUHRT (eds.), *Studies in Persian History: Essays in Memory of David M. Lewis* (Achaemenid History, 11; Leiden: Nederlands Instituut voor het Nabije Oosten, 1998), pp. xi + 306, including many illustrations. Nlg 129.00/$68.00/DM 114.00/FF 384.00. ISBN 90-6258-411-X.

An introduction explains the significance of Professor Lewis's work and puts into perspective the contributions in the volume (Kuhrt). J. Wiesehöfer shows how the diary of a seventeenth-century visit to Persepolis by von Mandelslo was distorted in publication to conform to contemporary ideas about the Persians. Two articles discuss the Old Persian and Elamite terms for tribute and conclude that, contrary to the statements of Herodotus, the aristocracy of Persis seems to have paid tribute (H. Sancisi-Weerdenburg, G.G. Aperghis). C. Tuplin gives an important case study in the question of relating Greek to Persian evidence in his discussion of the alleged seasonal migration of the Achaemenid kings (finding that no definitive answer is forthcoming on the specific question). H.G.M. Williamson provides a critique of J. Weinberg's well-known thesis of a *Bürger-Tempel-Gemeinde* and concludes that the Jewish community was not treated differently by the Persian authorities from other groups in the region. P. Briant re-examines a Greek inscription from Sardes, concluding that rather than establishing a cult of Ahuramazda in the Persian period, it instead shows a Persian establishing a state in honour of the local Greek god Zeus. The question of Greek adoption of the Persian cult of Anahita is answered in the reverse: the cult of Artemis was 'Persianized' (Brosius). The Babylonian astronomical diaries (cf. *B.L.* 1998, pp. 36-37) throw light on the chronology of Artaxerxes II's wars (R.J. van der Spek). Three articles cover the seal of Ašbazana (Aspathines), a document mentioning a slave woman with 'Egyptian' inscribed on her wrist, and the pyramidal stamp seals from the Persepolis area (M. Garrison, M.W. Stolper, M.C. Root). There are also articles on Elamite grammar and the *lan* ritual in the Persepolis Fortification Texts. Altogether a fitting memorial to a great scholar of the Persian period.

L.L. GRABBE

CARRASCO, DAVÍD, *City of Sacrifice: The Aztec Empire and the Role of Violence in Civilization* (Boston: Beacon Press, 1999), pp. ix + 279. $27.50. ISBN 0-8070-4642-6.

This study considers the relationship of violence, religion and urbanization. Some early urban societies attempted to replicate the pattern of the cosmos in their cities, with an *axis mundi* at the centre, which becomes the sacred precinct. This was true of the Aztecs. The city, with all its symbolism, was also essential to warfare, and religious violence was integral to urbanization. The question of violence is one that has intrigued certain anthropologists (e.g., René Gerard), and some would see implications for ancient Israel from such societies as the ancient Aztecs, despite significant differences in the two cultures.

ED.

CARTER, CHARLES E., *The Emergence of Yehud in the Persian Period: A Social and Demographic Study* (JSOTSup, 294; Sheffield: Sheffield Academic Press, 1999), pp. 386. £55.00/$85.00. ISBN 1-84127-012-1.

This important book represents a thorough reworking of C.'s 1991 Duke University dissertation. He has already published some influential articles based on this material but, as he himself acknowledges, they are now superseded by this new synthesis. Driven by an interest in the social and economic history of Judah in the Persian period, he presents for the first time a thorough analysis of the settlement pattern of the province. This is based upon detailed study both of sites which have been excavated (ch. 3) and on those identified in area surveys (ch. 4). This is necessarily preceded not only by a general and well-informed introduction to the literary, historical, archaeological and social-science problems of the period, but in particular (ch. 2) by a discussion of the boundaries of the province. He argues carefully in favour of a 'small Yehud' theory, and this naturally has important consequences for the discussion to follow. The demographic results of his analysis are that in the first half of the Persian period, Yehud had a population of 13,350, and this rose to 20,650 in the second half. This represents an increase on his previously published estimates, reflecting discoveries of new sites in recent years, and he accepts (indeed, expects) that further revisions are likely to be needed within a very few years. Nevertheless, the pattern and nature of the settlement will probably not be affected, and this allows him to draw significant consequences in the final two chapters on such matters as the economy, constitution, social make-up and self-awareness of the population. In particular, Weinberg's 'Citizen-Temple-Community' model comes in for well-taken criticism. C. is right to observe that the Persian period is currently the focus of attention for many aspects of biblical study. Being grounded in carefully researched and thoroughly analysed empirical data which have not previously been available to most scholars, this book is required reading for anyone with interests in the history or literature of this formative period for the Hebrew Bible and early Judaism.

H.G.M. WILLIAMSON

CARTER, CHARLES E. and CAROL L. MEYERS (eds.), *Community, Identity, and Ideology: Social Science Approaches to the Hebrew Bible* (Sources for Biblical and Theological Study, 6; Winona Lake, IN: Eisenbrauns, 1996), pp. xviii + 574. $37.95. ISBN 1-57506-005-1.

The series aims to enable students to approach areas of scholarship through examples of the work of the pioneers and later original work, and also to be a convenience for scholars. This collection fulfils the dual aim satisfactorily. There is a substantial introductory essay by Carter outlining the place of social science approaches in the study of the Hebrew Bible. The reprints (excerpts from books as well as usually complete articles) are collected in two parts. The first section of Part 1 offers 'classic studies': Robertson Smith on sacrifice; Weber on ancient Judaism (several short extracts from the book); Causse on Judaism's progress from ethnic group to religious community; M. Douglas and also M. Harris on clean and unclean animals; G.E. Mendenhall on the Hebrew conquest; and N.K. Gottwald on assumptions and models in the study of pre-monarchic Israel. Next come 'critical perspectives' exercised on such studies: G.A. Anderson on understandings of sacrifice; R.A. Oden on the German historical tradition in biblical scholarship as an exercise in the sociology of knowledge; G.A. Herion on assumptions made in the reconstruction of Israelite history; A.D.H. Mayes on Weber and Gottwald; and N.P. Lemche on the use of 'system theory' and other models. Part 2 consists of 'case studies': collections of studies on two major foci of research, though the second is too diffuse to constitute a real 'case study'. We have under the heading of Israel's Emergence and Early Political Development: A. Malamat on charismatic leadership in Judges; J.W. Flanagan on chiefs in Israel; R.B. Coote and K.W. Whitelam on the emergence of Israel; and I. Finkelstein on the emergence of the monarch; and under Israelite Society and Institutions: R.R. Wilson on prophecy and ecstasy; T.W. Overholt on cross-cultural comparison in the case of prophecy; F.S. Frick on the relation between religion and social structure in early Israel; D.C. Hopkins on subsistence in early Israel; C. Meyers on the balance between male and female functions in early Israel; P. Bird on women in the cult; and D.L. Smith on the exclusivism of the returned exiles.

W.J. HOUSTON

COLLINGWOOD, R.G., *The Principles of History and Other Writings in Philosophy of History* (ed. with an introduction by W.H. Dray and W.J. van der Dussen; Oxford: Oxford University Press, 1999), pp. lxxxvii + 293. £48.00. ISBN 0-19-823703-0.

The importance of C. for historiography is widely recognized. It was known that he planned a work on the philosophy of history, to be his chief and crowning work, and some parts of a manuscript uncompleted at his death were published as part of the volume put together (by M. Knox) from posthumous papers as the influential volume, *The Idea of History*. There had been a good deal of speculation as to what the unpublished parts might contain, but the manuscript was not among the papers deposited in the New Bodleian and was thought to have been destroyed. Fortunately, it surfaced in 1995 and is now published here in complete form, along with a number of other unpublished essays (including 'History as the Understanding of the Present', 'Reality as History', 'Can Historians Be Impartial?', 'Notes on Historiography' and other conclusions to his lectures on nature and mind). A long introduction by the editors is helpful in setting this study in the context of Collingwood's overall work.

L.L. GRABBE

COOGAN, MICHAEL D., *The Oxford History of the Biblical World* (Oxford: Oxford University Press, 1998), pp. xii + 643 + 26 plates and many other illustrations and maps. £30.00/$49.95. ISBN 0-19-508707-0.

This extremely handsome volume, with many illustrations (26 in colour) and numerous maps and other aids to understanding, has eleven chapters, topped and tailed with Prologue and Epilogue. The 'biblical world' of the title is very generously understood, since the Prologue takes us back to the beginnings of civilization and the Epilogue reaches the Muslim conquest. Authors of individual chapters have generally been allowed free rein, and this leads to a good deal of repetition; there are three separate discussions of the 'Merneptah Stele'. Minimalist views of Israel's history are briefly discussed in the Preface, but firmly dismissed. The Preface is by Coogan; subsequent chapters are by W.T. Pitard ('Syria-Palestine in the Bronze Age'), C.A. Redmount ('Israel in and out of Egypt'), L.E. Stager ('The Emergence of Ancient Israel'), J.A. Hackett ('The Era of the Judges'), C. Meyers ('The Early Monarchy'), E.F. Campbell, Jr ('From the Death of Solomon to the Fall of Samaria'), M. Cogan ('From the Assyrian Conquest to the Fall of Babylon'), M.J.W. Leith ('The Persian Period'), L.J. Greenspoon ('Judaism in the Hellenistic Period'), A.J. Levine ('From Pompey to the First Jewish Revolt'), and D.N. Schowalter ('The Jesus Movement in the Roman World'). The Epilogue, by B. Geller, is concerned with 'Jews and Christians in the Roman Empire'. Some authors assume a good deal of previous knowledge; others more consciously aim at the educated general reader. Either way this is a most impressive collection.

R.J. COGGINS

DASSMANN, ERNST and WERNER H. SCHMIDT (eds.), *Jahrbuch für Biblische Theologie (JBTh)*, Band 14: *Prophetie und Charisma* (Neukirchen-Vluyn: Neukirchener Verlag, 1999), pp. xii + 291. DM 68.00/AS 496/SwF 62.00. ISBN 3-7887-1749-1.

This special issue (entirely in German) has a section on the Old Testament: prophecy as the self-critique of faith (W.H. Schmidt), prophetic word and prophetic book—on the reconstruction of the oral pronouncement of the prophets (J. Jeremias), the prophetic saying pronouncement and the written prophet Amos (I. Willi-Plein). A section on the NT looks at prophecy in Paul and the book of Revelation. A section on antiquity and the subsequent period has articles on prophecy in the early church, early Christian exegesis of the prophets, prophets and prophecy in post-biblical Judaism (G. Stemberger), and from an Islamic perspective. A final section is on the Reformation and modern times.

ED.

EISENSTADT, S.N., *Fundamentalism, Sectarianism and Revolution: The Jacobin Dimension of Modernity* (Cambridge Cultural Social Studies; Cambridge: Cambridge University Press, 1999), pp. xiv + 280. £40.00/$69.95; paper £14.95/$24.95. ISBN 0-521-64184-5; paper 0-521-64586-7.

E. is well known for his sociological work, especially his *Revolution and the Transformations of Society* (1978). Here he looks at the current growth of fundamentalism in Christianity, Judaism and Islam by studying fundamentalism and sectarianism in the great 'axial' civilizations of the past (those arising in the second half of the first millennium BCE). He argues against the view that these fundamentalist movements are an eruption of repressed traditionalist forces or anti-modernist movements. On the contrary, they are a form of modern political movement with strong Jacobin tendencies (by which is meant totalitarianism—even 'democratic' totalitarianism—in the name of public welfare) which believes that a utopian society can be created through political means. This strong Jacobin element is why such movements have much in common with communisitic movements (which are also Jacobin in nature).

ED.

EXUM, J. CHERYL (ed.), *Virtual History and the Bible* (Leiden–Boston–Cologne: E.J. Brill, 2000), pp. 204. Nlg 90.00/$53.00. ISBN 90-04-11555-2.

This collection asks the interesting question of 'what if'—what if certain events of history had been different in certain ways. After an introduction by the editor, the 'what if' question is put by contributors: Merneptah's scribes were telling the truth (K.W. Whitelam), the exodus and conquest had really happed (L.L. Grabbe), Judges had been written by a Philistine (S. Ackerman), David had not climbed the Mount of Olives (T.L. Thompson), we had no accounts of Sennacherib's third campaign (D. Edelman), Zedekiah had remained loyal to his master (N.P. Lemche), the Chronicler really did use the Deuteronomistic History (A.G. Auld), the Lord's anointed had lived (P.R. Davies), Luke had not met Theophilus (L.C.A. Alexander), Paul had travelled east instead of west (R. Bauckham), Jerusalem had not fallen (P. Perkins). Several other contributors phrase their topic a bit differently but with the same aim: how did Joram really die?, or the invention of militarism (E.A. Knauf), Israel, Assyrian hegemony and some considerations about virtual Israelite history (E. Ben Zvi), the loss of Armageddon or 621 and all that (R.P. Carroll), a case of benign imperial neglect and its consequences (J. Blenkinsopp), earliest Christianity in counterfactual focus (J.D. Crossan).

ED.

FRERICHS, ERNEST S. and LEONARD H. LESKO (eds.), *Exodus: The Egyptian Evidence* (Winona Lake, IN: Eisenbrauns, 1997), pp. 112. $24.95. ISBN 1-57506-025-6.

A short collection of 1992 Brown University conference papers, bibliographically updated to 1996, on the historicity of the Exodus as attested by Egyptian evidence. The contributors are Malamat (the Exodus, Egyptian analogies) and Yurco (Merenptah's Canaanite campaign and Israel's origins), both of whom see *indirect* Egyptian evidence for what seems to be a durative rather than a punctual Exodus event but one that peaks between the thirteenth and twelfth centuries BC, and those who consign the Exodus to folklore: Redford (observations on the sojourn of the *Bene-Israel*), Dever (is there any archaeological evidence for the Exodus?) and Weinstein (Exodus and archaeological reality). The summary by William Ward fails to collate the chief points of friction and agreement between the two groups. I was glad to find an extended critique of B. Wood by Weinstein and disappointed by Dever's failure to take stock of Halpern's emphasis on the distinction between 'conquering' and 'supplanting' in Joshua–Judges (*ABD*, V, p. 1124). The slight lopsidedness of the panel should have been remedied, for example by the addition of Mazar or the frequently cited Stager, or the sharply critiqued Bimson. Something should have been said about historiography and the suppression of the memory and traces of Akhenaten as contested, in the year of publication, by Hoffmeier's *Israel in Egypt* (*B.L.* 1998, p. 49) and by Assmann's *Moses the Egyptian*.

G. GLAZOV

GARNSEY, PETER, *Food and Society in Classical Antiquity* (Key Themes in Ancient History; Cambridge: Cambridge University Press, 1999), pp. xiv + 175. £35.00/ $54.95; paper £12.95/$19.95. ISBN 0-521-64182-9; paper 0-521-64588-3.

The author has written and edited a good deal on society in classical antiquity, including studies on food and famine. This book includes all aspects of food, eating, and diet, especially as they relate to culture and society. There is a section on Jewish dietary laws (pp. 91-95).

ED.

GOTTWALD, NORMAN K., *The Tribes of Yahweh: A Sociology of the Religion of Liberated Israel, 1250–1050 BCE* (The Biblical Seminar, 66; Sheffield: Sheffield Academic Press, 1999), pp. l + 916. £24.95/$35.00. ISBN 1-84127-026-1.

Many will welcome the reprint of what has become something of a pioneering classic. The author has added a 'preface to the reprint' (pp. xxvi-l) that looks at the reception of the book, more recent developments, and bibliography of the author to the present. An 'epilogue' provides additional notes to various sections, especially in response to criticisms of reviewers.

ED.

GRABBE, LESTER L., *Sacerdot, profeti, indovini, sapienti nell'antico Israele* (Milan: Edizioni San Paolo, 1998), pp. 350. N.P. ISBN 88-215-3558-4.

This is an Italian translation of the book reviewed in *B.L.* 1996 (p. 36). The author was not consulted about either the translation or any possible updating.

ED.

HESS, RICHARD S. and GORDON J. WENHAM (eds.), *Zion, City of Our God* (Grand Rapids, MI: Eerdmans, 1999; distributed in the UK by Alban Books, Bristol), pp. x + 206. $22.00/£12.99. ISBN 0-8028-4426-X.

This collection reviews many aspects of the role of Jerusalem in the First Temple period. The contributions are: J.M. Monson, 'The Temple of Solomon: Heart of Jerusalem' (illuminating comparisons especially with the Neo-Hittite 'Ain Dara temple); R.S. Hess, 'Hezekiah and Sennacherib in 1 Kings 18–20' (a literary approach to the A and B sections in 2 Kings 18); M.J. Selman, 'Jerusalem in Chronicles' (the Chronicler affirming Jerusalem's continuing significance after the Exile); G.N. Knoppers, 'Jerusalem at War in Chronicles' (challenging von Rad's view of the holy war in Chronicles as cultic); T. Renz, 'The Use of the Zion Tradition in the Book of Ezekiel' (transformation of the Zion tradition in the context of the Exile); P.E. Satterthwaite, 'Zion in the Songs of Ascents' (re-affirmation of the choice of Zion and David); K.M. Heim, 'The Personification of Jerusalem and the Drama of her Bereavement in Lamentations'; R. Doyle, 'Molek of Jerusalem?' (extensive consideration of comparative evidence). The editors, who are well known to members of the Society, have produced a valuable and well-focused collection. The blurb reminds us that Jerusalem is important to Jews and Christians: it is equally important to Muslims.

J.F. HEALEY

HJELM, INGRID, *The Samaritans and Early Judaism: A Literary Analysis* (JSOTSup, 303; Copenhagen International Seminar, 7; Sheffield: Sheffield Academic Press, 2000), pp. 318. £35.00/$57.50. ISBN 1-84127-072-2; ISSN 0309-0787.

Originally a prize-winning master's thesis, this marks a welcome addition to the few monographs on Samaritan studies. After surveying the modern study of the Samaritans and the native Samaritan literature (chs. 1–3), she looks at the Samaritans in Jewish, Christian and Hellenistic literature (ch. 4) and in Josephus (ch. 5). Chapter 6 is on how the Samaritans see themselves (relying primarily on John Macdonald's 'Chronicle 2' and Abu'l Fath). The final chapter is on moving from literary to historical reality (though it must be said that a lot of issues are also addressed in ch. 4 with historical questions in mind). For the author's first scholarly efforts, this study is commendable, especially in the breadth of coverage. This does not mean that one always agrees (e.g., the date and identity of the Simon in Ben Sira 50 is not as uncertain as her somewhat selective—indeed, slightly misleading—treatment implies [pp. 129-36]). Also, although the problems with using the Samaritans' own writings are acknowledged (especially on p. 272), this very late literature is sometimes set alongside much earlier sources with the vast difference in date apparently forgotten. Her bibliography is good (though she was apparently not aware of L.H. Schiffman's important article on the Samaritans in Tannaitic sources [*JQR* 75 (1984–85)] or my article on the Samaritans in the Hasmonean period in the *Society of Biblical Literature 1993 Seminar Papers*).

L.L. GRABBE

HOFFMEIER, JAMES K., *Israel in Egypt: The Evidence for the Authenticity of the Exodus Tradition* (Oxford: Oxford University Press, 1999 [1996]), pp. xix + 244. Paper £12.99. ISBN 0-19-513088-X.

This is the paperback edition of the book reviewed in *B.L.* 1998 (p. 49).

ED.

HORBURY, WILLIAM, W.D. DAVIES and JOHN STURDY (eds.), *The Cambridge History of Judaism.* III. *The Early Roman Period* (Cambridge: Cambridge University Press, 1999), pp. xlv + 1254 + 2 maps and 51 figures. £90.00/$140.00. ISBN 0-521-24377-7.

This volume completes the trilogy begun with Vol. 1 (*The Persian Age* [1984]) and Vol. 2 (*The Hellenistic Age* [1989]), reviewed in *B.L.* 1985 (p. 34), and 1991 (pp. 35-36) respectively. W.D. Davies has edited throughout; regrettably, John Sturdy, who assisted with Vol. 2, died before the completion of Vol. 3. The first four chapters tackle archaeological matters (M. Broshi, D. Bahat, E.M. Meyers, M. Williams), and the next four the social, economic and political history (E. Gabbe), the Diaspora (M. Smallwood), the role of non-Jews in Judaism (M. Smith), and the post-70 CE Jewish view of Gentiles (R. Loewe). There follow four studies on the synagogue (H. Bloedhorn and G. Huttenmeister; S.J.D. Cohen; S.C. Reif; W. Horbury), and a sequence on Pharisees (J. Schaper), Sadducees (G. Stemberger), Essenes (O. Betz), baptist sects (K. Rudolph), 'The troublemakers' (M. Smith), the Samaritans (S. Isser), and Galilaean and Judaean Judaism (M. Goodman). The contemporary Jewish view of Jesus is examined by W.D. Davies and E.P. Sanders, and of Paul by W.D. Davies. J.C. Paget writes on Jewish Christianity, and C.C. Rowlands on apocalyptic. J. Campbell presents an 'orthodox' view of Qumran, N. Golb his view of the Qumran writings as originating from Jerusalem. D.K. Falk studies prayer in the Qumran texts. C. Mondésert updates us on Philo, and L.H. Feldman on Josephus. S.J.D. Cohen examines second-century rabbis, and L.I. Levine the archaeological evidence for second- to third-century Hellenistic-Roman diaspora. J.G. Griffiths studies the legacy of Egypt in Judaism, and P.S. Alexander Jewish elements in gnosticism and magic.

Book List readers will pursue their own interests here; but students of Herod will enjoy Morton Smith's subtle revisionism, and those in pursuit of the historical Jesus will be rewarded by Davies and Sanders's careful study of what led to his death. Betz's description of the Essenes should be read alongside Campbell and Golb; the Qumran debate is not over yet. C.C. Rowlands contributes a very useful essay on apocalyptic. L.H. Feldman's review of Josephus studies shows the authority of a real master. In spite of occasionally careless sub-editing and geography (on p. 830 the River Jabbok is surprisingly located), this volume will be a valuable tool for years to come, and the publisher, editors and contributors deserve our warm congratulations and thanks.

J.R. BARTLETT

HORNBLOWER, SIMON (ed.), *Greek Historiography* (Clarendon Paperbacks; Oxford: Clarendon Press, 1996 [1994]), pp. xii + 286. £15.99. ISBN 0-19-815072-5.

The editor himself provides an outstanding introductory essay on the 'story' of Greek historiography and also writes about narratology and narrative techniques in Thucydides. Other topics, as well as subjects that cut across more than one essay, include Greek historiography from Hecataeus to Polybius; the effect of Herodotus's views about religion on his history; the question of oral tradition; 'invented tradition'; how pre-Alexander writers obtained their information about the western Mediterranean, and post-Alexander writers about the East; the influence of the contemporary situation of a writer on his evaluation of a past event. The specific examples are naturally taken from classical history, but for anyone interested in the current debate on the history of ancient Israel and to what extent the OT can be used as a source, this collection has a good deal of relevant material.

L.L. GRABBE

HORSLEY, RICHARD A., with JOHN S. HANSON, *Bandits, Prophets, and Messiahs: Popular Movements at the Time of Jesus* (Harrisburg, PA: Trinity Press International, 1999), pp. xl + 271. $16.00. ISBN 1-56338-273-3.

This is a reprint of the 1985 edition (not reviewed in the *B.L.*), with a new preface discussing the reception of the original book and some subsequent developments. The book gives a historical background and then discusses ancient Jewish social banditry, various popular royal and messianic movements, prophets and prophetic movements, and the 'Fourth Philosophy' (along with the Sicarii and Zealots). H.'s sociological interpretation has been widely influential, and it is good to have this in print in an affordable edition. However, it should be noted that various interpretations will be debated by specialists. For example, the question of whether 'social bandits' is a meaningful category has been answered in the negative by a recent study on the Roman empire (p. 161 below).

ED.

ILAN, TAL, *Integrating Women into Second Temple History* (Texte und Studien zum Antiken Judentum, 76; Tübingen: J.C.B. Mohr [Paul Siebeck], 1999), pp. xiii + 296. DM 168.00. ISBN 3-16-147107-5; ISSN 0721-875.

This, the third volume in a trilogy on Jewish women of the Second Temple and rabbinic periods (see *B.L.* 1996), is a stimulating and at times controversial study. Attention is focused on women, outside the domestic sphere, in political activity or at the centre of theological debate. With meticulous attention to detail I. explores the way women are presented in Josephus, Ben Sira and rabbinic literature, and demonstrates how stereotypes have distorted the actual role of women. She proposes a reconstruction of the relationship between women and the Pharisees from the first century BCE through the Second Temple period, and considers the dispute between Beit Shammai and Beit Hillel over the legal status of women. Skeletal remains of Jewish burials also provide material for the study of gender and social history in the period. From the Judean desert papyri she finds evidence for pre-marital cohabitation within a Jewish community and for divorce initiated by a Jewish woman. Among the more speculative articles is the suggestion, on the grounds of the colophon to the Greek Esther, that this book, together with Judith and Susanna, was composed as propaganda for Shelamzion's accession to the throne. Altogether a valuable study.

G.I. EMMERSON

ISHIDA, TOMOO, *History and Historical Writing in Ancient Israel: Studies in Biblical Historiography* (Studies in the History and Culture of the Ancient Near East, 16; Leiden–New York–Cologne: E.J. Brill, 1999), pp. xiv + 219. Nlg 127.82/$72.00. ISBN 90-04-11444-0; ISSN 0169-9024.

Here I. publishes a selection of essays from 1973–93. They have been revised to take account of more recent literature but not necessarily rethought as far as the argument is concerned. Some of the subjects are the lists of pre-Israelite nations, the leaders of the tribal league in the pre-monarchic period, the people of the land and the political crisis of Judah, the house of Ahab, and a number of essays relating to the Succession Narrative. I. admits that some would regard him as on the conservative side, and he does not seem to be aware of some of the discussion in the past five years.

ED.

ISSERLIN, B.S.J., *The Israelites* (London: Thames and Hudson, 1998), pp. 304 + 159 illustrations. £28.00. ISBN 0-500-05081-1.

I.'s aim is to fashion a detailed portrait of Israelite culture within its broader ancient Near Eastern setting. Part 1 considers Israel's land, origins, history, social structure; part 2 explores towns, agriculture, industry/crafts, trade, warfare; and part 3 discusses language/texts, religion and art. The framework for this entire discussion begins with the late thirteenth century BCE and ends in 586 BCE (with some forays into the Second Temple period). This attempt to portray Israel 'in the round' is a welcome contribution and the 74 colour photographs help to make this an attractive, informative publication for the general reader. I. knows the very existence of an 'ancient Israel' in the thirteenth century is now an issue rather than a presumed fact and this awareness does filter through into the text. Yet, for all I.'s bibliography of contemporary scholarship he often repeats conventional perspectives, doggedly referring to the Iron I population as 'Israelite' and falling foul of the temptation to paraphrase the biblical text when no other sources are available. Moreover, the decision to refer anonymously to 'scholarly attitudes' is frustrating. There is little use in telling the reader of scholars who think Abraham, Isaac and Jacob represent 'theoretical eponymous ancestors of tribal groups' when these scholars are not identified, leaving the reader to refer to an undifferentiated select bibliography.

D. GUEST

JARUZELSKA, IZABELA, *Amos and the Officialdom in the Kingdom of Israel* (Uniwersytet im. Adama Mickiewicza w Poznaniu, Serio Socjologia, 25; Poznań: Adam Mickiewicz University Press, 1998), pp. 240 N.P. ISBN 83-232-0910-3; ISSN 0554-8225.

The title of this study may mislead; it is not concerned with detailed exegesis of Amos, but is intended as a contribution to the socio-economic history of the United Monarchy. The author is a Polish scholar who has worked with A. Lemaire and has spent much time in Israel. She also readily acknowledges her debt to the earlier work of M. Weber, particularly in the analysis of the sociology of officialdom. A detailed appraisal of our knowledge of the history of the northern kingdom leads to a discussion of its economic development, with particular reference to demography, agriculture and the role of international trade. Epigraphic and archaeological evidence is assessed, with a full presentation of current scholarly disputes. Then, in the last chapter, four possible relevant passages in Amos are considered, with the suggestion that the prophet's indignation was especially roused by the officials' eagerness to seize the opportunity for self-enrichment that was brought about by rising prosperity. This implies, of course, that the final form of Amos can be taken as a reliable indicator of eighth-century conditions; the absence of precise descriptions of any of the official classes in Amos is also not regarded as a major problem. Despite these reservations this study can be commended as a balanced appraisal of an important aspect of ancient Israelite society. Résumés in French and Polish are appended, together with a table of errata; how readily available the work will be in the West is not clear.

R.J. COGGINS

JUNGRAITHMAYR, HERRMANN, *Das Orakel von Ife: Reflexion über das verborgene Afrika* (Sitzungsberichte der Wissenschaftlichen Gesellschaft an der Johann Wolfgang Goethe-Universität, Frankfurt am Main, Band, 36/4; Stuttgart: Steiner, 1998), pp. 175-201, including 10 plates. £32.00/SwF 32.00/AS 234. ISBN 3-515-07419-8.

The Ife of sub-Saharan Africa have a form of divination (called *Ifa*) which makes use of traditional sayings and songs preserved orally and also a complicated system of symbolic numbers. A version of an oracle called the 'Sixteen Cowries' was imported to the New World where it is widespread in black communities. Behind the Ifa system lies a differentiated cosmology which gives an insight into the inner-Africa world of hidden lives and thoughts.

ED.

KAMM, ANTONY, *The Israelites: An Introduction* (London and New York: Routledge, 1999), pp. x + 242, including 20 figures, 4 charts, 7 maps. £35.00; paper £11.95/$18.99. ISBN 0-415-18095-3; (paper) 0-415-18096-1.

This is a carefully produced book which has a good range of maps and illustrations. It intends to be an introductory work and is chronologically arranged; it makes use of a number of relevant comparative sources for OT study such as the

Amarna letters and the Ugaritic tables. However it takes as its base line the history of Israel as presented within the biblical material with the implicit assumption that this framework is acceptable for a work of documentary history. Occasionally the author acknowledges some of the major difficulties with this approach, such as the numbers of Israelites leaving Egypt in the Exodus and the uncertain archaeological support for the story of a speedy and near-complete conquest of Canaan found in Joshua. At critical points the author refers to archaeological evidence, offering one interpretation of this without citing the source for this evidence, leaving the reader incapable of checking out this interpretation (see, e.g., pp. 51, 63, 147). This book has been written by a classical scholar who presumably has not been exposed to the current scholarly debates concerning the genre of the biblical material as historiography. As an introduction it serves to inform students who have not read through the OT and related texts such as 1 and 2 Maccabees of the biblical picture of events but it does not clearly alert them to the need for a critical exploration of the OT.

M.E. MILLS

LEVINE, LEE I. (ed.), *Jerusalem: Its Sanctity and Centrality to Judaism, Christianity and Islam* (New York: Continuum; Poole, Dorset: Cassell, 1999), pp. xxvii + 516. $75.00/£50.00. ISBN 0-8264-1024-3.

This collection of studies is divided into six parts—Jerusalem in biblical tradition, in the Second Temple period, in the Byzantine period, in the early Middle Ages, in the mediaeval Jewish and Christian traditions, and in the late Middle Ages and modern era. *Book List* readers will concentrate mainly on the first two sections. However, the first section does scant justice to its theme, containing only three studies, two of which (Sara Japhet, Yair Zakovitch) focus largely on the Chronicler's version of Jerusalem's election or sanctification under David, while the third (W.W. Hallo) studies the Assyrian records of Jerusalem in Hezekiah's time, barely noting the ideological interests of the conference whose papers these were. The second section contains some excellent essays. L. offers a masterly discussion and a clear perspective of the interplay between Judaism and Hellenism in Hasmonaean-Herodian Jerusalem. Martin Goodman argues that in rebuilding the Temple Herod was banking on future tourist income from the Diaspora. Albert Baumgarten studies the messianic movements and figures, and locates John the Baptist firmly in Peraea, not Judah and Jerusalem. E.P. Sanders contributes a stunning short paper on Jerusalem and the Temple in the mind of Jesus, Paul, and Luke. Philip Alexander traces the doctrine of Jerusalem as the navel of the world to the Hasmonaean revolution, and sees the Hereford *mappa mundi* as deriving ultimately from the theological geography visible in *Jubilees*.

J.R. BARTLETT

LONG, V. PHILIPS, *Israels' Past in Present Research: Essays in Ancient Israelite Historiography* (Sources for Biblical and Theological Study, 7; Winona Lake, IN: Eisenbrauns, 1999), pp. xx + 612. $37.95. ISBN 1-57506-028-0.

This is a useful collection of articles illustrating some of the main issues in the current debate over historiography and ancient Israel. The choice of essays can be justified for the most part, though a number of conservative evangelical writings seem to be included because they support L.'s views, not because they have had much impact on the field. The five main sections are Israel's past in present research, the historiographical impulse among Israel's neighbours (a much better job could have been done on this section), Israel's history writing, writing Israel's history: the methodological challenge, and the historical impulse in the Hebrew canon. A general introduction, an introduction to the main sections, and a concluding essay help to orient the reader, but these do not always give a balanced picture of the present debate or the main issues in it. Although the first published volume of the European Seminar on Methodology in Israel's History is cited, L. fails to note the existence of the Seminar and its intent to address the methodological issues. Despite this collection's general usefulness, an opportunity has been missed to give an even-handed and reliable perspective on the state of the field and the directions it is taking.

L.L. GRABBE

MCINTOSH, SUSAN KEECH (ed.), *Beyond Chiefdoms: Pathways to Complexity in Africa* (New Directions in Archaeology; Cambridge: Cambridge University Press, 1999), pp. x + 176. £40.00/$64.95. ISBN 0-521-63074-6.

This collection challenges a number of assumptions made by some biblical scholars who make use of sociological models in their work. As the studies make clear, differences can be found in different areas, and no one model fits all situations; nevertheless, the development of complexity and its implications for society in many African areas does not follow the 'evolutionary model' so widely accepted. Hierarchies may be flexible, status may not lead to hierarchy, hierarchy may not have economic consequences, power relations do not necessarily follow an elite/non-elite dichotomy. A local or even regional chief may have primarily a ritual function without significant political or economic power. On the other hand, there are no necessary links between agriculture and political ranking: inequalities can occur in hunter-gatherer societies. The editor provides a commendable orientation to the themes found in the rest of the book. Any OT scholar tempted to impose a particular sociological model on ancient Israel/Judah should read this book first.

L.L. GRABBE

MCNUTT, PAULA, *Reconstructing the Society of Ancient Israel* (Library of Ancient Israel; Louisville, KY: Westminster/John Knox Press; London: SPCK, 1999), pp. xiv + 284. $27.00/£30.00. ISBN (Westminster) 0-664-22132-7; (SPCK) 0-281-05259-X.

The series in which this volume appears is rapidly becoming an excellent source (and resource) of well-analysed accounts of the current state of play in biblical scholarship. This volume provides a carefully argued set of analyses of the social dimensions of the biblical story, moving from the Iron Age I origins of ancient 'Israel'— note the Daviesian scare quotes!—to the Babylonian and Persian periods. There is an excellent first chapter in which M. judiciously discusses the vexed questions about sources (historical and otherwise), archaeological information, anthropology and sociology, social-scientific approaches to the Bible and the interpretative process, with excellent bibliographical notes. M. certainly knows her Davies (Philip rather than the other types of Davies in the Guild), so makes no major errors of judgment or balance that I can detect. Following the schematic order of the biblical narratives M. works her way through the Bible, looking at Iron Age I, IA, IB, then IC and II, the rise of the monarchy, then the period of the monarchy and finally the Babylonian and Persian periods. The overviews of the different debates for each period are also well presented. Within these discussions there is a wealth of observations on urban and rural settlements, labour production, land ownership, distribution of wealth (some good coverage of Max Weber in these matters), technology and many other germane issues. This is a very judiciously written book and one which can be recommended strongly to beginners in the field wishing to learn about the contours of the current state of the discipline.

R.P. CARROLL

MAISELS, CHARLES KEITH, *Early Civilizations of the Old World: The Formative Histories of Egypt, the Levant, Mesopotamia, India and China* (London and New York: Routledge, 1999), pp. xvi + 479, including many figures and tables. £40.00. ISBN 0-415-10975-2.

How the world's first civilizations came into existence is the subject of this very solid work, which is based on a series of lectures given by the author at the University of Bristol in 1992–93. The introductory chapter 1, 'How does the past illuminate the present?' is particularly useful and covers topics such as 'The Emergence of Archaeology as a Scientific Discipline', 'The Lands of the Bible (= Near East)', and 'Social Archaeology'. According to M., 'Archaeology, as it is practised toward the end of the twentieth century, is social archaeology, attempting to reconstruct from artefactual evidence the configuration of a previous society in order to discover how it functioned'. The author uses 'Childe's Checklist' to examine systematically the early civilizations of the Old World from the Late Palaeolithic period right through to urbanism and the rise of the state. This checklist is a list of criteria set out by V.G. Childe in a paper on 'Urban Revolution' (1950). The application of this checklist in the study of each early civilization reveals structural parallels, though in the case of the Harappan civilization there are gaps in our knowledge, which only urgent excavation can rectify. This is a well-organized book, packed with information and beautifully produced. It would have been wise to leave out the paragraphs on the decipherment of cuneiform and H.C. Rawlinson's contribution to it (p. 20), for Old Persian cuneiform and Mesopotamian cuneiform are different writing systems. Recent scholarship has confirmed in some detail that it was Edward Hincks, not Rawlinson, who deciphered Mesopotamian cuneiform. Furthermore the Behistun inscription played no role whatever in the decipherment.

K.J. CATHCART

PATAI, RAPHAEL, *The Children of Noah: Jewish Seafaring in Ancient Times* (Princeton, NJ: Princeton University Press, 1998), pp. xix + 228. $24.95. ISBN 0-691-01580-5.

L. Casson's *The Ancient Mariners* (2nd edn, 1991) and *Ships and Seafaring in Ancient Times* (1994) barely refer to Israelite activity, and P.'s posthumous book, developed from a work originally published in 1938, aims to fill a gap. P. examines Noah's ark, offers a short essay on sea-faring in the Bible, and then explores ship construction, types of ships, the crew, sea trade, ships in harbour and at sea, ships at war, sea law, similes and parables, sea legends and sailors' stories, ports, and Lake Kinneret. An appendix by J.M. Lundquist on 'Biblical Seafaring and the Book of Mormon' ends the book. P. recognizes that the biblical evidence for marine activity by monarchic Israel or Judah is meagre (*pace* 1 Kgs 10.11, 22), but relies heavily on the Oniyahu seal ship illustration and on the knowledge shown in Ezekiel 27. The book's content depends greatly on Hellenistic, midrashic and talmudic sources, and evidences those rather than biblical periods. There is much fascinating, but question-provoking, detail. Thus P. accepts the queried translation 'peacocks' (1 Kgs 10.22, p. 12); he thinks that the Madeba map shows pontoon bridges on the Jordan (pp. 44-45), though the mosaic suggests rather a rope or pole across the stream preventing the ferry from being carried downstream (cf. Avi-Yonah, *The Madeba Mosaic Map*, 1954, p. 35). P. makes Eshmunazar of Sidon Ptolemy I's contemporary (p. 154); but Eshmunazar II has long been dated to the fifth century BC (see Gibson, *Syrian Semitic Inscriptions*, III, pp. 101-102). However, the book, though dated, is a treasure house, especially on Jewish attitudes to the sea, and should not be missed.

J.R. BARTLETT

PETZOLD, KARL-ERNST, *Geschichtsdenken und Geschichtsschreibung: Kleine Schriften zur griechischen und römischen Geschichte* (Historia-Einzelschriften, 126; Stuttgart: Franz Steiner, 1999), pp. 629. DM 236.00/SwF 236.00/AS 1723. ISBN 3-515-07458-9.

If you think that Greek and Roman history has little to do with the OT, think again!: there are those who are now arguing that the Deuteronomistic History is modelled on Herodotus—or even Livy. In this context, the collection here (many of the essays reviews, all in German) is very much relevant. The first part on historical thinking and historical writing is the most important, with a good many items on Polybius who is the historian perhaps the most explicit about what he is doing. There are also a number of essays and reviews relating to the annalists. The important essay on Cicero and history should be compared with that of P.A. Brunt (*Studies in Greek History and Thought* [1993], pp. 181-209). The other two sections (on Greek and Roman history respectively) tend to focus on specialist issues, though the review of *Cambridge Ancient History* VIII should be noted.

L.L. GRABBE

RAPPORT, ROY A., *Ritual and Religion in the Making of Humanity* (foreword by Keith Hart; Cambridge Studies in Social and Cultural Anthropology, 110; Cambridge: Cambridge University Press, 1999), pp. xxiii + 535. £45.00/$64.95; paper £16.95/$19.95. ISBN 0-521-22873-5; (paper) 0-521-29690-0.

When diagnosed with terminal lung cancer, the late R. devoted his attention to completing this work which had been developing for several decades. In the foreword it is claimed that R.'s is the first to address systematically the problem posed by Durkheim: science has driven religion from the modern world without being able to fulfil the function of religion. The bulk of R.'s study is on ritual, covering such topics as sanctification, the idea of sacred space, and time, but it has a higher aim. R. ultimately proposes a 'post-modern science' that would allow a place for natural religion/theology.

ED.

ROGERSON, JOHN, *Chronicle of the Old Testament Kings: The Reign-by-Reign Record of the Rulers of Ancient Israel* (London: Thames and Hudson, 1999), pp. 208 + 260 illustrations. £19.95. ISBN 0-500-05095-3.

This is a remarkable book. What looks like a popular, coffee-table book in a general series on Chronology of the Pharaohs, Popes, Roman Emperors, Russian Tsars and Chinese Emperors turns out to be a sophisticated introduction to the problems of Israelite history. From the opening pages, R. provides a sensitive and sophisticated introduction to the results of recent critical scholarship on the problems of the historicity of the biblical traditions, the relationship of archaeology, and the problems of chronology, as well as the literary sensitivity necessary for appreciating the biblical traditions. Nor is it confined to the monarchic period, but ranges from the central characters of the Patriarchs and Judges to the Second Temple period. It is lavishly and beautifully illustrated, including an excellent photograph of the Tel Dan inscription on the opening page. Hopefully, this will bring the results of current scholarship to the general public as well as providing a fine introduction for undergraduate students. Although, of necessity given the nature of the series, it is focused on the 'great men' of history, it offers a much more up to date and sophisticated analysis than many standard histories of ancient Israel currently in use.

K.W. WHITELAM

SMALL, JOCELYN PENNY, *Wax Tablets of the Mind: Cognitive Studies of Memory and Literacy in Classical Antiquity* (London and New York: Routledge, 1997), pp. xviii + 377. £60.00/$100.00. ISBN 0-415-14983-5.

This is a fascinating book. The author is a classical archaeologist who is also interested in cognative theory. She attempts here to explore the relationship between literacy, orality and memory in antiquity. This entails investigation of a great many topics often overlooked: how books were written, organized and 'published'; how documents and other information were stored and retrieved; how writing was done and the tools and equipment used; how libraries were set up; ancient techniques of memory. Although much of the data is from the classical world, there are likely to be many parallels with ancient Israel and the Near East.

ED.

SNEED, MARK R. (ed.), *Concepts of Class in Ancient Israel* (South Florida Studies in the History of Judaism, 201, The Hebrew Scriptures and their World; Atlanta: Scholars Press, 1999), pp. xiii + 126. $44.95. ISBN 0-7885-0571-6.

This collection of essays arose from an SBL section session in 1997. The ambiguous title means to refer to how the writers conceive of class in ancient Israel, but there are hints of how people in ancient Israel conceived of class. The question is increasingly important in the social study of the Hebrew Bible, but no consistent view emerges from this book. There is no general introduction, but S.'s own essay includes a very brief survey of research. N.K. Gottwald writes on class relations in Nehemiah 5. S.R. Mandell argues that the picture of a classless Israel projected in Genesis–Kings is itself the fantasy of a privileged class, rather like Marie Antoinette playing at shepherdesses. P.R. Davies sees the majority of the Hebrew Bible as the work of a scribal class, and the late literary fictions such as Esther, Ruth and the Song of Songs as emerging from a new leisured merchant class. S. finds only two classes in ancient Israel: masters and slaves. R.A. Simkins tries to use Genesis 2 to analyse the relationship between class and gender in early Israel, but finds only gender and no classes. N.P. Lemche denies that such a thing as class exists in ancient Israel, substituting the patron–client relationship. Responding, J. Berlinerblau subjects each of the six essays to careful and always justified criticism, and calls for biblical sociology to engage seriously with sociological theory.

W.J. HOUSTON

SPARKS, KENTON L., *Ethnicity and Identity in Ancient Israel: Prolegomena to the Study of Ethnic Sentiments and their Expression in the Hebrew Bible* (Winona Lake, IN: Eisenbrauns, 1998), pp. xiv + 344. $37.50. ISBN 1-57506-033-7.

This is a reworked dissertation, under the direction of John Van Seters, from the University of North Carolina, Chapel Hill which addresses one of the key issues in biblical studies today. S. claims to have adopted a 'minimalist' perspective while accepting that there is more historical information to be gleaned from the Hebrew sources than some minimalists admit. He rejects attempts to isolate and identify ethnic groups through archaeology because distinctive pottery types and similar kinds of evidence cannot show whether ethnic ancestry served an important role for the modality in question. He explores, mainly through specific biblical texts, the reasons why ethnicity beame an important component of Israelite national identity when ethnicity appears to have played a relatively minor role in the national identity of surrounding ancient Near Eastern states. He attempts to trace a chronological development in Israelite ethnicity from the simple to the complex from the Merneptah stele, the Song of Deborah, which he dates to the ninth century, through the prophetic corpus from the eighth to the sixth centuries. The argument turns on his confidence in terms of dating various texts, although S. is well aware of the problems and possible objections to such an approach. This is a theoretically well-informed study which offers a valuable introduction to complex material on ethnicity. Although S. describes his work as a prolegomena, it will form an important point of reference for further discussions of this critical issue, whether biblically or archaeologically focused, which will require careful engagement.

K.W. WHITELAM

THOMPSON, THOMAS L., *The Bible in History: How Writers Create a Past* (London: Jonathan Cape, 1999), pp. xix + 412. £25.00. ISBN 0-224-03977-6.

The main thrust of this book is that the OT belongs to the Hellenistic world and represents an identity document for Judaism. The stories of the past are just that, and serve the purposes of the community to which they belong rather than any supposed historical intention. In three major sections, the author covers how stories talk about the past, how historians create a past, and the Bible's place in history. In terms of method and approach the author too often tilts at windmills. In terms of concrete results the book is too full of sweeping assertions and generalizations: can the work of critical scholarship in its attempts to create a literary history of the various part of the biblical text be simply ignored in favour of a view which, apparently, sees no significant difference between one kind of text and another, all having the same (origin and?) purpose in the desire of Hellenistic Judaism to create its own identity?

A.D.H. MAYES

VAN DE MIEROOP, MARC, *Cuneiform Texts and the Writing of History* (Approaching the Ancient World; London and New York: Routledge, 1999), pp. ix + 106 + 6 plates. £40.00/$65.00; paper £13.99/$22.99. ISBN 0-415-19532-2; (paper) 0-415-19533-0.

This tightly packed volume is an excellent introduction to the skills required and the pitfalls encountered in the modern writing of Mesopotamian history. The chapters deal in turn with 'the first half of history', the main genres of texts at the historian's disposal, with due account given to their limitations; 'History from Above', that is the 'official' history put about by kings (and therefore inherently suspect); 'History from Below', that is the procedures required to glean historical information from the thousands of commercial and legal documents unearthed; these are followed by chapters on the writing of economic history and gender studies and history, ending with a conclusion. Apart from its intrinsic interest, the book is full of wise cautions that deserve to be taken seriously by those biblical historians who continue to believe that they are telling it as it happened by merely paraphrasing the Deuteronomist and the Chronicler.

N. WYATT

WELLS, RONALD A. (ed.), *History and the Christian Historian* (Grand Rapids, MI: Eerdmans, 1998; distributed in the UK by Alban Books, Bristol), pp. vi + 248. $23.00. ISBN 0-8028-4536-3.

This collection of essays attempts to address the concerns of 'Christian historians'. Some of the issues addressed and questions asked are the following: What difference does a Christian perspective make? Historical narrative and truth-telling in a postmodern age; critical historical judgment and faith. Some specific topics addressed concern men, women and God; missionology and the crises of history; and historiography as it relates to Baptists in the American South, American Puritan studies, religion in rural America, and Northern Ireland. A final section addresses questions of teaching history. There are some relevant issues and interesting points here, but one cannot help feeling that some of the essays are ultimately an apologetic for exercising a conservative bias.

ED.

4. TEXTS AND VERSIONS

ABEGG, MARTIN, JR, PETER FLINT and EUGENE ULRICH (trans. and with commentary), *The Dead Sea Scrolls Bible* (Edinburgh: T. & T. Clark, 1999), pp. xxii + 649. £24.95. ISBN 0-567-08715-8.

This is a most welcome volume, long a desideratum: a collection of the various biblical manuscripts and other textual witnesses to the OT in a convenient form. It is also good to have the continuous text rather than just a series of notes of where the Scrolls differ from the MT or another standard version. There are some dangers in such a collection, of course; for example, the impression might be gained that the Qumran community had one text, whereas in some cases there was clearly textual variety, and which books might have belonged to its 'canon' (if this word is even appropriate) will be debated. The editors/translators are aware of this and attempt to explain the situation in a useful introduction. Specialists may have reason to disagree on this or that point (e.g., there is not a shred of evidence that the Pharisees had anything to do with the development of the text or canon), but on the whole it is helpful, informative and balanced. Evidence of textual variety is also indicated in notes in which variations from the particular manuscript(s) followed at any point in the main text are given in the footnotes. The books of *Jubilees*, *1 Enoch*, *the Epistle of Jeremiah*, Ben Sira and Tobit are also included; not all would agree, but the editors justify their decision. There are introductions to each book and helpful explanatory notes here and there in the text. Sometimes one could suggest more (e.g., it might have been made clearer that the reading '75' in Exodus 1.5 is based on a different counting of persons than the MT '70'), but this would always be true, whoever produced a work like this. The one real criticism from a production point of view is that the heading at the top righthand page should have had the name of the particular biblical book on that page; at present one must flip back and forth to find the book to which a particular passage belongs. But, again, this is a very welcome work that fills a significant gap. Now all we need is a companion volume with the actual original text!

L.L. GRABBE

ERBES, JOHANN E., *The Peshitta and the Versions: A Study of the Peshitta Variants in Joshua 1–5 in Relation to their Equivalents in the Ancient Versions* (Acta Universitatis Upsaliensis, Studia Semitica Upsaliensia, 16; Uppsala: Uppsala University Library, 1999), pp. 374. N.P. ISBN 91-554-4459-8; ISSN 0585-5335.

This Uppsala dissertation is concerned with the relation between readings in the Peshitta and readings in the MT and in the LXX and other versions. The author, who was responsible for the text of Joshua in the Leiden Peshitta, has attempted to avoid working from any preconceived theory, but rather to take full account of all the textual data and to let that speak for itself. Thus, on the one hand, he discusses all variants within the Peshitta (except those that are inner-Syriac variants with no possibility of versional contact) and, on the other hand, compares these readings with the complete range of evidence from the Hebrew and the versions, not just with the readings adopted in pre-existent critical texts. E. sets out his aims and his methodology in a short introduction and gives a brief summary of his results at the end. But the great bulk of his work is taken up with a 'Sequential Commentary' in which 459 individual Peshitta readings in Joshua 1–5 are subjected to minute analysis in relation to readings in the ancient versions. The latter are organized in three blocks: the Jewish sphere (primarily the MT, mediaeval Hebrew MSS, Targum Jonathan), the Septuagint sphere (primarily the Septuagint, the Syro-Hexapla, the Coptic, the Ethiopic), and the Vulgate. E.'s main conclusions are that the Peshitta most often follows the MT, that it sometimes follows the LXX in readings that can only have originated in the LXX, and that, within Joshua 1–5, it was not influenced by the Targum. It is helpful to have the evidence for these conclusions set out so fully, and E. makes some interesting comments on individual readings in the Peshitta and in other versions. But it may be wondered whether the way in which the material is presented, in which there is a considerable degree of repetition and a number of special symbols are used, really is—as E. intends—a help to the reader.

M.A. KNIBB

GRABER, STEFAN, *Der Autortext in der historisch-kritischen Ausgabe* (Frankfurt–Bern–New York: Lang, 1998), pp. 240. SwF 30.00. ISBN 3-906759-60-1.

Much of this book is tangential to OT studies, but it raises some pertinent questions, if only as a reminder that it is difficult enough to produce critical editions of relatively modern texts where autograph manuscripts are available, let alone of biblical materials. The study arises from G.'s methodological reflections on his own completion of the historical-critical edition of J.H. Pestalozzi's writings, and the final chapter is a demonstration of how these principles have been put in practice in that edition. Those engaged in such work will find his scrupulous consideration of how to reconcile and represent inconsistencies or apparent errors in the authorial text itself and the early editions an impressive, perhaps even daunting, model. A broader readership will find that the outline history of text criticism in the first chapter gives a useful context to biblical developments. His later consideration of the historical development and social characteristics of the readership and market for critical editions (pp. 164-76) is intriguingly relevant to the growing interest in the Bible as market commodity. An extensive bibliography is supplied.

H. PYPER

GUTJAHR, PAUL C., *An American Bible: A History of the Good Book in the United States, 1777–1880* (Stanford: Stanford University Press, 1999; distributed outside the USA by Cambridge University Press), pp. xix + 256. $39.50/£25.00. ISBN 0-8047-3425-9.

This is a magnificently produced book, copiously illustrated and finely argued. It is in my judgment just the kind of book which more biblical scholars should be writing rather than the tediously tiresome reams of commentaries on already over-commentaried biblical books which are the stock-in-trade of the profession. G. is Assistant Professor of English and American Studies at Indiana University. This is the kind of book I would be proud to have written and wish that I had the ability to produce work so good in conjunction with a publisher of such splendid quality. I commend it strongly to all SOTS members and *Book List* readers. It is very much a study of the changing fate of the Bible as part of the developing print culture in the first century of America's independent existence. A fate represented by the shift of the Bible from the centre of the country's print culture and, while it remained a best-seller, it ceased to tower over that culture or even indeed to remain the central written text of burgeoning American culture. Among the great strengths of the book are its focus on the cultural materiality of Bible production, including translation, in the century under scrutiny and also a study of popular fiction involving the Bible, featuring the *Book of Mormon*, novels too many to mention here and a fine treatment of Lew Wallace's *Ben-Hur*. Some of the consequences of this popular fiction-alizing focus on the Bible entailed ways of avoiding engaging with the Bible in all its dense complexity. As for his postscriptal conclusion about the way the Book is never truly alone because it is 'constrained by its own materiality: how it is set in type, formatted, commented upon in marginalia, illustrated, bound and distributed… A book *is* judged by its cover, as well as by all aspects of its content and method of conveyance', now ain't that the truth! I thought this a magnificent book. This is how biblical scholarship should be done. Brilliant. I loved it.

R.P. CARROLL

HANHART, ROBERT, *Studien zur Septuaginta und zum hellenistischen Judentum* (ed. Reinhard Gregor Kratz; Forschungen zum Alten Testament, 24; Tübingen: J.C.B. Mohr [Paul Siebeck], 1999), pp. x + 298. DM 198.00. ISBN 3-16-147101-6; ISSN 0940-4155.

This German work is divided into the sections on the origin and history of the LXX (three articles, including one on the LXX and Lucianic recension of 2 Esdras [= the Greek translation of Ezra–Nehemiah] in relation to the Old Latin); the essence of the LXX (four articles, including the meaning of the LXX for the definition of 'Hellenistic Judaism', the interpretation of Dan. 11.29 as an indication of translation technique, Isa. 9.1[8.23]–7[6]); the effects of the LXX (criteria of historical truth in the Maccabean period—on the historical meaning of the world empire teaching in Daniel, on the place of Judaism in the history of ideas, two articles on the *status confessionis* of Israel in the Hellenistic period, the meaning of the LXX in the NT period); the continuing influence of the LXX (the LXX as a problem of textual history, history of research and theology, the history of LXX research in Göttingen, P.A. de Lagarde and his critique of theology), and a bibliography of H.

ED.

HARL, MARGUERITE, CÉCILE DOGNIEZ, LAURENCE BROTTIER, MICHEL CASEVITZ and PIERRE SANDEVOIR (eds.), *Les Douze Prophètes 4–9: Joël, Abdiou, Jonas, Naoum, Ambakoum, Sophonie* (with the collaboration of R. Dupont-Roc, T. Roqueplo, F. Roux; La Bible d'Alexandrie, 23.4-9; Paris; Cerf, 1999), pp. 417. N.P. ISBN 2-204-06265-0; ISSN 1243-1982.

The Twelve Prophets have been divided among several volumes of the Bible d'Alexandrie; this, the first volume to appear in print, will eventually be the third, and the first volume *Osé*, will contain a general introduction to the Twelve by Takamitsu Muraoka. The six prophetic books translated and annotated here are all treated separately, but the treatment in each case is similar, and conforms to the pattern set for the series as a whole. An introduction presents the Greek version both in its own right and in relation to the MT and to the Greek Bible as a whole; linguistic comments are followed by a survey of the reception of the book in early Jewish and Christian writers. The introduction to *Jonas* includes a section on iconography; that on *Naoum* argues that the divergences between the Greek and MT, far from indicating the incompetence of the translator, point to legitimate interpretative choices. A discussion of the *Prayer of Ambakoum* draws attention to the existence of a second translation, the so-called Barberini version, which shows some affinities with Symmachus, but this rival text is not translated or commented on. An excursus by Harl studies the meaning and history of the word lemma used as the heading of a prophecy.

N.R.M. DE LANGE

HARLÉ, PAUL (ed.), with the collaboration of THÉRÈSE ROQUEPLO, *Les Juges* (La Bible d'Alexandrie, 7; Paris: Cerf, 1999), pp. 286, including 1 map. N.P. ISBN 2-204-06147-6; ISSN 1243-1982.

The Greek book of Judges, H. declares, evinces a new approach to translation several generations after the translation of the first six biblical books. Where the translators of the Hexateuch sought to find Greek equivalents for the words of the Hebrew original, the translator or translators of Judges attempted to imitate the Hebrew language in Greek. The result is a Greek with a distinctive 'colour' which marks it out from other Greek writing of its time. In the introduction the Greek translation is subjected to a careful study, a separate chapter being devoted to the Canticle of Deborah, which circulated also in a collection of canticles. An account of ancient readings of Judges begins with the Bible itself, and continues through Josephus and Philo to the Christian authors Origen and Theodoret of Cyrrhus. Josephus rewrites the history of the Judges, hellenizing the language, excising certain episodes judged too alien to the Greek temper, and rearranging the order of events to yield a more satisfactory historical narrative. The Greek text used by Josephus was of Antiochian type, and H. speculates that the text may have been sent to Josephus in Rome from Antioch.

N.R.M. DE LANGE

PLAUT, W. GUNTHER (ed.), *Die Tora in jüdischer Auslegung: Band 1 Bereschit/ Genesis* (trans. and ed. Annette Böckler; Gütersloh: Chr. Kaiser/Gütersloher Verlagshaus, 1999), pp. 472. DM 64.00/AS 467/SwF 45.50. ISBN (set) 3-579-02645-3; (vol. 1) 3-579-02646-1.

This is the first volume of a translation of P.'s *The Torah: A Modern Commentary* published by the Union of American Hebrew Congregations in 1981. It contains a preface by the provincial rabbi of Hanover and by P. himself who emigrated from Germany in the 1930s. The commentary is designed for lay readers, including non-Jews. The format puts the Hebrew text on the top right-hand page, with a German translation underneath, accompanied by clarifications of individual words or verses and some textual notes. Sometimes the left-hand page is devoted to a longer comment about the overall story or pericope. Often, however, no lengthier comment is included, and the left-hand page is laid out like the right-hand, with only short notes. The Hebrew text seems to be a photographic reprint of the Bomberg text and is often not all that clear or aesthetically pleasing. The translation is that of Moses Mendelsohn but revised to modernize the language and to take account of new textual understandings. The Haftarah readings are also included, with a brief introduction in each case but no commentary.

ED.

SALVESEN, ALISON, *The Books of Samuel in the Syriac Version of Jacob of Edesa* (Monographs of the Peshitta Institute Leiden, 10; Leiden–Boston–Cologne: E.J. Brill, 1999), pp. xlviii + 170 (Syriac) + 125 (Eng.). Nlg 251.22/$140.00. ISBN 90-04-11543-9; ISSN 0169-9008.

About AD 700 Jacob produced his own version of the books of Samuel using different traditions, including the Peshitta, Syrohexapla, and the LXX in its various forms. This unique text does not seem to have had very wide acceptance. The relationship of Jacob's text to the other traditions has already been investigated recently, and S. gives only a brief summary of this. She also has an excursus on the use of Samuel in Jacob's other writings, and an excursus on names in his version of Samuel. Most of the volume is given over to the Syriac text (computer generated but with a form of the script closely following Jacob's own) and an English translation.

ED.

SEPMEIJER, FLORIS (ed.), *A Bilingual Concordance to the Targum of the Prophets, Vol. 12: Jeremiah (I)* (Leiden: E.J. Brill, 1998), pp. 322. Nlg 222.50/ $131.00. ISBN (vol. 12) 90-04-11012-7; (set) 90-04-10284-1.

SEPMEIJER, FLORIS (ed.), *A Bilingual Concordance to the Targum of the Prophets, Vol. 13: Jeremiah (II)* (Leiden: E.J. Brill, 1998), pp. 309. Nlg 222.50/ $131.00. ISBN (vol. 13) 90-04-11013-5; (set) 90-04-10284-1.

SEPMEIJER, FLORIS (ed.), *A Bilingual Concordance to the Targum of the Prophets, Vol. 14: Jeremiah (III)* (Leiden: E.J. Brill, 1998), pp. 363. Nlg 222.50/$131.00. ISBN (vol. 14) 90-04-11014-3; (set) 90-04-10284-1.

FINLEY, THOMAS (ed.) *A Bilingual Concordance to the Targum of the Prophets, Vol. 15: Ezekiel (I)* (Leiden: E.J. Brill, 1999), pp. 317. Nlg 231.39/$129.00. ISBN (vol. 15) 90-04-11015-1; (set) 90-04-10284-1.

FINLEY, THOMAS (ed.), *A Bilingual Concordance to the Targum of the Prophets, Vol. 16: Ezekiel* (II) (Leiden: E.J. Brill, 1999), pp. 330. Nlg 231.39/$129.00. ISBN (vol. 16) 90-04-11017-8; (set) 90-04-10284-1.

FINLEY, THOMAS (ed.), *A Bilingual Concordance to the Targum of the Prophets, Vol. 17: Ezekiel (III)* (Leiden: E.J. Brill 1999), pp. 361. Nlg 231.39/$129.00. ISBN (vol. 17) 90-04-11018-6; (set) 90-04-10284-1.

Since the first volume of the *Bilingual Concordance*, an impressive and most useful instrument of research, appeared in 1995 the editors have shown admirable diligence and speed in advancing their plan to publish volumes on all the Former and the Latter Prophets (see *B.L.* 1997, p. 51: 1998, p. 61). The editors of the volumes on *Jeremiah* and *Ezekiel* under review here maintain the high standard that has been shown in the production of the earlier volumes. In accordance with the principle formulated in the first volume in the series, the editors of these volumes use Sperber's edition as the text of the Targum. But both Sepmeijer, in his preface to *Jeremiah*, and Finley, in his preface to *Ezekiel*, note that they have incorporated corrections to Sperber's edition which were supplied by Jerome Lund of the team compiling *The Comprehensive Aramaic Lexicon* at the Hebrew Union College, Cincinnati. However, there seems to be no way of discovering where corrections of Sperber's text have been introduced. The statistical information supplied by the *Concordance* will offer invaluable assistance to the student of the Targums. We learn, for example, from p. 223 of vol. 1 of *Jeremiah*, that the word *gabra* occurs 139 times in the Targum of Jeremiah; on six occasions there is no corresponding word in the Hebrew text; in 125 passages the Hebrew correspondent is *'ish*, 'man', once the Hebrew *Vorlage* has *ba'l*, 'lord, owner', on seven occasions the Hebrew word translated is *geber*, 'young man'. Information like this enables us to evaluate the targumist's consistency or lack of it in translating particular Hebrew words or terms. The statistics can also give us an insight into the targumist's theological views. Thus, for example, if we wish to find out how the authors of the Targums of Jeremiah and Ezekiel understood the term *shekina*, 'Shekinah', we can check out this word in Sepmeijer's or Finley's works. These two editors have made a worthy contribution to the important *Bilingual Concordance* and their practical works which put so much information at the disposal of scholars will become necessary tools for anyone seriously interested in the Targums of Jeremiah and Ezekiel.

M. MAHER

STIPP, HERMANN-JOSEF, *Deuterojeremianische Konkordanz* (Arbeiten zu Text und Sprache im Alten Testament, 63; St Ottilien: Eos 1998), pp. vi + 193. DM 28.00. ISBN 3-88096-563-3.

This concordance continues S.'s interest in the light that may be shed on Jeremiah's literary history by a close study of its distinctive phrases (see *B.L.* 1996, p. 48). Do certain lexical strings expose redactional developments, or affirm a text's essential unity? S.'s presentation of the data moves beyond what one might find by performing searches in computerized Bible programs. He wishes, rather, to sketch the range of possible influences that may be detected in the 'deuteronomic' phraseology of the book. S. also furthers his interest in the relationship between LXX and MT forms of the book, and differences are accordingly noted in the concordance proper. The end result is something like the appendix to Weinfeld's *Deuteronomy and the Deuteronomic School* (or Bright's oft-cited article from *JBL* 70 [1951]) on steroids. A given word heads a list broken up by settings in which that word occurs, cited in context from Jeremiah, plus the references only of comparable phrases from elsewhere in the Hebrew Bible. Clearly, this will be of interest for those working closely with the text of Jeremiah; and, in themselves, the lists prove nothing one way or the other. But S.'s diligence—even perseverance—in collecting this material may well assist the research of others.

D.J. REIMER

TALSHIR, ZIPORA, *I Esdras: From Origin to Translation* (SBLSCS, 47; Atlanta: Society of Biblical Literature, 1999), pp. xii + 305. $57.00. ISBN 0-88414-006-7.

T. has been published articles on 1 Esdras for many years, and she indicates that a major text-critical commentary is in preparation. It is therefore welcome that she has decided here to gather together the results of her research on three particular topics. The first concerns the perennial problem of the composition of the book: is it a complete work in its own right, a fragment of a larger work, or a translation of an earlier form of Chronicles–Ezra–Nehemiah? She argues resolutely in favour of the first of these possibilities, seeing the purpose of the whole to be the preservation of the story of the three guardsmen (which many other scholars regard as a secondary interpolation), together with sufficient context to make clear the significance which it attributes to Zerubbabel. This is the least satisfactory chapter in the book. Her own proposal is asserted rather than argued, and although it accounts well for some of the transpositions of material in Ezra 1–6, there are other parts of 1 Esdras whose inclusion is not so well explained. It is also disappointing that she was not able to make more than passing mention of the monograph of D. Böhler (cf. *B.L.* 1999, pp. 96-97), though she promises a full rebuttal of his diametrically opposite view in the future. The second chapter deals with text-critical issues, and argues on the basis of much well-presented evidence that the *Vorlage* of 1 Esdras and the MT of Chronicles–Ezra–Nehemiah each developed independently in the course of their prior transmission. The third chapter discusses the nature of the work as a translation, again with careful analysis and clear presentation of a wealth of detailed evidence. To adopt old-fashioned terminology, T. is stronger in lower than in higher criticism.

H.G.M. WILLIAMSON

THUESEN, PETER J., *In Discordance with the Scriptures: American Protestant Battles over Translating the Bible* (Oxford: Oxford University Press, 1999), pp. xi + 238. £16.99. ISBN 0-19-512736-6.

This fascinating history of controversies over Bible translations focuses on the RSV and its aftermath (chs. 3–4) and the NIV (ch. 5). However, T. has an introductory chapter on the beginnings of Bible translating in the sixteenth century and another chapter on the Revised Version. Much of the controversy concentrated on one verse, Isa. 7.14, for which the RSV had used 'young woman'. Although the RSV was defended by some notable Evangelical scholars (e.g., at Fuller Theological Seminary), it was dissatisfaction with this that led to the NIV whose translators had to subscribe to belief in the inerrancy of Scripture. T. notes that Zondervan publishers negotiated for exclusive rights and provided advances to fund the project, even though the publisher had been an enthusiastic distributor of the RSV: 'Zondervan's dual loyalties reflected pecuniary as well as theological motives, but such was the pragmatism of the American Bible business' (p. 148).

ED.

TOV, EMANUEL, *The Greek and Hebrew Bible: Collected Essays on the Septuagint* (VTSup, 72; Leiden–Boston–Cologne: E.J. Brill, 1999), pp. xxxviii + 570. Nlg 265.00/$148.00. ISBN 90-04-11309-6; ISSN 0083-5889.

This publishes 38 of T.'s essays on the LXX (the great majority of those he has written), in six sections: General Studies, Lexicography, Translation Technique and Exegesis, the LXX and Textual Criticism of the Hebrew Bible, the LXX and Literary Criticism of the Hebrew Bible, and Revisions of the LXX. Few if any living scholars have done more to investigate the place of the Greek versions in the textual criticism of the Hebrew Bible, and to have most of his studies collected together is a great service to scholarship. The studies were written between 1971 and 1997 and have all been revised. In some cases, discussion in the original articles can now be omitted or shortened because of the more recent treatment in T.'s *Text-Critical Use of the Septuagint* (*B.L.* 1982, p. 38; 1998, p. 62) and *Textual Criticism of the Hebrew Bible* (*B.L.* 1993, p. 53: 1998, p. 62). The section on literary criticism is extremely important because it demonstrates how the traditional dividing line between 'lower' and 'higher' criticism cannot always be drawn. One regrets the lack of indexes. The fact that this is volume 72 of *VT* Supplements is surely no coincidence!

ED.

ULRICH, EUGENE, *The Dead Sea Scrolls and the Origins of the Bible* (Studies in the Dead Sea Scrolls and Related Literature; Grand Rapids, MI: Eerdmans, 1999; distributed in the UK by Alban Books, Bristol), pp. xviii + 309. $25.00/£15.06. ISBN 0-8028-4611-4.

U. has been the chief editor of the biblical scrolls from Qumran in the DJD series, and the fourteen articles reprinted in this volume reflect his longstanding concern with the evidence provided by the Qumran biblical scrolls, and more generally with the textual history of the Hebrew Bible and of the LXX. The articles were originally published between 1980 and 1998, the majority in *Festschriften* or in volumes of papers from conferences, and there is a certain degree of overlap between them. Four of the articles in the first part of the volume have as a primary focus the significance of the pluriform character of the biblical texts from Qumran, and particularly the significance of multiple literary editions of biblical texts, both for our understanding of textual history and for our understanding of the 'canonical process'. Two further articles in this section offer a valuable critique of the views of Cross, Talmon and Tov concerning the history of the biblical text, and of the view that there is a distinctive 'Qumran practice' of orthography and morphology, while two other articles focus respectively on the palaeo-Hebrew manuscripts from Qumran Cave 4 and on 4QDan^a and 4QDan^b. The second part of the volume is concerned with the biblical scrolls from Qumran, the LXX, and the Old Latin. It contains articles on the LXX manuscripts from Qumran, on Josephus's text of Samuel, two articles on Origen's Hexapla, and two on the Old Latin. U. writes with knowledge and authority on questions of both text and canon, and it is good to have these articles republished together in this convenient form.

M.A. KNIBB

WEITZMAN, M.P., *The Syriac Version of the Old Testament: An Introduction* (University of Cambridge Oriental Publications, 56; Cambridge: Cambridge University Press, 1999), pp. xv + 355. £50.00/$79.95. ISBN 0-521-63288-9.

This comprehensive introduction to the Peshitta argues strongly in favour of much greater consistency and coherence among the Syriac translators than is sometimes acknowledged. Evidence for this consistency W. finds especially in the authors' translation technique, which is exhaustively analysed and copiously illustrated with examples drawn from the whole Peshitta version. W. argues that the translators worked from a Hebrew *Vorlage* which shared a common ancestor with MT, and which differed from the *Vorlage* of LXX: he thus broadly agrees with Emanuel Tov that Peshitta can be assigned to the 'same basic category as MT', and that its value for textual criticism of the Hebrew Bible should not be over-rated. The translators somewhat sporadically consulted LXX, the evidence suggesting that those who made most use of that version were also the most likely to adopt 'modern' Syriac vocabulary (rather than more ancient and venerable expressions, or Syriac words reminiscent of the original Hebrew). Peshitta translation redolent of Aramaic Targum, however, cannot sustain the thesis that the Peshitta translators drew upon written Targums; nor does it support the theory that the extant Syriac represents a 'simplified' version translated from an Aramaic Targum. W. shows at length how similarities between Targum and Peshitta arose through polygenesis, coincidence, or from the translators' familiarity with a common stock of widely known Aramaic traditions of exegesis.

His close attention to translation technique leads W. to discern the hands of some fifteen different translators, putting into Syriac the books of the Hebrew Bible in their canonical order. Thus he suggests that later translators made use of their precursors' work: he allows for consultation among the translators, and indicates that their work was finished within a relatively short time span (c. 150–c. 200 CE). Following investigation of the ideas and theology peculiar to the version, he concludes that the Peshitta version was made at Edessa, by Jews belonging to a distinctly non-rabbinic community isolated from other Jews, who converted to Christianity and brought their version with them. Finally, the Peshitta manuscript tradition is (as might be expected from a fine textual scholar) painstakingly scrutinized: one of the many important conclusions resulting from this scrutiny is the (surely correct) deduction that the manuscripts show no evidence for an 'earlier' Peshitta which could be likened to an Aramaic Targum.

It will be obvious that a short review cannot do anything like justice to a major and impressive achievement of this kind. Certainly students of Peshitta will find themselves disagreeing with W. over this or that detail; but such debate will itself only enhance the significance of this remarkable introduction to the Peshitta. There is nothing else written on the Syriac version as a whole which comes close to emulating this work. In his Foreword to the book, Robert Gordon describes W.'s work as 'a landmark study', and it stands before us as a fitting memorial to a great scholar.

C.T.R. HAYWARD

WIEDER, LAURANCE (ed.), *The Poets' Book of Psalms: The Complete Psalter as Rendered by Twenty-Five Poets from the Sixteenth to the Twentieth Centuries* (Oxford Paperbacks; Oxford: Oxford University Press, 1999 [1995]), pp. xxiii + 311. £9.99/$15.95. ISBN 0-19-513058-8.

This book is for biblical scholars of a literary bent. Originally published in 1995 by HarperCollins, an introduction of eleven pages gives a short history of the translation of the psalms into English. Among the poets chosen only three have more than ten poems selected, one of whom is W. himself, another being Mary Sidney Herbert with 28. The most familiar is probably George Herbert's rendering of the twenty-third psalm, 'The king of love my shepherd is'—his only contribution. To enable cross-referencing the Authorized Version of the psalter is printed in full, separately at the end. The pieces printed are poems inspired by each psalm. George Herbert's poem is closest to the Hebrew—some seem to have only a suggestive connection! But these are poems inspired by the Hebrew psalms, not paraphrases or poetic versions: some indeed seem far from the psalm itself, not least W.'s own contributions. Thus, as understanding of the Hebrew original will not be helped, this volume is to be recommended to readers with an interest primarily in English literature rather than Hebrew language and philology.

J.G. SNAITH

WIJESINGHE, SHIRLEY LAL, *Jeremiah 34,8-22: Structure and Redactional History of the Masoretic Text and of the Septuagint Hebrew Vorlage* (Logos, 37, 1–2; Colombo, Sri Lanka: Centre for Society and Religion, 1999), pp. xii + 233. $18.00. ISSN 1391-0582.

This study in redaction criticism of Jer. 34(41).8-22 forms part of a doctoral dissertation defended at the Catholic University of Louvain and completed under the direction of P.-M. Bogaert. The author argues that a 'shorter text', consisting of vv. 13, 14a*, 14b-20, can be identified behind the short text represented by the reconstructed Hebrew *Vorlage* of Jer. LXX 41.8-22, and that in the former the historical background is the Josianic reform, but that in the latter Zedekiah has been made responsible for the transgression of the covenant as a means both of explaining the disparity between the promise to Zedekiah in Jer. LXX 41.5 and his fate as described in Jer. LXX 52.10-11 and of explaining why the exile of 598 occurred. In these two texts the author takes the reference to the calf to be to the golden calf incident. In the long text represented by Jer. MT 34.8-11 the reference to the calf has been made into a reference to the covenant ceremony of Genesis 15 as a means of showing that the effects of transgressing the covenant were limited to the Zedekian generation which had entered into the covenant regarding slavery, and thus did not affect the future kingship and (particularly) priesthood with whom Yahweh would conclude an inviolable unilateral covenant (Jer. MT 33.14-26). The author supports his arguments by a detailed analysis of the literary structure of the three versions of the text with which he is concerned.

M.A. KNIBB

ZIEGLER, JOSEPH, *Susanna, Daniel, Bel et Draco* (ed. Olivier Munnich; foreword by R. Smend; Septuaginta, Vetus Testamentum Graecum 16/2; Göttingen: Vandenhoeck & Ruprecht, 2nd edn, 1999), pp. 407. DM 188.00. ISBN 3-525-534469.

The 1954 edition is partially revised to take account of developments and finds in the past half century. Because further portions of Pap. 967 have been found, the 'LXX' (Origenic) text has been revised by Munnich. The 'Theodotion' text is reprinted from the previous edition; however, a long appendix by Detlef Fraenkel (pp. 170-214) discusses the fragments of this text found since the first edition, along with a collation of the data. These were not thought significant enough to warrant the expense of a revised text. Considering the amount of interest in the Greek versions of Daniel in recent years (cf. *B.L.* 1989, p. 47; 1996, pp. 44-45; 1997, p. 51), this revised edition is most welcome.

L.L. GRABBE

5. EXEGESIS AND MODERN TRANSLATIONS

BAILDAM, JOHN D., *Paradisal Love: Johann Gottfried Herder and the Song of Songs* (JSOTSup, 298; Sheffield: Sheffield Academic Press, 1999), pp. 368. £55.00/ $90.00. ISBN 1-84127-022-9; ISSN 0309-0787.

Originally a German doctoral dissertation, 'this work claims to be the first comprehensive published study of the preoccupation of... Herder (1744–1803) with the Song of Songs... It argues that, despite Herder's claims to the contrary, his own cultural position is revealed in his translations and his unique interpretation of the work as the voice of pure, paradisal love' (p. 9). The work describes Herder's approach to poetry and the Bible, his work as a translator, and his reception, interpretation and translations of Song. Of particular interest is the author's line-by-line commentary on Herder's translations (pp. 235-90). It is significant that, contrary to the prevailing view of the period, he defended the literal as against the allegorical interpretation of Song, although he did not consider it to be a drama. For comparative purposes, the translations of the Song by Herder, Luther and Goethe are provided in appendices. A bibliography and indexes are also supplied. It is refreshing to read a study of Song from the perspective of German language and literature, particularly when all the German passages quoted are glossed.

W.G.E. WATSON

BALTZER, KLAUS, *Deutero-Jesaja* (KAT, 10/2; Gütersloh: Gütersloher Verlagshaus, 1999), pp. 680. DM 220.00/AS 1606/SwF 198.00. ISBN 3-579-04291-2.

B.'s sumptuous commentary on Isaiah 40–55 will undoubtedly establish a landmark in the study of these sixteen chapters of the book and place all future students in his debt. Not least his judicious review of more than a century of research, his bibliographies and fair-minded assessments of different solutions to problems, coupled with detailed text-critical and lexicographical comments make this volume an indispensable resource. So far as B.'s own proposals are concerned the following are worthy of note: in literary form all sixteen chapters are regarded as a liturgical drama, with a prologue in 40.1-31, followed by six separate dramatic acts, concluding with an epilogue in 55.1-13, which celebrates a pilgrimage festival to the Holy City. The four Servant Passages are formed from a combination of biographical experience and a typified recollection of the figure of Moses. They form an integral feature of the larger liturgical drama of the book. Throughout there is extensive appeal to other canonical texts, not only from the collection of Isaiah prophecies, but also from Jeremiah, Ezekiel and the Pentateuch. This presupposes a library providing access to them and a tradition of interpretation. Essentially B. regards Deutero-Isaiah as comprising a single, carefully constructed, text which displays homogeneity and coherence. While not ruling out the familiar assumed time of origin in the mid-sixth century, c. 540 BCE, he makes a strong case for dating it a century later, seeing reflected in it the political conflicts and the renewal of Jerusalem in Nehemiah's time. Altogether the volume belongs to the category of essential reference works for the serious librarian and researcher.

R.E. CLEMENTS

BARBIERO, GIANNI, *Das erste Psalmenbuch als Einheit: Eine synchrone Analyse von Psalm 1–41* (Österreichische biblische Studien, 16; Frankfurt–Bern–New York: Lang, 1999), pp. 785. SwF 61.00. ISBN 3-631-33854-6; ISSN 0948-1664.

The author sees the first book of the Psalms (1–41) as having its own character, coherence and development of theme. His aim is to demonstrate this by a close reading and structural analysis of the final text, somewhat in the tradition of Ridderbos, Schökel, Auffret and Girard. He shows the close relationship of Pss. 1 and 2, which together form the book's prologue, and then finds a series of four structural units (Pss. 3–14, 15–24, 25–34, 35–41). In these units, the prologue's theme of 'kingdom' appears first as man's royal position in creation, then the office of the Lord's Anointed, then the sovereignty of the Lord, and finally the role of the Servant. The work of analysis is carried through with clarity and good reference to the relevant literature, and the resultant large book will be a useful tool for consideration of the relationship between psalms and groups of psalms.

J.H. EATON

BARTHOLOMEW, CRAIG G., *Reading Ecclesiastes: Old Testament Exegesis and Hermeneutical Theory* (AnBib, 139; Rome: Pontifical Biblical Institute, 1998), pp. vii + 319. Lire 45,000/$30.00. ISBN 88-7653-139-4.

The sub-title is perhaps more representative of the nature of this book than the lead title. It is a revised version of a 1996 Bristol University PhD which seeks to use the interpretation of the book of Ecclesiastes, both past and present, as a foil for discussing every conceivable hermeneutical theory as a way of moving 'towards a correct interpretation of this perplexing book'. This 'correct' interpretation turns out to be one in which 'the philosophical scaffolding of OT studies' is 'shaped by a Christian perspective upon reality'. The author is completely up-front in his approach, arguing that 'transformational Christian perspective in OT hermeneutics is incompatible with the antithetical philosophical pluralism present in the academy' (whatever that might be!). Ecclesiastes is taken to be an 'ironic exposure' of 'an empiricistic epistemology which seeks wisdom through personal experience and analysis with the "glasses" of the fear of God'. But if it has such a subtle and positive message, then the history of interpretation would suggest that, contrary to B.'s strong assertion, the author of Ecclesiastes was rather incompetent at communicating with his readers. Readers sympathetic with B.'s starting point might find the book of some value but, in the end, even they might find it difficult to see what is distinctly 'Christian' about the few attempts at exegesis which he actually provides.

A.P. HAYMAN

BAUER, ANGELA, *Gender in the Book of Jeremiah: A Feminist-Literary Reading* (Studies in Biblical Literature, 5; Frankfurt–Bern–New York: Lang, 1999), pp. xiii + 203. SwF 29.00. ISBN 0-8204-3899-5; ISSN 1089-0645.

B. takes as her starting point Jeremiah's specific call to women to 'Hear...the word of Yahweh' (9.19) and goes on to consider all the passages containing imagery that might be considered to be associated with women's lives. Those passages referring to the womb, giving birth, prostitution, marriage, divorce, rape and so on, are all given a feminist-literary treatment. A new perspective is gained by seeing these passages grouped together in this way. B. searches for 'male' and 'female' voices in Jeremiah and discovers (perhaps not surprisingly) that for the most part, 'male voices surround female voices' (p. 159). However, there are also reversals of this pattern, and these counter-traditions leave the way open for a changed perception of the book's message. B.'s work has its base more in the biblical text than in feminist theory, which means that she is more in the tradition of scholars such as Trible and Bird than feminists who have moved more towards gender and cultural studies. B. manages to avoid some of the clichés sometimes appearing in this kind of scholarship, and the result is an interesting reading of Jeremiah that can be recommended both to Jeremiah scholars and those with an interest in feminist biblical interpretation.

C. SMITH

BELLIA, GIUSEPPE and ANGELO PASSARO (eds.), *Libro dei Proverbi: Tradizione, redazione, teologia* (Casale Monferrato: Edizioni Piemme, 1999), pp. 260. Lire 32,000. ISBN 88-384-4377-7.

The book is a collection of papers read at a conference on the Book of Proverbs held at Palermo in June 1998. The eleven Roman Catholic authors set themselves the task of exploring new approaches to the structure, redaction and social background of the book. R. Clifford finds a semblance of unity in the way chs. 1–9 contextualize compilations of familiar aphoristic material. H.-W. Jüngling discovered a remarkably well-developed structure in the first 'Solomonic' collection (10.1–22.16) and subjected one unit, 10.28–11.7, to a detailed formal analysis, finding evidence of cross-references to the prophetic literature. Inspired by the recent monograph of S.L. Harris (*Proverbs 1–9: A Study of Inner-Biblical Interpretation* [*B.L.* 1997, p. 64]), Passaro explored the intertextual links between Prov. 1.8-19 and Gen. 37.12-36 concluding, somewhat too rapidly one suspects, on the direct dependence of the former on the latter. A summary investigation of the historical and anthropological setting of the individual compilations, with special reference to the social context of the exercise of moral authority, led Bellia to set chs. 1–9 against the background of a well-developed, complex and predominantly lay urban society. L. Viganò discovered relevant examples of the sapiential in the form of legends in the Ugaritic texts, H. Simian-Yofre suggested the meaning 'sarcasm' for the term מליצה (ליץ>), and M. Gilbert argued that the 'valiant woman' ('woman of substance'?) of Prov. 31.10-31 is more a role model for practical and religious wisdom than a personification of Wisdom. P. Beauchamp and P. Iovino followed some of the well-known lines leading from the personification of Wisdom and the parable as symbolic narrative to the New Testament. A. Minissale and E. Puech, finally, contributed useful discussions of, respectively, the LXX of Proverbs and relevant Qumran material.

J. BLENKINSOPP

BERRIGAN, DANIEL, *Jeremiah: The World, The Wound of God* (Minneapolis: Fortress Press, 1998), pp. xii + 195. $18.00. ISBN 0-8006-3138-2.

Jeremiah here receives the same treatment as Fr Berrigan has recently accorded to Isaiah (1996), Ezekiel (*B.L.* 1999, p. 61), the Psalms (*B.L.* 1999, pp. 61-62) and Daniel (1998). In short the book is not a commentary in the historical-critical sense but a reader's response to the biblical text by a poet and radical activist in the light of his deeply held convictions about the need to speak up against prejudice, violence, the misuse of power, and every other sort of *sheqer* in today's world. It has a number of features to which the present reviewer is allergic, not least single-sentence paragraphs and the gross over-use of exclamation marks. But B.'s poetical paraphrases of the text are often striking, and a man who has himself frequently been at odds with his government and his superiors and has endured imprisonment for his beliefs (notably over Vietnam and nuclear warfare) is not surprisingly able to bring some distinctive insights to bear on the text of Jeremiah. A passionate and personal book.

B.P. ROBINSON

BRENNER, ATHALYA (ed.), *Ruth and Esther: A Feminist Companion to the Bible (Second Series)* (The Feminist Companion to the Bible [Second Series], 3; Sheffield: Sheffield Academic Press, 1999), pp. 271. £16.95/$28.50. ISBN 1-85075-978-2.

Following the very successful series of the Feminist Companion to specific biblical books, a second series takes up the books of Ruth and Esther (although it would be more appropriate to leave Esther out since out of fourteen articles only two are exclusively devoted to this book). While the first series explored in some depth gender relationships in Ruth, the second series is more illustrative of a broad range of feminist methodologies, leaving some of the gender debates behind and exploring some contemporary social issues such as immigration, alienation and grief (Honig: 'Ruth, The Model Emigree: Mourning and the Symbolic Politics of Immigration'). The book of Ruth is seen as providing a model for contemporary rural women in Germany (Silber's article). Fischer's article provides a link to the first series in its examination of female authorship and positing Ruth as a Torah exegete (in Part I: Aspects of the Ruth Scroll). Fontaine's article, based on an illustration of a Jewish mediaeval manuscript representing Ruth with a cat face among women with bird faces (the men are men!) belongs to the history of interpretation. The second part is made up of papers given at the Semiotics and Exegesis Session, in SBL 1997 and is also characterized by a diversity of readings with contemporary resonances (e.g. Dube's article, the Unpublished Letters of Orpah to Ruth read from an African woman's view point or Donaldson, from a native American's). One of the attractive features of this book is to make available in English both new and foreign material. The diversity and creativity of feminist readings is once again illustrated in this series.

A. JEFFERS

BRENNER, ATHALYA (ed.), *Judges: A Feminist Companion to the Bible (Second Series)* (The Feminist Companion to the Bible [Second Series], 4; Sheffield: Sheffield Academic Press, 1999), pp. 174. £16.95/$28.50. ISBN 1-84127-024-5.

This second collection (for the first, see *B.L.* 1995, p. 57) includes essays by Lillian Klein (on Achsah as a model for Israelite womanhood), Claudia Rakel (on the intertextual relationship between Jdt. 16.1-17, Judg. 5.2-31 and Exod. 15.1-19), Shulamit Valler (on the story of Jephthah's daughter in early Midrash), Phyllis Silverman Kramer (on later rabbinic understanding of the story of Jephthah's daughter, and the treatment of the major themes of the story in painting), Carol Smith (on differing feminist understandings of Delilah), Renate Jost (a feminist reading of the prayer of Samson in Judges 16), concluding with essays by Ilse Müllner and Alice Bach (on sexual violence against women in Judges 19 and Judges 21). The editor distinguishes this collection from the earlier by drawing attention to the heavy emphasis on intertextuality in the later volume, and on the significance of Judges in relation to the social and anthropological analysis of gender relations both within and outside the Bible.

A.D.H. MAYES

BRUEGGEMANN, WALTER, *Isaiah 1–39* (Westminster Bible Companion; Louisville, KY: Westminster/John Knox Press, 1998), pp. x + 314. £20.00. ISBN 0-664-25524-8.

BRUEGGEMANN, WALTER, *Isaiah 40–66* (Westminster Bible Companion; Louisville, KY: Westminster/John Knox Press, 1998), pp. x + 263. $18.00. ISBN 0-664-25791-7.

These two volumes belong together in a series aimed at mediating contemporary scholarship to a readership of lay persons and study groups. The format concentrates on theological exposition, noting the changing approaches adopted by recent scholars towards the text, with attention to the coherence of all 66 chapters and the reception-history of the book within both Christian and Jewish tradition. There is therefore careful attention to the importance of the text among the sixteenth-century Christian Reformers, with Calvin to the fore, and its relevance for the presentation of a biblical doctrine of God as Creator and Goal of human history. The exposition points to the relevance for the present day of the book's emphasis on a world order of peace and justice with the overthrow of all forms of tyranny, whether military, political or economic. Exploration of the basic themes of God-given hope as the only antidote to human despair, the concept of exile as a human, and not simply Jewish, challenge and the need for a re-integration of theological exegesis with social commitment characterize both volumes.

R.E. CLEMENTS

CLIFFORD, RICHARD J., *Proverbs* (OTL; Norwich: SCM-Canterbury; Louisville, KY: Westminster/John Knox Press, 1999), pp. xvi + 286. £28.50/$25.00. ISBN 0-664-22131-9.

Many previous commentators have laid considerable emphasis upon connections between Proverbs and foreign literature, most notably the instructions and sayings collections of Egypt and Mesopotamia. Indeed, William McKane's commentary in the OTL series devoted around a third of its pages to examining those texts and re-arranged parts of Proverbs, for purposes of discussion, in accordance with a scheme derived from the foreign works. This new commentary in the same series attempts no such re-organization and presents no more than a brief sketch of the relevant non-Israelite material. This certainly makes the commentary easier to use, but it does not signal any lack of enthusiasm for foreign texts and traditions as guides in the interpretation of Proverbs. Indeed, the most distinctive feature of this work is its attempt to understand wisdom and some other concepts against a background of Mesopotamian mythological ideas. The interpretation of various passages is influenced by this approach: in 26.16, for instance, the seven men to whom the fool considers himself superior are identified with the seven sages of Mesopotamian tradition, rather than simply as 'many' men. More significantly, C. takes personified wisdom in chs. 1–9 to be portrayed as an *ummānu*, a royal advisor, and ties this, principally by means of a late text from Uruk, to the story in Berossus of humans being taught civilization by the beast Oannes. Wisdom, on this reading, reflects Mesopotamian mythological ideas about the transmission of divine wisdom to humans. However, it seems far from certain that the role of *ummānu* had such mythological significance in Mesopotamia, and the evidence evinced for knowledge of such ideas in Syria-Palestine is, frankly, unconvincing. C. also associates the 'foreign woman' with stories of goddesses who offer themselves to mortals—a link which is not at all apparent. Although interesting, then, these suggestions seem highly speculative, and leave one wondering once more what it is about Proverbs that drives so many commentators to consider every context for it except that of early Judaism. Mythological backgrounds aside, this commentary offers few new solutions to the many problems in Proverbs, but it does achieve a good balance between detailed discussion of the text and language, on the one hand, and investigations of structure and presentation, on the other. In general, then, this is a useful and very accessible book, but one which is marred by its repeated, but unnecessary and poorly supported attempts to read Proverbs in terms of Mesopotamian mythology.

S. WEEKS

COATS, GEORGE W., *Exodus 1–18* (FOTL, 2A; Grand Rapids, MI: Eerdmans, 1999; distributed in the UK by Alban Books, Bristol), pp. xiv + 178. $24.00/£15.99. ISBN 0-8028-0592-2.

C., like the FOTL project as a whole, belongs to a strand of American scholarship which has maintained its links with German historical criticism when others have abandoned it for methods drawn from the study of contemporary literature. Here his life-work on the Exodus, Moses and wilderness traditions is distilled readily into the format required by the series, with treatments both of the composition of the whole narrative (or rather of its major sources J and P) and of its individual pericopae seen as examples of recurring minor genres and formulae. Although C. has fashioned his insights into the form of a commentary, his objective analysis of the text offers much to enrich the work of others. Sadly the disability of recent years prevented him from publishing this work before the appearance of major new works with their distinctive approaches or revising it to take adequate account of them. The editors of the series have done their best by adding occasional annotations and lists of recent publications. C.'s account of the structure and growth of the Exodus tradition fully deserves to stand alongside more recent studies by E. Blum, J. Van Seters and K. Schmid as a serious alternative to them.

G.I. DAVIES

CONRAD, EDGAR W., *Zechariah* (Readings: A New Biblical Commentary; Sheffield: Sheffield Academic Press, 1999), pp. 220. £35.00/$57.50; paper £13.95/$23.75. ISBN 1-85075-899-9; (paper) 1-85075-900-6; ISSN 0952-7656.

Those familiar with C.'s earlier work, particularly his *Reading Isaiah* (enthusiastically welcomed in *B.L.* 1993, p. 57) will have some idea of what to expect here. This is not a historical-critical study, and the customary division into 'Proto'- and 'Deutero'-Zechariah is not followed. Instead, the whole book of Zechariah is read in its literary context, which is essentially that of the Twelve, seen as a 'collage'. There are many intertextual insights and a recurring motif is the way in which 'prophets' are now seen as figures of the past who have given way to 'messengers'; a possible linkage with Haggai here is drawn out in a particularly interesting way. The visions are not to be seen as portraying a new and fantastic world, but emanate from Zechariah's 'real' world, that of the Jerusalem temple. C. stresses that we should not regard what he offers here as the only possible reading, but he undoubtedly offers rich insights into this puzzling book.

R.J. COGGINS

CREACH, JEROME F.D., *Psalms* (Interpretation Bible Studies; Louisville, KY: Geneva Press, 1999), pp. vii + 106. $7.00. ISBN 0-664-50021-8.

The series in which this booklet appears is designed to provide simplified aids for personal or group study, as practical companions to volumes in the *Interpretation Commentary* series (John Knox Press), in this case *Psalms* by J.L. Mays (1994). The subject-matter is treated in ten 'units', in which, besides a survey of types of psalms, nine psalms are taken as examples of different types and, to some extent, of different ways of looking at them. The style of presentation is generally non-technical, but further resources (Mays or other commentators) are often referred to. Three units perhaps stand out: those on Psalm 121 (emphasizing the implicit 'portrait of God'), Psalm 8 (focused on human responsibility for creation) and Psalm 137(which takes anger seriously). The author revealingly hints at problems his readers may have in feeling with the speakers in all those psalms which rise 'from the depths of great suffering, oppression and persecution', not likely to be familiar to 'most North American Christians' (p. 2). He suggests use of these psalms in intercessory prayer for those less fortunate, but his examples are comfortably distant from the readers he seems to envision.

R.P.R. MURRAY

DAVIES, GORDON F., *Ezra and Nehemiah* (Berit Olam, Studies in Hebrew Narrative and Poetry; Collegeville, MN: Michael Glazier [Liturgical Press], 1999), pp. xxii + 138. $29.95. ISBN 0-8146-5049-X.

Ezra and Nehemiah are here read not primarily as a source of historical information from a little-documented period nor, as so often, as little more than 'an ill-sorted scrapbook', but in terms of rhetorical criticism, of the kind introduced into NT studies by G.A. Kennedy and others. So Ezra 4, for example, often the despair of historical analysts, is here seen as a rhetorical unit. Parallels and differences between the Exodus situation and that of the community under Persian rule are explored. Free use is made of the traditional terminology of classical rhetoric, but it might have been helpful to explore more fully the applicability of these terms to Hebrew narrative structures. (The possibility that Ezra–Nehemiah reached their final form in the Hellenistic period is touched upon only in passing.) The series in which this appears had earlier volumes on 1 Kings (*B.L.* 1998, p. 96) and 1 Samuel (*B.L.* 1999, pp. 71-72); see also p. 81 below.

R.J. COGGINS

DIAMOND, A.R. PETE, KATHLEEN M. O'CONNOR and LOUIS STULMAN, *Troubling Jeremiah* (JSOTSup, 260; Sheffield: Sheffield Academic Press, 1999), pp. 463. £50.00/$85.00. ISBN 1-85075-910-3; ISSN 0309-0787.

The SBL Book of Jeremiah Group here presents the substance of several years' work to the wider world. Only four of the 21 contributors are based outside the USA (two from the UK, one each from Australia and Denmark). Diamond provides an editorial overview of the whole (plus some insights into the workings of the group); there follow sections on (1) Text- or (2) Reader-centered readings, (3) theological proposals, and (4) summary responses from two well-seasoned and distinctly flavoured Jeremiah commentators (Brueggemann and Carroll). In Section I, L. Stulman looks at the prose sermons in Jeremiah 1–25; M. Kessler examines the function of Jeremiah 25 and 50–51 in the book (these chapters, along with ch. 1, crop up repeatedly in the volume); R.P. Carroll's first contribution reflects on Jeremiah 25; N.C. Lee exposes an interest in Abel in Jeremiah and Lamentations; Diamond and O'Connor look at gendered coding in Jeremiah 2–3; J. Hill investigates 'time' in Jeremiah

25; E.K. Holt examines the composition of Jeremiah 37–44; M.C. Callaway focuses on Jeremiah 37–38; A.O. Bellis unpacks the poetry of Jeremiah 50; and M.A. Sweeney looks at structure and redaction in Jeremiah 2–6. In Section II, Carroll's second offering looks at intertextuality and ideology in the 'Book of J'; W.R. Domeris offers a socio-linguistic reading of the book; R.F. Person engages McKane's idea of a 'rolling corpus'; R.D. Wells investigates the MT 'revision' of Jeremiah concerning the expectations of the exiles; A. Bauer examines female imagery in Jer. 4.29-31; taking a different approach, J. Barton casts his net widely in describing Jeremiah in apocryphal and pseudepigraphic texts. My impression from Sections I and II is that both approaches offer insights, but 'text-centered' approaches seem the more successful route: the beefier essays in the 'reader-centered' section share much with the essays in Section I! Most of the essays in Section III, Theological Proposals, derive from a panel session on Leo Perdue's *The Collapse of History* (Perdue, L. Boadt, D.T. Olson, and T.W. Overholt participating). In addition, W. Brueggemann reflects on Baruch in Jer. 43.1-7; O'Connor describes a fractured picture of a God-who-cries in Jeremiah 2–9. Altogether, a varied and valuable collection, for which this group should be thanked.

D.J. REIMER

FARMER, WILLIAM R. (ed.), *The International Bible Commentary: A Catholic and Ecumenical Commentary for the Twenty-First Century* (Collegeville, MN: Liturgical Press, 1998), pp. lii + 1918 + 16 maps. $99.95. ISBN 0-8146-2454-5.

Devised as a successor to *A Catholic Commentary on Holy Scripture* (1953), this commentary is *Catholic*, in that it covers the Catholic canon of Scripture, and carries the *Nihil Obstat* and *Imprimatur*; *catholic*, in that its contributors come from all over the world, and in that it is being published 'simultaneously in English and Spanish and in other languages as well'; it is *ecumenical*, in that it 'intends to profit as fully as possible from the contributions of non-Catholic exegesis and exegetes' (one of its Associate Editors is not a Catholic). Its intended readership is primarily 'all the educated faithful, especially pastors and teachers'. Indeed, its (limited) concordance is titled 'Pastoral Guide for the Use of the Bible in Preaching'. Of particular note are the 'General Articles', the essays on 'Selected Pastoral Concerns', and the introductions to the various parts of the canon, all of which take up over a quarter of the whole text. That the selected pastoral concerns include liberation, women's biblical studies, justice, work and poverty, ecumenism, anti-Semitism and the Bible and ecology reveal the commentary's attempt to be twenty-first century in its outlook. Inevitably, the comments on individual passages are brief, but overall this is a fine piece of work.

C.H. KNIGHTS

FOX, MICHAEL V., *A Time to Tear Down and a Time to Build Up: A Rereading of Ecclesiastes* (Grand Rapids, MI: Eerdmans, 1999; distributed in the UK by Alban Books, Bristol), pp. xvii + 422. $30.00/£18.99. ISBN 0-8028-4292-5.

We have here a *magnum opus* on Ecclesiastes from an author who has written much on wisdom literature and Ecclesiastes in particular. More than a revision of his 1987 book (as originally intended), this volume explores the positive side of Qohelet's work—unusual enough to attract attention in itself! Various authors later than his earlier volume are discussed before he plunges headlong into Qohelet's contradictions which are claimed to be part of the author's real intention. He criticizes those who try to make the argument consistent by emendation. Separate sections are given to key terms like *ḥebel, r'ût rûaḥ* and *'āmāl*, to justice and to toil and pleasure. Qohelet's argumentation is seen to be experiential, concentrating on the main issues of life, toil and pleasure. Sundry references are made to the French existentialist writer Albert Camus, and the work is excellently researched. The preface has useful discussions of the puzzling topics of literary structure and genre. Translation and commentary fill 219 pages. There are two excursuses on time in the 'catalogue of times' and on ageing and death. A valuable product of the life-time work of a distinguished scholar, this will be a good book to have on one's bookshelf.

J.G. SNAITH

FRETHEIM, TERENCE E., *First and Second Kings* (Westminster Bible Companion; Louisville, KY: Westminster/John Knox Press; London: SCM Press, 1999), pp. x + 228. $18.00/£13.95. ISBN 0-664-25565-5.

This is a companion primarily aimed towards the layman or leader taking Bible studies based on the NRSV text (included as about a sixth of the book). Emphasis is on the theology and on divine judgment and prophetic promise throughout. There is little on the editorial process and David's covenant is regarded as conditional. It is good on God and political structures, wisdom, justice and prayer and serves as a clear introduction to the books, concentrating more on the dramatic events than on the chronicles of more than forty kings over almost four hundred years. The comment on God's use of deception (Micaiah, 1 Kgs 22; cf. ch. 13) is well judged and helpful. Note, too, the significance of these books for Christian faith and practice today. The rhetorical strategy of Kings is emphasized with its calls for change by and in its readers ancient and modern.

D.J. WISEMAN

FRIES, JOACHIM, *'Im Dienst am Hause des HERRN': Literaturwissenschaftliche Untersuchungen zu 2 Chr 29-31, Zur Hiskijatradition in Chronik* (Arbeiten zu Text and Sprache im Alten Testament, 60; St Ottilien: Eos 1998), pp. xv + 427. DM 48.00. ISBN 3-88096-560-9.

This work, presented to the Catholic Theological Faculty of the University of Würzburg in 1997–98, bears very distinctly the marks of a doctoral dissertation with as many as 48 lists and tables. After a general consideration of the Hezekiah tradition in the OT, the author gives a synopsis of three relevant chapters in 2 Chronicles. He then proceeds to his more detailed observations on these chapters, taking into account historical, textual, literary and syntactic issues. His textual analysis leads him to accept the evidence of the MT after comparing it with the Peshitta. Following an analysis of the pericope as literary composition, F. presents a detailed account of sentence structure, giving attention to both nominal and verbal sentences. The main conclusion drawn after his scrutiny of such details is that the pericope is a theological composition which has been constructed according to a calendrical scheme. The use of such schema is confirmed by apocalyptic writings and by Qumran literature. The first month is concerned with temple and cult, the second with the Passover and the third with priests and Levites. This is not an easy book to handle, and its main thesis is open to debate and challenge.

G.H. JONES

GRAHAM, M. PATRICK and STEVEN L. MCKENZIE (eds.), *The Chronicler as Author: Studies in Text and Texture* (JSOTSup, 263; Sheffield: Sheffield Academic Press, 1999), pp. 422. £50.00/$85.00. ISBN 1-84127-057-1; ISSN 0309-0787.

This is intended as a sequel to *The Chronicler as Historian* (*B.L.* 1998, pp. 80-81) and has three sections. In Overviews of Chronicles: aspects of source criticism as theory and method in the history of research (K. Peltonen), the Chronicler as redactor (McKenzie), the question of the books' main source (A.G. Auld), a rhetorical approach (R.K. Dale), the fabula of the books (J.W. Wright). In Themes in Chronicles: as an interpreter of Scripture (W.M. Schniedewind), royal misappropriations in Kings and Chronicles (G.N. Knoppers), when the foreign monarch speaks (E. Ben Zvi), foreigners, warfare and Judahite identity (A. Siedlecki), what the books have to say about the psalms (H.N. Wallace). In Texts in Chronicles: reading the account of Saul's death in 1 Chronicles 10 (J.M. Trotter), dialogism of the books (C. Mitchell), the purpose of the psalm in 1 Chronicles 16 (K. Nielsen), David and God in 1 Chronicles 21 (N. Bailey), utopian politics in 2 Chronicles 10–13 (R.T. Boer), 2 Chron. 26.20-23 as literary and theological interface.

ED.

GRÜNWALDT, KLAUS, *Das Heiligkeitsgesetz Leviticus 17–26: Ursprüngliche Gestalt, Tradition und Theologie* (BZAW, 271; Berlin and New York: de Gruyter, 1999), pp. x + 439. DM 218.00. ISBN 3-11-016279-2; ISSN 0934-2575.

This book is a cross between a commentary on and a critical study of the structure, date and theology of the Holiness Code (Lev. 17–26). As befits a Habilitationsschrift it begins with a review of the study of the Holiness Code from its identification by Graf in 1866 to the present. Unlike some who have doubted the separate identity of the Code, G. argues that it is a coherent entity embedded in the P source. The next major chapter is devoted to distinguishing between the redactional material from the editor of H and his earlier source material. After a brief discussion of the structure of H, G. gives a long and thorough exegesis of the code as it was before the redaction, and then he discusses how the code was changed by the redactor's theological insertions: this section comprises more than half the book. The book closes with G.'s critical conclusions. H's apparent dependence on many parts of the OT, including Ezekiel and second Isaiah, means it is post-exilic. It was probably the constitution for the Second Temple, drafted by a layman in 520–515 BC. Its theology revolves around election, holiness and the land, and its message is still relevant to the church today. This is a work of thorough scholarship, but some of the critical conclusions seem hasty and pay little attention to dissenters such as I. Knohl.

G.J. WENHAM

HOLLERICH, M.J., *Eusebius of Caesarea's* Commentary on Isaiah: *Christian Exegesis in the Age of Constantine* (Oxford Early Christian Studies; Oxford: Oxford University Press, 1999), pp. ix + 230. £40.00. ISBN 0-19-826368-6.

Eusebius's claim to lasting fame is based on his church history and his panegyric on the Emperor Constantine. His more numerous works of biblical scholarship (including commentaries on the Psalms and on Isaiah) are much less well known. H. argues—and here perhaps protests too much—that the Isaiah commentary is a surer guide to Eusebius's real theological and political beliefs in the immediate aftermath of Nicaea than the later works which deliberately buttress the Constantinian settlement. Of particular interest are the comparison drawn between Eusebius as interpreter of Isaiah and earlier Christian exegetes, especially Justin and Origen, which reveal him as neither a slavish follower of the Alexandrian exegetical tradition nor wholly divorced from that tradition. H. concludes that Eusebius uses this commentary as 'a vehicle for [the Church's] institutional self-celebration' (p. 33), and as a vehicle for renewed Christian anti-Jewish polemic at a time when Constantine was reversing the traditional Roman policy of toleration towards Judaism. This is a useful attempt at establishing the *Sitz im Leben* of a text which has only relatively recently been fully reconstructed.

D.V.N. BAGCHI

HOUTMAN, CORNELIS, *Exodus: Vol. 3, Chapters 20–40* (trans. Sierd Woudstra; Historical Commentary on the Old Testament; Leuven: Peeters, 2000), pp. xiv + 737. BEF 2100/EUR 52.00. ISBN 90-420-0805-X.

The publication of this, the third and final volume of the English version of this well-regarded commentary (see *B.L.* 1987, p. 50, 1990, p. 56, 1997, pp. 65-66 for the publication of the three volumes of the original Dutch running to more than 1630 pp.—not to mention H.'s large-scale study of the Book of the Covenant noted in *B.L.* 1998, p. 150—and *B.L.* 1995, p. 66 for the English translation of vol. 1) must be the occasion for warm congratulation to the author, his translator and his publishers. Opportunity has been taken of the English translation for some updating of the bibliographical apparatus. As in the earlier volumes, an exhaustive account of the secondary literature which can scarcely be bettered opens up a huge range of possibilities of understanding, H. himself steers a judicious course of 'final form' interpretation (e.g. on Exodus 32–34, 'the exegesis of the three chapters is only done justice if the content is regarded as a unified whole', an interpretation not without its problems). 2000 as year of publication seems entirely fitting for what is undoubtedly a summative study which will stand as a landmark for years to come.

W. JOHNSTONE

HUNTER, ALASTAIR G., *Psalms* (Old Testament Readings; London and New York: Routledge, 1999), pp. xiii + 298. £17.99. ISBN 0-415-12770-X.

This is a witty, sophisticated book that aims to enable those without specialist knowledge of Hebrew to shape their own commentary on the Psalms. H. elects not to offer his own translation of the Hebrew texts, but to work with a widely accepted English version. Thus, after scrutiny of various versions, particularly their renderings of Psalm 29, he opts for the NRSV with KJV 'kept within reach' (p. 32). (My impression was that the JB and NJB came out of his analysis in best light.) Even so, H. still uses his own specialist knowledge to 'tweak' the translations at various points. Part 1, Theory and Practice, demonstrates H.'s acute awareness of the ambiguities involved in interpreting the Psalms. He playfully combines modern and postmodern hermeneutics through his sevenfold approach: (1) assess the implications arising from linguistic or text-critical analysis; (2) compare the text with similar material from other ancient Near Eastern cultures; (3) draw in readings of a historical, cultic/liturgical and sociological character; (4) reflect on the poetical and rhetorical structures of the psalm; (5) develop a first-level reading which may take into account the first four 'aspects'; (6) apply modern hermeneutical techniques, particularly deconstruction; and (7) invite a personal and subjective appropriation of the psalm (p. 63). This method is then fleshed out in Part 2 through readings of individual psalms (2, 8, 24, 74, 82). Finally, in Part 3, the method is applied to the Psalms of Ascent. H. makes a good case for viewing this group as having 'a genre coherence as a whole'; argues that they have an idealistic interest in themes associated with messiah, priest and Zion; and suggests that they may have been commissioned by one of the early Hasmonaean rulers (pp. 234, 247). It must be said that the most opaque section of the book is the discussion of 'post-structuralism', 'super-structuralism' and 'deconstruction' (pp. 82-94). That said, I found his deconstruction most stimulating and challenging. With unerring skill H. locates the blindspots in the psalmists' rhetoric and logic.

D.J. BRYAN

KASSIS, RIAD AZIZ, *The Book of Proverbs and Arabic Proverbial Works* (VTSup, 74; Leiden–Boston–Cologne: E.J. Brill, 1999), pp. xiv + 318. Nlg 205.00/$114.00. ISBN 90-04-11305-3; ISSN 0083-5889.

This slightly revised 1997 Nottingham thesis is one of the few studies to compare the OT book of Proverbs with Arabic proverbial tradition. Many comparisons have been made with Egyptian and Mesopotamian literature because of its being closer in time to the OT and of potentially direct or indirect influence on the OT. But there is nothing to preclude comparison with literature without a direct connection since one can compare them in such areas as social setting, literary and oral construction, thought patterns, transmission and the like—all relevant to a better understanding of the biblical book of Proverbs (cf. F. Golka, *The Leopard's Spots* [*B.L.* 1994, p. 87]). After an introductory chapter and one on the Solomonic wisdom tradition, successive chapters discuss the important themes of royal sayings, speech and silence, and wealth and poverty. A chapter on traditio-historical aspects (comparisons, numerical statements, parallelism, admonition) concludes the study.

ED.

KÖHLMOOS, MELANIE, *Das Auge Gottes: Textstrategie im Hiobbuch* (Forschungen zum Alten Testament, 25; Tübingen: J.C.B. Mohr [Paul Siebeck], 1999), pp. ix + 386. DM 178.00. ISBN 3-16-147140-7; ISSN 0940-4155.

The book represents the author's Hamburg doctoral dissertation written under the supervision of H. Spieckermann and aims to investigate which strategies are applied to guide the reader to an interpretation of the book of Job. The biblical book is viewed as a post-exilic intertextual document, which does not necessarily belong to sapiental circles and voices critique of the official religion in Judah. The central theme of the book of Job is the question of the presence of God so that God and not Job becomes the main character. To do justice to the unique character of Job, K. uses U. Eco's theory of the guidance of the reader (*Leserlenkung*) for her investigation. Such a model allows us to recognize the individual structure of a text according to genre and contents and the possibility of combining such individual structure with form-critical insights. After a chapter on the question of the growth of the book, Eco's theory is applied and combined with historical critical insights in chs. 4–6, dealing with Job 1–3, 3–31 and 38.1–42.7. The work is a fine example of how literary theory can successfully be combined with historical critical scholarship. Scholarship on Job will profit greatly from K.'s detailed study.

A.C. HAGEDORN

KOSSMANN, RUTH, *Die Esthernovelle: Vom Erzählten zur Erzählung: Studien zur Traditions- und Redaktionsgeschichte des Estherbuches* (VTSup, 79; Leiden–Boston–Cologne: E.J. Brill, 2000), pp. ix + 400. Nlg 185.00/$109.00. ISBN 90-04-11556-0; ISSN 0083-5889.

The tradition-history of Esther seems to have become a favourite subject for investigation in recent years. This represents a further attempt to suggest how the present-day Hebrew version reached its form. K. proposes that the book originated in three non-Jewish narratives: the marriage or Vashti narrative (Esther 1–2), and two court tales, the Haman-Mordechai narrative and the Haman-Mordechai-Queen narrative (reconstructed from the remainder of the book). These three were combined into a 'pre-Esther' narrative encompassing chs. 1–7. A 'Jewish redaction' led to a 'proto-Alpha text' which included the episodes of the persecution of the Jewish people and the issuing of an edict. From this was created the 'proto-MT' by editing and the addition of a 'Purim layer' and ch. 9. The 'proto-LXX' was produced by combining the proto-AT and the proto-MT. A critique of K. De Troyer (cf. *B.L.* 1998, p. 57) and D.J.A. Clines forms part of the argument.

ED.

LABAHN, ANTJE, *Wort Gottes und Schuld Israels: Untersuchungen zu Motiven deuteronomistischer Theologie im Deuterojesajabuch mit einem Ausblick auf das Verhältnis von Jes 40–55 zum Deuteronomismus* (BWANT, 143; Stuttgart: Kohlhammer, 1999), pp. 320. DM 70.00/SwF 64.00/AS 515. ISBN 3-17-015894-5.

Working from the recognition that the Deuteronomic and Deutero-Isaianic literary traditions represent two separate, but significantly parallel, streams of theological thought that emerged in the exilic/early post-exilic period, L. traces the influence of the former upon the latter. Although both traditions share fundamental interpretations of national defeat as a consequence of national guilt and Israel's exile as punishment, the covenant-focused nationalism of the Deuteronomic movement contrasts with the universalism and hope of salvation for the nations expressed by Deutero-Isaiah. So the body of the study is made up of a critical examination of passages in Isaiah 40–55 which reflect, or contrast, with Deuteronomic ideas. A primary concern to reconcile these differences is found in Isaiah 55, to which close attention is given and which is seen as an epilogue to the Deutero-Isaianic collection. The location of chs. 40–55 within the compass of the larger Isaiah book then raises further questions, as do the contrasts with the Priestly aspects of the Ezekiel tradition and the Jeremiah editing. L. retains a strong inclination to see the contrasts between Deuteronomy and Deutero-Isaiah as emanating from regional differences, with Deutero-Isaiah representing a Babylonian/exilic milieu. The study raises many question, besides answering some, but overall sets out constructively to identify and compare two of the major streams of theological thought which have shaped the Hebrew Bible.

R.E. CLEMENTS

LELIÈVRE, ANDRÉ and ALPHONSE MAILLOT, *Commentaire des Proverbes: III chapitres 1–9* (Lectio Divina, Commentaires, 8; Paris: Cerf, 2000), pp. 313. FF 229.00. ISBN 2-204-06365-7; ISSN 0750-1919.

This commentary is being issued in disjointed form, the first two volumes (covering 10–18 and 19–31) having been reviewed in *B.L.* 1997 (p. 69) by R.N. Whybray. A general introductory volume was also reviewed in *B.L.* 1994 (p. 65). In addition to the verse-by-verse commentary this volume has an excursus on 'Sophie la Sagesse' (the question of whether there are several figures of wisdom in 1–9, personification of wisdom, the wisdom of Prov. 8 and Job 28, wisdom and Qohelet, wisdom in the proverbs of Ahiqar, Lady Wisdom and the Egyptian Maat, and the influence of Lady Wisdom on later Jewish and Christian writings). There are also three further lists: an index of ancient Near Eastern writings cited in the first three volumes of this commentary; a list of French translation equivalents for the Hebrew vocabulary of the first three volumes, and a bibliography (on vol. 3 but supplementing vols. 1–2). The authors take the not-uncontroversial position that the figure of wisdom borrows from the image of Maat.

ED.

LINAFELT, TOD, *Ruth*, and TIMOTHY K. BEAL, *Esther* (Berit Olam, Studies in Hebrew Narrative and Poetry; Collegeville, MN: Liturgical Press, 1999), pp. xxv + 90; xxii + 130. $34.95. ISBN 0-8146-5045-7.

This work is part of the multi-volume commentary, other volumes of which have already been reviewed in the *B.L.* (see p. 73 above). The first part of the commentary is devoted to Ruth, and in this part of the work L. offers an 'unsettling' interpretation of the book which is built on the ambiguity and complexity which he has noted in the biblical text. What this means in practical terms is that he refuses to settle on a single, unequivocal meaning of a particular word, phrase or theme, since he prefers to underscore the dual or multiple meanings which he detects in the narrative. He also argues that the book is intended as an interlude between Judges and Samuel, so that he dates the book in late pre-exilic or early post-exilic times. In the second part of the work B. offers a commentary on the text by means of the use of rhetorical criticism, by which he questions the text thoroughly. He has also focused on the narrative structure of the book. By these methods he has sought to investigate the tensions and ambivalences in the text, so that he can emphasize the particular over the general in order to bring out what the text actually says, as well as what it does not say. The result is a new and lively interpretation of Esther which should appeal to all.

F. GOSLING

LINDEN, NICO TER, *The Story Goes... I The Stories of the Torah* (trans. J. Bowden; London; SCM Press, 1999), pp. viii + 296. £14.95. ISBN 0-334-02764-0.

This is indeed, as the translator acknowledges in an afterword, a 'remarkable book'. A re-telling of the stories of the Torah with imaginative and poignant detail, it has arisen in part from the author's preaching ministry over the years, but it is by no means a mere slushy paraphrase. Although it is written from a Christian and a devotional perspective, it respects the OT as a work of Scripture in its own right, and in its reading of the biblical text it is evidently though unobtrusively indebted to critical scholarship. It also draws frequently on Jewish tradition in its efforts to illuminate the significance of the text. Such a combination of scholarship, imagination and perceptive devotional wisdom is truly remarkable. In terms of the material covered in the book, Genesis fares better, and, I think, its re-tellings are more effective, than the rest of the Torah; of 287 pages of narrative re-telling, 191 are devoted to Genesis, leaving the remaining 96 to be divided between Exodus–Deuteronomy. However, it must be said that after the Exodus narrative proper there is relatively little narrative that lends itself to this kind of treatment; and the pericopes from this part of the text that are treated are approached with the same kind of gentle rigour and sensitivity as those from Genesis. Whilst not a 'conventionally scholarly' piece of writing, it is a book that will provoke and move as well as illuminate its readers.

D. ROOKE

LOVE, MARK CAMERON, *The Evasive Text: Zechariah 1–8 and the Frustrated Reader* (JSOTSup, 296; Sheffield: Sheffield Academic Press, 1999), pp. 265. £49.00/ $82.00. ISBN 1-84127-020-2; ISSN 0309-0787.

This book is a good read but any reader hoping for illumination regarding the meaning of Zechariah 1–8 will be disappointed. L. admits at the outset that he does not understand the text and concludes by labelling Zechariah 'incomprehensible'. However, *en route* to this conclusion he takes his readers on a journey of exploration during which one recognizes resonances between words and imagery found in Zechariah and elsewhere in the Hebrew Bible. L. demonstrates the ways in which meanings drawn from one narrative context may enhance the interpretation of another text but at the same time may cause an interpreter to suppress meanings that were legitimately drawn from a different narrative. Some sections of Zechariah 1–8 receive detailed attention, others were virtually ignored. Issues such as authorial intent, historical background, textual development, implied audience(s), theology are not discussed. The book concentrates on a particular method of postmodern narrative criticism and as such is an excellent example of both the value and the limitations of this methodology. This book is accessible to all readers as all Hebrew words (and foreign language quotes) are translated; indeed L.'s style should enable non-Hebraists to appreciate the arguments being made on the basis of the Hebrew text.

J.E. TOLLINGTON

MA, WONSUK, *Until the Spirit Comes: The Spirit of God in the Book of Isaiah* (JSOTSup, 271; Sheffield: Sheffield Academic Press, 1999), pp. 247. £43.50/$70.00. ISBN 1-85075-981-2; ISSN 0309-0787.

In this revised dissertation from Fuller Theological Seminary, M. has the reasonable plan of studying in turn what is said about the Spirit in the pre-exilic, exilic and post-exilic parts of the book of Isaiah, and then in a fourth chapter discussing the picture which emerges from the canonical book as a whole. It is an obvious and sensible way of trying to do justice to both the diachronic and synchronic aspects of this complex work. The substance is somewhat less exciting than the programme promises to be. The exegesis of each relevant passage in turn ranges further afield than is strictly necessary for the task in hand, and there is something of an unimaginative concern to relate what is said about the Spirit in each case to one or another of no less than six pre-Isaianic 'Spirit Traditions'. There is sometimes also a lack of sensitivity to the peculiar nuances which Isaiah brings to his usage; for instance, can the Spirit 'resting' on the figure in ch. 11 be so quickly aligned with the charismatic endowment of the judges and early kings? Despite this, some useful observations are made along the way, and the major conclusion to emerge is that the Spirit traditions gain in eschatological significance through the book and that this is reflected still more in its finished form. In view of current trends in the study of Isaiah, it is likely that there will be more such studies of major themes in future.

H.G.M. WILLIAMSON

MARSHALL, CELIA BREWER, *Genesis* (Interpretation Bible Studies; Louisville, KY: Geneva Press, 1999), pp. viii + 104. $7.00. ISBN 0-664-50038-2.

The ten chapters in this work (each devoted to a particular passage from Genesis) are intended for 'adults and older youth' either in church groups or in individual study, and there is a ten-page guide for group leaders. The style is colloquial and often refers to situations in modern life to illustrate the issues raised by the biblical passages, and each chapter ends with several 'Questions for Reflection'. There are some diagrams and photographs, references for further reading, and quotations relevant to the passages discussed.

J.A. EMERTON

MCKEATING, HENRY, *The Book of Jeremiah* (Epworth Commentaries, Peterborough: Epworth, 1999; distributed by SCM Press, London), pp. vii + 231. £9.95. ISBN 0-7162-0526-2.

M. has decided to stick closely to the aim of the original Epworth series back in the 1950s and 1960s, that of serving the needs of preachers. This is not, though, the sort of commentary for preachers that is full of homiletical prosings. It gives them the tools they need, and the occasional nudge, rather than doing their job for them. M. relies heavily on the work of the historical critics, though their names are seldom mentioned. His starting-point is always an exposition of, so far as it can be discovered, the meaning of the original author(s). (Where he thinks it cannot be identified he says so and quickly passes on.) He does not side-step the problems that critics have found in the book of Jeremiah. He believes that the Deuteronomists and perhaps others have clearly had quite a hand in the composition of the book as we have it, but that their influence, though real, was limited: 'we are still in touch, however uncertainly, with the man from Anathoth' (p. 76), whose rejection of animal sacrifice, for example, has not been edited out by later hands. This is a well-informed, clear and well-written commentary. There is a brief guide to further reading.

B.P. ROBINSON

MELLOR, ENID B., *Proverbs* (The People's Bible Commentary; Oxford: Bible Reading Fellowship, 1999), pp. 255. £7.99. ISBN 1-84101-07105.

After a very brief introduction to wisdom literature the text of Proverbs is here divided into 109 brief sections, envisaged as daily readings, each concluded with a topic for thought and/or a prayer. (Presumably the daily readings need not be continuous; more than three months on Proverbs will not be everyone's ideal diet of Bible reading.) Its lack of continuity makes Proverbs one of the most difficult biblical texts to provide a basis for non-technical commentary, but M. is a skilful communicator and has a good knowledge of the text and of the secondary literature, and her enthusiasm for her task comes over strongly. Incidentally, several other volumes in this series have been published since its inception in 1996, but appear not to have been noticed in *B.L.*

R.J. COGGINS

MURPHY, ROLAND E., OCarm, *The Book of Job: A Short Reading* (New York and Mahwah, NJ: Paulist Press, 1999), pp. vii + 137. $14.95. ISBN 0-8091-3889-1.

This book aims to make Job easily accessible by offering an overview rather than dwelling in long commentary mode on a text that can be seen as repetitious. It is thus an attempt to draw out the essence of the book of Job and stress its enduring appeal and relevance. There is an introduction formulated in question form, such as 'Is Job a historical figure?' The answer given to this is that whilst the Job of the Prologue and Epilogue may have had some historical existence, that of the dialogue is a literary character. The uncertainty of different scholarly opinions comes across in this section. M. then returns to some of these introductory issues, e.g. the literary-critical one, in one of his summary sections towards the end of the book. On the issue of authorship he is keen to treat the book as a unity and yet there is a recognition of the possibility of composite authorship so that while M. is keen to read the book of Job at a sitting, he acknowledges the disjointedness that forces us into literary-critical categories. An example is his treatment of the Elihu speeches—he urges us to 'take him [Elihu] for what he is and add him to the mix' (p. 79), but later admits that 'the chapters devoted to him could have been dropped without any great loss' (pp. 110-11). This book is readable and informed, a particularly good starting-point for those coming to Job for the first time. One can tell that this is written by a scholar very familiar with the book. There is a short section noting the inspiration that Job has generated during history and among artists and writers. There is also a section on the theological themes of the book, considering God, creation and worldview (the heavenly court and Sheol ideas), retribution (seen as not the main point of Job) and spirituality (including the role of testing in this story and others, of the Abraham story). The book ends with a 'Postil' in which the individuality of the reader's response is stressed, almost an apology for the personal nature of this slightly quirky but eminently readable little book.

K.J. DELL

MURPHY, ROLAND E. and ELIZABETH HUWILER, *Proverbs, Ecclesiastes, Song of Songs* (New International Biblical Commentary, Old Testament Series, 12; Peabody, MA: Hendrickson; Carlisle: Paternoster, 1999), pp. xv + 312. $11.95. ISBN (Hendrickson) 1-56564-221-4; (Paternoster) 0-85364-733-X.

Murphy has contributed the commentary on Proverbs in this volume, while Huwiler has written those on Ecclesiastes and Song of Songs. In line with the overall intentions of the series, both scholars have provided critical treatments and made some attempt to link the texts to the concerns of modern Christian readers. Murphy's opinions on Proverbs have, of course, been set out at greater length elsewhere, but his presentation here does pack considerable detail into a short space, while remaining lucid and accessible. Huwiler is necessarily more constrained, given less than half the volume to cover the notorious complexities of Ecclesiastes and the Song of Songs. She manages, nevertheless, to produce very good short treatments of the two texts. In order to achieve relatively detailed verse-by-verse commentary, both writers seem to have made sacrifices in their introductory sections; this limits the usefulness of the volume for readers seeking a broader understanding. In general, though, it is to be welcomed as a useful and reliable resource for students and non-specialists.

S. WEEKS

NEWSOME, JAMES D., *Exodus* (Interpretation Bible Studies; Louisville, KY: Geneva Press, 1998), pp. vii + 134. $7.95. ISBN 0-664-50020-X.

The volume follows the general pattern of its series, which is designed 'for adults and older youth…for either personal or group study' (as such it includes at the end the series' standard ten-page 'Leader's Guide'). Ten representative 'units' are selected (2.1-10; 3.1–4.17; 7.1-24; 12.1-51; 14.1-31; 19.1-25; 20.1-7; 20.8-17; 32.1-35; 34.1-35) in order 'to capture the sweep of the whole biblical book'. The salient features of each section are considered, especially their theological significance— and difficulties; connections with NT are noted, where appropriate; each unit ends with 'questions for reflection'. Side boxes provide illuminating quotations, bibliographical leads, definition of terms, and so on. The volume must be adjudged highly successful in its aim: it is well written, informative and provocative of reflexion on contemporary relevance. While one might have initial quibbles at the selection of passages and the balance between them (and enduring doubts that the material is taken rather too much at face value), the presentation amply vindicates the choice: links are made with the wider context both within and beyond Exodus so that, on the whole (the discussion of the tabernacle is, however, meagre), the import of the whole book is conveyed.

W. JOHNSTONE

PROPP, WILLIAM H.C., *Exodus 1–18: A New Translation with Introduction and Commentary* (AB, 2; New York: Doubleday, 1999), pp. xl + 680. $44.95. ISBN 0-385-41804-6.

The first volume of P.'s commentary is a most welcome addition to the scholarly literature on Exodus. Above all, it presents a clear, independent and judicious discussion of the many exegetical problems in the book and earlier treatments of them, not least in Jewish scholarship of all periods. It is also the first commentary to be able to deal fully with manuscript evidence from Qumran and it has some fresh things to say about the sources of Exodus, attributing much to E that is usually ascribed to J. Such symbols may seem dated to some, but a review of current Pentateuchal criticism is promised as one of several Appendices to appear in the second volume; another will deal with historical questions. There is an extensive bibliography, but it strangely omits C. Houtman's major commentary. The one real weakness of this volume is the translation of the text, which is extremely literal to the point of stiltedness and sometimes unintelligibility. P. has a theory about translation which insists on resurrecting dead metaphors and representing the most alien features of Hebrew idiom: for example, 'Now all the soul coming from Jacob's *thigh* was seventy *souls*' (1.5). Such renderings belong, if anywhere, in parentheses in the notes.

G.I. DAVIES

REDDITT, PAUL L., *Daniel, Based on the New Revised Standard Version* (New Century Bible Commentary; Sheffield: Sheffield Academic Press, 1999), pp. xxvi + 211. £12.95/$19.95. ISBN 1-84127-009-1.

It is perhaps not inappropriate that a commentary on Daniel should mark the resurrection of the New Century Bible series! An Introduction deals with (a) authorship and date; (b) historical background; (c) unity, genres and languages; (d) literary history; (e) plot; (f) the figure of Daniel and the reader; (g) canon; and (h) message. R. argues that the book emanated from a group of Diaspora Jews who counted themselves among the 'wise', who moved from Babylon to Jerusalem after control was taken by Antiochus III and who subsequently became an apocalyptic group under the regime of Antiochus Epiphanes. There is a unity to the book in the sense that it was the product of the same ongoing group. R. explains the change of language by suggesting that by December 167 the writer for the group had switched from Aramaic to Hebrew. The layout and the arrangement of the material are 'user friendly'. For each section there is a general introduction, a verse-by-verse commentary, and a comment on the theology of the section. The verse-by-verse commentary relates to the NRSV; from time to time there are references to the Hebrew/Aramaic. It is strange that the phrase 'abomination that desolates' (the preferred translation of NRSV) is not given in bold type at 9.27 (p. 163) and that elsewhere in the volume the phrase 'transgression that makes desolate' from 8.13 is preferred (e.g. on pp. 10, 29, 24, 30 and 34 of the Introduction), except in the index of subjects which gives the more traditional 'abomination of desolation'!

A.H.W. CURTIS

RENZ, THOMAS, *The Rhetorical Function of the Book of Ezekiel* (VTSup, 76; Leiden–Boston–Cologne: E.J. Brill, 1999), pp. xvii + 298. Nlg 204.95/$114.00. ISBN 90-04-11362-2; ISSN 0083-5889.

This Bristol thesis (supervisors G.J. Wenham and P. Joyce) aims to analyse Ezekiel as a vehicle of communication ('rhetoric' being defined as the 'art of persuasion'). The different parts of the book form a single rhetorical unit, addressing a single rhetorical situation: the exilic community. The final editor has worked as an author to try to dissuade the exilic community from defining itself by the Jerusalem of the past nor in Babylon of the present; rather, he wants the surviving community to define itself by the future promised by Yhwh, which includes a return from exile and a nation focused on God's temple. A variety of techniques are employed, including the use of legal traditions, emotive language, the 'dry bones' of 37.1-14, and the careful use of terms to designate the community.

ED.

RÖSEL, CHRISTOPH, *Die messianische Redaktion des Psalters: Studien zu Entstehung und Theologie der Sammlung Psalm 2–89* (Calwer Theologische Monographien, 19; Stuttgart: Calwer, 1999), pp. ix + 241. DM 88.00/SwF 80.00/AS 642. ISBN 3-7668-3627-7.

This dissertation from Marburg examines the view that Psalms 2–89 formed a collection prior to the completed Psalter, and that the collection had been redacted to express faith in the restoration of the Davidic dynasty. The discussion proceeds patiently through all the relevant details, including the 'Elohistic redaction' of Psalms 42–83, the arrangement of headings, the duplication of some passages, the stages of the collection's growth, and the passages thought to be redactional additions. The conclusion affirms such a deliberate messianic redaction of the collection, and a similar work is also traced in the redaction of the whole Psalter. This dissertation will be valued as a careful, incisive survey and assessment of a mass of data for the growth and purpose of the psalm collections.

J.H. EATON

SAKENFELD, KATHARINE DOOB, *Ruth* (Interpretation: A Bible Commentary for Teaching and Preaching; Louisville, KY: Westminster/John Knox Press, 1999), pp. xii + 91. $21.95. ISBN 0-8042-3149-4.

This commentary seeks to treat the story as a drama of ordinary life but against the background of divine providence. Because of her experiences in Asia S. is interested in the theological power of the story in the community of faith, as well as its sociological dimensions. Alternative interpretations are given at various points.

ED.

SCHNIEDEWIND, WILLIAM M., *Society and the Promise to David: The Reception History of 2 Samuel 7:1-17* (Oxford: Oxford University Press, 1999), pp. x + 229. £30.00. ISBN 0-19-512680-7.

The project of the book is to examine how the divine promise to David in 2 Samuel 7 was understood and reinterpreted at various moments of Hebrew history down to the fall of the Second Temple. S.'s special emphasis is that key texts like this not only take on changing meanings in new social circumstances but are themselves influential in changing societies. This is a very early text, produced as a justification for the United Monarchy under David and Solomon (p. 46), subsequently becoming the ideology that held together the Israelite state (pp. 28, 168). Its influence can be seen in Isaiah, Amos and Hosea, in the various layers of the Deuteronomistic History, in Second Isaiah, the Chronicler's Work, Zecharaiah, Sirach, the Psalms of Solomon and the Dead Sea Scrolls. This tracing of what is often called 'inner-biblical exegesis' is not infrequently discursive, loosely edited, and a little predictable; and it must be open to question whether texts can have as much influence on real-life politics as the author would think.

D.J.A. CLINES

SIMON, URIEL, *Jonah* (trans. Lenn Schramm; The JPS Bible Commentary; Philadelphia: Jewish Publication Society, 1999), pp. xliii + 52. $34.95. ISBN 0-8276-0672-9.

The original Hebrew edition appeared in 1992 in the series Mikra LeYisra'el (some volumes of which have been reviewed in the *B.L.*), and this translation is from a revised and expanded Hebrew text. The translation of the biblical text is that of the New Jewish Publication Society translation, though modified where the author has understood the text differently. The author tries to combine the insights of the traditional Jewish commentators and modern biblical exegesis. He goes against a number of recent commentators in not seeing the book as ironic satire.

ED.

SOMMER, BENJAMIN D., *A Prophet Reads Scripture: Allusion in Isaiah 40–66* (Contraversions; Stanford: Stanford University Press, 1998; distributed outside the USA by Cambridge University Press), pp. xiii + 355. $49.50/£30.00. ISBN 0-8047-3216-7.

This is one of a growing number of studies in intertextuality. Different kinds of reference to earlier biblical material are analysed, the focus of the present study being mainly on allusion. Characteristic methods found in Deutero-Isaiah include the 'split-up pattern', where a phrase in the source is split into two parts, separated by intervening material, sound play, word play and word order. The use of the earlier material may be in confirmation, reprediction, repetition, reversal or polemic. Jeremiah is the source to which most allusions are found, followed by First Isaiah, a smaller number of allusions to other prophetic material, some to Psalms and Lamentations, and some to Deuteronomy and the earlier Pentateuchal traditions. The study is judicious, although not all readers will be convinced that some of the smaller allusions are conscious and deliberate. Some wider conclusions are drawn about the extent of the Deutero-Isaianic corpus (it includes 34–35 and 56–66), its relation to First Isaiah (less close than to Jeremiah), and Deutero-Isaiah's transitional role between prophecy and scribal exegesis. This stimulating and important study can usefully be compared with that of Willey (*B.L.* 1998, p. 98).

A. GELSTON

STARBUCK, SCOTT R.A., *Court Oracles in the Psalms: The So-called Royal Psalms in their Ancient Near Eastern Context* (SBLDS, 172; Atlanta: Scholars Press, 1999), pp. xx + 271. $37.00. ISBN 0-88414-000-8.

This well-researched volume surveys the history of scholarship on the royal psalms, finding too much imprecision in both definition and scope, and with copious reference to the ancient Near Eastern royal hymnody for comparison attempts a new typology, with special reference to those containing oracular material. S. notes that alone among ancient Near Eastern royal texts of similar kind, the Psalms are at one remove from their original royal cultic context, indicated by the systematic omission of specific royal names, and the fact that there is no common *traditio*. They deal rather with the institution than with the office-holder. The discussion is extremely nuanced, since S. is happy to recognize the survival of ancient material from the monarchical period.

N. WYATT

STEINS, GEORG, *Die 'Bindung Isaaks' im Kanon (Gen. 22): Grundlagen und Programm einer kanonisch-intertextuellen Lektüre: mit einer Spezialbibliographie zu Gen. 22* (Herders Biblische Studien, 20; Freiburg im Breisgau: Herder, 1999), pp. x + 302. DM 88.00/AS 642/SwF 84.00. ISBN 3-451-26916-3.

This Münster *Habilitationsschrift* (1998) seeks to meet a need arising from belief in the importance of the biblical canon for exegesis: although 'canonical criticism' and the 'canonical approach' stress the importance of the canon, they do not provide a method for exegetes. S. suggests as a method 'kanonisch-intertextuelle Lektüre' and illustrates the method by applying it to Genesis 22. He limits his application to other places in the Pentateuch: Gen. 12.1-9; 21.1-21; Exod. 3–4; 19–24; 29.38-46; Lev. 8–9; 16; Deut. 8.2-6; 12. He concludes that the 'story anticipates, via the experience of Abraham, what…Israel will undergo on Mount Sinai, namely, the presence of God in the obedience of the Torah and in the ritual of the whole burnt-offering' (p. 238). His method is synchronic in character and depends on the acceptance of the canon as a criterion for interpretation, but he also argues that his conclusions have a bearing on the historical origin of Genesis 22: that it is a unity and is one of the latest parts of the Pentateuch. The book has an English summary and a bibliography.

J.A. EMERTON

STRIEK, MARCO, *Das vordeuteronomistische Zephanjabuch* (Beiträge zur biblischen Exegesis und Theologie, 29; Frankfurt–Bern–New York: Lang, 1999), pp. 281. SwF 31.00. ISBN 3-631-33607-1; ISSN 0170-8716.

S. argues that a first redaction of the book of Zephaniah, taking up the 'Day of Yahweh' oracles of the prophet against certain specific groups in Judah and Jerusalem and foreign nations, was made round about 604 BCE. This redaction, possibly made by Zephaniah himself, extended the oracles to the whole of Judah and Jerusalem, and indeed the whole earth (e.g. 1.14b-16), linked the 'Day of Yahweh' theme to the concept of a sacrifice (1.7b-8a), stressed the nearness of the 'Day', saw its initial fulfilment in the overthrow of Nineveh (2.15) and urged its readers to repentance (2.3b), reflecting on how people might be saved from its wrath (1.18; 2.3b). An exilic Deuteronomistic redaction identified Zephaniah as a prophet of the word of God and supporter of the Josianic reform (1.1, 4b-5), identified the 'Day of Yahweh' with the events of 587 BCE and gave theological reasons for it (3.1, 7). Various post-exilic additions appear to reflect the interests of a certain group who saw themselves as the 'humble' remnant (2.3a; 3.11-13), identify the parallels between the Day of Yahweh and the flood (1.2-3a) and envisage ultimate deliverance for the Jewish diaspora (3.10-11, 18-19, 20). This is a careful, well-informed and well-argued work which needs detailed reading before passing quick judgments. Suffice it to say that, if the presuppositions and methods of redaction criticism in general, and this writer's use of them in particular, are questioned, the results become less secure. That some such process lies behind the book is undeniable. But can we be sure of it in this detail?

R. MASON

VAN SETERS, JOHN, *The Pentateuch: A Social-Science Commentary* (Trajectories, 1; Sheffield: Sheffield Academic Press, 1999), pp. 233. £45.00/$79.00; paper £16.95/ $28.00. ISBN 1-84127-027-X; (paper) 1-84127-036-9.

This is the first volume of a new series, in which further contributions are promised on the Deuteronomistic and Chronistic histories, the wisdom traditions and prophecy. The dictionary defines 'trajectory' as 'the path of an object moving under the action of given forces'. The 'forces' in this case being the author's original ideas, as developed over the years in his lengthy series of studies in the Pentateuch. After a chapter discussing the Pentateuch as a whole, the next two sections almost inevitably survey the history of research on the Pentateuch, with special reference to the period from 1975. The more original part of the book consists of the five following chapters, where the author expounds and defends in turn his particular views of Deuteronomy, J, P and Law in the Pentateuch. Thus the whole represents a summary of his current position on the nature of the Pentateuch in general, which, as he notes, often differs considerably from views represented in other introductory works. The author has deliberately written for the student and the novice and his concise, uncluttered and stimulating presentation will admirably meet their needs. But more experienced scholars will equally profit from a perusal of this lively and invariably challenging study.

J.R. PORTER

VLAARDINGERBROEK, JOHANNES, *Zephaniah* (Historical Commentary on the Old Testament: Leuven: Peeters, 1999), pp. xxviii + 222. BEF 1600. ISBN 90-429-0755-X.

The editors of this series lay great stress on the 'historical' in the title, wanting to produce commentaries which take the historical context of both the prophet's original words and ministry, as well as that of successive redactions seriously, while giving primacy to its final form. They also want to give attention to the history of interpretation of the book, both within the OT itself, the NT and in subsequent exegesis. An extensive bibliography is followed by a translation in which different typefaces distinguish between words of the prophet and later additions. A full introduction heralds a passage-by-passage survey in which a section, 'Essentials and Perspectives', highlights the heart of the meaning and its contemporary relevance, while another, 'Scholarly Exposition', offers a full and detailed exposition of the Hebrew text. This is an excellent volume in the series, with its full survey of previous scholarly work and its careful investigations of all aspects of the text. One wonders at the declared aim of accessibility to a 'wide readership' when, even in the general sections, large chunks of German quotation are left untranslated while others presuppose a knowledge of Hebrew. But G. is a reliable and clear guide and this commentary (a readable translation of the original Dutch) will be a splendid tool for all working on the prophets in general and Zephaniah in particular. The lack of indexes is unfortunate.

R. MASON

VOLGGER, DAVID, *Verbindliche Tora am einzigen Tempel: Zu Motiv und Ort der Komposition von 1.2 Kön* (Arbeiten zu Text und Sprache im Alten Testament, 61; St Ottilien: Eos, 1998), pp. vi + 418. DM 46.00. ISBN 3-880096-561-7.

This *Habilitationsschrift*, presented to the Catholic Theological Faculty of the University of Würzburg in 1997/98, examines the theme and provenance of 1 and 2 Kings. Three main textual complexes are analysed: Jerusalem under Solomon (1 Kgs 1–11); the Samaritan temple (1 Kgs 16.21–2 Kgs 11); the Josianic Reformation (2 Kgs 22f.). A final chapter discusses the relevance of Ezra/Nehemiah for our understanding of the books of Kings. V. maintains that the main thrust of these books is their claim that the Jerusalem temple is the only legitimate cultic centre where Yahweh, as God of heaven and earth, can be truly worshipped with accompanying sacrifices. The text has originated from around 400 BC, after the time of Ezra and Nehemiah and after the correspondence between the colony at Elephantine and the homeland. The priesthood of Jerusalem was in a politically strong position in post-exilic times (fifth–third centuries BC) and was responsible for the dominant theme and final shape of 1 and 2 Kings. The textual analysis in this work has been carefully and successfully executed. In presenting his argument V. has taken into account previous analyses and takes issue with some of his predecessors in the field. It is a cogent and interesting work.

G.H. JONES

WEEMS, ANN, *Psalms of Lament* (foreword by W. Brueggemann; Louisville, KY: Westminster/John Knox Press, 1995; large print edn, 1999), pp. xxii + 113. $14.95. ISBN 0-664-25831-X.

This is a large print edition of a book published in 1995 and noticed in the 1996 *Book List* (pp. 70-71). It is not what readers of the *Book List* might expect from the title in that it is not a study of the Lament *Gattungen* in the Hebrew Bible. It is in fact a collection of 50 compositions, in the *genre* of the lament psalm, written by poet Ann Weems as an expression of her emotions after her 21-year-old son was killed. The initial prompting to write these laments came from Brueggemann, who contributes a Foreword in which he notes some of the features of the biblical laments, their significance for an understanding of the faith of Israel, and the possible effects of engaging in this sort of prayer. These moving modern poems are a testimony to the psalmists' ongoing power to inspire, not least by their willingness to complain (using W.'s words in her Lament Psalm 24), 'It is not fair, O God!'

A.H.W. CURTIS

WÉNIN, ANDRÉ, *Isaac ou l'épreuve d'Abraham: Approche narrative de Genèse 22* (Le livre et le rouleau, 8; Brussels: Editions Lessius, 1999; distributed by Cerf, Paris), pp. 102. N.P. ISBN 2-87299-086-0.

This exposition of Genesis 22 'dans la ligne de l'analyse narrative' includes a study of the chapter's structure. The test to which Abraham is subjected in v. 2 is thought to be ambiguous: he is to take Isaac to the land of Moriah either to 'offer him there as a burnt offering' or to 'take him up there for [i.e. to witness] a burnt offering'. The story is expounded in terms of Abraham's need to decide which inter-pretation to obey and of the reader's wondering, until the climax of the story, which decision he has made. The story has a double conclusion: the second message from heaven in vv. 15-18, and the return to Beer-sheba in v. 19, where the failure to men-tion Isaac is thought to signify a change in his relationship to Abraham. Finally comes a reflection on Abraham's willingness to give back to God God's gift of a son.

J.A. EMERTON

WHARTON, JAMES A., *Job* (Westminster Bible Companion; Louisville, KY: West-minster/John Knox Press; London: SCM Press, 1999), pp. viii + 191. $16.00/£12.50. ISBN 0-664-25267-2.

This Westminster Bible Companion is essentially a personal response to the book of Job informed with scholarly findings and yet not limited by them. As W. writes in his comment on Job 1.1-5 after airing a few traditional scholarly questions gen-erally posed to this passage, 'the goal of this book is to concentrate on what is most clearly understandable in Job rather than on unresolved scholarly questions'. (p. 13). There is a focus therefore on the themes of the book of Job a fresh emphasis, for ex-ample, on the issue of integrity as a theme, the integrity of both Job and God. W. sees 'the Satan's' question as containing the question, 'Is Job corruptible?' He stresses the risk God is taking in staking his integrity on Job and sees the upholding of his integrity as a justification for God's 'angry' speeches from the whirlwind. There is an unusual handling of the speeches of the friends in this book, in the grouping together of Eliphaz's speeches (a good method as it gets across a sense of the argument as a whole) but not of the speeches of the others. Further, when intro-ducing ch. 28, W. characterizes the speeches as 'this long siege of arguments and counterarguments that finally lead nowhere' (p. 113)—I wonder whether all schol-ars would agree. The comments on each passage are of varied length, ranging from a paragraph to a number of pages. There is an introductory section on the function and structure of the book, on the fact that there is a variety of names for God in the book and on the links of Job with the suffering servant figure of Deutero-Isaiah. This is a 'reader' to accompany Bible study and stresses the relevance of Job today. There is a limited bibliography and further reading section. This is, however, a very read-able and thoughtful contribution to Job studies.

K.J. DELL

WILDBERGER, HANS, *Isaiah 13–27: A Continental Commentary* (trans. T.H. Trapp; Minneapolis: Fortress Press, 1997), pp. x + 624. $65.00. ISBN 0-8006-9509-7.

The first volume of this translation, covering Isaiah 1–12, was noticed in *B.L.* 1993 (p. 70). The fascicles of the original of this volume were noted as they ap-peared in *B.L.* 1975 (p. 53), 1976 (p. 43), 1977 (p. 54), and 1979 (p. 64). The bibli-ographies, as before, have been supplemented as far as 1979 from W.'s third volume. However, the translator announces his intention to update them further in his third volume. It is pleasing to be able to welcome the appearance of a further part of this commentary in English. However, the translation has not improved much in quality. It still tends to be wooden, often unidiomatic and sometimes carelessly misleading: for example, on p. 424 W. appears to be made to say that *mal'akim* means 'undertaking, business, wares'. These blemishes do not detract from the value of the commentary, with its immense fund of detail, especially on textual, historical and redactional matters. It is, of course a product of its era, and new insights require new types of commentary: one misses particularly any sense of the text as a whole. But on his own ground W. will be hard to beat.

W.J. HOUSTON

ZAKOVITCH, YAIR, *Das Buch Rut: Ein jüdischer Kommentar* (trans. Andreas Lehnardt, with an introduction by Erich Zenger; SBS, 177; Stuttgart: Katholisches Bibelwerk, 1999), pp. 192. DM 47.80/SwF 45.50/AS 349/Eur 24.44. ISBN 3-460-04771-2.

This packs a good deal of helpful information into a small format. Translated from a Hebrew original, it deals with the Hebrew text in a way not normally expected in a more popular commentary. Although a point is made that rabbinic literature is included in the commentary, only about two dozen references are actually found, along with about another dozen to *Ruth Rabbah* alone. But there is much of interest, and the translation is smooth and readable, with a reasonable secondary bibliography.

ED.

6. LITERARY CRITICISM AND INTRODUCTION (INCLUDING HISTORY OF INTERPRETATION, CANON AND SPECIAL STUDIES)

ABMA, E., *Bonds of Love: Methodic Studies of Prophetic Texts with Marriage Imagery (Isaiah 50:1-3 and 54:1-10, Hosea 1–3, Jeremiah 2–3)* (Studia Semitica Neerlandica, 40; Assen: Van Gorcum, 1999), pp. x + 281. Nlg 140.00. ISBN 90-232-3509-6.

Essentially this book is a study of imagery. The first 50 pages or so deal with background issues and method. Under the first heading are topics such as metaphor, the marriage metaphor (including sacred marriage, but very briefly) and feminist approaches. Methodological issues raised include whether the approach to these texts should be synchronic (as the author prefers) or diachronic, the fact that prophecy is largely in verse and what kind of audience was being addressed. A five-stage model of interpretation is then provided and there are some notes on translation and layout. A chapter is devoted to each of the three prophets in question and a final chapter describes the implications of biblical marriage imagery. A bibliography and indexes are supplied but there is no topic index. The work is marked by clarity of presentation (for example, whole passages are reprinted to make their structure evident) and clear argument in dialogue with other scholars.

W.G.E. WATSON

ALMOND, PHILIP C., *Adam and Eve in Seventeenth-Century Thought* (Cambridge: Cambridge University Press, 1999), pp. ix + 240. £35.00/$54.95. ISBN 0-521-66076-9.

It was a delight to find the Eden story forthrightly billed, by a literary scholar from Brisbane, as 'the central myth of Western culture'—a claim that is made good, for that foundational seventeenth century in England at least, in this erudite and scintillating book. The myth of Adam and Eve was seminal, A. argues, for all aspects of cultural life in that age, for debates on monarchy and democracy, on androgyny, libertinism and polygamy, and no less for reflections on vegetarianism, agrarian communism, gardening and the meaning of work. With this book in hand, the biblical scholar alert to the influence of the Bible will be reminded of its significance not only for Milton and Calvin and Herbert and Thomas Browne, but also for Muggletonians and Levellers, dieticians, transvestites, philologians, sceptics, voyagers and exponents of the Puritan art of love. This is a book to lift the spirits of any biblical scholar feeling marginalized by the values of the new entrepreneurial academy.

D.J.A. CLINES

ARNOLD, BILL T., *Encountering the Book of Genesis* (Encountering Biblical Studies; Grand Rapids, MI: Baker Book House, 1998), pp. 234. $24.99. ISBN 0-8010-2177-4.

Encountering Biblical Studies aim to be undergraduate texts which 'are written from an evangelical point of view, in the firm conviction that the Scripture is absolutely true and never misleads us' (p. 11). This book is not an exegetical analysis of Genesis, but a survey which draws out theological significance. The aim is to present factual content; historical, archaeological, geographical and cultural background; hermeneutical principles; and to substantiate the Christian faith. Also, the writers hope to instil a love for the Scriptures and enhance piety: for example, there is advice on ethical conduct about sex and on personal faith. The book is well laid out and illustrated: each section begins with an outline and objectives of the passage under discussion, and ends with study questions and key terms. There is discussion of such issues as science and creation. The book is conservative; for example, the flood is regarded as a historical event. The final chapters look at the authorship of Genesis, biblical criticism, and there is a survey of modern scholarship of the Pentateuch. Although the book is a good general introduction to Genesis, I expect that many undergraduates will want something more detailed.

P.J. HARLAND

ARNOLD, BILL T. and BRYAN E. BEYER, *Encountering the Old Testament: A Christian Survey* (Encountering Biblical Studies; Grand Rapids, MI: Baker Book House, 1999), pp. 512. $49.99. ISBN 0-8010-2176-6.

The aim of Encountering Biblical Studies is noted in the review above. This introduction to the OT starts by discussing canon, inspiration, history, archaeology and geography, and then has sections on each corpus of literature and book. The aim is to present factual content; historical, archaeological, geographical and cultural background; hermeneutical principles; and to substantiate the Christian faith. The writers hope to instil a love for the scriptures, enhance piety, and they offer advice on ethical conduct and personal faith. The book is beautifully produced and illustrated: each section begins with an outline and objectives, and ends with study questions and key terms. A CD-ROM is attached. The book is conservative; the view that the book of Isaiah is the work of one author is favoured, as is a sixth-century date for Daniel, and Jonah is regarded as historical. Although this is a good general introduction to the OT, undergraduates will need a much more detailed text book.

P.J. HARLAND

AUFFRET, PIERRE, *Là montent les tribus: Etude structurelle de la collection des Psaumes des Montées, d'Ex 15, 1-18 et des rapports entre eux* (BZAW, 290; Berlin–New York: de Gruyter, 1999), pp. xiv + 301. DM 178.00. ISBN 3-11-016694-1; ISSN 0934-2575.

The veteran structural analyst of the Psalms here adds another substantial work to his very long list of contributions of this kind. The psalms treated are the Ascents (120–134), and their structures are minutely observed and recorded with many ingenious diagrams; they are studied individually, in their sequence, in various groupings, and as a total collection. There is also analysis of Exod. 15.1-8 and Acts 15.3-4, correlated with the foregoing psalms, since they are all texts celebrating a march to the temple. Our author's intention is to offer his method of study as one resource among those which the commentator draws on for his general exegesis. Many will feel, however, that the intricate detail is somewhat daunting, and they would be glad of more help from the author, through general summaries and evaluation, in passing over from his analysis to consequent exegesis.

J.H. EATON

AXSKJÖLD, CARL-JOHAN, *Aram as the Enemy Friend: The Ideological Role of Aram in the Composition of Genesis—2 Kings* (ConBOT, 45; Stockholm: Almqvist & Wiksell, 1998), pp. 183. SEK 184.00. ISBN 91-22-01815-8.

This is a very helpful review of the roles of Aram[eans] in Pentateuch and Former Prophets. The first main chapter discusses the origin of Aram (Gen. 10), Aram's twelve tribes (22.20-24), the wooing of Rebekah (24), Jacob and Laban (28.10–32.3), Balaam (Num. 22–24), and the 'wandering' Aramean of Deut. 26.5. Of all its neighbours, Aram is most similar and closely related to Israel. The next chapter focuses on the nations and the Davidic empire, with particular attention paid to 2 Samuel 8 and Judges 3; while the third introduces the theme of Aram as Yahweh's instrument, with reference to Cushan-rishathaim, Hadadezer, Rezon and Ben-hadad. The rest of the volume develops this theme at greater length with reference to the (Elijah and) Elisha chapters in Kings under the somewhat curious category 'Aram as a Confederated Instrument of YHWH'. The lengthier ch. 4 explores the role of Aram in the execution of Ahab and in the purification of Israel. Then the epilogue of the Aramean story (2 Kgs 8.16–16.9) is traced in ch. 5. The brief sixth chapter sketches the distinction between ideological and factual history in terms of 2 Kgs 9–10 and the Tel Dan stele; and general conclusions are drawn. Even where it does not convince, the discussion is regularly stimulating; and it is an important enough contribution simply to have put this topic on the agenda.

A.G. AULD

BACH, ALICE (ed.), *Women in the Hebrew Bible: A Reader* (London and New York: Routledge, 1999), pp. xxvi + 539. £18.99. ISBN 0-415-91561-9.

This reader contains a wide selection of essays that covers a long period and a wide variety of viewpoints. The important names in feminist biblical scholarship over the last two decades are all there—ranging from scholars such as Trible, Bird, and Meyers, who are sometimes seen as being more conservative, to those who have pushed the boundaries of the field further, such as Bal, Exum, and Bach herself. It also includes articles by male scholars, notably Milgrom, Fishbane and Sasson. Jews, Christians and those professing no religious faith are all represented. This volume will be a good resource for those teaching courses on women in the Bible or feminist biblical interpretation. It would, however, have benefited from an introduction that contained a more thorough scholarly analysis of the different strands and developments in the discipline that are reflected so well in the volume's contents. B.'s introduction has a disturbingly polemical tone that conveys a sense that the reader is being bullied into reading texts in a particular way. For example, the reader is instructed to 'ask [a list of] feminist questions [presented by B.] while [she is] reading the ancient texts' (p. xxiii). The above notwithstanding the book is to be recommended as an extremely useful collection.

C. SMITH

BAKER, DAVID W. and BILL T. ARNOLD (eds.), *The Face of Old Testament Studies: A Survey of Contemporary Approaches* (Grand Rapids, MI: Baker Book House; Leicester: Apollos [Inter-Varsity Press], 1999), pp. 512. $34.99. ISBN 0-85111-774-0.

Any student (or teacher, for that matter) wanting an up-to-date survey of OT studies over the past 30 years or so could do little better than this volume. Although written from a Western, academic and evangelical perspective, the surveys of the various aspects of our discipline are thorough, succinct and judicious, and generally give fair coverage to non-evangelical approaches. Most of the essays are very readable and relevant, and some are superb (such as those by Gordon Wenham and Walter Moberly). Inevitably, however, one or two of the pieces are something of a disappointment (particularly those on archaeology and epigraphy), and the authors do not always seem quite clear for whom they are writing (for other evangelicals, or for readers of all persuasions?), and some recent developments, such as feminism and postcolonialism, receive little or no attention. These criticisms apart, this collection shows that evangelical OT scholarship is alive, well, informed and incisive.

C.H. KNIGHTS

BERG, HORST KLAUS, *Altes Testament unterrichten: Neunundzwanzig Unterrichtsvorschläge* (Stuttgart: Calwer; Munich: Kösel, 1999), pp. 392. DM 49.90/SwF 46.80/AS 364. ISBN (Calwer) 3-7668-3620-X; (Kösel) 3-466-36511-2.

The book provides the teacher of religious education with 29 sample lessons to teach OT to primary school and intermediate school pupils within the German school system. The sample lessons are structured according to eleven main topics (creation, primeval history, patriarchal narratives, freedom and the land, Torah, Ruth, kings, prophets, Babylonian exile, Psalms, Job). Each chapter contains theological and didactic considerations before moving on to the sample lessons. Songs (some of them in English), prayers, sketches and pictures complement each chapter. Whether the sample lessons will work cannot be judged from reading the book alone. Nevertheless it contains numerous ideas on how to make children familiar with the often strange world of the Hebrew Bible, but the teacher could have expected a bit more up to date bibliography for tackling the exegetical problems.

A.C. HAGEDORN

BERGEN, WESLEY J., *Elisha and the End of Prophetism* (JSOTSup, 286; Sheffield: Sheffield Academic Press, 1999), pp. 200. £37.50/$60.00. ISBN 1-85075-949-9; ISSN 0309-0787.

B. has contributed a remarkably attractive reading of the Elisha cycle of stories. He introduces his way of reading in three short chapters (pp. 11-41), with Bal, Stern-berg, Alter, Fewell and Gunn, Culley, Miscall, Josipovici, and Exum as guides, warnings, and discussion partners—and elements of the Elisha material already as illustrations. The bulk of the volume then reads Elisha, pericope by pericope, con-cluding (pp. 162-74) with sections on Elijah's return (2 Kgs 9–13) and on proph-etism after Elisha (2 Kgs 14–25). Some conclusions are then briefly drawn. B.'s thesis, all the more compelling for its modest presentation, is that the portrayal of Elisha deliberately belittles both him and prophetism in general: the role of prophet as alternative to monarch is explored in the narrative, only to be rejected. Elisha and his word are powerful, but there is little divine initiative in the story. He does act to save king and people in time of distress, but 'his role...never supersedes the royal office'—not even when he acts to replace one king by another.

A.G. AULD

BEST, ROBERT M., *Noah's Ark and the Ziusudra Epic: Sumerian Origins of the Flood Myth* (Fort Myers, FL: Enlil Press, 1999), pp. 304. £38.00. ISBN 0-9667840-1-4.

B. claims a BS in physics and a 'successful' decipherment of the numbers in Gen-esis 5. The 'key' is to note that the ratios of the antediluvians' 'ages at death' and 'ages at son's birth' were the same as ours, implying that they had our life spans, but that these were mistranslated by the various scribes responsible for the Sumerian King Lists and Genesis 5. As the few dozen phrases common to the Genesis and five ancient Near Eastern flood narratives suggest interdependence, B. attempts to recon-struct the original legend by emphasizing the naturally possible, the technically fea-sible and the archaeologically consistent. He concludes that the legend originally involved a Sumerian king who was transporting 270 animals on a cattle barge in 2900 BC but got caught in a local river flood after a six-day thunderstorm (cf. www.noahs-ark-flood.com). The method is clear and the valuable insights are many, but B. fails to engage with textual issues (cf. the discussion of Gen. 5 with Wenham) and this impedes serious reading. The book frequently prompts Monty-Python-esque questions, many of which are answered in the appendices. Here is one I would like answered: If 'the whole world (only) looked flooded because all dry land was beyond the horizon' (p. 52), even for birds (p. 56), shouldn't the average flight-heights and distances of doves and ravens be calculated to refine the original esti-mations of the flood's extent? The question sounds like one suited for someone with the patience of Job or the humour of a knight in Monty Python's *In Search of the Holy Grail.*

G. GLAZOV

BIRCH, BRUCE C., WALTER BRUEGGEMANN, TERENCE E. FRETHEIM and DAVID L. PETERSEN, *A Theological Introduction to the Old Testament* (Nashville: Abingdon Press, 1999), pp. 475. $40.00. ISBN 0-687-01348-8.

This text grew out of seminary teaching in which the Bible is not just a description of ancient faith but also a theological resource for contemporary confessing communities. The emphasis is therefore theological and canonical (the Protestant canon, since the Deutero-canonical books are omitted). The 'story of Israel' as found in Genesis to 2 Kings is followed as the backbone of the work, with appropriate sections from the Latter Prophets and Writings brought in at different points. Each chapter has a set of 'key topics' and 'key texts' listed. Some comments are made about historical matters, but these are generally superficial (e.g. the discussion of the theories of the settlement on pp. 181-83). In such an approach, there is danger that problematic aspects of the text will be skated over; however, some attempt is made to avoid this. For example, the view of Joshua that the 'Canaanites' should be destroyed is recognized to be an ideology not necessarily to be commended (pp. 189-97). It could be argued that the text should not always be seen in a positive light and that sharper recognition of its negative aspects should be introduced, but this will obviously be a moot point. No doubt many students studying to become clergy will find this a very useful book for bringing the text into their teaching and preaching ministry.

ED.

BLACK, FIONA C., ROLAND BOER and ERIN RUNIONS (eds.), *The Labour of Reading: Desire, Alienation, and Biblical Interpretation* (SBLSS, 36; Atlanta: Scholars Press, 1999), pp. xii + 417. $30.00. ISBN 0-88414-011-3.

The essays in this volume were written in honour of Robert C. Culley, and seek to provide fresh and unconventional approaches to the biblical text in ways continuous with Culley's own work. The essays are grouped under two headings. Part 1: Pleasurable Labour/Laborious Pleasure: 'Seraphim and Poetic Process' (Francis Landy), 'What is my Beloved? On Erotic Reading and the Song of Songs' (Black), 'To Love the Lord: An Intertextual Reading of John 20' (Adele Reinhartz), 'In the Eye of the Beholder: Wishing, Dreaming, and Double Entendre in the Song of Songs' (J. Cheryl Exum), 'Sing Us One of the Songs of Zion: Poetry and Theology in the Hebrew Bible' (Robert B. Robinson), 'Imagining Arrival: Rhetoric, Reader, and Word of God in Deuteronomy 1–3' (Susan Slater), 'Yearning for Jerusalem: Reading Myth on the Web' (David M. Gunn), 'Reading the Land: Holy Land as Text of Witness' (Burke O. Long). Part 2: Writers, Power and the Alienation of Labour: 'David is a Thing' (Boer), 'A Bettered Woman: Elisha and the Shunammite in the Deuteronomic Work' (David Jobling), 'Reading Story in Judges 1' (Susan Niditch), 'Icelandic and Israelite Beginnings: A Comparative Probe' (Norman K. Gottwald),

'On Reading the Story of the Man of God from Judah in 1 Kings 13' (John Van Seters), 'The Labour of Sharing' (John Dominic Crossan), 'The Killing Fields of Matthew's Gospel' (Gary A. Phillips), 'Labouring with Abusive Biblical Texts: Tracing Trajectories of Misogyny' (Pamela J. Milne), 'Playing it Again: Utopia, Contradiction, Hybrid Space and the Bright Future in Micah' (Runions), 'In Job's Face/ Facing Job' (Edward Greenstein). There is also a bibliography of works by Culley. There are no indexes.

R.W.L. MOBERLEY

BRAUN, JOACHIM, *Die Musikkultur Altisraels/Palästinas: Studien zu archäologischen, schriftlichen und vergleichenden Quellen* (OBO, 164; Freiburg: Universitätsverlag; Göttingen: Vandenhoeck & Ruprecht, 1999), pp. xi + 388, including 106 pp. of photos. SwF 115.00. ISBN (Universitätsverlag) 3-7278-1246-X; (Vandenhoeck & Ruprecht) 3-525-53664-X.

This book has waited a long time to see the light of day (the author gave its date of publication as 1996 in his article in the *Oxford Encyclopedia of Archaeology in the Near East!*), but the wait has been worthwhile. Covering the period from the late fourth millennium BCE to the fourth century CE and based upon an exhaustive examination of archaeological material which is richly illustrated in the book, this is the most comprehensive treatment of its subject that is likely to appear for a very long time. The fact that it deals with ancient Israel/Palestine brings some surprises, the biggest of which is the almost complete absence of archaeological evidence for musical instruments or activities in the Babylonian-Persian period (586–333 BCE). This contrasts signally with what is found in Ezra, Nehemiah and Chronicles, books which suggest that this period is a high-point for music in ancient Israel. This lack of archaeological evidence is not regarded as an accident, although the author cannot explain it. Another surprise is the diversity of Samaritan musical instruments up to the fourth century CE, including the earliest evidence in the whole area for a pneumatic organ. The discussions of the relevant artefacts take full account of the varying possibilities of their interpretation, and the book acknowledges how little can be known about the whole subject. Nevertheless, the book will repay careful reading by specialists in various areas, not the least by lexicographers. The *ḥālîl*, it seems, is more likely to be some kind of oboe than a flute, while the *nével* is not a harp but a kind of large lyre. Excellent indexes to biblical and post-biblical sources and to technical terms in Hebrew and German enhance the usefulness of this encyclopaedic work.

J.W. ROGERSON

BULTMANN, CHRISTOPH, *Die biblische Urgeschichte in der Aufklärung: Johann Gottfried Herders Interpretation der Genesis als Antwort auf die Religionskritik David Humes* (BHT, 110; Tübingen: J.C.B. Mohr [Paul Siebeck], 1999), pp. ix + 222. DM 128.00. ISBN 3-16-147164-4; ISSN 0340-6741.

In the history of interpretation Johann Gottfried Herder has been classified as a pioneer of the aesthetic interpretation of the OT, whose exegesis of Genesis 1 saw it as a poetic account of a dawning day, and who substituted poetry for theology. By the end of Dr Bultmann's *Habilitationsschrift* a different picture has emerged. Herder is reinstated as a theologian who sought to counter the deistic and reductionist enlightenment accounts of religion by means of an exegesis of Genesis 1, which took it seriously as revelation of God the creator and which defined humankind in relation to God. To be sure, the revelation was not in terms of natural science information about the world and its origins, and its main function was to awaken the human faculty of language and poetic expression; but it was nevertheless a poetry 'die aus einer wirklichen, ursprungshaften Beziehung zwischen Gott und Mensch erwachsen ist' (p. 187). The route to this conclusion is not only an exhaustive examination of Herder's *Älteste Urkunde des Menschengeschlechts* and its forerunner, rediscovered only in 1980, *Über die ersten Urkunden des Menschlichen Geschlects. Einige Anmerkungen.* Herder's early literary critical works are reviewed, as is critical work on the opening chapters of Genesis in the seventeenth and eighteenth centuries prior to Herder, some of it carried out by largely forgotten British exegetes. Crucial for the argument, however, is the work of David Hume, part of which Herder accepted, but whose reductionist conclusions about the origin of religion Herder could not follow, and which caused him to propose a theological alternative based upon his exegesis of Genesis 1. There are briefer treatments of Herder's interpretation of Genesis 2–3, of reactions to Herder's position by Hamann and Kant, neither of which was favourable, and of developments post-Herder, to de Wette. The book is not only a model of how to study individual scholars who have been influential in the history of interpretation; the questions that it raises are fundamental to hermeneutics in any generation, which means that the book has an importance well beyond the history of interpretation.

J.W.ROGERSON

BUREN, PAUL M. VAN, *According to the Scriptures: The Origins of the Gospel and of the Church's Old Testament* (Grand Rapids, MI: Eerdmans, 1998; distributed in the UK by Alban Books, Bristol), pp. ix + 147. $16.00/£9.99. ISBN 0-8028-4535-5.

Elegantly written, suggestive and provocative, this posthumous publication argues that the primitive Christian gospel was discovered by interpreting the Easter events in light of the Hebrew scriptures. Key among the latter are the *aqedah* of Genesis 22 (the rejected son) and Psalm 89 (the rejected king). The 'events' are more difficult to identify. It is, perhaps, surprising that an encounter between the disciples and Jesus alive again after being crucified does not feature among the possibilities considered. This does, however, explain B.'s difficulty in understanding why the concept of resurrection should have appealed to the 'discoverers' of the gospel (p. 28). Still, his hypothesis challenges the church's lectionary neglect of its OT. It also makes possible some measure of rapprochement between Christians and Jews, because Christians are free to recognize the christological reading of the scriptures as simply one possible reading without denying the eternal covenant between God and Israel and the reading it contains. Both readings are authentic, and emerge out of the distinctive history of each community. In brief compass B. addresses many contentious issues. Readers will find here much clear thinking as well as stimulus to do some of their own, whether or not they find B.'s own proposals persuasive.

D.J. REIMER

BURKES, SHANNON, *Death in Qoheleth and Egyptian Biographies of the Late Period* (SBLDS, 170; Atlanta: Scholars Press, 1999), pp. ix + 298. $45.00. ISBN 0-88414-005-9.

This book (1) insists that Qoheleth is obsessed with death; (2) that some Late-Period ancient Egyptian (auto)biographies also treat death as humanity's end-point; (3) that neither Qoheleth nor Egypt borrowed from the Greeks, but all three exhibit parallel cultural shifts. Point (1) seems to be over-emphasized—in Qoheleth, death is certainly the great leveller, but the futility of all human activities when without purpose or divine anchorage seems a closer focus. As for point (2), the author can only cite three examples alongside his chosen date for Qoheleth (Persian period), one of seventh century BC, one (far too late!) of first century BC, and only one c. 320 BC. All three lament premature deaths, hence they doubt the afterlife's reality. They in no wise mirror the scope of Qoheleth; older Egyptian texts are more comprehensive. Point (3) is well taken (chronologically, Greeks more probably borrowed from the East), but the theme of cultural change and crisis seems in part overstated (J.Z. Smith's theories were best omitted). A careful thoughtful contribution, but a more 'heavyweight' treatment would be preferable.

K.A. KITCHEN

BUSS, MARTIN J., *Biblical Form Criticism in its Context* (JSOTSup, 274; Sheffield: Sheffield Academic Press, 1999), pp. 512. £55.00/$85.00. ISBN 1-85075-876-X; ISSN 0309-0787.

In this large and learned work, B. moves well beyond the simplistic perception that 'form-criticism' was the discovery of Hermann Gunkel—although he attracts deserved attention in a chapter devoted to an assessment of his work—and beyond the sorts of analyses that Rolf Knierim so usefully carried out. The 'context' of the book's title is essentially a historical one. After some introductory considerations, B. moves chronologically from the Graeco-Roman period through the eighteenth century in the first 150 pages. Scholarship of the nineteenth and twentieth centuries is examined through the work of particular groups—Jewish, or Catholic, or Protestant interpretation, and so on—with the final two chapters before the conclusion devoted to NT and OT respectively. B's work shows with clarity how much the reading is an activity carried out in a social context, as the distinctive literary features noticed and the notion of 'form' itself shift across time. The study also explores the nature of the relationship between reading the Bible and reading any other literature in a given period. A key idea for B. is this 'relational' element of form, a factor that has contributed to the vitality of this approach over the centuries. A brief note cannot hope to engage with the riches of this major study; anyone wishing to reflect on the nature of interpretation, biblical or otherwise, will benefit from reading it.

D.J. REIMER

COGGINS, RICHARD J., *Old Testament: Israel and the Great Powers* (External Programme; London: University of London, 1999), pp. 66. N.P.

This is a textbook for the BD degree at the University of London and its format and contents are shaped by that genre. It is for external students and offers them a study guide for the set texts in prophecy and related areas. Part 1 deals with basic study skills in the area of OT study, Part 2 relates to the broad historical setting of the texts and Part 3 works with the set books themselves. Although this is a concise guide, it clearly identifies the critical issues generated by scholarship in all three areas—from a historical perspective. It does not raise issues of narrative criticism, for instance because, as the author states, these methodologies are not formally taught within the course as it stands. The main notes on historical background and set texts are accompanied by short bibliographies which are of manageable size and include older books, newer works and some references to articles. There are summaries of learning outcomes for a student in each section together with suggested examination questions. With such complex and varied texts it may still be difficult for a student to understand the critical debates without some individual support, but this is a solid textbook from which to begin.

M.E. MILLS

COOK, JOAN E., *Hannah's Desire, God's Design: Early Interpretations of the Story of Hannah* (JSOTSup, 282; Sheffield: Sheffield Academic Press, 1999), pp. 134. £27.95/$46.50. ISBN 1-85075-909-X; ISSN 0309-0787.

This development of a PhD Dissertation at Vanderbilt University examines the story of Hannah in 1 Samuel 1–2 and the later retellings in the *Biblical Antiquities* of Pseudo-Philo, the Targum of the Prophets, and the rather more distant Lukan infancy narratives. In them is seen the model of the 'barren mother', three forms of which are identified: 'competition', 'the promise' and 'the request'. In addition the theological themes of divine guidance and human initiative are traced, and the relation of the early biblical interpretations to the historical background of the writers is discussed. Emphasis is placed on differences between the four narratives, notably in plot and characterization, and special attention is given to the songs, since it is here that the greatest changes are made by Pseudo-Philo and the Targum. The study is marked by great clarity and well-ordered argument, with a certain feminist emphasis: 'All three birth stories [Samuel, John, Jesus] highlight the divine role in the birth of a child, and in doing so, allude to God as divine mother' (p. 116).

C.S. RODD

CRENSHAW, JAMES L., *Education in Ancient Israel: Across the Deadening Silence* (Anchor Bible Reference Library; New York: Doubleday, 1998), pp. xi + 305. $34.95. ISBN 0-385-46891-1.

The author's concern is not with the level of literacy but with the epistemological question of the 'manner of learning and the horizon of knowledge'. Set within the ancient Near Eastern context, with much enlightening reference to Egypt and Mesopotamia, the contrasts with Israel are clear, the parallels less so. The questions of the 'where? who? and how?' of education are considered, the last involving much interesting (sometimes humorous) evidence: what resistance was there on the part of the young, and why is the student's the missing voice? 'All knowledge is sacred'; it is both human discovery and divine gift. Although ultimately many uncertainties about the method and content of Israelite education remain, we are greatly in the author's debt for this highly readable study which not only illuminates the past but challenges the present.

G.I. EMMERSON

DALY-DENTON, MARGARET, *David in the Fourth Gospel: The Johannine Reception of the Psalms* (AGJU, 47; Leiden–Boston–Cologne: E.J. Brill, 2000), pp. xiv + 375 + frontispiece. Nlg 200.00/$117.75. ISBN 90-04-11448-3; ISSN 0169-734X.

Originating as a PhD thesis supervised by Seán Freyne at Trinity College, Dublin, this study argues for the importance of the psalmist David as a model for Jesus. The particular image of David as temple founder, musician and prophet have shaped the citations from the Psalms in the Fourth Gospel. More than three quarters of the explicit OT citations in the Fourth Gospel are from the Psalms, a far greater ratio than in any of the Synoptic Gospels.

ED.

DENNIS, TREVOR, *Looking God in the Eye: Encountering God in Genesis* (London: SPCK, 1998), pp. xiii + 104. £7.99. ISBN 0-281-05003-1.

This short book consists of an exposition of seven narrative portions from Genesis, with the stated aim of examining 'the intimacy of God, and…our human response to that intimacy'. As such, it is as much a devotional as an academic piece of writing, although the author refers to some contemporary scholarship on Genesis, and also provides his own translations of the passages he examines. This is not the only such volume of narrative exposition he has produced, but it is not as striking as some of his other work. The earlier chapters, particularly those on Adam and Eve (Gen. 2.4b–3.24) and Cain and Abel (Gen. 4.1-16), are the best, with more originality and insight and genuine wrestling with difficult theological issues. By contrast, some of the later ones are rather laboured, and have the feel of trying very hard to say something new about the passages without necessarily succeeding—sometimes, it must be said, because of the author's own doctrinal presuppositions. The translations too are literalistic and (perhaps deliberately) unsophisticated, giving the same impression of less-than-successful striving for novelty. In sum, while narrative exposition is a valid and valuable enterprise, this particular example of it is rather disappointingly superficial.

D. ROOKE

DENNIS, TREVOR, *Face to Face with God: Moses, Eluma and Job* (London: SPCK, 1999), pp. xvi + 125. £8.99. ISBN 0-281-05203-4.

This volume is a sequel to an earlier work (above) examining the encounters between humans and God in Genesis. This present work engages with such encounters in the rest of Torah, in Judges and in Job. In each chapter the author follows a common style, that of a slow and careful reading of the story of the human–divine meeting. The biblical text is broken into small sections for which a new translation from the Hebrew is given; the section is then discussed for the light it sheds on the relationship between God and us. Whereas Moses' encounters with God in Torah provide models of pathos and passion, that of Eluma, Manoah's wife, offers a comic picture in which the laughter of women's voices can be heard, as Eluma's perception of the divine nature of her visitor is matched with the obtuseness of her husband. The prologue to Job has some comic moments as well as deeply serious ones which foreshadow the mysterious depth of the deity revealed in the whirlwind speech, meeting with whom leaves Job speechless. This is a book of biblical spiritual reading, accessible to all readers with an interest in the OT. Notes refer the reader to scholarly studies which the writer has consulted.

M.E. MILLS

DORSEY, DAVID A., *The Literary Structure of the Old Testament: A Commentary on Genesis–Malachi* (Grand Rapids, MI: Baker Book House, 1999), pp. 330. $34.99. ISBN 0-8010-2187-1.

After introducing methods of structural analysis, D. examines all the books of the Hebrew Bible. His aim is ambitious: to divine the original structure as intended by the author (there is a tendency to see one author where others sometimes see more). He is aware of the dangers of trying to impose structure upon text and making the latter fit the former, and of the 'problem of subjectivity'—though he is not readily daunted by these caveats. He contends that structure not only aids emphasis, with which few would disagree, but also reveals meaning, yet some conclusions may easily, perhaps more easily, be reached by reflection on the content of the text, for example, that the Pentateuch is really a Hexateuch. D.'s evangelical standpoint repeatedly informs his writing, for example, in his reluctance to rearrange text, urging instead its re-examination in order to discover its 'true structure'. One suspects that such matters as dittography do not figure large in his approach, that he tends to desire (assume?) a single author of a book, and sees the author employing rather more literary artifice than others have discerned. He particularly finds chiasmus. However, against this, it must be conceded that his persuasive powers are considerable. (He is aware of this tendency it seems, as in his joking assertion that a chiastic structure could, with a bit of imagination, be imposed on the Old Testament as a whole!) It is not a commentary—despite the subtitle—in the conventional sense.

M.D. GRAY

DOUGLAS, MARY, *Leviticus as Literature* (Oxford: Oxford University Press, 1999), pp. xviii + 280. £25.00. ISBN 0-19-815092-X.

Since her chapter in *Purity and Danger* (1966) on Leviticus, D. has been one of the most creative interpreters of that book. Her latest work develops some themes broached in her earlier studies, while quietly dropping others. D. relies heavily on modern Israeli scholarship for her historical and exegetical reading of Leviticus, but on broader interpretative issues she uses anthropological methods to introduce insights of her own. D. holds that Leviticus is analogical in its mode of thought, that is, it draws repeated analogies between different spheres of life and activity. For example, the tripartite division of the tabernacle matches the three zones of holiness on Mount Sinai. Sacrificial animals exhibit a threefold division in their bodies: relatively unholy outer meat, holy fat and very holy inwards. The choice of Israel is mirrored in the choice of certain species as sacrificial, while declaring most animals unclean protects them from human exploitation. D. sees analogies in the classification of human impurity, impurity in garments, and in houses. She argues that the threefold division of the tabernacle is echoed in the threefold division of the book of Leviticus itself: the laws in chs. 1–7, 11–24, 25–27 are separated by narratives which act like the curtains of the tabernacle separating the holy of holies from the holy place from the courtyard. A short review cannot do justice to the wealth of interesting ideas in this work, which will need to be taken into account by future readers of Leviticus.

G.J. WENHAM

DUNDES, ALAN, *Holy Writ as Oral Lit: The Bible as Folklore* (Lanham, MD: Rowman & Littlefield, 1999), pp. vii + 131. $40.00/£43.00; paper $15.95/£11.95. ISBN 0-8476-9197-7; (paper) 0-8476-9198-5.

This short work by an eminent American folklorist, now turning to the Bible for his domain, intends 'to demonstrate that the Bible is...folklore', obvious from the fact that it 'clearly manifests the basic distinctive criteria of folklore: namely, multiple existence and variation' (pp. 1-2). The bulk of the book illustrates this claim from numerous examples of doublets of various genres across both the OT and the NT, highlighting the type of variance. The main interest of this work is that it draws attention, in an easily readable form, to the still largely unresolved issue of the significance of oral tradition and folklore genres to the biblical composition and, in particular, the presence of variants in it. However, the lack of meaningful engagement with already existing scholarship on the matter, or with the problems of the development of the biblical text, and the rushed coverage of both Testaments, resulting at times in little more than a compilation of duplicate texts under the undifferentiated heading 'folklore', gives the book an introductory, 'surveyish' quality and raises questions concerning its intended audience. The work does not do justice to the author's previous scholarship.

A. NAHKOLA

EVANS, ROBERT, *Using the Bible: Studying the Text* (Exploring Faith: Theology for Life; London: Darton, Longman and Todd, 1999), pp. x + 133. £7.95. ISBN 0-232-52344-4.

The series to which this book belongs is designed for people who want to take Christian theology seriously, is deemed to be suitable for those who have already taken Christian basic courses (such as *Alpha* and *Emmaus*) and has been adopted by the Church Colleges Certificate Programme offered by Anglican Colleges as credit-bearing modules. So from a scholarly viewpoint, this book might be thought of as belonging more to the propaganda end of biblical studies than to the 'pure milk' and 'strong meat' of engaged radical scholarship. But as a book for sixth formers or for those contemplating further study at college or university it strikes me as being eminently suitable as an introduction to reading the Bible in the company of believing scholars, with a few more daring souls included (e.g. P.R. Davies). Various biblical texts are selected for comment and there is a good running commentary on different translations of the Bible in terms of how they translate the selected texts. Lots of boxed sections draw readers' attention to important principles of interpretation and there is throughout the book an intelligent guide to some of the more recent approaches to biblical hermeneutics which would prepare readers well for deeper study (e.g. ideological analysis, socio-historical investigation, feminist perspectives). As a teaching tool I thought this to be an excellent little volume and would commend it to all pre-college and pre-university would-be students of the Bible. It could make for a much easier transition into the arcana of contemporary biblical scholarship.

R.P. CARROLL

FERRY, JOËLLE, *Illusions et salut dans la prédication prophétique de Jérémie* (BZAW, 269; Berlin–New York: de Gruyter, 1999), pp. xiii + 428. DM 218.00. ISBN 3-11-016239-3; ISSN 0934-2575.

The 'illusions' of the title of this Sorbonne thesis are the people's 'false' (*šeqer*) beliefs in security given by the temple (Jer. 7; 26), the possession of the law (8.8-9), or idols (2; 10.1-16); salvation, however, is the gift of Yahweh himself (30–31). The bulk of the book consists of detailed studies of these passages, with translation, textual criticism and literary and redactional analysis making large use of vocabulary studies to assign verses to one redactional level or another. F. finds a core of material in each text from Jeremiah himself, but also more than one level of deuteronomistic redaction nearly everywhere. She briefly characterizes the theological tendency of each level, but has no interest in more recent approaches to the text: it is remarkable in these days to find a woman scholar reading Jeremiah 2 without reacting to its exploitation of female sexuality. There are, however, plenty of interesting observations in detail. Regrettably, the publication has been delayed; the thesis was completed in 1992 and the only updating is the provision of a supplementary bibliography. Every single Hebrew quotation that crosses the line-break is printed in the wrong order, a disgrace to a scholarly publisher.

W.J. HOUSTON

FISCH, HAROLD, *The Biblical Presence in Shakespeare, Milton and Blake: A Comparative Study* (Oxford: Clarendon Press, 1999), pp. xiv + 331. £45.00. ISBN 0-19-818489-1.

The biblical presence in the title of Professor Fischs's book is not references or allusions to biblical passages in the poets discussed, but ways of reading and interpreting texts in accordance with or opposition to biblical 'world views'. In *Julius*

Caesar a Roman world is confronted by the biblical Christian Reformed world of the audiences. In *Anthony and Cleopatra* the Alexandrian and Roman worlds fail to define what it is to be human (as against Ezek. 36.26), while *Hamlet* explores the hermeneutics of remembering, in ways that evoke the OT. Milton's work in *Samson Agonistes* and *Paradise Lost* is a reflection upon midrashic discourse. Combining the idea of covenant and Abraham's questioning of God in Genesis 18, it defines interpretation as a covenant in which the text has authority while the interpreter has far-reaching interpretative freedom. In Blake, with his opposition to the Enlightenment and his exaltation of poetry, especially that of the OT prophets, to a unique mode of cognition the point is reached where the interpreter is all-important and poetry is self-validating. This is illustrated by a reading of Blake's engravings in which a comparison of the illustrations for Job 1 and Psalm 137 indicates that the former does not portray a peaceful, idyllic world, but a world oppressed by Urizen/ Elohim whom Job must overcome and abandon. Job does this by becoming Christ, as indicated, for example, in the engraving of Job and his daughters. This an extremely rich and rewarding book which, although primarily an exercise in literary criticism, contains many stimulating ideas about biblical hermeneutics.

J.W. ROGERSON

FRIEBEL, KELVIN G., *Jeremiah's and Ezekiel's Sign-Acts: Rhetorical Nonverbal Communication* (JSOTSup, 283; Sheffield: Sheffield Academic Press, 1999), pp. 535. £60.00/$90.00. ISBN 1-85075-929-7; ISSN 0309-0787.

This is a substantially revised and expanded version of a 1989 PhD supervised by Michael V. Fox. The author studies the prophets' proclamations, specifically their non-verbal features, from the perspectives of communication theory and rhetoric, in order to elucidate more fully both the messages and the transmission processes. His definition of 'sign-acts' is broader than what have often been called the 'symbolic actions' of the prophets, taking in for example the clapping of Ezek. 6.11-12 and the wailing of Ezek. 21.17-22. He devotes much attention to theory and method, without shirking very detailed exegesis of the relevant biblical texts. The author explores and rejects the view that the non-verbal sign-acts never really occurred but are, for example, merely literary motifs. He also rejects emphatically the more widespread view that such acts were inherently 'efficacious' or even in some sense magical, arguing rather that they were 'suasive' rhetorical vehicles for communicating 'message-contents' appropriate to the changing circumstances of Jerusalem and the Judahites. The volume is technical in its employment of the language of communication theory, but on the whole avoids becoming exclusive in its use of jargon. There is a large and well-presented bibliography; significant omissions are few but include A. Graffy's *A Prophet Confronts his People* and W. Houston's article on speech acts (*BibInt* 1993). At over 500 pages, the book would seem to have grown considerably over the decade since submission of the dissertation, and at times greater brevity might have made for more effective communication. Nevertheless, this constitutes a valuable contribution to study of the prophetic literature.

P.M. JOYCE

FRIEDMAN, RICHARD ELLIOTT, *The Hidden Book in the Bible: Restored, Translated and Introduced* (London: Profile Books, 1999), pp. xii + 404. £20.00. ISBN 1-86197-176-1.

F. here follows his best-selling book *Who Wrote the Bible?* with an equally lively study which claims to have rediscovered the first great prose writer of Western civilization. This work is traced to a single author in early monarchical Israel and is reconstructed from a careful and precise study of Genesis, Exodus, Numbers, Deuteronomy and the Former Prophets up to 2 Kings 1–2. Within the context of the Pentateuch the work resembles what has traditionally been designated J in critical scholarship. But, F. argues, J is only the first part of a more extensive prose work that culminates in narrative of the accession of Solomon to the throne of Israel in 2 Kings 1–2. The recovery of the work is outlined in the Introduction. A translation of it occupies the central part of the book. There follows an 'Afterword' drawing subtle literary and thematic relationships between the beginning of the narrative in the story of creation in Genesis 2 and its conclusion in 2 Kings 1–2. A further chapter is devoted to textual notes on the translation. An appendix contains a discussion of the converging evidence for the unity of the work, its antiquity, and a rejection of current attempts to attribute the earliest stages in the composition of the Pentateuch to a date as late as the exilic period or even later.

E.W. NICHOLSON

GARCÍA MARTÍNEZ, FLORENTINO and GERARD P. LUTTIKHUIZEN (eds.), *Interpretations of the Flood* (Themes in Biblical Narrative, 1; Leiden–Boston–Cologne: E.J. Brill, 1998), pp. xi + 202. Nlg 148.50/$83.00. ISBN 90-04-11253-7.

The essays here look at how the flood story was interpreted in later tradition, along with some modern perspectives on the story. The phrase 'the flood story' or equivalent should be added to most of the article topics listed here: Gen. 6.5–9.17 in the context of the ancient Near East (E. Noort), Apollodorus's account (J.N. Bremmer), was it known to the Greeks? (A. Hilhorst), the book of Jubilees (J.T.A.G.M. van Ruiten), the Dead Sea Scrolls (García Martínez), Gnostic mythology (Luttikhuizen), מבול in rabbinic tradition (W.J. van Bekkum), early Christian theology (H.S. Benjamins), scientific revolution—Thomas Burnet's system of natural providence (R. Vermij), considerations of a psychoanalyst (P.M.G.P. Vandermeersch). These papers were originally given in Dutch (except for one in German); most readers will be grateful for the translation here.

ED.

GOLKA, FRIEDEMANN W., *Jakob—Biblische Gestalt und literarische Figur: Thomas Manns Beitrag zur Bibelexegese* (Arbeiten zur Theologie, 91; Stuttgart: Calwer, 1999), pp. 152. DM 38.00/SwF 35.90/AS 277. ISBN 3-7668-3628-5.

Thomas Mann's Tetralogy *Joseph und seine Brüder*, which was published between 1933 and 1942, has understandably received more attention from *Germanisten* than from OT scholars. G. is an exception, and on the basis of his collaboration with *Germanisten* and courses that he has taught in Oldenburg, he has produced a valuable introduction to the first volume of Mann's masterpiece, *Die Geschichten Jaakobs*. An introductory chapter outlines, among other things, Mann's knowledge of the biblical scholarship then available, including Wellhausen, Gunkel and (surprisingly) the pan-Babylonian Alfred Jeremias. The main part of the book is an examination of the biblical texts as handled by classical and recent exegetes such as von Rad, Westermann, Blum and Golka himself, the results being compared with Mann's treatment. It emerges that, while Mann was well read in historical criticism, his handling of the text in its final form enabled him to anticipate generally, and in particular instances, some of the suggestions of Noth's *Überlieferungsgeschichte* and of Rendtorff and Blum's newer Pentateuchal criticism. Mann's use of Jewish sources, such as Bin Gorion's *Sagen der Juden*, is also examined. A general conclusion is that Mann, with the help of Jeremias's astral mythology, remythologized the story in his telling of it, a fact that explains his omission of the already highly mythologized story of Jacob's wrestling in Genesis 32. This is a stimulating book which indicates how much can be learned by biblical scholars from treatments of the Bible by great literary writers. G. encourages readers to return to Mann by deliberately referring to a readily available edition of *Die Geschichte Jaakobs*. His introduction will reward anyone who is minded to do so.

J.W. ROGERSON

GRAFFY, ADRIAN, *Alive and Active: The Old Testament beyond 2000* (Blackrock, Co. Dublin: Columba Press, 1999), pp. 192. £7.99. ISBN 1-85607-253-3.

The speaker who at a recent SOTS meeting asked for suitable A-Level OT textbooks to be written will not be disappointed with this volume. Indeed, this well-written introduction could usefully acquaint today's first-year theology and religious studies undergraduates who are often lacking in even the rudimentary knowledge of biblical texts. G. discusses the OT texts systematically, thematically and at times expositionally. References to postbiblical and other ancient Near Eastern texts are included. G.'s approach is obviously selective though he asks good and pertinent questions about the texts. His theological comments are not glib. However, some key texts (e.g. Leviticus—Deuteronomy) deserve more than the scant attention which they receive and the very occasional contemporary cross-cultural references could be further developed. Overall, one gets a clear impression that the OT can be alive and active through the interaction between its many colourful personalities and their different perceptions and understandings of God. This creator and liberating God is deeply concerned with justice and peace. Still, I have a nagging question: Can our familiar and apparently exhausted(?) understandings of this same God in all 'his' awe and mystery sustain us in the new century?

A.S.J. LIE

GREEN, BARBARA, *Like a Tree Planted: An Exploration of Psalms and Parables through Metaphor* (Collegeville, MN: Michael Glazier [Liturgical Press], 1997), pp. 160. $14.95. ISBN 0-8146-5869-5.

The author is a Dominican who teaches Scripture and spirituality in Berkeley.

She has here paired each of her eight psalms with a parable from Luke's Gospel; she deals with each pair in successive chapters, centring her comments on shared metaphor. The psalms treated are 1, 7, 8, 18, 23, 27, 39, 41, quoted in the translation of *The Liturgical Psalter* of the International Commission on English in the Liturgy, 1994 (Ps. 1 begins: 'If you would be happy, never walk with the wicked'). This is an interesting and original contribution in the area of spiritual development; it would be suitable as a stimulus to discussion.

J.H. EATON

GREEN, GARRETT, *Theology, Hermeneutics, and Imagination: The Crisis of Interpretation at the End of Modernity* (Cambridge: Cambridge University Press, 2000), pp. xii + 229. £37.50/$59.95. ISBN 0-521-65048-8.

This neat little book represents a revised and expanded version of the 1998 Edward Cadbury Lectures. While there is little here for the pure *altestamentlicher* scholar, those who are interested in general biblical hermeneutics vis-à-vis current interpretation theory will find much to engage their attention. Throughout the book there is a good 'owl's-eye' view of the philosophers (especially Kant, Hamann, Nietzsche, and so on) who have laid the groundwork for how we tend to read the Bible in the twilight of modernity. G.'s central focus is on Nietzsche, in particular the Nietzsche who is the sworn enemy of Christianity, even if he may be viewed as 'play[ing] the unwilling part of *advocatus Christi*'. The postmodern Nietzsche is then taken up into a discussion of the work of Jacques Derrida and Karl Barth (very much under the influence of Graham Ward's reading of these two redoubtable figures) in order to produce an account of Christian imagination in a postmodern world. G. does a brilliant job here of reading Barth in relation to Derridean *différance* or, I should say, reading some of the interstices of Barth's magisterial *Die kirchliche Dogmatik* in order to show how Barth embraces *différance*. Hans Frei's notion of 'narrative eclipse' also plays a big part in his reading of the matter, as does Auerbach's famous demand for *Deutungsbedürftigkeit*. 'If the meaning of the text is always open ended, then it follows that there can be no escape from interpretation, and interpretation requires the active engagement of the imagination' (p. 175). G. concludes that 'God has chosen to reveal himself in the world in a manner accessible only to imagination', so that 'from the standpoint of the faithful imagination of the Christian believer, the fantasies of God are more real than the realities of men' (p. 206). I wonder if that conclusion is postmodern enough to rescue the premodern enterprise of Christian imagination and its readings of Scripture? I do however commend the book as a good read.

R.P. CARROLL

GRIMM, MARKUS, *'Dies Leben ist der Tod': Vergänglichkeit in den Reden Ijobs— Entwurf einer Textsemantik* (Arbeiten zu Text und Sprache im Alten Testament, 62; St Ottilien: Eos, 2998), pp. xii + 250. DM 38.00. ISBN 3-88096-562-5.

This detailed study of lexico-semantic relationships among words connected with life and death in the speeches of Job presents analyses of numerous and diverse words in order to generate various diagrams that try to capture the semantic fields of life and death. Although the result is something of a *tour de force* in respect of the big picture of life and death in Job, the description is founded on so many small-scale analyses of individual words and verses that there are inevitable omissions and simplifications. Moreover, the constant shifting of lexical attention means that the work never quite attains either to an exegetically based discourse on life and death in Job or to a usable lexicographical description, but remains an undigested PhD. It is, nonetheless, an impressive piece of scholarship and well indexed, so that one can easily access (in piecemeal fashion) information about such Hebrew voca-bles as *'ereṣ, bāśār, dām, derek, hālak, √ḤYY, ḥereb, yārad, √MWT, nepeš, 'āpār, 'eṣem, √QBR, šᵉ'ōl* and *šūb*, as well as linguistic terms.

J.F. ELWOLDE

GROTTANELLI, CRISTIANO, *Kings and Prophets: Monarch Power, Inspired Lead-ership, and Sacred Text in Biblical Narrative* (Oxford: Oxford University Press, 1999), pp. x + 210. £42.00. ISBN 0-19-507196-4.

This is a collection of ten essays, published between 1977 and 1993, several of them translated from Italian for this volume. The essays have less to do with history than they have with literature, tradition and mythology. The author adopts a typo-logical approach which allows him to set aside questions of historical particularity and range widely over the mythologies and literatures of the classical and ancient Near Eastern worlds, bringing together common themes and motifs relating to a variety of topics. Thus an essay on 'Charismatic Possession and Monarchic Ratio-nalization' examines the relevant biblical texts in the context of non-biblical ac-counts of the origin of state order, while another on 'Healers and Saviors of the Eastern Mediterranean in Preclassical Times' examines the common traits of non-royal healers and saviours and their relationship to kings in the biblical and Greek worlds. These are all interesting and significant essays reflecting an intimate famil-iarity with a wide range of ancient Near Eastern and classical materials.

A.D.H. MAYES

HEIMERDINGER, JEAN-MARC, *Topic, Focus and Foreground in Ancient Hebrew Nar-ratives* (JSOTSup, 295; Sheffield: Sheffield Academic Press, 1999), pp. 286. £50.00/ $85.00. ISBN 1-84127-014-8; ISSN 0309-0787.

H. seeks to bring the latest insights of linguistic and discourse analysis studies to bear on the grammatical, stylistic and literary characteristics of 'Old Hebrew' (his term preferred to 'Biblical' or 'Classical Hebrew') narratives, something under-taken by a 'still too small group of pioneering scholars' (p. 7). After a useful open-ing chapter on the present 'state of play' in such studies he investigates the para-graph, sentence and clause, grammatical and stylistic structures by which Hebrew narrators emphasize topic and theme (ch. 3), bring concepts and character ('refer-ents') to their readers' attention and maintain them there (ch. 4), manage to focus on certain presuppositions (ch. 5) and employ various techniques to bring aspects of the narrative into the foreground. H., with his 'organizational' approach to the texts (see p. 72) reacts throughout the book to the more 'structural' approach of Longacre, with his rigid views of plot structure and insistence that in Old Hebrew the *vayyiqtol* clause was the bearer of the main, highlighted action, while other constructions (e.g. the noun clause plus *qatal* form) carried the background material. Liberally illustrating his own much more flexible approach from biblical narratives, accompanied by instructive diagrams and charts, H. argues for a more complex and varied use of the devices by which the narrators achieved their aim. It is tempting for those who are not among the 'too few' to have made use of such studies to say that they had already intuitively divined some of this without such detailed analysis and without peppering their pages with the grapeshot of jargon so prominent in the armoury of contemporary literary scholars. But that would be unfair. To have one's attention directed to such things is to gain immeasurably in one's appreciation of Hebrew narrative and H. is to be congratulated on producing such an informative, balanced, and, in fact, readable a book.

R. MASON

HEITHER, THERESIA and CHRISTIANA REEMTS, *Schriftauslegung—Die Patriarchenerzählungen bei den Kirchenvätern* (Neuer Stuttgarter Kommentar: Altes Testament, 33/2; Stuttgart: Katholisches Bibelwerk, 1999), pp. 172. DM 36.00. ISBN 3-460-07332-2.

The first part of this useful book (by Reemts) gives a beautifully lucid account of the way that Christian preaching was received in pagan antiquity, and of the exegetical and hermeneutical strategies which the Fathers adopted towards the biblical text in their works of apologetic and scriptural commentary. Readers of *B.L.* will find part two of the book (by Heither) of particular interest, given growing scholarly interest in postbiblical interpretations of Scripture. Heither demonstrates how the theoretical principles of interpretation adopted by the Fathers, discussed in the first part of the book, were applied to Patriarchal stories in Genesis: particular attention is paid to Genesis 12, 15, 17, 21–22, 26–32, 37–50. Examples of exegesis of both Eastern and Western Fathers are offered in translation, accompanied by commentary which lays open the concerns and goals of the patristic use of the Bible. An English version of this book would be of considerable value in introducing undergraduates to Patristic exegesis.

C.T.R. HAYWARD

HENZE, MATTHIAS, *The Madness of King Nebuchadnezzar: The Ancient Near Eastern Origins and Early History of Interpretation of Daniel 4* (Supplements to Journal for the Study of Judaism, 61; Leiden–Boston–Cologne: E.J. Brill, 1999), pp. xii + 295. Nlg 155.00/$91.50. ISBN 90-04-11421-1; ISSN 1384-2161.

The first chapter is devoted to the story in the text of Daniel, and the second to the reconstructed background in Babylonian history (namely, the reign of Nabonidus and 4QPrayer of Nabonidus). The bulk of the study is given over to how the legend was interpreted in rabbinic Judaism and the Syriac Christian tradition, plus Hippolytus and Tertullian. Some of the Syriac writers were able to derive the basis of their asceticism from the story in Daniel.

ED.

HILL, JOHN, *Friend or Foe? The Figure of Babylon in the Book of Jeremiah MT* (Biblical Interpretation Series, 40; Leiden: E.J. Brill, 1999), pp. ix + 239. Nlg 138.83/$78.00. ISBN 90-04-11434-3; ISSN 0928-0731.

This work is a thorough consideration of the theme or figure of Babylon on the book of Jeremiah. This valuable study presents a literary interpretation of Babylon in Jeremiah MT, and is much needed since there has been a neglect of this figure in studies on Jeremiah. The author has sought to fill this gap by providing us with a work which explores this theme in the entire book. The author has moved beyond historical-critical approaches and has shown that this metaphor is central to a synchronic reading of this book. The work itself shows that Babylon is a multi-layered metaphor: on the one hand it is the archetypal enemy of both Judah and its God; on the other hand it is metaphorically identified with Judah. The work also explores the concept of the unended exile, and shows how this idea, so central to post-exilic Judaism, is also to be found in the book of Jeremiah. The work refers to the original languages in a script that is pleasing to read; the English text is that of the NRSV. The bibliography is well organized and up to date.

F. GOSLING

HUSSER, JEAN-MARIE, *Dreams and Dream Narratives in the Biblical World* (trans. Jill M. Munro; The Biblical Seminar, 63; Sheffield: Sheffield Academic Press, 1999), pp. 197. £14.95/$19.95. ISBN 1-85075-968-5.

This is an English translation of the French article 'Songe' that appeared in the *Supplément au Dictionnaire de la Bible* (*B.L.* 1998, pp. 2-3). The text has not been revised, but the bibliography has been updated and adapted for English-speaking readers. It should be noted that this is not his more thorough monograph (in French) on dreams in the OT which was reviewed in *B.L.* 1995 (p. 92). However, the present study, although rather shorter, covers dreams from other parts of the ancient Near East more comprehensively and thus serves as a useful supplement to the 1994 book.

ED.

KLAUS, NATHAN, *Pivot Patterns in the Former Prophets* (JSOTSup, 248; Sheffield: Sheffield Academic Press, 1999), pp. 310. £35.00/$57.50. ISBN 1-85075-912-X; ISSN 0309-0787.

The pivot pattern 'is an elaborate multi-lateral chiastic structure with a pivot at its centre and with its remaining elements distributed on both of its sides in mirrored symmetry enabling the narrator to conclude his story the way he began' (p. 13). In his brief survey of previous research on this form of chiasmus K. is particularly critical of J.P. Fokkelman but seems unaware of works by R. Meynet (see *B.L.* 1999, pp. 200-201) and other recent work, notably, M.J. Boda, 'Chiasmus in Ubiquity: Symmetrical Mirages in Nehemiah 9', *JSOT* 71 (1996), pp. 55-70. He then outlines (all too briefly) his own approach, which is to examine short passages in terms of repetition, paying particular attention to the central or pivotal section. He then applies this method to prose texts, described according to genre, in five chapters. Many of these examples are convincing or at least intriguing (e.g. 1 Sam. 3.17) but many others seem rather weak, and the one example from verse (Amos 5.4-6) is not new. There is a long concluding chapter. In general the presentation is rather vague and the whole book (quite obviously a doctoral thesis) should have been tightened up considerably before publication. Even so it provides material for discussion on 'the Bible as literature' (p. 289).

W.G.E. WATSON

KUGEL, JAMES L., *The Bible as It Was* (Cambridge, MA: Harvard University Press, 1999 [1997]), pp. xx + 680. Paper £12.50. ISBN 0-674-06941-2.

This is the UK edition of a book originally published in 1997. It was not reviewed in the *B.L.*; however, the revision of it (*Traditions of the Bible*) was reviewed in *B.L.* 1999 (p. 109). The advantage of this reprinted earlier edition is that it is in paperback and much cheaper than the revision.

ED.

LARSSON, GÖRAN, *Bound for Freedom: The Book of Exodus in Jewish and Christian Traditions* (Peabody, MA: Hendrickson, 1999), pp. xviii + 334. $24.95. ISBN 1-56563-083-1.

This commentary is notable as the product of—among other experiences—a dozen years' teaching Hebrew Bible and Rabbinic Literature at the Swedish Theological Institute, Jerusalem, and the many contacts with Jewish and other scholars that locus afforded. The result is an impressive weaving together of comments on the material in Exodus, rabbinic sources, and the experience of Jews in the last century (the author is recipient of an award for 'encouraging greater understanding and respect between Christians and Jews'). Somewhat disappointingly Exodus is read insistently in its 'final form', though, in the opinion of this reader, a diachronic study would have enhanced the very helpful linkages made with Jewish observance of Passover and Pentecost. The claim that '[a]ll through the book of Exodus, a great familiarity with the culture and religion of Egypt can be detected' is maximized. While the work will undoubtedly be read with profit by students and scholars, the author himself states that the work is designed 'primarily for Bible readers, teachers and ministers' as well. Alongside its many exegetical insights, it does indeed contain quality homiletical materials from the *double entendre* of the title to the quotation from Wiesel, 'the opposite of love is not hate, but indifference', and the comparison of the luckless Israelite *šôṭ^erîm* in Exodus 5 with Jewish 'Kapos' at Auschwitz.

W. JOHNSTONE

LEVISON, JOHN R. and PRISCILLA POPE-LEVISON (eds.), *Return to Babel: Global Perspectives on the Bible* (Louisville, KY: Westminster/John Knox Press, 1999), pp. xiv + 234. $19.95/£12.99. ISBN 0-664-25823-9.

This edited volume represents a nice idea well executed. Thirty essays by various biblical scholars from Latin America, Africa and Asia, some of them well known, represent perspectives from these areas of the world on a number of selected biblical texts. Thus on the Hebrew Bible we have José Miguez-Bonino, Solomon Avotri and Choan-Seng Song on Gen. 11.1-9, Jorge Pixley, François Kabasele Lumbala and George M. Soares-Prabhu on Exod. 20.1-17; J. Severino Croatto, Hannah W. Kinoti and Cyris Heesuk Moon on Ps. 23.1-6; Elsa Tamez, Lumbala and Song on Eccl. 3.1-8; Pixley, Lumbala and Moon on Isa. 52.13–53.12. On the NT side—when, oh when, will we get a book which gets the biblical proportions right, avoids implicit (covert) supersessionism and makes the division 80-20 instead of 50-50?—we have Croatto, Kinoti and Helen R. Graham on Mt. 5.1-12 ; José Cárdenas Pallares, Kinoti and Soares-Prabhu on Jn 1.1-18; Míguez-Bonino, Patrice M. Siyemeto and Graham on Acts 2.1-42; Tamez, Lumbala and Daniel C. Arichea on 1 Cor. 15.1-58; Pixley, Timothy G. Kiogora and Song on Rev. 21.1–22.5. At times the different cultural perspectives make for a good tension between text and cultural reception which generates thought and reflection, whereas at other times it is more difficult to see what the cultural perspective has added to our understanding of the reception of the text. An attractively neat volume, nicely produced and quite thought-provoking in a low-key way. The two editors are to be congratulated on its appearance. Well worth reading too.

R.P. CARROLL

LEW, DANIEL J., *Three Crucial Questions about the Last Days* (Carlisle: Paternoster; Grand Rapids, MI: Baker Book House, 1998), pp. 168. £9.99/$11.99. ISBN (Paternoster) 0-85364-962-6; (Baker) 0-8010-5820-1.

This book is very much in the context of evangelical Christianity and its views about eschatology and the return of Christ. Many of the standard passages (both OT and NT) and interpretations are rehearsed. However, it urges caution and ultimately concludes that we cannot know the future—a rather moderate position in the milieu from which it comes.

ED.

LIENHARD, JOSEPH T., SJ, *The Bible, the Church, and Authority: The Canon of the Christian Bible in History and Theology* (Collegeville, MN: Michael Glazier [Liturgical Press], 1995), pp. xi + 108. $9.95. ISBN 0-8146-5536-X.

A relatively brief but well-informed account of the scholarly consensus on the formation of the NT canon. L. writes from the position of a convinced Catholic and sees the canonization of Scripture in wholly positive terms: no 'curse of the canon' here! On the way he argues for biblical interpretation as properly the task of the Church, and gently criticizes Protestant approaches, especially historical criticism.

There is nothing new in this discussion, but it is a good introduction to a complex subject.

J. BARTON

LIPTON, DIANA, *Revisions of the Night: Politics and Promises in the Patriarchal Dreams of Genesis* (JSOTSup, 288; Sheffield: Sheffield Academic Press, 1999), pp. 241. £46.00/$75.00. ISBN 1-85075-958-8; ISSN 0309-0787.

L.'s notably polished and assured revision of her Cambridge PhD thesis is a study of what she terms the 'patriarchal dreams' (Gen. 20.1-18; 28.10-22; 31.10-13; 31.24) and the 'covenant of the pieces' (Gen. 15.1-21). She omits the dreams in the Joseph narrative as she judges them to represent an Israelite attempt to reflect Egyptian practice. Those left are subject to a thorough close reading and are found to act as foci for a number of common themes. In particular, each explains the divine plan behind some delay in the fulfilment of the promise of the land. L. reads these episodes as having been inserted by exilic writers to bring 'hope by patriarchal precedent' (p. 245) to their audience. She deals confidently and ably with a wide-ranging literature. No doubt wisely, she specifically exchews any engagement with psychoanalytic interpretations, although this may leave unexplored intriguing resonances with Freud's concept of the dream text and its relations to anxiety and wish-fulfilment. Be that as it may, L.'s work brings a new clarity to a surprisingly neglected topic.

H.S. PYPER

LUTTIKHUIZEN, GERARD P. (ed.), *Paradise Interpreted: Representations of Biblical Paradise in Judaism and Christianity* (Themes in Biblical Narrative, 2; Leiden– Boston–Cologne: E.J. Brill, 1999), pp. xiii + 218. Nlg 145.44/$81.00. ISBN 90-04-11331-2.

This collection of essays traces the concept of paradise from the Median word *paridaeza* (Old Persion *paridaida*) through the LXX, the Eden story in Genesis and Ezekiel, *1 Enoch*, *Jubilees*, the Dead Sea Scrolls, rabbinic and qabbalistic literature, early Christian and Gnostic literature, mediaeval concepts, to Milton. A brief preface gives a précis of each essay but without any attempt to pull together any common threads or conclusions. There is an index of ancient texts but not of modern authors.

ED.

MARGUERAT, DANIEL and YVAN BOURQUIN, *How to Read Bible Stories: An Introduction to Narrative Criticism* (with the collaboration of M. Durrer; trans. John Bowden; London: SCM Press, 1999), pp. ix + 190 + illustrations. £12.95. ISBN 0-334-02778-0.

The books of the 'How to Read' series have established themselves as accessible introductions to areas of theological study for lay people. This one is in effect a comprehensive textbook on narrative criticism with examples from biblical narratives. The examples are predominantly from the NT, but with a good sprinkling from the

OT. The approach is essentially technical, surprisingly different from most books on the narrative criticism of the Hebrew Bible, yet the style is remarkably lucid and readable. The chapters review successively narrator and various sorts of reader, story and discourse, closure, plot, characters, setting, narrative time, narrative commentary, and the roles of text and reader. Dozens of technical terms of narratology are defined, often pictorially as well as verbally, including such monstrosities as *intradiegetic* and *extradiegetic* (no, you'll have to read the book to find out). Exercises are set at the end of each section, with answers at the back of the book(!), along with a glossary, bibliography and indexes. All this strongly suggests that the book would be more useful for students than for its intended readership, and I shall keep my copy for reference. The translation flows well, but haste occasionally results in an incomprehensible sentence.

W.J. HOUSTON

MILLS, MARY E., *Historical Israel: Biblical Israel: Studying Joshua to 2 Kings* (Cassell Biblical Studies Series; London: Cassell, 1999), pp. x + 146. £9.99. ISBN 0-304-70474-1.

The book has three major sections. The first examines the links between the texts Joshua to 2 Kings and the Israel of history via an analysis of three main debates: models of Israelite origins, societal structures in Israel and the united monarchy controversy. The second section considers the narrative art at work in these texts and the contribution of literary approaches. M. introduces some main features of narrative criticism and its exponents before moving on to a chapter on tragedy in the Deuteronomic History (DH). She closes this section with a further chapter on the strategies of female readers, their evaluations of the construction of women within the DH and resistant readings. The third section examines the theological themes of the texts, including a discussion of ideological criticism, a chapter on the character of God and a further chapter on the Deuteronomist's construction of Biblical Israel. There is a useful, short bibliography and an index. Through these discussions, M. focuses succinctly on the pivotal issues, identifies the crux of various scholarly positions, contrasting these positions helpfully and without prejudice, while deftly pointing the reader to further reading. Given that this is such a slim volume, one might expect that brevity leads to simplicity. This is not the case. M. is to be commended for covering the areas of study in a concise but thorough manner, writing with a clarity that makes this a very attractive introductory textbook for students. In the foreword, John Barton commends this book as one which concentrates equally on the historical, literary, sociological and theological dimensions of the Joshua to 2 Kings narratives, summarizing major scholarly work in these four areas and making that information available to a wider audience. I endorse this view.

D. GUEST

MOYISE, STEVE, *Introduction to Biblical Studies* (Cassell Biblical Studies; London: Cassell, 1998), pp. viii + 113. £9.99. ISBN 0-304-70091-6.

This is a basic introduction to the biblical scholar's toolbox which draws material from both Testaments, but mainly the New. It gives a (necessarily) brief account of historical and source criticism, the quest for the historical Jesus, the social scientific approach, rhetorical criticism and various readings, e.g. liberation, feminist. It introduces the idea of textual variants (indicating its intended readership: 'Which version is the Word of God?') and concludes with a glimpse of meaning, deconstruction and intertextuality. The book is clearly written and gives suggestions for further reading at the end of each section. It would be useful reading for absolute beginners.

M. BARKER

NASUTI, HARRY P., *Defining the Sacred Songs: Genre, Tradition and the Post-Critical Interpretation of the Psalms* (JSOTSup, 218; Sheffield: Sheffield Academic Press, 1999), pp. 231. £35.00/$57.50. ISBN 1-84127-028-8; ISSN 0309-0787.

The author pleads for a psalm interpretation which takes account of the reception and interpretation of the Psalms down all the centuries. The discussion, however, centres on genre, and many thought-provoking comments are made about the fundamental aim and nature of genre definition. Gunkel's system is viewed from the perspectives of later work (Mowinckel, Westermann, Brueggemann), and then more broadly in relation to the canonical approach of Childs and Wilson. There is also reference to Ricoeur and to work in the humanities generally, but always our author returns to his point that genre has been a concern throughout the whole history of psalm interpretation. And always, he says theological understanding of the psalms has interacted with the way they have been grouped. For those who would reflect on the value of genre study in relation to the continued religious use and theological significance of the Psalms, this will be worthwhile reading, all the better for its accessible style.

J.H. EATON

NAY, RETO, *Jahwe im Dialog: Kommunikationsanalytische Untersuchung von Ez 14,1-11 unter Berücksichtigung des dialogischen Rahmens in Ez 8-11 und Ez 20* (AnBib, 11; Rome: Pontifical Biblical Institute, 1999), pp. xii + 424. Lire 50,000/ $30.00. ISBN 88-7653-141-6.

This volume is a revised version of a dissertation submitted at the Pontifical Biblical Institute in 1997, under the supervision of H. Simian-Yofre. The author investigates Ezek. 14.1-11 from the point of view of analysis of the encounter between Yahweh and the prophet with his people, in the light of material in the great vision account of chs. 8–11 and the bold historical review of ch. 20, chosen because these sections share with 14.1-11 the motif of the elders of Israel, of particular importance in N.'s understanding of Ezekiel. He emphasizes that, while it is Yahweh who speaks in the prophetic oracle, nonetheless both prophet and people exercise an active influence on Yahweh's mode of speech. The divine word responds to the situation of the prophet and those associated with him, and thus there is genuine interaction and dialogue. N. largely eschews the technical discourse of communication theory and handles matters in a more traditional form-critical and literary-critical manner, with frequent theological insights. There are some affinities with an earlier Rome dissertation, namely A. Graffy's *A Prophet Confronts his People*. But N. certainly makes a distinctive contribution, in his rigorous exploration of issues of method and in his massively detailed textual and exegetical discussion of 14.1-11, including examination of 27 other scholarly treatments of passage, from Origen to Leslie Allen.

P.M. JOYCE

ORTON, DAVID E., *Prophecy in the Hebrew Bible: Selected Studies from* Vetus Testamentum (Brill's Readers in Biblical Studies, 5; Leiden–Boston–Cologne: E.J. Brill, 2000), pp. x + 282. Nlg 59.50/$35.00. ISBN 90-04-1116-0-3; ISSN 1389-1170.

As the title indicates, this is a selection of 19 articles on prophecy from *VT*. This includes a number of oft-cited and classical studies: Micah in dispute with the pseudoprophets (A.S. van der Woule), the Elijah-Elisha sagas (R.P. Carroll), 2 Kings 3 and genres of prophetic literature (B.O. Long), ancient Near Eastern patterns in prophetic literature (M. Weinfeld), the prophecies of Isaiah and the fall of Jerusalem (R.E. Clements), 1 Kings 13 on true and false prophecy (D.W. Van Winkle). S.B. Parker gets in twice: possession trance and prophecy in pre-exilic Israel and official attitudes toward prophecy at Mari and in Israel.

ED.

PFEIFFER, HENRIK, *Das Heiligtum von Bethel im Spiegel des Hoseabuches* (FRLANT, 183; Göttingen: Vandenhoeck & Ruprecht, 1999), pp. 272. DM 128.00. ISBN 3-525-53867-7.

P. opposes the dominant voice of the commentators who continue to portray secondary material in Hosea as marginal, who attribute to the prophet himself the majority of the contents of the book, and who depict Hosea as a precursor of the Deuteronomists. He endorses the move in more recent criticism to see much more of the book as a product of much later periods; and finds particularly helpful the categories of *Fortschreibung* and *Redaktion* as used in M. Nissinen's study of Hosea 4 and 11 (AOAT, 1991; but not noted in the *B.L.*). He restricts his attention to Hos. 8.5-6, 10.5-6 and 13.2. Beth-aven (5.8) is a city rather than a cultic site; and *byt-'l* (10.15) is a corruption of *byt-yśr'l*. In the original form of these three passages, Hosea's critique of Bethel was like Amos's, or like Micah's of Zion. The base texts were modified in turn by pre-exilic tradents, Dtr or post-Dtr criticism of Bethel, exilic Bethel theology, and later post-exilic polemic against images. This very clearly presented and careful study was a Berlin dissertation. The final six pages summarize the argument in some 65 theses.

A.G. AULD

PHAM, XUAN HUONG THI, *Mourning in the Ancient Near East and the Hebrew Bible* (JSOTSup, 302; Sheffield: Sheffield Academic Press, 1999), pp. 221. £35.00/ $57.50. ISBN 1-84127-029-6; ISSN 0309-0787.

Inspired by her early life in Vietnam, P. examines the place of mourning rites through an analysis of Lamentations 1–2 and Isa. 51.9–52.2, comparing them with the mourning rites known from elsewhere in the ancient Near East. She finds the outlines of the mourning ceremony in these texts and is able to explain many of the textual details by means of the rites. She sees her principal contribution in connection with the figure of the 'comforter'.

ED.

PIPPIN, TINA, *Apocalyptic Bodies: The Biblical End of the World in Text and Image* (London: Routledge, 1999), pp. xiv + 160. £45.00/$75.00; paper £14.99/$24.99. ISBN 0-415-18248-4; (paper) 0-415-18249-2.

This study attempts to approach the end of the world from a variety of perspectives: body criticism, ideological criticism, and horror and fantasy theory. P. draws on a variety of ancient and modern texts, and also on art, music and popular culture. Her concluding chapter is entitled 'The Joy of (Apocalyptic) Sex'; however, her concluding sentences are negative: 'What remains is the misogyny and exclusion by a powerful, wrathful deity. In the Apocalypse, the Kingdom of God is the kingdom of perversity.' Many of those who study apocalyptic literature would agree with neither the concluding subject content nor her conclusions, but there is stimulating material here, however you look at it.

ED.

RAMÍREZ KIDD, JOSÉ E., *Alterity and Identity in Israel: The* גר *in the Old Testament* (BZAW, 283; Berlin–New York: de Gruyter, 1999), pp. xi + 187. DM 128.00. ISBN 3-11-016625-9; ISSN 0934-2575.

The author of this Hamburg dissertation pursues his subject in three chapters on philological issues, on the legal status of a *ger* in Deuteronomy (pre-exilic) and the Holiness Code (post-exilic), and on the metaphorical use of the word in Deut. 10.19b and Lev. 25.23. The exegetical observations are summarized in a concluding chapter on the 'peculiar concern for the *ger* in the OT' and the 'progressive theologization of the notion of foreignness' (pp. 109-33). The *ger* in Deuteronomy is described as an 'immigrant' who is neither a 'native member of the Israelite community' nor a 'non-Israelite' (p. 46). According to the author, he may represent a class of refugees from the Northern Kingdom or a class of impoverished people who emerged from an assumed process of urbanization during the eighth to seventh centuries BCE (pp. 43-46). The command to love the *ger* in Deut. 10.19a is seen to be a late addition by 'Diaspora-oriented theologians' and thus understood in close parallel to references in the Holiness Code to 'non-Jews who joined Jewish communities during the Persian period' (p. 68). The book ends with some 50 pages of bibliography and indices.

C. BULTMANN

ROFÉ, ALEXANDER, *Introduction to the Composition of the Pentateuch* (The Biblical Seminar, 58; Sheffield: Sheffield Academic Press, 1999), pp. 152. £12.95/ $19.95. ISBN 1-85075-992-8.

This is a useful introduction of a traditional kind to the composition of the Pentateuch. Its first chapter 'Tradition and Criticism' outlines the reasons why the tradition of Mosaic composition of the Pentateuch was gradually undermined by the rise of criticism. Chapter 2 on the documentary hypothesis identifies and characterizes the well-known documents JEDP. Chapter 3 is concerned with the relative and absolute dating of the documents and contains a special discussion of the work of the distinguished Israeli scholar, Y. Kaufmann, especially concerning the origins and dating of Deuteronomy and of the priestly material of the Pentateuch. The fourth and final chapter 'Challenges to the Documentary Hypothesis' introduces form-criticism and the history of tradition method and illustrates the way in which these methods necessitate going beyond the literary sources to the earlier history of the literature and traditions of the Pentateuch. The book concludes with a summary of the impact of form-criticism, traditio-historical research, and literary analysis upon our understanding of the Pentateuch.

E.W. NICHOLSON

ROGERSON, J.W., *An Introduction to the Bible* (London: Penguin Books, 1999), pp. xi + 232 + 4 maps. £7.99. ISBN 0-14-025261-4.

This work should quickly establish itself as a core text for introducing students to basic questions about the Bible. Knowledge of the biblical material is often sketchy or non-existent today, and the author therefore takes little for granted. He explains carefully why we have so many versions of the Bible at present, and how the Bible came to be written in the first place. He gives summaries of the material in the OT, Apocrypha and NT. There is a chapter on the vexed issue of canon, and concluding chapters on ways of studying and reading the Bible today. The language of this textbook is straightforward and jargon-free. Nevertheless, R. does not dodge serious or difficult questions facing the modern reader. This is an excellent resource for students beginning an exploration of the Scriptures.

M. TUNNICLIFFE

SÄRKIÖ, PEKKA, *Exodus und Salomo: Erwägungen zur verdeckten Salomokritik anhand von Ex 1-2; 5; 14 und 32* (Schriften der Finnischen Exegetischen Gesellschaft, 71; Finnische Exegetische Gesellschaft in Helsinki; Göttingen: Vandenhoeck & Ruprecht, 1998), pp. vi + 185. DM 68.00/AS 496/SwF 63.80. ISBN (Helsinki) 951-9217-26-6; (Göttingen) 3-525-53648-8; ISSN 0356-2786.

S. proposes a complex history of the growth of the text of the chapters in Exodus indicated in the title of his work. A pre-priestly edition (which he terms 'J') is based on pre-Deuteronomistic traditions in 1 Kings 1–12. These offer covert criticism of Solomon in the person of Pharaoh and equally surreptitious glorification of Jeroboam under the guise of Moses, Pharaoh/Solomon's victim and liberator of enslaved Israel. The audience for this presentation was the fugitives of the former northern kingdom of Israel in the seventh century as they tried to come to terms with their new relationship with the House of David, given their former experience of oppression at its hands under Solomon. P knows no such veiled historiography and, influenced by the Chronicler's almost exclusive glorification of Solomon, is concerned simply with the deliverance of Israel from oppression. A final redaction of the P edition (fifth century?) resumes the covert criticism of Solomon in re-touches to Exod. 13.17–14.31. This ingenious discussion raises a host of questions about dating and interrelationship of passages: for instance, not all will share S.'s recognition of parallels between Exodus and 1 Kings beyond Exod. 1.11 and 32.1-6, let alone his proposals for source criticism.

W. JOHNSTONE

SCHEARING, LINDA S. and STEVEN L. MCKENZIE (eds.), *Those Elusive Deuterono-mists: The Phenomenon of Pan-Deuteronomism* (JSOTSup, 268; Sheffield: Sheffield Academic Press, 1999), pp. 288. £50.00/$85.00. ISBN 1-84127-010-5; ISSN 0309-0787.

Nine of the thirteen essays collected here were given as papers in the Deuterono-mistic History section at the 1996 meeting of the SBL; two have previously ap-peared, and two others were specially commissioned for the volume. The two earlier publications are those of R. Coggins and N. Lohfink (the latter translated from the French for this volume), both of which, from different angles, deal with the ques-tion of pan-deuteronomism. Coggins is concerned with the meaning of the term 'deuteronomistic', while Lohfink goes on to consider also the question of a 'deuter-onomistic movement'. A third introductory essay, by Robert Wilson, expands on the ambiguities present in scholarly use of the term 'deuteronomistic'. The next sec-tion of the book, with essays by J. Blenkinsopp, A.G. Auld, R.A. Kugler and J.L. Crenshaw, addresses the issue of deuteronomistic material in the Pentateuch, the former Prophets, the Latter Prophets and the Writings, respectively. The last section consists of particular case studies, covering the possibility of deuteronomistic redac-tion in the Sinai pericope (J. Van Seters), the relationship of Deut. 30.1-10 and Jer. 31 (M.Z. Brettler), deuteronomistic redaction of Jeremiah (T.C. Römer), deuterono-mistic ideas in Ezekiel (C.L. Patten), deuteronomistic redaction of Micah (S.L. Cook), and the question of deuteronomistic redaction in the Twelve, with particular reference to Micah, Zephaniah and Obadiah (E. Ben Zvi).

A.D.H. MAYES

SCHULTZ, RICHARD L., *The Search for Quotation: Verbal Parallels in the Prophets* (JSOTSup, 180; Sheffield: Sheffield Academic Press, 1999), pp. 395. £50.00/$85.00. ISBN 1-85075-496-0; ISSN 0309-0787.

Intertextuality and inner biblical quotation have been major concerns in recent biblical study, so that this Yale dissertation completed under B.S. Childs seems very topical. Its starting-point is the recognition that linkages between different prophetic passages have been widely recognized but rarely subjected to precise analysis. In

Part I of his study S. offers an extremely useful survey of earlier study of the theme, concentrating mainly on Isaiah, and has little difficulty in showing the methodological inadequacy of much of that work. Less satisfactory is Part II, 'Quotation in Non-Prophetic Literature' where in fewer than 100 pages we are rushed through ancient Near Eastern literature (Egypt, Mesopotamia and Ugarit), early Judaism, with reference particularly to Sirach and the *Hodayoth*, proverbial sayings in the OT, and quotation in Western literature. Such a survey is interesting but raises far more questions than it answers. Finally, Part III outlines a new approach, stressing the need for both diachronic and synchronic assessment of the material, and applying the method to a number of passages, with Isaiah again the main concern—either cross-references within Isaiah itself or linkages between Isaiah and other prophetic books. S. shows that no single approach is appropriate for them all. The book ends with a note of 'problems, perspectives and prospects' and a very extensive bibliography. There is much of interest here, but it should be noted that the dissertation was submitted in 1989; more recent studies are referred to but in a somewhat marginal way. The *JSOT* Supplement number also suggests that considerable delays have taken place; the adjacent numbers in the series were published in 1994.

R.J. COGGINS

SCHÜSSLER FIORENZA, ELISABETH, *Rhetoric and Ethic: The Politics of Biblical Studies* (Minneapolis: Fortress Press, 1999), pp. xi + 220. $19.00. ISBN 0-8006-2795-4.

The main purpose of this book is to expound a 'new' method (paradigm) of textual interpretation, the rhetorical-emancipatory, which is to be contrasted with the three other current paradigms: the doctrinal-fundamentalist, the 'scientific positivist', and the postmodernist. It is still being developed, and whether it turns out to be really new remains to be seen (it looks postmodernist to me), but much of the content of this book is distinctly *déjà vu*, with the usual Schüssler Fiorenza hobby-horses (e.g. the obsession with victimhood) and the bizarre neologisms (theologians for centuries have recognized the inadequacy of our language to speak about the divine, without having to invent a strange form like 'G*d'). Her claims to have been marginalized rather jar in someone who holds a Harvard chair and is widely read, listened to, and quoted—or perhaps she has her tongue in her cheek?

ED.

STERNBERG, MEIR, *Hebrews between Cultures: Group Portraits and National Literature* (Indiana Studies in Biblical Literature; Bloomington–Indianapolis: Indiana University Press, 1999), pp. xxiii + 730. $59.95. ISBN 0-253-33459-4.

Another major volume from the magisterial pen (word processor) of Meir Sternberg, author of the formidable *Poetics of Biblical Narrative: Ideological Literature and the Drama of Reading* (*B.L.* 1987, p. 78). This new volume is, in my judgment, just as formidable, but being even longer it is therefore another major challenge to readers' capacity for reading sustained and dense argument. A ludicrously short notice such as this is an insult to S.'s magnificent work, but perhaps it is better than nothing! Using a technique he calls 'intercultural poetics' S. sets out to answer the question 'who were the Hebrews?' by a close scrutiny of all the biblical narratives bearing on such a topic. Starting from the words *yehudi, yisra'el, ibrit* S. gets to work on the Hebrew Bible and ranges far and wide in his brilliantly sustained exegetical arguments, even though concentrating on the book of Genesis. Moving from the Pentateuch codes to a Jeremian coda, S. concludes, among a number of conclusions, that 'If the Pentateuch bondage enactment (like the Moses psychodrama earlier or the Samuel trio after) diagnoses and eventually contains the ethnocultural Hamite Other within the self, then the Jeremiah finale reveals a self that has become this Other: a self translation in excess of the worst Hebrewing tradition. Not even at his lowest, for example, Moses' challenger and the pro-Philistine camp, or at his lowest in the downgrader's eyes, has any Israelite sunk to the nadir of Hamiteness before' (p. 632). In other words, the Israelites have become mere Hebrews. It is a most powerful reading of the biblical narratives and, among so many other insightful analyses, provides a *tour de force* reading of the Pentateuchal material on the law of slaves (in its varying forms). I do not expect to encounter a better or more comprehensive treatment of the vexed laws on slaves (including Jer. 34) nor would I hope to read a more sustained series of exegetically based arguments seeking to make sense of the Hebrew Bible. S. is magnificent, his book stunning and his arguments will be generating discussion and disagreement among biblical scholars for decades to come. Read the book before it comes out in paperback, then buy it and rework you way through a fabulous labyrinth of attentive textual readings and join the debate.

R.P. CARROLL

STEUSSY, MARTI J., *David: Biblical Portraits of Power* (Columbia, SC: University of South Carolina, 1999), pp. xi + 251. $34.95. ISBN 1-57003-250-5.

David is a complex character even when viewed solely from the Deuteronomistic accounts of his career. When the major references to him in the OT are combined a great variety of portraits emerge. S. examines three major sources—the Deuteronomistic history, the books of Chronicles and the book of Psalms, finding in each of these texts a separate model of how the king is perceived. The military leader of Samuel is both hero and villain, whereas the Chronicler focuses on the idealistic leadership of David in a temple-centred society. In Psalms the 'voice' of David is heard in prayer, mirroring sometimes the military commander beset by enemies and, sometimes, the cultic leader. S.'s study is a synchronic reading of these texts, seeking to deepen understanding of the complexity of literary presentation of character on the part of the non-specialist. She shows contact with the current state of scholarship in the field of Davidic studies through end-notes and a full bibliography, allowing the reader to pursue further issues such as the historical significance of the sources concerning David.

M.E. MILLS

SUGIRTHARAJAH, R.S., *Asian Biblical Hermeneutics and Postcolonialism: Contesting the Interpretations* (The Biblical Seminar, 64; Sheffield: Sheffield Academic Press, 1999), pp. 148. £10.95/$13.95. ISBN 1-85075-973-1.

This collection explores the relationship between hermeneutics and postcolonialism from seven complementary angles. 'From Orientalism to Postcolonialism' helpfully separates Asian biblical interpretation in the colonial era into three essential modes—'Orientalist', 'Anglicist' and 'Nativist'—and then sketches the dimensions of a newly nascent 'postcolonial' approach. Chapter 2, 'The Indian Textual Mutiny of 1820', looks at how the Bengali Brahmin Raja Ramohun Roy used the Bible in debates with Baptist missionaries (so demonstrating how colonizers can never predict how their texts are going to be selectively appropriated and transformed in a process of 'transculturation'). Chapters 3 and 4 concentrate on NT commentaries and Bible translations produced in India during the colonial period, exploring how they totalize indigenous cultures, domesticate potentially radical texts, and promote a general attitude of quietism towards imperial authority—then ch. 5, 'Orientalism, Nationalism and Transnationalism', widens the frame, and shows how the experience of imperialism affects translations and commentaries that are not produced within an explicitly colonial context. (Ample quotations show how Joachim Jeremias's *Parables of Jesus* abounds in Orientalist stereotypes of 'the East' and I suspect that it would not be too difficult to find similar examples in OT scholarship). Chapter 6, 'Jesus in Saffron Robes' takes on Western individualist understandings of Jesus and histories of the early church that act 'as if the Mediterranean world were a quarantined zone that had not been infiltrated by Eastern religious thinking'; and ch. 7 returns to the theme of postcolonial biblical hermeutics, and the problems of living between the 'East' and the 'West'. This book raises questions that impact on the whole field of Biblical Studies. The worst thing that could happen would be for it to be confined to a ghetto of 'postcolonial' studies, so reinscribing the marginality that the author so powerfully contests.

Y. SHERWOOD

SUGIRTHARAJAH, R.S. (ed.), *Vernacular Hermeneutices* (The Bible and Postcolonialism, 2: Sheffield: Sheffield Academic Press, 1999), pp. 148. £12.95/$19.95. ISBN 1-85075-943-X.

The contributions are divided into two sections. Part I, Indigenizing the Narratives, includes Laura Donaldson on 'Reading Ruth Through Native Eyes', Gerald West on 'Indigenous Reading Resources from a South African Perspective', Dalia Naya-Pot on 'Naomi, Ruth and the Plight of Indigeneous Women' and David Tuesday Adamo on 'African Cultural Hermeneutics'. Part II, Reinstating the Local, includes Sugirtharajah on 'Thinking about Vernacular Hermeneutics Sitting in a Metropolitan Study', George Mulrain on 'Hermeneutics in a Caribbean Context' and M. Thomas Thanjaraj on 'The Bible as Veda: Biblical Hermeneutics in Tamil Christianity'. Like Segovia and Tolbert's *Reading From This Place*, the collection asks what it would mean to detach oneself from the 'superintending tendencies of the Western intellectual tradition' and to foreground the different vernacular heritages of the authors (as Surgirtharajah asks, quoting Kirin Narayan, 'If you can sprinkle texts with fancy French terms, what's wrong with a little Sanskrit?'). Adamo's essay on the use of the protective and therapeutic Psalms suggests that such interpretation can give us very different understandings of familiar texts. Donaldson and Naya-Pot's divergent readings of Ruth show that 'indigenous' readings of biblical texts can be neither predicted nor homogenized.

Y. SHERWOOD

UFFENHEIMER, BENJAMIN, *Early Prophecy in Israel* (trans. David Louvish; Publications of the Perry Foundation for Biblical Research in the Hebrew University of Jerusalem; Jerusalem: Magnes Press, 1999), pp. 591. $55.00. ISBN 965-223-977-1.

This is in many ways an odd book. It combines a great deal of stimulating and interesting material with some views and interpretations that are strangely out of touch with current scholarship, indeed, sometimes a bit naïve. Part of the late U.'s aims is to challenge the views of Wellhausen which he sees as still unduly influential; on the other hand, he himself is strongly influenced by Kaufmann and Buber, as he plainly tells us, and although he is not uncritical of them, it would help explain a conservative stance toward the tradition that most scholars would now find unacceptable (e.g., the early origin of monotheism). The chapter on Moses often quotes Albright as evidence for ideas that current scholarship would no longer generally accept, and the 'Hittite treaty form' is used as proof for the early character of the Sinai tradition (an argument long rejected by mainstream scholarship). Israel arose from semi-nomads settling down, and the jubilee year was genuinely observed. The early prophets tend to be treated as an undifferentiated mass who prepared 'the way for the emergence of classical prophecy', as if 'classical prophecy' was a different social (as opposed to literary) phenomenon. Yet the first chapter which surveys prophecy in the ancient Near East (even if Neo-Assyrian prophecy is omitted) and the chapter on mantic and magical elements are both interesting and useful, and many observations through the text look at data in a new light. Specialists in prophecy will find much to disagree with here, but they can—and should—still read it with a good deal of profit.

L.L. GRABBE

UTZSCHNEIDER, HELMUT, *Michas Reise in die Zeit: Studien zum Drama als Genre der prophetischen Literatur des Alten Testaments* (Stuttgarter Bibelstudien, 180; Stuttgart: Katholisches Bibelwerk, 1999), pp. 200. EUR 24.44/DM 47.80/AS 349/ SwF 45.50. ISBN 3-460-04801-8.

The unevennesses of the book of Micah have led to many different scholarly proposals; here a new suggestion is made. Micah 1.1–4.7 is seen as a dramatic poem, (not a full-length play; it is too brief for that), with a Prologue (1.2-7) and two Acts (1.8–2.5; 2.6–4.7), set in Jerusalem in the days of the eighth-century kings named in the opening verse, but readable by and applicable to the community from a much later date (the 'Reise in der Zeit' of the title). Before setting out his reading in detail, U. provides a full discussion of other scholars' proposals for a 'dramatic' understanding of prophetic material; Watts and House receive particular attention. By comparison his reading owes much more to the Aristotelian categories of *mythos*, *lexis* and *opsis*. Particular attention is paid to Mic. 4.5, and the inadequacies of a concessive or adversative reading of that verse rejected in favour of a universalist understanding. The view of 4.7 as a conclusion is explained, but obviously problems remain because of the lack of support for a closure at that point. This book will not 'solve' the problems of Micah, but certainly sheds some interesting new light upon them.

R.J. COGGINS

VAUGHN, ANDREW G., *Theology, History, and Archaeology in the Chronicler's Account of Hezekiah* (Archaeology and Biblical Studies, 4; Atlanta: Scholars Press, 1999), pp. xviii + 240. $39.00. ISBN 0-7885-0594-7.

In this excellent monograph the relationship between extra-biblical historical data and the Chronicler's account of Hezekiah's reign is addressed. The reliability of 2 Chron. 29-32 has been questioned, on the one hand because the material is not included in the Deuteronomistic History, and on the other because of the Chronicler's tendency to glorify reputably pious kings. V. has demonstrated that the account of Hezekiah's economic measures resulting in a reign of prosperity is historically reliable. It was due not simply to a siege function but to the general establishment of a strong kingdom. The buildup had happened over a number of years, and may be taken as an indication that Hezekiah may have exceeded the status of Josiah. For this information the Chronicler was dependent on a historical source or a historical memory. Admittedly the Chronicler's ideology is obvious, but he has coupled his theological exposition with historical remembrance. V. thus rejects the view that the Chronicler's work is not to be considered as historiography. A substantial part of the work is devoted to the study of *lmlk* jars which, it is claimed, were limited to this period and testify to Hezekiah's economic buildup. A historical reconstruction of the reign of Hezekiah, and also a better assessment of the historicity of Chronicles, have been made possible through this study.

G.H. JONES

VERMEYLEN, JACQUES, *Ten Keys for Opening the Bible* (London: SCM Press, 1999), pp. x + 182. £8.95. ISBN 0-334-02781-0.

This volume by a well-known Catholic OT scholar has been rapidly translated from the French original (also published in 1999) by the indefatigable John Bowden. The title is somewhat misleading, for the focus is almost entirely on the OT, with occasional mention of the NT. In addition, the ten keys turn out simply to be the ten chapters, which cover various aspects of the OT (approaches to reading, geography, canon, history, literature—including apocryphal books, the relation of Jesus to the Scriptures). The tension between the ostensive setting and a critically reconstructed history is indicated through an intriguing threefold discussion of 'the biblical narrative', 'the [historical] facts' and 'interpretation' (the wider implications of text). Perhaps in the interests of simplification historical judgments are made with great confidence, without reference to other points of view (in fact, no other book on the Bible is mentioned!). Occasional passages are recommended for reading, while at one point a few questions are asked. However, the pedagogic dimension is limited and the book's main achievement is to introduce the OT in the light of historical criticism and within a general positive affirmation of its value for believers.

P. JENSON

WATTS, JAMES W., *Reading Law: The Rhetorical Shaping of the Pentateuch* (The Biblical Seminar, 59; Sheffield: Sheffield Academic Press, 1999), pp. 189. £14.95/ $19.95. ISBN 1-85075-997-9.

This book includes and develops essays previously published in *JSOT*, *VT*, *HUCA*, *JBL* and *BI*. Using insights of rhetorical criticism W. develops the thesis that the Pentateuch is a deliberative discourse designed to motivate future behaviour. He examines the close interplay between laws and the narratives to determine how the Pentateuch attempts to persuade its readers to obey its injunctions. The stories of Israel's behaviour in the wilderness serve to show the importance of obeying the laws. This appeal for obedience is reinforced by motive clauses with the laws, repetition of laws on important subjects (e.g. the sabbath), and by the blessings and curses that conclude different biblical collections. The attribution of many laws to God underlines that they deserve serious attention. W. argues that the Pentateuch's rhetorical structure derives from a tradition of public reading of the law which reaches back at least into monarchy times, but it received its definitive form when the Persians encouraged their subjects to promulgate laws on religious matters. This explains its concentration on worship rather than secular issues. W.'s work is valuable in drawing attention to aspects of OT law that tend to be overlooked, but he shows the coherence of law and narrative only to a limited extent, and he says little about how the long narratives in Genesis and Exodus that preface the laws contribute to the overall rhetoric of the Pentateuch.

G.J. WENHAM

WEEKS, STUART, *Early Israelite Wisdom* (Oxford Theological Monographs; Oxford: Oxford University Press, 1999), pp. xii + 212. £14.99. ISBN 0-19-827007-0.

The book reviewed in *B.L.* 1994 (p. 102) has now been issued in paperback.

ED.

WEST, GERALD O., *The Academy of the Poor: Towards a Dialogical Reading of the Bible* (Interventions, 2; Sheffield: Sheffield Academic Press, 1999), pp. 182. £10.95/$14.95. ISBN 1-85075-758-5.

W.'s approach to a 'dialogical reading' of the Bible arises from his work as Director of the Institute for the Study of the Bible in Natal, a joint project connecting biblical scholars at the School of Theology in Pietermaritzberg with communities of the poor and marginalized. Several chapters offer a theoretical account of how such collaborative work is done. The essence of it is 'reading with' the 'ordinary readers' in poor communities, which avoids both merely 'listening to' them (and thus tending to romanticize their 'pre-critical' approaches) and also 'speaking for' them (which is patronizing). In the closing chapters W. reports on the practicalities of this kind of liberationist Bible study, and includes one particularly fascinating transcript of a study based on Lk. 4.16-22. The book should be of interest to all who engage in biblical study beyond the bounds of the academic community.

J. BARTON

WILK, FLORIAN, *Die Bedeutung des Jesajabuches für Paulus* (FRLANT, 179; Göttingen: Vandenhoeck & Ruprecht, 1998), pp. xii + 461. DM 128.00. ISBN 3-525-53863-4.

If one of the criteria for assessing the importance of Isaiah for Paul is the sheer size of a monograph on the subject, then Isaiah's role in the Pauline corpus, and indeed in Christian origins in general, cannot be over-emphasized, a view heartily endorsed by the present reviewer. After a brief general introduction on aim, method and previous research, the material is divided into four parts. Part II, the longest part, discusses what text of Isaiah Paul uses (Greek), for what purpose he uses him (to provide authority and proof), and in what connection (the Gospel of Christ, his own self-understanding as Apostle, the role of Israel and the Jews, the Parousia). Part III on *Kontextrezeption* discusses Paul's awareness of the context in which each quotation or allusion is located in Isaiah, and argues that consequently he cannot have been using any kind of florilegium. Parts IV and V, the shortest but most interesting and readable sections, then attempt to deduce Paul's special christological understanding of the book of Isaiah as a whole, and its role in the evolution of Paul's theology. There are copious footnotes on almost every page, a 33-page bibliography, and indexes of biblical, Jewish and Christian texts.

J.F.A. SAWYER

Zimmer, Frank, *Der Elohist als weisheitlich-prophetische Redaktionsschicht: Eine literarische und theologiegeschichtliche Untersuchung der sogenannten elohistischen Texte im Pentateuch* (Europäische Hochschulschriften, Reihe 23; Theologie, 656; Frankfurt–Bern–New York: Lang, 1999), pp. 343. SwF 33.00. ISBN 3-631-34200-4; ISSN 0721-3409.

In the first chapter of this doctoral dissertation, Z. surveys the long standing debate over the existence and character of E. He concludes that, while the postulate of an independent elohistic historical work should be rejected, the passages that can be described as E texts, which revise and re-order older materials, display common literary characteristics. He then proceeds to a detailed literary analysis of Genesis 20–22 which has always been viewed as central for the theory of an elohistic source. This leads on to perhaps the most original part of Z.'s work where he describes what he considers the distinctive theological concepts of the E texts, particular understandings of the 'fear of God', of Israel, the heathen and the deity, as well as a characteristic elohistic ethic. Next Z. turns to consider the concerns of the circle or circles in which the elohistic material was produced. These he sees as basically representatives of older Wisdom thought but also profoundly influenced by the message of early classical prophets, such as Amos and Hosea: the Elohist is thus 'between Wisdom and Prophecy'. However, he rejects the widely held view of close links between the elohistic source and eighth-century northern prophecy. Rather, the origin of the material was in seventh-century Judah and its reinterpretation of traditional themes reflects the religious and social tensions of that epoch. Granted that Z.'s methodological presuppositions will not find favour with everyone, nevertheless his wide-ranging discussion presents a number of interesting suggestions and insights which deserve serious consideration.

J.R. PORTER

7. LAW, RELIGION AND THEOLOGY

ANTHANASSIADI, POLYMNIA and MICHAEL FREDE (eds.), *Pagan Monotheism in Late Antiquity* (Oxford: Clarendon Press, 1999), pp. vii + 211. £40.00. ISBN 0-19-815252-3.

This fine volume assesses the evidence that some pagans in the later Roman empire espoused notions close to monotheism. The editors are both experts in late Roman thought and philosophy, and most of the contributions deal with the more theological strands within late antique paganism. An introductory chapter by Martin West points out the polytheism to be found in the Hebrew Bible and the contradictory gropings towards monotheism in the early Greek philosophical tradition, but most of the other contributions deal with pagan thought in the later Roman empire, much of it systematized in reaction to the theories of Christianity with which the editors seek to compare the pagan texts they study. The exception is a brilliant chapter by Stephen Mitchell which provides a remarkably fresh insight into the cult of Theos Hypsistos. Mitchell provides a full appendix of the documentary evidence for the cult (most of it epigraphic) and observes that the problems faced by scholars over more than a century in identifying which of these dedications to the highest god are Jewish or Christian and which are pagan must indicate the simple truth that these pagans believed that they worshipped the same God as did the Jews and Christians, and that this belief was shared by the Jews and Christians themselves. The corollary, that the spread of monotheism through Christianity and Islam was based on a prior widespread acceptance of the notion throughout the Roman empire, is attractive, although it remains striking that these pagan monotheists continued to worship other gods (albeit sometimes under the guise of angels) in a way that Jews and Christians ostentatiously declined to do: in the eyes of pagans, the oddness of Jews and Christians lay almost always not in what they believed but in what they refused to do. Thus, although Mitchell is right to say that 'angel worship was an important symptom of monotheistic belief' (p. 103), it is striking that in Judaism and Christianity this symptom usually failed to manifest itself.

M. GOODMAN

ASSMANN, JAN and GUY G. STROUMSA (eds.), *Transformations of the Inner Self in Ancient Religions* (Studies in the History of Religions [*Numen* Book Series], 83; Leiden–Boston–Cologne: E.J. Brill, 1999), pp. 437. Nlg 205.00/$114.00. ISBN 90-04-11356-8; ISSN 0169-8834.

This collection of 24 essays is divided into two parts. Part I is on Confession and

Conversion and has essays on the conversion paradigm (F. Stolz), repentence in Jewish texts, and on conversion, penance, etc., in ancient Egypt, Sassanian Iran, and Gnostic, Hermetic and Christian texts. Part II is on Guilt, Sin and Purification and covers ancient and late antique Egypt, archaic Greece, and Roman, Zoroastrian, Christian and Manichean topics. Articles of particular interest include dimensions and transformations of purification ideas (F. Stolz), salvation in Ezek. 36.16-32 (M. Greenberg), Yom Kippur in apocalyptic and the roots of Jesus' high priesthood, and the seat of sin in early Jewish and Christian sources.

ED.

AVERY-PECK, ALAN J. and JACOB NEUSNER (eds.), *Judaism in Late Antiquity: Volume 4. Special Topics: (1) Death, Life-After-Death, Resurrection and the World-to-Come in the Judaisms of Antiquity* (Handbuch der Orientalistik: Erste Abteilung, Der Nahe und Mittlere Osten, 49. Band; Leiden–Boston–Cologne: E.J. Brill, 2000), pp. xi + 342. Nlg 190.00/$112.00. ISBN 90-04-11262-6; ISSN 0169-9423.

Fourteen essays by distinguished scholars lay out a very large sample of ancient Israelite thought that intersected on a single subject, to answer the question 'one Judaism or many?' The intention is also 'to open questions of method through the study of evidence and cases'. Neusner's impassioned introduction promotes a historical critical (specifically 'documentary') method of textual analysis, and attacks previous approaches to the description of Judaism as fatally flawed: these are characterized as the nominalists (S.J.D. Cohen); the harmonistic (E.P. Sanders, 1992); and the theological (G.F. Moore, J. Bonsirven, E.E. Urbach and E.P. Sanders, 1997). This debate overlaps with the familiar controversy about the merits of historical criticism of biblical texts. The editors clearly believe there are many Judaisms, but readers are left to evaluate this collection for themselves. It comprises essays on (1) the legacy of Scripture (the biblical silence about the afterlife, the Psalms, the 'death after death', the Wisdom literature); (2) Judaic writings in Greek (apocalyptic, Apocrypha/Pseudepigrapha, Philo and Josephus); (3) the Dead Sea Scrolls; (4) earliest Christianity; and (5) rabbinic Judaism (including inscriptional evidence). An intriguing presentation of beliefs often 'held with some reticence and expressed with vagueness'.

K.J.A. LARKIN

BALENTINE, SAMUEL, E., *The Torah's Vision of Worship* (Minneapolis; Fortress Press, 1999; distributed in the UK by Alban Books, Bristol), pp. xiv + 266. $26.00/£15.99. ISBN 0-8006-3155-2.

Biblical scholars, especially Protestant ones, have tended to neglect the insights of the Pentateuchal legislation about religious ritual or to regard it as a decline from the teaching of the prophets. B. wishes to reverse this trend. He attempts a holistic (or canonical) reading of the Pentateuch in its final form, and tries to show that it reflects ideas of the service of God as a cosmic liturgy, centred on the sabbath and expressed especially through the ministry of the priesthood. He claims further that this vision of the meaning of worship has deep resonances for our own age, and needs to be grasped as thoroughly by Christian thinkers as it already is by many Jews. There is a useful survey of the modern study of Israel's worship, and also a detailed study of the political background to the final redaction of the Pentateuch in the Persian period. B. characteristically mentions possible source-divisions within the material studies, but argues that the final redactors have sought to express a coherent 'vision' in the way they have arranged and deployed the materials at their disposal. He rejects the idea that the Pentateuch contains anything unplanned or accidental. As well as being a thoughtful guide to Old Testament ideas of worship the book is thus also a good illustration of what can be achieved by redaction or rhetorical criticism, and of what we may expect to find in works committed to a 'canonical' perspective. Unfortunately there is no bibliography, though the footnotes show mastery of a mass of secondary literature. This is an important contribution both to the study of worship in ancient Israel and to the current debate about hermeneutical approaches to the text.

J. BARTON

BARR, JAMES, *The Concept of Biblical Theology: An Old Testament Perspective* (London: SCM Press, 1999), pp. xvii + 715. £25.00. ISBN 0-334-02752-7.

Professor Barr's major statement on biblical theology has been eagerly awaited. Here B. draws on a lifetime of scholarship to describe, analyse and assess many significant issues concerning the Christian theological use of its Bible, especially the OT. The volume is comprised of 34 substantive chapters (and a brief conclusion) which fall roughly into two parts with a transition around chs. 18–19. The first 250 or so pages are the most systematic and programmatic: here B. spells out an approach to biblical theology using many conversation partners as a foil to sharpen his own proposals. The second part reverses this arrangement so that critical discussions of the work of various scholars take centre stage, informed always by B.'s own ideas. He warns the reader against looking for 'his' biblical theology in these pages: *caveat lector*! What B. sketches, models, encourages is the relating of the OT within Christianity 'to the total work of salvation...not only through what it is in itself but also indirectly through the tradition of interpretation which grew up from it' (p. 279). This necessarily involves at a minimum the judicious handling of historical, exegetical, and doctrinal considerations (cf. p. 492) in the pursuit of 'biblical theology'. This is also a book about good guys and bad guys: B. is generous with praise, scathing in critique. While sometimes this is expected (the latter for Childs), sometimes it is not (the former for Eichrodt). It would take much more than a note to engage adequately with this sprawling yet probing collection: Professor Barr can be assured that anyone interested in 'biblical theology' will find much here that is helpful (p. 607), and much for which to be grateful.

D.J. REIMER

BATSCH, CHRISTOPHE, ULRIKE EGELHAAF-GAISER and RUTH STEPPER (eds.), *Zwischen Krise und Alltag: Antike Religionen im Mittelmeerraum/Conflit et Normalité: Religions anciennes dans l'espace méditerranéen* (Potsdamer Altertumswissenschaftliche Beiträge; Stuttgart: Franz Steiner, 1999), pp. 287. DM 96.00/SwF 96.00/AS 701. ISBN 3-515-07513-5.

This volume contains papers in French and German delivered to a conference held in Potsdam in June 1997. Contributions fall into four sections. In the first (Religion and cults in the Mediterranean region), J. Rüpke writes on religion in the larger states; C. Auffarth on festivals; C. Batch on the *Urim* and *Tummim* in second temple Judaism; A. Zografou on the triple Hecate; and M. Sebaï on religion in Thugga (North Africa). In the second (Religious language and terminology) S. Crippa discusses sybillic and magicians' ritual terminology; C. Nasse writes on the meaning of *hostia consultatoria*; and A.V. Siebert on Roman cultic instruments. In the third (Priests and cultic personnel) U. Egelhaaf-Gaiser examines the personal religious life of lower orders of temple priests; J. Schneid, priestly 'books' and learning; and R. Stepper, the role of *Pontifex Maximus* from Caesar to Nerva. The final section (Religion and politics) is devoted to studies by V. Sauer on religion as a category in late Republican political life; A. Glock on Propertius 4.2; C. Kunst on religious elements in the imperial domestic environment; U. Reimer on Flavius Clemens and his move from Roman consul to Christian martyr, and P. Barceló on the implications of Constantine's edict.

N. WYATT

BAUCKHAM, RICHARD, *God Crucified: Monotheism and Christology in the New Testament* (Didsbury Lectures 1996; Carlisle: Paternoster, 1998), pp. x + 79. £9.99. ISBN 0-85364-944-8.

The thesis of this monograph is set out in three short chapters. The first explores the character of Jewish monotheism in the first century CE. The author emphasizes the unbridgeable divide between God as creator and ruler, and all other powers. He considers the role of so-called 'intermediary figures' to be no help whatsoever in charting the development of early Christology. Such figures as angels or exalted patriarchs are never seen to share the attributes of God—monolatry is the standard of Second Temple Judaism. In contrast to these non-divine figures, the hypostatic Word or Wisdom are intrinsic to the identity of God. B. argues further that it was the intention of the NT authors to include Jesus in the unique divine identity, as Jewish monotheism understood it. Thus there is a 'high' Christology from the very beginning, rather than a series of incremental steps. Christian faith did not move from an early purely functional to a later ontological understanding of the person of Christ. He explores the use of Ps. 110.1 as the most frequently cited verse in the NT. In the final chapter he seeks to show how an integrated early Christian reading of the material in Isaiah 40–55 developed. He uses texts such as the hymn in Philippians 2 and texts from Revelation and John. This work is a bold attempt to show that 'orthodox' Christology existed from the earliest days of Christianity, and that it was compatible with Jewish monotheism. These Didsbury lectures are the author's first thoughts on the matter, and a more detailed study is promised.

M. TUNNICLIFFE

BAVINCK, HERMAN, *In the Beginning: Foundations of Creation Theology* (ed. John Bolt; trans. John Vriend; Grand Rapids, MI: Baker Book House, 1999), pp. 293. $15.99. ISBN 0-8010-2190-1.

This work is the second instalment in the Dutch Reformed Translation Society's translation of B.'s classic *Gereformeerde dogmatik*, which was originally published in 1928. This volume is the second section of his magisterial work to be produced by the Society, the first being a translation of the eschatology section (*The Last Things: Hope for this World and the Next*, ed. John Bolt [1996]). The present volume is a translation of vol. 2, ch. 5, 'Over de wereld in haar oorspronkelijke staat' (Concerning the World and its Original State), and is a restatement of the Reformed doctrine of creation. As such it contains treatments of topics such as evolution, Darwinism and the age of humanity, but it also seeks to explore other elements of the doctrine of creation such as angels and the spiritual world, the image of God in humans, the destiny of creation and humanity, and God's providential care of creation. For this edition every chapter is provided with a summary at its beginning and additional editorial notes have been provided by the editor. Additionally, the bibliography has been brought up to date. Since B. died as long ago as 1921 his work may not be known to readers of the *B.L.*; however, this volume is worthy of further study, at least because of the exhaustive treatment of the doctrine in question.

F. GOSLING

BECKING, BOB and MARJO C.A. KORPEL (eds.), *The Crisis of Israelite Religion: Transformation of Religious Tradition in Exilic and Post-Exilic Times* (OTS, 42; Leiden: E.J. Brill, 1999), pp. vi + 311. Nlg 198.33/$111.00. ISBN 90-04-11496-3.

The volume broadly deals with the question of religious continuity or discontinuity between the monarchic and post-monarchic periods of Judaean history, and originated in a conference held in Utrecht in 1998. The virtual reversal of the biblical portrait, and those scholarly writings that follow it goes back to De Wette and later to Wellhausen, but has only in recent years re-emerged as a central issue and in a radical new guise, in which the connection between Iron Age Israelite and Judaean religions and the religion of Persian and Hellenistic Yehud is minimized. Significantly, there are two kinds of papers in this volume: those which address what is seen as a problem necessitating the deconstruction of the tradition of the corpus of biblical texts, and those which offer a theology of the texts. There is a violent, yet unacknowledged tension between the approaches. Here, Becking, Grabbe, Uehlinger, Niehr and Stern offer papers of the first kind, and Japhet, Dietrich, Van Seters, Korpel, M. Dijkstra, Schüngel-Straumann, Tollington, van Grol and Williamson the latter, which therefore dominate. Becking introduces the issues very well, and many of the papers take up the challenge in a lively and informative way. But the volume still groans under the weight of traditional biblical exegesis, as if that could illuminate questions that for so long it has largely obscured. In this sort of agenda, one can no longer work purely deductively from unreliable texts.

P.R. DAVIES

BERGANT, DIANNE, *The Earth is the Lord's: The Bible, Ecology, and Worship* (American Essays in Liturgy; Collegeville, MN: Liturgical Press, 1998), pp. 71. $6.95. ISBN 0-8146-2528-2.

There has been great interest in recent years in things ecological and this book adds yet another facet to the debate. This slim volume presents itself as part of a series of essays 'on current research in liturgy'. But rather than a straight essay in liturgy this book is of interest to OT scholars as it focuses on OT texts dealings with creational issues. There are five chapters; each one presents a group of passages, linked by a common theme, and followed by a short reflection on how it might be integrated within liturgy and the reality of our lives. (1) 'A New World View' looks at environmental concerns and at the impact of science and technology in our world while (2) 'Creation and Re-creation' calls for the celebration of sacred time and space. (3) 'Nature: Friend or Foe?' looks at some of the OT's view of nature (Ps. 104; 148; Hosea). (4) 'Creation and Morality' emphasizes Deuteronomic covenant and Wisdom of Solomon. Finally, (5) 'On that Day' examines some trends in the eschatological tradition (Zephaniah, Jeremiah and Joel). Given the relatively short space it is impossible to explore all aspects of creation. And although the subject matter is broached with enthusiasm, it is sometimes a little disappointing (see its uncritical acceptance of the fertility cults, for instance). When feminist insights might be used to strengthen and deepen her point, the author does not take them up (e.g. the section on Hosea in ch. 3). But despite this it is a useful resource to add to the increasing material on creation and ecological concerns in the OT.

A. JEFFERS

BERLEJUNG, ANGELIKA, *Die Theologie der Bilder: Herstellung und Einweihung von Kultbildern in Mesopotamien und die alttestamentliche Bilderpolemik* (OBO, 162; Freiburg: Universitätsverlag; Göttingen: Vandenhoeck & Ruprecht, 1999), pp. xii + 547 + plates. SwF 155.00. ISBN (Universitätsverlag) 3-7278-1195-1; (Vandenhoeck & Ruprecht) 3-525-53308-X.

The author's expressed aim is to show how the biblical passages referring to the 'idols of the nations' are illuminated by the theory and practice of the Mesopotamian rituals for the production of cult-images. The limitations adopted for the work are clearly defined, excluding comparable Egyptian material. The whole complex survey is presented with admirable clarity, both in its overall layout and in detail, helped by excellent summaries at the end of main sections. The word-studies are valuable in themselves: the initial treatment of *Bild* and its semantic field, the very illuminating account of the archetypal *me* and their ontological status, and the studies of the Sumero-Akkadian and Hebrew terminology.

The main sections present, first, general information about Mesopotamian cult images, how they were described in contemporary texts and the terms used. Next

comes the longest section, on the dedication of the images by the rituals of washing
and opening the mouth. These are described in detail, with explanation of their intended effects, the priestly agents, the prayers and incantations, the ritual actions
and the application of the rituals also to non-anthropomorphic sacred symbols.
Finally the work focuses on the cult-images in Palestine and the OT, first on the
general situation, the evidence of archaeological finds and of descriptions or references in the Bible, then the biblical polemic against cult-images, its terminology,
the roles of the king (with an excursus on the question of Assyrian policy in con-
quered territories), of the people and priests and of the craftsmen. The passages
deriding their labours in the prophetic books and Psalms are discussed in detail.
Only at the end, in less than two pages, is there any reference to the biblical passages (especially prophetic call narratives) in which purification and opening of the
mouth feature, in ways which suggest that Yahwists were not ignorant of their neighbours' sophisticated theology, and could transpose elements of it to human medi-
ators. The final summary is followed by texts of the dedication ritual, first in transliteration, then in translation, of the Nineveh and Babylonian versions; then nine
pages of photographs and drawings and an exhaustive bibliography.

R.P.R. MURRAY

BINDER, DONALD D., *Into the Temple Courts: The Place of the Synagogues in the
Second Temple Period* (SBLDS, 169; Atlanta: Scholars Press, 1999), pp. xix + 566.
$60.00. ISBN 0-88414-008-3.

B.'s book aims to 'pull together all of the pre-70 evidence in order to present it
comprehensively and systematically' and to provide 'the existing data along with a
critical analysis and interpretation of that data so that the reader can make...judg-
ments...' about his thesis that synagogues functioned as widely prevalent exten-
sions of the Temple, and not in any way as rivals to it. B.'s powerful introduction
deals with methodological problems and recent trends (pp. 1-22). Thereafter, B.
surveys and discusses the evidence from literary sources, papyri, inscriptions, archi-
tectural remains, and thoroughly explores terminology, synagogue functions and
functionaries, as well as giving detailed, illustrated accounts of Palestinian and Diaspora synagogues. Frequently, he deals with evidence at first hand but often relies on
secondary sources, and in the building of his case these sources are, on occasion,
misread or misrepresented. B. argues his case well and presents a balanced, though
traditional, account of the Second Temple synagogue while also introducing the relevant sources and the scholars involved in the debate over synagogue origins. As a
reviewer, I read the book from beginning to end, but believe that the lack of indexes
renders other types of use of the book much more difficult.

H.A. MCKAY

BLOMBERG, CRAIG L., *Neither Poverty nor Riches: A Biblical Theology of Material Possessions* (New Studies in Biblical Theology, 7; Leicester: Apollos [Inter-
Varsity Press], 1999), pp. 300. £12.99. ISBN 0-85111-516-0.

I was put off by B.'s introductory remarks. In stating that 25 per cent of global population will quickly fall below any reasonable poverty line, he adds: 'While indigence, false religion and corruption certainly account for some of this plight, many of the poor are the victims of natural disasters, famine or drought'. *False* religion today! No surprise that this book comes clearly within the (conservative) evangelical mode. Following Don Carson's (the series editor) assumptions about biblical theology, B. quite admirably surveys the OT (first two chapters), inter-testamental literature and the NT on material possessions, wealth and poverty and their interrelatedness to well-rehearsed notions of covenant, reconciliation and stewardship. There is nothing radical by way of conclusions, not even in its challenge to the current affluence among American Christians. However, credit must be given to B.'s personal testimony in attempting to live out a simple and almost debt-free lifestyle with his practice of the graduated tithe. Serious questions remain. There is hardly any discussion of international debt relief or the Jubilee 2000 campaign. Do Western Christians really want to change their lifestyle? Wherein lies salvation/liberation for those very destitute poor who have nothing to begin with?

A.S.J. LIE

BROWN, WILLIAM P., *The Ethos of the Cosmos: The Genesis of Moral Imagination in the Bible* (Grand Rapids, MI: Eerdmans, 1999; distributed in the UK by Alban Books, Bristol), pp. xviii + 458. $35.00/£21.99. ISBN 0-8028-4539-8.

This extensive and ambitious work investigates how the various pictures of creation helped shape the moral character of the ancient Israelite faith community, and what this might have to say to modern Christian believers. The particular textual focuses are Genesis 1–3, Isaiah 40–55, Proverbs and Job. B. argues that any given account of creation reflects something of the moral perceptions of the community that produced it. Conversely a model of creation imparts those ethical values to future generations in the ongoing tradition. In short, creation and community interact. Bridging the fields of ethics and biblical studies (predominantly OT but also—rather superficially—NT), this is ultimately a work of constructive Christian theology, with an eye to modern ecological challenges. By an OT specialist, who has previously written on the wisdom literature, it stands in the mainstream of biblical scholarship, in a moderately conservative critical manner. On the ethical side, there is an acknowledged debt to Stanley Hauerwas, especially in the themes of moral community, character and narrative ethics. It is well documented and elegantly written, if at times a little wordy. B perhaps overstates the originality of his project, but the sustained detail with which he carries most of it through is generally impressive.

P.J. JOYCE

BRUEGGEMANN, WALTER, *The Covenanted Self: Explorations in Law and Covenant* (Minneapolis: Fortress Press, 1999), pp. xi + 148. $18.00. ISBN 0-8006-3176-5

These nine exegetical studies are devoted to themes relating to tensions between law and grace. Obeying the law in the modern world is the pathway to a new freedom through the covenanted personality which discovers itself in relating to other persons and to the larger realm of society. They display the author's skill in relating biblical themes—largely drawn from the decalogue and Psalms—to contemporary issues and provide a useful basis for discussion groups.

R.E. CLEMENTS

CAZELLES, HENRI, *La Bible et son Dieu* (new edn, revised and enlarged; Collection 'Jésus et Jésus-Christ', 40; Paris: Desclée, 1999), pp. 252. FF 150. ISBN 2-7189-0949-9.

This is new and revised edition of a work of 1989, which does not appear to have been reviewed in the *B.L.* The basic text seems substantially the same but, in the footnotes, C. frequently takes account of studies which have appeared since the first edition. In an interesting new preface, he lists what he considers as seven assured results of biblical scholarship which govern his own approach. There is a distinctive Israelite religion but this can only be understood against the ancient Near Eastern background, particularly the institution of sacral monarchy which Israel adopted from its neighbours; the traditional documentary theory should not be abandoned, especially the recognition of the deuteronomic and priestly historical syntheses as independent works, both of which desacralize political authority and reflect the shock of the events of 722 and 587 BC; equally significant is the destruction of the Temple in AD 70, which caused the study of the Torah to become central for both the Jewish and Christian communities. These themes are developed in some fourteen chapters, beginning with the pre-biblical world and moving on to discussions of the personal deity of Abraham, the God of the covenant, God as Israel's national deity and the God of the king. There follow chapters dealing with the prophetical concept of a God of justice and the messianic ideas in the psalms, with God and the Temple and God as creator, as holy and as the source of wisdom. Finally, there is a comparatively brief chapter on the period of the NT and the early church, considering Jesus as the fulfilment of messianic expectations and the witness to him of both the Bible and the Koran. Hence this is a wide-ranging work, but one marked by admirable clarity and the mastery of exposition characteristic of the author.

J.R. PORTER

CLARKE, ERSKINE (ed.), *Exilic Preaching: Testimony for Christian Exiles in an Increasingly Hostile Culture* (Harrisburg, PA: Trinity Press International, 1998), pp. vi + 137. $13.00. ISBN 1-56338-246-6.

This collection of 12 essays/sermons is primarily addressed to the American context where the churches are constantly struggling with their existence and meaning in the face of the relentless onslaught of (post-?) modernity and rapid technological change. Can the churches continue to exercise a hitherto vibrant social and moral role when their own position has been so domesticated and thus relegated to the realm of private religion? In a sense, this is a question applicable to the worldwide church. In selectively employing the biblical metaphor of the 'exile' with different shades of meaning, three essays each (all previously published in the *Journal for Preachers*) by Walter Brueggemann, Stanley Hauerwas, Barbara Brown Taylor and

William Willimon attempt to help readers (re)discover their 'soul' in a context where faith has been marginalized. Although the essays and especially the fast-paced sermons are soundly 'biblical' and sufficiently 'earthed', I fail to see how they might help us even to begin engaging with the realities of our multi-faith world. We do well to remember that Christians do not have a monopoly of familiar religious metaphors.

A.S.J. LIE

DAVIES, JON, *Death, Burial and Rebirth in the Religions of Antiquity* (Religion in the First Christian Centuries; London and New York: Routledge, 1999), pp. xiii + 246. £16.99/$24.99. ISBN 0-415-12990-7; (paper) 0-415-12991-5.

The declared aim of this book is to show that Christianity successfully defined an identity for itself on matters to do with death (p. 1). It begins with the important observation that one must understand the creation stories of any culture if one is to understand its attitudes to death. There follows a (necessarily) brief survey of Egyptian, Zoroastrian, Mesopotamian and Canaanite beliefs about death, followed by sections on Jewish and Roman burial customs and epitaphs and finally Christian martyrdom and burial. This is a fascinating but untidy collection of material, which does not achieve its declared aim. There is only the briefest of references to the Hebrew creation stories (half of p. 68) and no discussion at all of the NT texts dealing with rebirth, nor with the important mystical texts from Qumran. 'First look for the basic values of a society, then for its material reality' (p. xi) is a fine ideal, but the basic values of Christianity are conspicuously missing from this book. Rebirth for Christians is not a post-mortem experience.

M. BARKER

DICK, MICHAEL D. (ed.), *Born in Heaven, Made on Earth: The Making of the Cult Image in the Ancient Near East* (Winona Lake, IN: Eisenbrauns, 1999), pp. xii + 243. $35.00. ISBN 1-57506-024-8.

'Idolatry' is a dirty word. All too often the use of cult images is dismissed by many biblical scholars as just another perversion in popular religion. Increasingly it is becoming recognized that it was probably normative in pre-exilic religion in Israel and Judah, though not without vigorous aniconic opposition in some quarters (traceable in the rise and final triumph of the so-called 'Yahweh-alone' movement). Anyone familiar with religious practice in many parts of the ancient and modern worlds will know that images were or are the ultimate symbol of the divine presence. Puzzled by various features of the prophetic parodies of the making of divine images, D. has undertaken a thorough study of such passages, which is elegantly counterpointed by essays on the making of the cult image in Mesopotamia (D. with C. Walker), and on the theology of the cult statue in Egypt (D. Lorton). These in turn are nicely set in context by a provocative study of images in present-day South India (J.P. Waghorne).

N. WYATT

DOYLE, ROBERT C., *Eschatology and the Shape of Christian Belief* (Carlisle: Pater-noster, 1999), pp. x + 342. £19.99. ISBN 0-85364-818-2.

This book sets out to show how eschatology has been and still is fundamental to Christian theology. Written for students new to the subject, it sets out with admirable clarity the basic issues: personal resurrection, the role of the church, the hope for universal renewal. Beginning with the Bible, but mainly the NT, he offers a brief survey of the development of Christian thought in this area: before Chalcedon, Augustine, the Middle Ages including Aquinas and Joachim of Fiore, the Refor-mation, discussing Luther and Calvin, and then millennial beliefs since the sixteenth century. The last two sections deal with Barth, Liberation Theology and Moltmann, and then the doctrine of hope. There is a good bibliography.

M. BARKER

FITZPATRICK-MCKINLEY, ANNE, *The Transformation of Torah from Scribal Advice to Law* (JSOTSup, 287; Sheffield: Sheffield Academic Press, 1999), pp. 200. £35.00/ $57.50. ISBN 1-85075-953-7; ISSN 0309-0787.

Originating in a doctoral thesis at Trinity College, Dublin, this book usefully reviews the debate regarding the nature of the biblical legal collections. Scepticism regarding the positivist model (which takes the laws to have been actually applied in courts in ancient Israel) has been widespread since a similar issue came to promi-nence with the work of Kraus and Finkelstein on the ancient Near Eastern texts. The author takes the view that the biblical collections, similarly, represent the lit-erary products of a scribal elite. Her version of this theory, however, is extreme, making little allowance for any antecedent oral tradition. She relies heavily upon two highly controversial theories: that of the legal historian Alan Watson, that legal change is primarily the product of foreign influence rather than internal social devel-opment, and that of Calum Carmichael, on the genesis (or at least formulation and arrangement) of the biblical laws in reaction to the narrative tradition. Her work may serve as a useful stimulus to those wedded to neither extreme.

B.S. JACKSON

FRETHEIM, TERENCE E. and KARLFRIED FROEHLICH, *The Bible as Word of God: In a Postmodern Age* (Minneapolis: Fortress Press, 1998), pp. vii + 135. $15.00. ISBN 0-8006-3094-7.

This book records the dialogue between the two authors which formed the 1995 Hein/Fry lectures, part of an annual series given in the seminaries of the Evan-gelical Lutheran Church in America. The question both were asked to address was what meaning could be given to the concept of biblical authority in an age of crit-ical pluralism. Each contributes a lecture and offers a brief response to the other. Froelich, a church historian, looks to Lindbeck and Ebeling to support his con-tention that the Bible offers 'a Christian mother tongue' (p. 39), a language which deserves trust because it is authored by God. Fretheim takes issue as an OT scholar with Froelich's suspension of suspicion, arguing the experience, confirmed by inner-biblical example, demands that the reader says 'No' to aspects of the OT's portrayal of God, leaving himself open to Froelich's counter that the postmodern reader becomes the source of authority. The difference is unresolved but the authors provide well-grounded and very readable arguments within their theological parameters which students might use to re-enact, but also to broaden, the debate.

H. PYPER

GREIDANUS, SIDNEY, *Preaching Christ from the Old Testament: A Contemporary Hermeneutical Method* (Grand Rapids, MI: Eerdmans, 1999; distributed in the UK by Alban Books , Bristol), pp. xvii + 373. $22.00/£12.99. ISBN 0-8028-4449-9.

If Christ is at the heart of Christian preaching, how can preachers address the OT, which was written before the coming of Jesus Christ? G. discusses this complex question in considerable detail. He first deals with inadequate resolutions of the tension (e.g. allegory, dismissal of the OT). There follows an illuminating historical survey of how key theologians have preached Christ from the OT. Over against Luther's christological and Calvin's theocentric approach, G. advocates 'the redemptive-historical christocentric method', where Christ stands in the centre of redemptive history. Six other ways may also lead from the OT to Christ (promise-fulfilment, typology, analogy, longitudinal themes, contrast). The final part of the book suggests a practical ten-step method for writing a christocentric sermon. G.'s overall case is well made, and he shows a preacher's skill in analysis and selection of quotations. His conclusion may be rather one-sided (is there no place for a theocentric sermon or one related only to the OT?), but this is a comprehensive treatment that will be of interest to biblical theologians as well as preachers.

P. JENSON

HANNAH, DARRELL D., *Michael and Christ: Michael Traditions and Angel Christology in Early Christianity* (WUNT, 2, Reihe 109; Tübingen: J.C.B. Mohr [Paul Siebeck], 1999), pp. xv + 289. DM 98.00. ISBN 3-16-147054-0; ISSN 0340-9570.

A significant section of this book (Part II) investigates the Michael tradition in Second Temple and rabbinic literature. The work seems to be well done and is another example of the sudden explosion of recent works on the question of 'angel worship', 'angel christology' and monotheism.

ED.

HAUGHT, JOHN F., *God after Darwin: A Theology of Evolution* (Boulder, CO: Westview Press, 2000), pp. xiii + 221. $25.00/£19.50. ISBN 0-8133-6723-9.

There has been a variety of reactions in the century and a half since Darwin published his *Origin of Species*. Many religious apologists have rejected evolution, and many scientists have seen the only possible conclusion from Darwin to be atheism. H. is one of that growing number of theologians who not only accept evolution, with all its consequences, but embrace it as a means of reflecting on the nature of creation and God. This is a sophisticated but accessible study and represents the sort of 'science and religion' book that we should see more of.

ED.

HEGER, PAUL, *The Three Biblical Altar Laws: Developments in the Sacrificial Cult in Practice and Theology, Political and Economic Background* (BZAW, 279; Berlin –New York: de Gruyter, 1999), pp. xi + 463. DM 198.00. ISBN 3-11-016474-4; ISSN 0934-2575.

Even the subtitle of this volume hardly prepares the reader for the scope and sig-nificance of this book. Structuring his argument around a detailed analysis of the meanings of and historical relationships between the altar laws of Exod. 20.21-23, Deut. 27.2-8 (the former a temporary mound altar going back to nomadism, the latter a permanent altar with *avanim shelemot*), and the bronze altar of Exod. 27.1-8, viewed in the light of the (frequently conflicting) archaeological record as well as related biblical texts, the author succeeds in integrating a history of the cult, the theological ideas associated with it, and the political/economic circumstances in which development occurred. Particular topics considered include the various uses of stone (for pillars, tablets, execution, circumcision, sacrifice), the 'horns' of the altar (seen as symbolizing the four corners of the earth), the reforms of Ahaz and Josiah (the last seen as self-defeating), and developments in the sacrificial cult in both practice and theology right down to rabbinic perspectives after 70 CE. Few future studies in the history of Israelite religion will be able to ignore this book.

B.S. JACKSON

HOFFMANN, HEINRICH, *Das Gesetz in der frühjüdischen Apokalyptik* (Studien zur Umwelt des Neuen Testaments, 23; Göttingen: Vandenhoeck & Ruprecht, 1999), pp. 367. DM 148.00. ISBN 3-525-53377-2.

The impetus for undertaking this study was to better understand the Pauline con-cept of law (for purposes of Christian–Jewish dialogue), but the study of the Jewish material was already of such a size that this ultimate question was omitted except for a short note at the end. The subject of this study has tended to be neglected for studies of the concept of law in rabbinic literature, the Jewish Greek writings, or the Qumran literature. After a long introductory section tracing the study of apocalyptic for the past two centuries, the role of law in the main Jewish apocalyptic writings (plus an appendix on *Jubilees*) is studied. The question of what to include could nat-urally be debated. For example, H. includes the *Testament (Assumption) of Moses* (rightly in my opinion, contra some recent scholars such as J.J. Collins), but then why not the *Testament of Abraham*? In these texts, H. notes the close connection be-tween cult and law, wisdom and law, and the heavenly and earthly law (which includes the calendar), as well as the prominence of Deuteronomistic features. They generally assume that reward or punishment for obedience will be finally meted out at judgment (if not before) and that the righteous are the obedient (not necessarily the physical Israelites). There is also the paradoxical view that the evil inclination of human nature leads inevitably to disobedience, yet each individual is still fully responsible for the acts committed. A final section looks briefly at the concept of law in the Qumran texts and the relationship between the apocalyptic and the Pauline concepts of law. Unfortunately, there are no indexes.

L.L. GRABBE

HÜBNER, HANS and BERND JASPERT (eds.), *Biblische Theologie: Entwürfe der Gegenwart* (Biblisch-Theologische Studien, 38; Neukirchen-Vluyn: Neukirchener Verlag, 1999), pp. 221. DM 48.00/AS 350/SwF 44.50. ISBN 3-7887-1753-X.

The essays in this volume arise out of a theological forum at the Hofgeismar Lutheran Academy which aimed to explore the question of a biblical theology and the relationship of the two Testaments. However, there was also the desire to make the contributions accessible to those who were not professional theologians. The essays (all in German) are on why a biblical theology (Hübner), sketches of a contemporary biblical theology (T. Söding), speech about the people of God as a biblical category (J. Hausmann), the Bible as the book of God's developing unity (U. Mauser), biblical theology and church history (B. Jaspert), and NT theology and cultural anthropology (J. Riches).

ED.

HURTADO, LARRY W., *At the Origins of Christian Worship: The Context and Character of Earliest Christian Devotion* (Didsbury Lectures, 1999; Carlisle: Paternoster, 1999), pp. xi + 138. £9.99. ISBN 0-85364-992-8.

Based on the Didsbury Lectures 1999, this is a stimulating and comprehensive analysis of the setting and the development of early Christian worship in the rich religious diversity in the pagan world of the Roman Empire, and in contemporary synagogue practice. A concluding chapter reflects on the significance of the material for Christian worship today. While this volume will be of primary interest to NT scholars, there is much here to provoke wider interest. There is a very useful comprehensive bibliography.

R. DAVIDSON

JANOWSKI, BERND and MATTHIAS KÖCKERT (eds.), *Religionsgeschichte Israels: Formale und materiale Aspekte* (Veröffentlichungen der Wissenschaftlichen Gesellschaft für Theologie, 15; Gütersloh: Chr. Kaiser/Gütersloher Verlagshaus, 1999), pp. 298. DM 88.00/AS 642/SwF 78.50. ISBN 3-579-01816-7.

This collection of papers, originally delivered at a conference in 1997, falls into two sections. In the first, concerned with the formal aspects of the book's theme, W. Zwickel's opening essay surveys a number of recent German works on Israel's religious history: he feels that they tend rather to represent OT theologies and fail to produce an Israelite religious history in the true sense. Similarly, the following chapter by H. Niehr sets out to define the constitutive elements of such a history, seeing the fundamental issue as to whether it is primarily to be based on the OT or on other independent evidence. The second section comprises five studies of various material aspects of pre-exilic Israelite religion. In an extensively illustrated essay, J. Jeremias and F. Hartenstein take up the much discussed question of 'Yahweh and his Ashera' in the context of the relationship between official and popular religion in the period of classical prophecy. M. Albini, beginning from Amos 5.8, examines the significance of the Pleiades for Israel's religion and A. Berlejung discusses the character of the OT debate about images. K. Koch asks how far Israel's religion belongs to the ancient Near East, concentrating on ideas of kingship. Finally, E. Zenger seeks to elucidate the religious implications of Psalm 82 when viewed in the context of the Asaph psalm collection.

J.R. PORTER

JONES, D. GARETH, *Valuing People: Human Value in a World of Medical Technology* (Carlisle: Paternoster, 1999), pp. xi + 241. £12.99. ISBN 0-85364-991-X.

An anatomist at the Univeristy of Otago gives an account of his Christian ethics and matters dependent upon biomedical technology. It is a follow-up to two previous books *Brave New People* (1984) and *Manufacturing Humans* (1987). *Valuing People* is written in an engaging and accessible style, helped greatly by the organization of topics. Rather than discussing clinical ethics in detail, the narrative describes the human life-cycle (from embryo to the end of life) and the biomedical technologies that cause ethical dilemmas at different points. J. argues that developments in medical technology mean that human well-being is now more than an absence of overt pathology. However, medicine has not become merely a matter of technique. It serves a social role, and for this reason must be linked to a moral framework. For J. this framework should affirm human value and dignity according to the biblical principle that human beings are created in God's image. Christians, he argues, have a responsibility to argue for the rightful place of biomedical technologies in our societies.

P. DEAREY

KLINGBEIL, MARTIN, *Yahweh Fighting from Heaven: God as Warrior and as God of Heaven in the Hebrew Psalter and Ancient Near Eastern Iconography* (OBO, 169; Freiburg: Universitätsverlag; Göttingen: Vandenhoeck & Ruprecht, 1999), pp. xii + 361. SwF 108.00. ISBN (Universitätsverlag) 3-7278-1250-8; (Vandenhoeck & Ruprecht) 3-525-53678-X.

This book is based on a Stellenbosch doctoral dissertation supervised by I. Cornelius and reflects the iconographical approach to the OT found in the works of O. Keel and his disciples. Having established that there are 507 occurrences of metaphorical language for God in the Psalter, which he divides into 17 main metaphorical groups, K. concentrates on the metaphors of God as warrior and God of heaven. He studies these motifs in eight selected passages, Ps. 18.8-16, 21.9-13, 29.3-9, 46.7-12, 65.10-14, 68.15-22, 83.14-18 and 144.5-8. Having given a detailed textual analysis of these eight passages, he discusses depictions of deities as warriors or gods/goddesses of heaven in ancient Near Eastern, especially Syro-Palestinian and Mesopotamian, iconography. Finally, he endeavours to integrate the iconographical evidence previously discussed with the eight psalmic passages, showing how it can serve to illuminate them. The iconographical depictions of smiting deities and so on are certainly interesting in their own right and do to some degree help to concretize the biblical imagery. Whether this kind of iconographical study revolutionizes OT study as much as the Keel school imagines may, however, be doubted.

J. DAY

KNIGHT, GEORGE A.F., *Christ the Center* (Grand Rapids, MI: Eerdmans; Edinburgh: Handsel, 1999), pp. viii + 88. $12.00/£7.95. ISBN (Eerdmans) 0-8028-4624-6; (Handsel) 1-871828-38-4.

In this study K. revisits the theme which has played a dominant role in his critical and theological thinking over the past 50 years—witness his 1957 book *A Christian Theology of the Old Testament*. He argues for the distinctive Hebrew mind set, expressed both in linguistics and in psychology, and in its doctrine of God, as leading naturally into the Christian doctrine of the trinity, rooted in the incarnation and resurrection of Jesus, and as providing the basis of the life and witness of the church. Those who share his critical and religious assumptions will find here much to interest them in a well-written and highly personal book. Those, both Jews, Christians and others, who do not share his assumptions, will question the validity of some of the linguistic and philosophic arguments, wonder at his highly selective use of early rabbinic sources and his all-too-brief dismissal of religious pluralism.

R. DAVIDSON

KÖRTING, CORINNA, *Der Schall des Schofar: Israels Fests im Herbst* (BZAW, 285; Berlin and New York: de Gruyter, 1999), pp. xii + 389. DM 198.00. ISBN 3-11-016636-4.

As the subtitle indicates, this is an investigation of the autumnal festivals of the Day of Blowing Trumpets, the Day of Atonement, and the Festival of Tabernacles or Booths. The study is in rough (presumed) chronological order, with the first section on pre-exilic texts (primarily Exod. 23.14-19; 34.18-26; Deut. 16), exilic (Lev. 16; 23; Ezek. 45.18-25), post-exilic (Num. 28–29; Neh. 8), with a final section on the book of *Jubilees*, the *Temple Scroll* and the Mishnah. There are no startling conclusions, but this attempt to trace the development of thinking and practice covers a good deal of ground and has a commendable bibliography (though missing is J.L. Rubenstein, *History of Sukkot* [*B.L.* 1996, p. 89]),

ED.

KRAŠOVEC, JOŽE, *Reward, Punishment, and Forgiveness: The Thinking and Beliefs of Ancient Israel in the Light of Greek and Modern Views* (VTSup, 78; Leiden–Boston–Cologne: E.J. Brill, 1999), pp. xxxvi + 957. Nlg 360.00/$212.00. ISBN 90-04-11443-2; ISSN 0083-5889.

Using literary analysis, K. seeks not only to investigate the subjects of reward, punishment and forgiveness but to relate them to the modern world. There are four large sections devoted to a literary analysis of the subjects in the Pentateuch, the Former Prophets, the Latter Prophets, and the Writings. Part 5 is on the concept of punishment in ancient Greece, and Part 6 gives a comparative assessment in the light of modern theories. There are helpful summaries along the way to guide the reader through the mass of analysis and commentary, but ultimately the question is whether such a massive study is justified. The conclusions are hardly startling.

ED.

LAFONT, SOPHIE, *Femmes, droit et justice dans l'antiquité orientale: Contribution à l'étude du droit pénal au Proche-Orient ancien* (OBO, 165; Freiburg: Universi-tätsverlag; Göttingen: Vandenhoeck & Ruprecht, 1999), pp. xv + 562. SwF 148.00/ DM 178.00/AS 1300. ISBN (Universitätsverlag) 3-7278-1226-5; (Vandenhoeck & Ruprecht) 3-525-53339-X.

This book, written from the point of view of the history of law, analyses criminal laws regarding women in the ancient Near East. The spectrum of laws examined is very broad from the Sumerian corpus attributed to Ur-Namma in the third millennium BCE to the Babylonian Hammurapi Code, Neo-Babylonian, Assyrian and Hittite codes at the end of the second millennium, down to biblical laws. It posits an oriental common law bound by a common identify and principles founded upon common institutions—yet not a fixed unmovable set. The reviewer is not entirely convinced by the author's distinction into sexual (rape, adultery, incest, and so on) and social infringements (abortion, grievous bodily harm, blasphemy, robbery) which constitutes the two main sections. On the positive side, it is noteworthy to signal that some (free) women had access to public and semi-public offices and were treated as professional people in their own right (the wet nurse and the pub tender). However, there are no great surprises when it comes to assess the research as a whole: in order to be either respected or respectable a woman had to be subject to patriarchal control. Her social status, and therefore the way she was dealt with by the law, depended on it. One useful aspect of the book is that the legal texts under consideration are transliterated and translated. As to the index, it would benefit from further sub-classifications, that is, according to the various codes of ancient Near Eastern laws. But with its sheer abundance of footnotes, and a very complete bibliography, this book constitutes a valid resource for all who are interested in biblical law and especially in the law regarding women.

A. JEFFERS

LENOWITZ, HARRIS, *The Jewish Messiahs: From the Galilee to Crown Heights* (Oxford: Oxford University Press, 1998), pp. ix + 297. £36.00. ISBN 0-19-511492-2.

A chapter considers Jesus of Nazareth, Bar Kokhba, and some other early examples of messianic figures, but the information is fairly basic and not always reliable (though the author has clearly made an effort to use recent studies). The main interest of this study will be the later messianic figures in Judaism, as far as the present-day (e.g. a section on Rebbe Schneerson who has been hailed by some of the Lubav-itch movement as the messiah). Each chapter has a bibliographical note and there are some endnotes; however, some of the references are given in the text only and not otherwise repeated (e.g., G. Scholem's well-known study on Shabbatai Zvi).

ED.

LUNDIN, ROGER, CLARENCE WALHOUT and ANTHONY C. THISELTON, *The Promise of Hermeneutics* (Carlisle: Paternoster; Grand Rapids, MI: Eerdmans, 1999), pp. xii + 260. £14.99/$20.00. ISBN (Paternoster) 0-85364-900-6; (Eerdmans) 0-8028-4635-1.

The contributions by Lundin and Walhout have nothing specific to say about the OT, but have implications for the wider debate about how to interpret the Bible. Lundin provides a sophisticated defence of tradition, over against the Cartesian inheritance of the orphaned individual. Walhout discusses several features of narra-tive, particularly the relationship between fiction and history. He argues that prob-lems arise when the reference of a text (the world of the text) is confused with the relation of that world to the real world (mimesis). Thiselton's contribution is the longest and most directly related to the Bible (primarily NT). He has a helpful dis-cussion of reader-response criticism, and seeks to develop a hermeneutic that avoids the problems of mechanical repetition on the one hand and uncontrolled subjec-tivism on the other. Resources for this quest include Jauss's reception theory and a hermeneutics of promise, developed with the help of speech-act theory. The schol-arship and sophistication of the three authors makes these essays worthy of a wide circulation, including among those who would not accept the broadly conservative character of the perspectives that are developed.

P. JENSON

MACCOBY, HYAM, *Ritual and Morality: The Ritual Purity System and its Place in Judaism* (Cambridge: Cambridge University Press, 1999), pp. xii + 231. £37.50/ $59.95. ISBN 0-521-49540-7.

This clear and careful account of the ritual purity system of the Bible and the rabbinic writings will be warmly welcomed by all those who find the topic inter-esting but less than self-explanatory. M. himself draws attention to some common misconceptions, which seem to be particularly common among writers on the NT. The scarcity of reference to purity laws in the NT is taken as an indication that Jews at the time were far from being obsessed with the topic, as they are sometimes made out to have been. Impurity was, in most cases, not considered sinful, but rather a fact of life, often the result of circumstances beyond one's control or even of merito-rious acts. It was directly related to the sanctity of the temple, and by implication of Israel as the priestly people.

N.R.M. DE LANGE

MILLAR, J. GARY, *Now Choose Life: Theology and Ethics in Deuteronomy* (New Studies in Biblical Theology, 6; Grand Rapids, MI: Eerdmans, 1999), pp. 216. $24.00. ISBN 0-8028-4407-3.

This is the American edition of the book reviewed in *B.L.* 1999 (p. 136).

ED.

MINETTE DE TILLESSE, C. (ed.), *Revista Bíblica Brasileira*, Ano 15, No. 4 (Fortaleza, Brazil: Nova Jerusalém, 1998), pp. 433-615. $50.00 (US) p.a.

MINETTE DE TILLESSE, C. (ed.), *Revista Bíblica Brasileira*, Ano 16, Nos. 1-3: C. Minette de Tillesse (trans.), *Apócrifos do Antigo Testamento*, vol. I (Fortaleza, Brazil: Nova Jerusalém, 1999), pp. 491. $50.00 (US) p.a.

Issue 15.4 consists of classified reviews of a cosmopolitan spread of books, mainly biblical (OT, pp. 433-98; NT pp. 498-559), with shorter sections on intertestamental, patristic and contemporary theological and pastoral works. On p. 595 the new arrangement of incorporating the *B.L.* in an issue of *JSOT* is warmly applauded.

With indefatigable energy, R.P. Minette de Tillesse has set about translating H.F.D. Sparks's *The Apocryphal Old Testament* (1984) into Portuguese. Issue 16.1-3 covers everything from *Jubilees* to the *Testament of Job* (Sparks, pp. 1-648). For the most part the 'translator/adaptor' (p. 5) closely follows Sparks's translations, but he occasionally adopts alternative readings (this is usually made clear in footnotes). To make the texts easier to follow he has introduced subheadings, in effect, as he says, a mini-commentary. He has also updated Sparks's bibliographies in places (p. 10, nn. 4 and 5), and has added a short general bibliography (p. 16). A paragraph of the preface (Sparks, p. xvi) has been omitted on p. 13, and on p. 15 the date should be December 29, not 20—minor blemishes in a most commendable undertaking to make these important texts available and comprehensible to a wide Brazilian readership.

J.M. DINES

MOTZ, LOTTE, *The Faces of the Goddess* (Oxford: Clarendon Press, 1997), pp. viii + 280. £25.00/$35.00. ISBN 0-19-508967-7.

A mixture of patternistic thinking, New Age fashion, and the infinite capacity of human gullibility, to which intellectual currents even Jung and some contemporary feminists have not been immune, have led to sweeping generalizations about the universality of the 'mother' archetype, and the discovery of a mother goddess in every corner of the world, commonly represented in contemporary myth as subsequently subordinated to patriarchy in the growth of complex societies. M. endeavours to counter this with a more nuanced view of feminine symbols and divine roles, ranging widely for her examples. In the sections dealing with the ancient near Eastern World (Mesopotamia, Anatolia and Greece), however, her ability to break free of the paradigm is less than successful. Various historical problems are glossed over, in a too-broad-brush approach to be of use. Furthermore, poor old Asherah does not even get a look in!

N. WYATT

NEWMAN, CAREY C., JAMES R. DAVILA and GLADYS S. LEWIS, *The Jewish Roots of Christological Monotheism: Papers from the St Andrews Conference on the Historical Origins of the Worship of Jesus* (Supplements to Journal for the Study of Judaism, 63; Leiden–Boston–Cologne: E.J. Brill, 1999), pp. xi + 373. Nlg 195.00/ $115.00. ISBN 90-04-11361-4; ISSN 1384-2161.

The origins of monotheism have been of considerable interest in recent years, as well as the origins of the Christology found in the NT. The papers from this conference mainly focus on the latter part of this interest. One of the editors provides an introductory study putting the problem into perspective (Davila), followed by concepts of Jewish monotheism in the Hellenistic world (M. Mach), the throne of God and the worship of Jesus (R. Bauckham), worship and monotheism in the *Ascension of Isaiah* (L.T. Stuckenbruck), the high priest and the worship of Jesus (M. Barker), the worship of divine humanity and the worship of Jesus, 11QMelchizedek and the epistle to the Hebrews, and a number of other articles, mainly relating to the NT and early Christianity and Gnosticism.

ED.

NEWMAN, JUDITH H., *Praying by the Book: The Scripturalization of Prayer in Second Temple Judaism* (SBL Early Judaism and Its Literature, 14; Atlanta: Scholars Press, 1999), pp. x + 283. $49.00. ISBN 0-7885-0564-5.

In this revised version of a 1996 Harvard doctoral dissertation, supervised by James Kugel, the author demonstrates how prayer became an increasingly important feature of Jewish religious life after the Babylonian Exile and how its formulation was strongly influenced by the knowledge and use of earlier Hebrew traditions. She offers her own definition of what constitutes a prayer and uses literary-critical, linguistic and historical methods to analyse a selection of texts, particularly 1 Kings 8, Nehemiah 9, Judith 9 and *3 Maccabees* 2. She points to the central role of the historical review, the typological appropriation of past events, and the reference to characters as archetypes in such prayers and comments on their literary models, formal patterns and incorporation of earlier language. Of particular importance are the link she successfully establishes between liturgy and exegesis and her convincing description of how Jewish prayer underwent major development in the Second Temple period. Qumran is left to its specialists and the references to later Jewish and Christian prayer are fairly rudimentary. The body of the research is contained in chs. 2–4, while the remaining parts of the volume provide useful, if a trifle repetitive, summaries of its conclusions, as well as a helpful history of scholarship on prayer and liturgy. The volume is attractively written, richly annotated and well indexed.

S.C. REIF

ÖHLER, MARKUS (ed.), *Alttestamentliche Gestalten im Neuen Testament: Beiträge zur biblischen Theologie* (Darmstadt: Wissenschaftliche Buchgesellschaft, 1999), pp. 224. DM 58.00/SwF 52.50/AS 423. ISBN 3-534-13836-8.

Eleven scholars, predominantly in their thirties and working in the area of OT theology, have put together a series of short summarizing reports on the passages in the OT canon, the literature of Second-Temple Judaism, and—rather more fully—the NT, which deal with the figures selected. These are: Adam, the protagonists of Genesis 4–6, Abraham, Isaac and his sons and Joseph, the leading women in the narrative of Genesis 20–29, Moses, Joshua and the Judges, Melchizedek, Levi and Aaron, Saul, David and Solomon, Elisha and Elijah and finally and oddly, Balaam, Balak, Korah and Jezebel! The selective bibliographies, listing almost exclusively publications in German, are the only obviously useful feature of this curious volume.

C.J.A. HICKLING

OTTO, ECKART, *Das Deuteronomium: Politische Theologie und Rechtsreform in Juda und Assyrien* (BZAW, 284; Berlin–New York: de Gruyter, 1999), pp. x + 432. DM 198.00. ISBN 3-11-016621-6; ISSN 0934-2575.

For more than a decade, O. has been a dominant figure in the study of biblical and ancient Near Eastern law, contributing a series of monographs and establishing the important *Zeitschrift für altorientalische und biblische Rechtsgeschichte* (Harrassowitz). At first he concentrated on the 'Covenant Code', studying in particular its systematics in comparison with those of the Laws of Eshnunna and Hammurabi. Latterly, he has turned to Deuteronomy, for which (as in the earlier work of Weinfeld) the principal focus of comparison (and, indeed, direct historical connection) is Assyrian. Here, he compares the reformatory agendas of Deuteronomy and the Middle Assyrian Laws, both of which transfer matters of private law into the public sphere, but within the context of quite different political/theological ideologies. Deuteronomy itself reflects a series of identifiable stages, starting with a reformulation of the Covenant Code. This is a substantial study, designed in part as a preparatory work for the author's commentary on Deuteronomy in ATK.

B.S. JACKSON

PETERSON, DAVID (ed.), *Witness to the World* (Carlisle: Paternoster, 1999), pp. xvii + 138. £12.99. ISBN 0-85364-954-5.

This volume contains the papers delivered at the Second Annual School of Theology at Oak Hill College in 1998. They represent evangelical theology's response to the need to commend the Christian faith in a postmodern world. Two of the papers will be of particular interest to biblical scholars; Alan Storkey's 'The Bible's Politics', rightly castigating evangelic lack of interest in this field, and Andrew Hartropp's 'Biblical Justice and Modern Economic Life', drawing heavily on the biblical theological basis for ethics and the prophetic demand for justice.

R. DAVIDSON

POORTHUIS, M.J.H.M. and J. SCHWARTZ (eds.), *Purity and Holiness: The Heritage of Leviticus* (Jewish and Christian Perspectives, 2; Leiden–Boston–Cologne: E.J. Brill, 2000), pp. xv + 371. Nlg 195.00/$114.75. ISBN 90-04-11418-1.

This investigates the subject from a variety of points of view. The editors give a useful introduction, after which the subject is surveyed in historical sequence through the biblical, post-biblical, mediaeval and modern periods, including the dynamics of purity in the priestly system (J. Milgrom), impurity of land animals (M. Douglas), Israel's holiness (B. Schwartz), Chronicles' narrative on Uzziah's leprosy (P. Beentjes), Rudolph Otto revisited (Poorthuis), impurity disputes in first-century Judaism and the NT (E. Ottenheijm), non-priestly purity according to his-torical and archaeological findings (E. Regev). In addition, a variety of articles look at various aspects of the subject in the NT, rabbinic Judaism, and later Christianity and Judaism.

ED.

RYRIE, ALEXANDER, *Silent Waiting: The Biblical Roots of Contemplative Spiritu-ality* (Norwich: Canterbury Press, 1999), pp. xii + 212. £8.99. ISBN 1-85311-257-7.

This study provides an overview of some roots of modern contemplative spiritu-ality which are to be found in the Hebrew Bible. Particular attention is given to the themes of 'meditation', 'night vigil', 'silence' and 'standing before God'. A major part of the work involves a survey of the Hebrew verbs used for 'waiting' as ex-plored in the Psalms. There is a wider discussion also of the way in which the activity of God is portrayed and the implications of God's 'face' being either seen or hidden. The second major part of the book makes connections with forms of contemplative prayer today. The author does not argue for a straight, unbroken line between the biblical and modern practices. Nevertheless he draws parallels with the writings of the eastern desert fathers in an attempt to show that contemplative prayer, though much influenced by Greek concepts, has its roots in Hebraic forms of spirituality. It is a reflective piece of work which is nevertheless based on a wide reading of modern studies of the texts in question.

M. TUNNICLIFFE

SAWYER, JOHN F.A., *Sacred Languages and Sacred Texts* (Religion in the First Christian Centuries; London: Routledge, 1999), pp. x + 190. £50.00/$85.00; paper £16.99/$27.99. ISBN 0-415-12546-4; (paper) 0-415-12547-2.

This is a fast moving book, clearly written and packed with information, and it delivers what its cover promises: 'a comprehensive study of the role of languages and texts in the religions of the Greco-Roman world'. It deals with the many lan-guages spoken in the Greco-Roman world, and then with the phenomenon of sacred languages and the power these gave to their respective hierarchies. S. makes inter-esting observations on the extent of literacy in the ancient world and the crucial role of Christianity in promoting literacy. The chapters on canon and translation are good, especially the observations on the element of interpretation in any translation, and he then offers a glimpse of the more esoteric business of etymologies, sacred names and, for example, *gematria*. This book, although simply written and assuming no prior knowledge, is not just for beginners. Many will profit from it.

M. BARKER

SCHENK-ZIEGLER, ALOIS, Correctio fraterna *im Neuen Testament: Die 'brüder-liche Zurechtweisung' in biblischen, frühjüdischen und hellenistischen Schriften* (FzB, 84; Würzburg: Echter Verlag, 1997), pp. xii + 492. DM 56.00/AS 409/SwF 53.00. ISBN 3-429-01979-6; ISSN 0935-9764.

This monograph is based on a dissertation accepted by the Catholic Theological Faculty of the Eberhard-Karls University in 1995. It explores the theme of 'broth-erly admonition' through word and word-field studies in the OT, where, besides a detailed exegesis of Lev. 19.17 which later chapters show to be particularly forma-tive, most attention focuses on the prophetic literature and especially on the wisdom literature; in 'early Jewish' writings, namely the Dead Sea Scrolls, the *Testaments of the Twelve Patriarchs*, the *Letter of Aristeas*, and the 'rabbis', where the princi-ples of selection are not entirely clear; in Plutarch's *Moralia*; and finally in the NT where besides a few passages in Matthew and Luke, and in James, the Pauline corpus occupies most attention. The analysis is thorough, with proper attention to both MT and LXX where appropriate, and interaction with a wide secondary litera-ture, but it remains at the descriptive level and there is, for example, little explo-ration of the structures and self-understanding within which the texts functioned. As is common in studies of this nature, the ultimate aim appears to be towards delineat-ing the form of admonition appropriate in Christian communities—the more author-itarian attitude of the Pastoral Epistles with their tendency towards discipline and exclusion is not favoured—but the exercise of tracing 'background' has taken over, and is conducted without pre-emptive judgments or comparison. The result is a use-ful analysis of the relevant texts within the 'word-field' approach, although some will find that approach intrinsically restrictive and weak on historical, social and theological contextualization.

J. LIEU

SCHREINER, JOSEF, *Das Alte Testament verstehen* (Die Neue Echter Bibel: Ergän-zungsband zum Alten Testament, 4; Würzburg: Echter Verlag, 1999), pp. 248. DM 48.00/SwF 46.00/AS 350. ISBN 3-429-02079-4.

Understanding the OT, according to this companion volume to the Catholic *Neuer Echter Bibel*, is less a matter of beginning from a prior hermeneutical theory and more a matter of letting the OT speak for itself. This raises, in the first part of the book, questions about the limits and canonicity of the OT, its relation to other liter-ature of the ancient Near East, and the implication of the fact that, for the church, it is bound up together with the NT. These questions are tackled from the point of view of the close relationship between the Bible and the community that produced it, with attention to inner interpretation within the OT itself, as well as its interpre-tation in the Septuagint and the NT. The second part deals with key constituents of the OT's 'profile', such as the word of Yahweh, and leads to a discussion of the infallibility and authority of the OT, which are defined in respect to what is needed for human salvation. The third section deals with approaches to the OT, including Wolfgang Richter's linguistic method, canonical criticism, liberation theology, feminist interpretation and the psychological interpretation of Drewermann. Of these, only liberation theology receives anything like general approval; the other methods are seen as one-sided and tendentious, although not without value. The book is obviously written with German Catholic students in mind, as reference to Papal encyclicals makes clear. It also relies on a fairly traditional critical interpretation of the history of Israel. However, its wide coverage of a range of important topics will be of interest to anyone who is concerned with the place of the OT within Christian theology.

J.W. ROGERSON

SCHWARTZ, BARUCH J., תורת הקדושה: עיונים בחוקה הכוהנית שבתורה [*The Holiness Legislation: Studies in the Priestly Code*] (Publications of the Perry Foundation for Biblical Research in the Hebrew University of Jerusalem; Jerusalem: Magnes Press, 1999), pp. 452. $20.00. ISBN 965-493-033-1.

S., a graduate of Columbia and the Jewish Theological Seminary of America in New York, completed his education at the Hebrew University of Jerusalem, where he now lectures. He has produced here an expanded, amended and updated version of a 1987 doctoral dissertation that represents the best in the Jewish Bible scholarship of Israel and North America. He offers a close and critical examination of Leviticus 17–19 which holistically ranges over linguistic, literary, historical, legal and theological themes to expound the text and to explain its place in the larger Levitical and Pentateuchal contexts. He denies that chs. 17–26 represent an independent code of law with the kind of practical legislative dimension found in other ancient Near Eastern literature. For him these chapters are a literary creation that reflects the covenantal relationship between God and Israel and strives for a major educational impact on the spirituality of the Jewish people. He therefore opts to refer to 'holiness legislation' rather than the 'Holiness Code' and characterizes it as an expansion and development of the priestly traditions with a significant degree of independent thought and expression and some earlier legal content. The broader priestly material belongs to the First Temple period but parts of it were later revised in the light of the holiness legislation. The indexes and the short title catalogue are excellent but there is no English summary of the findings, only translated chapter headings.

S.C. REIF

SCORALICK, RUTH (ed.), *Das Drama der Barmherzigkeit Gottes: Studien zur biblischen Gottesrede und ihrer Wirkungsgeschichte in Judetum and Christentum* (Stuttgarter Bibelstudien, 183; Stuttgart: Katholisches Bibelwerk, 2000), pp. 240. DM 59.00/AS 431/SwF 56.00/Eur 27.15. ISBN 3-460-04831-X.

This collection arises out of a symposium in honour of Erich Zenger's sixtieth birthday. There are essays (all in German) on the subject of God's mercy and justice in a variety of areas: the eschatology of Lamentations (O. Fuchs), the divine image in the ancient Near East and the OT (B. Janowski), Psalm 103 as a bridge between Jews and Christians (C. Dohmen), the book of Joel (M.-T. Wacker), reality and the 'I' in Qohelet (H.-P. Müller), the 'gospel' in the First Testament (R. Rendtorff), the tensions between mercy and justice in rabbinic exposition, focusing on the Psalms (G. Bodendorfer), reciprocity as a category of meaning in rabbinic Judaism (B. Ego), and Pharisaic Sabbath observance in the travel reports of Luke (K. Löning).

ED.

ZIMMERLI, WALTHER, *Grundriss der alttestamentlichen Theologie* (Theologische Wissenschaft 3/1; Stuttgart–Berlin–Cologne: Kohlhammer, 7th edn, 1999), pp. 230. DM 44.60/AS 326/SwF 41.00. ISBN 3-17-016081-8.

This first appeared in 1972, with minor revisions for the 2nd (1975) and 4th (1982) editions. This appears to be a reprint of the 4th edition.

ED.

8. THE LIFE AND THOUGHT OF THE
SURROUNDING PEOPLES

BAUER, JOSEF, ROBERT K. ENGLUND and MANFRED KREBERNICK, *Mesopotamien: Späturuk-Zeit und Frühdynastische Zeit: Annäherungen 1* (ed. Pascal Attinger and Markus Wäfler; OBO, 160/1; Freiburg: Universitätsverlag; Göttingen: Vandenhoeck & Ruprecht, 1998), pp. 627 + 2 maps. DM 258.00. ISBN (Universitätsverlag) 3-7278-1166-8; (Vandenhoeck & Ruprecht) 3-525-53797-2.

SALLABERGER, WALTHER and AAGE WESTENHOLZ, *Mesopotamien: Akkade-Zeit und Ur III—Zeit: Annäherungen 3* (ed. Pascal Attinger and Markus Wäfler; OBO, 160/3; Freiburg: Universitätsverlag; Göttingen: Vandenhoeck & Ruprecht, 1999), pp. 414 + 1 map. DM 174.00. ISBN (Universitätsverlag) 3-7278-1210-9; (Vandenhoeck & Ruprecht) 3-525-53325-X.

The German title of this important new series is unfortunately ambiguous (*Approximations? Advances?*), and the editors merely state that it is neither cultural histories nor handbooks, but is meant to cover philology and history. The freedom thus given to the learned authors has been fully and beneficially exploited. The first two volumes to appear cover the earlier and later parts of third-millennium BC Mesopotamia. The central centuries are no doubt to be covered in vol. 2, but future plans are not revealed. The various chapters are well up to date and full, so that the history can be used in preference to the latest Cambridge Ancient History, but much of the philology requires expertise in third-millennium scripts and knowledge of Sumerian and Akkadian. However, the last few decades have seen tremendous advances in the understanding of the earliest ('proto-cuneiform') script, and R.K. Englund, one of the main workers in this field, has given in vol. 1 pp. 15-233, in English, the first detailed statement of what is now known, striving to make it intelligible without presuming first-hand knowledge of the material. This is a fundamental source for the origin of writing.

W.G. LAMBERT

BREWER, DOUGLAS J. and EMILY TEETER, *Egypt and the Egyptians* (Cambridge: Cambridge University Press, 1999), pp. xviii + 218. £35.00/$54.95; paper £12.95/$19.95. ISBN 0-521-44518-3; (paper) 0-521-44984-7.

Egypt is particularly well served by popular introductory works of high quality. This new and well-written addition to the genre ranges over all aspects of life in pharaonic antiquity, from religion and politics to technology and writing, and is enriched with useful surveys of the history of antiquarianism and its development into Egyptology. Each chapter has a short list of further readings, which are also listed together at the end. Glossary and index are provided.

N. WYATT

BRYCE, TREVOR, *The Kingdom of the Hittites* (Oxford: Oxford University Press, 1998), pp. xvii + 464. £45.00. ISBN 0-19-814095-9

This volume offers a history of the Hittites, taking account of recent discoveries and discussion, and providing material not otherwise available in a single volume in English, supported by full publication references. The author is an Australian scholar who has made individual contributions over a number of years, and this substantial work, written in a clear readable style, is welcome. He begins with an account of the origins and forerunners of the Hittites in Anatolia, including a good summary of the Old Assyrian merchant colonies, the activities of which have marginal analogies for the Patriarchal narratives. The main part of the volume (chs. 4–12) is a detailed history of the Hittites in the second millennium but, apart from reference to treaties as important historical sources (with general remarks, pp. 51-53), significant of course from the point of view of covenant, the most relevant part for OT studies is the chapter dealing with the fall of the kingdom and its aftermath (ch. 13). There is brief treatment of the Sea Peoples (pp. 367-74, including Philistines), of the so-called Syro-Hittite states, northern neighbours of Israel (pp. 384-85; a useful summary having been given, pp. 54-57, of the Luwians who were an important element among them), and, briefly, of Tabal (Tubal), Muski (Meshech) and related groups. There is brief discussion of the Hittites of the OT (pp. 385, 389-91), a distinction being drawn between the Syro-Hittites and a possible Hittite-influenced Canaanite tribal group.

T.C. MITCHELL

COLE, STEVEN W. and PETER MACHINIST (eds.), with contributions by SIMO PARPOLA, *Letters from Priests to the Kings Esarhaddon and Assurbanipal* (State Archives of Assyria, 13; Helsinki: Neo-Assyrian Text Corpus Project, 1998), pp. xxx + 221 + illustrations. $49.50. ISBN 951-570-437-5; paper 951-570-436-7.

This volume of letters from particular priests addressed to the Assyrian kings is part of the series editing and translating the state archives of Assyria. The introduction is informative regarding the type of general information to be derived from the letters, for example, complaints about theft and corrupt priestly practices in the temples, and information regarding temple sacrifices, rituals, making divine images, and the divine processions and sacred marriage rites. Some points are also relevant to biblical scholarship, such as references to surpluses of sacrificial meat being consigned to the 'storehouse for pickled meat' (nos. 18 and 22); one surmises that something similar must have existed in Jerusalem. Also of interest is a letter (no. 66) referring to being treated by both types of therapists, namely the 'exorcist' (*mašmaššu*) and 'physician' (*asû*), and another letter (no. 73) complains of an ailment resulting from contact with women, called the 'hand of Venus (Dilbat)' disease. One letter (no. 45) includes a proverb: 'a young man who caught the tail of a lion sank in the river, but one who caught the tail of the fox was saved'. There is much good material here.

M.J. GELLER

DIETRICH, MANFRED and OTTO LORETZ (eds.), *Ugarit-Forschungen: Internationales Jahrbuch für die Altertumskunde Syrien-Palästinas*, vol. 30 (Münster: Ugarit-Verlag, 1998 [1999]), pp. xiv + 972. N.P. ISBN 3-927120-74-X.

The following five articles (of 37) touch on biblical matters. M. Anbar considers covenant language in Exodus 24 in the light of texts from Mari, and J. Fox looks at the Ugaritic *ybmt limm* in the light of biblical *'ēmîm*. O. Lipschits discusses Nebuchadrezzar's policies in Anatolia and the fate of the Judahite kingdom; H. Niehr examines an underworld deity found in Ugarit, Phoenicia and Israel, and in a review article O. Loretz looks at history/histories of religion covering Syria and Canaan, and Israel and Judah.

N. WYATT

DIRVEN, LUCINDA, *The Palmyrenes of Dura-Europos: A Study of Religious Interaction in Roman Syria* (Religions in the Graeco-Roman World, 138; Leiden–Boston–Cologne: E.J. Brill, 1999), pp. xxiv + 360 + 19 figures and 23 plates. Ngl 230.00/ $135.50. ISBN 90-04-11589-7; ISSN 0927-7633.

The specific topic of this Leiden doctoral study under K. van der Toorn and H. Drijvers is of the worship carried out by Palmyrenes who had settled in Dura-Europos in the first few centuries of the Common Era. A very important part of the study is devoted to a systematic catalogue of the archaeological remains of Palmyrene culture in Dura-Europos. D. finds that the Palmyrenes consisted mainly of two groups, military personnel and merchants. Both groups preserved a strong religious tradition from their original home, though each favoured different deities. The Palmyrene deities worshipped in Dura-Europos were only a small number of those in Palmyra itself, all being civic deities whereas the family deities had been dropped from the cult. The Palmyrenes also participated in the official religion of Dura-Europos. On the other hand, Palmyrene deities do not seem to have influenced worship of the majority population at Dura-Europos. This is an important sociological study on the question of religious interaction.

L.L. GRABBE

EDWARDS, MARK, MARTIN GOODMAN and SIMON PRICE (eds.), in association with CHRISTOPHER ROWLAND, *Apologetics in the Roman Empire: Pagans, Jews, and Christians* (Oxford: Oxford University Press, 1999), pp. x + 315. £48.00. ISBN 0-19-826986-2.

Christian apologetics in the Roman empire have often been studied. This collection tries to achieve a balance by looking also at Jewish and even 'pagan' forms of apologetic in the first three centuries of the Roman empire. An introduction by the editors surveys the subject. Essays include Acts of the Apostles (L. Alexander), Josephus's treatise *Against Apion* (Goodman), Christian apologetic as anti-Judaism in Justin's *Dialogue with Trypho* (T. Rajak), Greek apologists, Latin apologists, Origen's treatise *Against Celsus*, Philostratus on Apollonius, Eusebius's apologetic writings, and the Constantinian circle.

ED.

FLÜCKIGER-HAWKER, ESTHER, *Urnamma of Ur in Sumerian Literary Tradition* (OBO, 166; Freiburg: Universitätsverlag; Göttingen: Vandenhoeck & Ruprecht, 1999), pp. xvii + 383 + 25 plates. SwF 120.00. ISBN (Universitätsverlag) 3-7278-1229-X; (Vandenhoeck & Ruprecht) 3-525-53342-X.

This book is a dissertation submitted to the Faculty of Arts at Berne University. It presents new standard editions of the hymns of Urnamma (formerly read Urnammu), founder of the Third Dynasty of Ur, but also deals with the composition and development of Sumerian royal hymns in general. Chapters 1–4 are short and are concerned with historical background, Sumerian hymns, the typology and orthography of the texts, historical correlations, and continuity and change in royal hymnography. Chapter 5 contains the critical editions of the Urnamma hymns and takes up more than half the book. This is clearly a work for Sumerologists and only the truly fearless biblical scholar will approach it. However, the new translation of 'Urnamma's Death' will be useful for those interested in lamentation literature (see also the discussion of this text and lamentation literature in ch. 4). The study of these hymns has advanced considerably since the earlier works of A. Falkenstein, G. Castellino and J.J.A. van Dijk. Building on these and the more recent research of C. Wilcke, J. Klein and others, F.-H. has made a substantial and impressive contribution to our understanding of Sumerian hymns.

K.J. CATHCART

GAGER, JOHN G., *Curse Tablets and Binding Spells from the Ancient World* (Oxford Paperbacks; Oxford: Oxford University Press, 1999 [1992]), pp. xv + 278. Paper £12.99. ISBN 0-19-513482-6.

In antiquity one dealt with an enemy by the use of written spells or incantations (*defixiones* or *katadesmoi*). About 1500 of these from the millennium between 500 BCE and 500 CE have been preserved. More than 150 of these are made available here in English translation, with bibliography and discussion. They are broadly categorized, with separate chapters on sex, love and marriage; legal and political disputes; business, shops and taverns; pleas for justice and revenge; antidotes and counterspells. There is also a chapter on testimonies to the existence of these spells. This welcome reprint in paperback format will make the study more widely available.

ED.

GOLLNICK, JAMES, *The Religious Dreamworld of Apuleius'* Metamorphoses: *Recovering a Forgotten Hermeneutic* (Editions Sciences Religieuses; Waterloo, Ontario: Wilfrid Laurier Press, 1999), pp. xiii + 174. £28.95. ISBN 0-88920-300-8.

Several recent works have demonstrated the importance of dreams in the ancient world (see above p. 114; *B.L.* 1995, pp. 92, 134). G. argues that in the classic work of Apuleius, the dream is an important vehicle for the religious teaching of the book. He brings in Freud, Jung and some modern studies of dreaming but points out that the ancient concept of dreams provided a richer context. A dream can be seen as a separate literary genre which gives a different quality from other sorts of narrative, which will affect its interpretation (perhaps there is a connection with the recent interest in fanasty?). G. traces the place of dreams and dream interpretation in the Graeco-Roman world. Knowledge of dreams in the biblical and Jewish literature can only be enhanced by such studies as this one.

ED.

GRAF, DAVID F., *Rome and the Arabian Frontier: From the Nabataeans to the Saracens* (Variorum Collected Studies Series, CS594; Ashgate: Variorum, 1999), pp. xvi + 348. £59.50. ISBN 0-86078-658-7.

This volume usefully reproduces studies by G. variously dated between 1978 and 1995; Graf adds a preface reviewing his work in the light of subsequent research. The Nabataeans are given Mesopotamian origins (1990), the Decapolis is seen as a buffer zone created by Pompey against the Hasmonaeans rather than against the Nabataeans (1986), and Greek civic life emerged here only under Augustus (1994). 'The Syrian Hauran' (1992) reviews J.M. Dentzer's volumes on the Hauran. The Nabataean army, *pace* Strabo and Josephus, was not inferior to neighbouring armies, and after 106 was absorbed into the Roman army (1994). G. explores the Via Nova Traina between Petra and Aqaba, locating its milestones (1995), refers '*l ḥwr* in a Nabataean inscription to the original name of Ḥumayma (1992), and argues that the Ḥijaz was not included in the Roman province of Arabia Petraea (1988). His earliest offering (1978) demonstrates late second-century Roman diplomacy with Thamudic tribes evidenced by the Rawwāfa inscriptions; a later article (1989) on Rome and the Saracens sees Roman fortifications in North Arabia as directed against internal unrest rather than supposed nomadic invasions from the desert. These well-researched pieces are reproduced photographically, with original typefaces, typographical errors, and pagination; the index refers to pages within each chapter.

J.R. BARTLETT

GRÜNEWALD, THOMAS, *Räuber, Rebellen, Rivalen, Rächer: Studien zu* Latrones *im römischen Reich* (Forschungen zur antiken Sklaverei, 31: Stuttgart: Franz Steiner, 1999), pp. x + 269. DM 85.00/SwF 85.00/AS 621. ISBN 3-515-07489-9.

Much has been written in recent years about the concept of 'social banditry' drawing on the model of E.J. Hobsbawm, and the concept has been widely used to understand certain movements within Second Temple Judaism. This monograph challenges a good number of such studies (e.g. the book by Horsley and Hanson, p. 44).

G. argues that there were four types of 'bandit', including 'real bandits'. The literature also envisages two ideal types, the 'real bandit' and the 'noble bandit' (i.e., the
Robin Hood type of 'social bandit'); however, the 'noble bandit' is a literary construct, not a social description. Indeed, Hobsbawm's 'social bandit' did not exist in
antiquity but is a creation of Roman writers. That is, various historical personages
existed who were bandits (or rebels or rivals or avengers—as the title indicates), but
their evaluation as 'noble' is a literary interpretation. There is not a factual difference between the activities of the two types, only how they were viewed by different writers. This challenging study should be read by all students of the society
of ancient Israel and Judah.

L.L. GRABBE

HOROWITZ, WAYNE, *Mesopotamian Cosmic Geography* (Mesopotamian Civilizations, 8; Winona Lake, IN: Eisenbrauns, 1998), pp. xiv + 410, including 10 plates.
$52.50. ISBN 0-931464-99-4.

There is much to be said about Mesopotamian cosmology, and this book tries to
say it all. It draws from a variety of sources, some well known and others not, including astronomical texts, esoteric texts, mythology and epic literature, historical
texts and incantations. There is no clear order to the presentation of the large amount
of material in this study, although biblical parallels are pointed out whenever possible. Most useful is the edition and translation of the Babylonian Mappa Mundi in
this context, as well as the discussion of the astronomical texts Mul-Apin and the
'Astrolabes', in which the theoretical framework of these texts is clearly explained.
The second part of the book explains the Sumerian and Akkadian terminology for
heavens, earth and underworld. It should be noted, however, that the cosmology described here is Akkadian cosmology best attested in second and first millennium
sources, and may not reflect Sumerian cosmology of an earlier period, that is, the
third millennium BCE. It is also worth noting that there is no Mesopotamian Dante,
and that no one ancient text was specifically devoted to the presentation or explanation of contemporary Mesopotamian cosmology.

M.J. GELLER

JONES, NICHOLAS F., *The Associations of Classical Athens: The Response to Democracy* (New York and Oxford: Oxford University Press, 1999), pp. xvii + 345 + 6 figures. £40.00. ISBN 0-19-5121759.

This is a detailed study of the various forms of association which developed in
Athens during the fifth and fourth centuries, presenting them as a response to the
impact of the ideology of democracy on actual opportunities for participation for
the majority of a highly politicized population; for example, they might offer an
alternative arena for political commitment, channels of access to influence central-
ized government, or a medium for articulating a sense of commonality with other
scattered groups. The analysis proceeds through detailed, often dense, study of the
evidence for the structure, development and roles of *demes*, *phylai* and phratries,
as well as of the more disparate 'clubs, schools, regional and cultic associations'.

Throughout, for example in the various discussions of the role of women, what becomes clear is the careful reading and methodological precision required before reaching any over-arching conclusions. Those more familiar with the history of Israel, and even with suggestions that the rise of the synagogue may be paralleled to the importance of Greek associations, will be struck by the radically different socio-political context and by the dangers of too easily 'translating' terms (*phyle*; *genos*), concepts and structures from one social and historical context to another.

J. LIEU

JONG, ALBERT DE, *Traditions of the Magi: Zoroastrianism in Greek and Latin Literature* (Religions in the Graeco-Roman World, 133; Leiden–New York–Cologne: E.J. Brill, 1997), pp. xii + 496. Ngl 314.00/$184.00. ISBN 90-04-10844-0; ISSN 0927-7633.

In two preliminary chapters, J. gives a clear and level-headed account of the problems which beset any attempt to compare knowledge of Zoroastrianism in Greek and Latin texts with what is known from Old and Middle Persian sources. There are many disagreements among specialists which put current OT debate in the shade, and since the primary sources are so late, for the most part, it is extremely difficult to pin down such historical development as must have taken place over the centuries. Moreover, the danger of circularity can hardly be avoided; on the one hand, the classical sources may help to unravel parts of this history, while on the other it is only on the basis of the history that a judgment can be made about the reliability of the classical authors in the first place. Since all this is clearly acknowledged, one approaches the two main chapters with a degree of confidence that the conclusions drawn will be soundly based. In the first, J provides a translation and detailed discussion of the relevant passages in five Greek authors (Herodotus, Strabo, Plutarch, Diogenes Laertius and Agathias). In the second, he provides a thematic analysis, in eight major sections (the pantheon, ritual, priests, and so on), of all references in Greek and Latin sources (some repetition is thus unavoidable). In both chapters, of course, evidence from Persian sources is fully utilized. As might be anticipated, no general conclusions about reliability one way or the other can be drawn; each author and passage needs to be studied carefully on its own merits. But even when allowance has been made for many an uncertainty, the independent value of the classical sources for a critically based reconstruction of Zoroastrianism in antiquity remains. Although there is little direct reference to the OT, this scholarly and responsible collection and analysis of a mass of data will be appreciated by all with particular interests in the Achaemenid period.

H.G.M. WILLIAMSON

KLAUCK, HANS-JOSEF, *The Religious Context of Early Christianity: A Guide to Graeco-Roman Religions* (trans. Brian McNeil; Studies of the New Testament and its World; Edinburgh: T. & T. Clark, 2000), pp. xxvii + 516. £34.95. ISBN 0-567-08693-3.

This surveys Graeco-Roman religions, with chapters on civic and domestic religion (sacrificial cults, religious associations, cults of the dead), the various mystery cults, popular beliefs (astrology, soothsaying, miracles, magic), the cult of rulers and emperors, philosophy and religion (Stoicism, Epicureanism, Middle Platonism) and Gnosticism. As will be clear, there is considerable comparative material for ancient Israelite and Near Eastern religion, as well as early Judaism.

ED.

KLENGEL, HORST and JOHANNES RENGER (eds.), *Landwirtschaft im Alten Orient: Ausgewählte Vorträge der XLI. Rencontre Assyriologique Internationale Berlin, 4.– 8.7. 1994* (Berliner Beiträge zum Vorderen Orient, 18; Berlin: Dietrich Reimer Verlag, 1999), pp. [8 +] 402. DM 79.00. ISBN 3-496-02652-9.

This conference volume contains 37 papers, and while the title speaks of 'Alten Orient' the Assyriological bias results in a majority being restricted to, or primarily concerned with, Mesopotamia. One is specifically devoted to the OT: E. Otto on 'Die Ackerbau in Juda im Spiegel der alttestamentlichen Rechtsüberlieferungen', dealing with the agricultural background of the law requiring ploughland to be left fallow every seventh year. However, other papers, some extremely specialized and learned, cover Palestine in dealing with the Near East generally. A number of authors have complained at the typographical defects in the book.

W.G. LAMBERT

LEICK, GWENDOLYN, *Who's Who in the Ancient Near East* (London and New York: Routledge, 1999), pp. xv + 229 + 4 maps. £19.99/$29.99. ISBN 0-415-13230-4.

This is a typical *Who's Who* in arrangement: a list of important or noteworthy people from the ancient Near East in alphabetical order. It covers all the areas from Egypt and Anatolia to Arabia and western Iran, from the earliest sources to Hellenistic times. Each entry has biographical and historical notes and concludes with most welcome references to further scholarly reading given in detail in the bibliography. It is a compilation from the best recent sources and is generally reliable. The dates given, however, are too often precise and unqualified. Thus nearly all the kings of Israel and Judah after Solomon are given exact dates without even a 'c.', dates taken from the *Cambridge Ancient History* without its qualifications. There is also a glossary of terms not necessarily known to general readers. A useful book for students and others wanting quick and easy access to information.

W.G. LAMBERT

MCDOWELL, A.G., *Village Life in Ancient Egypt: Laundry Lists and Love Songs* (Oxford: Clarendon Press, 1999), pp. xvii + 279. £40.00. ISBN 0-19-814998-0.

The village of workmen who produced the tombs of kings at Deir el-Medina in Egypt has been the subject of many studies and documentaries. This exemplifies the village life by giving over 200 documents in translation from the site, along with some comments. The collection is introduced by a chapter giving the background and history of what is known about the site and the people who worked there, but most of the text is devoted to the documents which give remarkable insight into the daily life of the people who lived and worked there for half a millennium during the New Kingdom (c. 1550–1050). A set of notes at the end gives references to each chapter, section by section and document by document.

ED.

MILES, RICHARD (ed.), *Constructing Identities in Late Antiquity* (Routledge Classical Monographs; London and New York: Routledge, 1999), pp. ix + 262. £45.00/ $75.00. ISBN 0-415-19406-7.

The 'crisis of identity' has been a feature of the last two decades, both in society and in scholarly research. This collection of essays has the late Roman Empire as its focus, but the points made will have relevance to the question in other contexts. The essays cover such subjects as gender, Christian versus pagan, barbarian versus Graeco-Roman, the secular destruction of statues (with implications for Christian action), the use of classical forms by a Christian writer. There is the curious case of Porphyry of Tyre who taught in Rome but shows no knowledge of Latin or Western philosophy, where the Orient is often mentioned but only after being filtered through Greek lenses. The image of the judge is a useful example of the multi-faceted way in which a figure might rightly be viewed.

ED.

POLLOCK, SUSAN, *Ancient Mesopotamia: The Eden that Never Was* (Case Studies in Early Societies; Cambridge: Cambridge University Press, 1999), pp. xii + 259. £32.50/$49.95; paper £10.95/$17.95. ISBN 0-521-57334-3; (paper) 0-521-57568-0.

This very readable volume deals with the developments that occurred in ancient Mesopotamia over the course of the three millennia from c. 5000 to 2100 BCE. After a brief survey of archaeological work in Mesopotamia, the author outlines the theoretical framework within which she works. Her approach is one informed by political economy, paying attention to economic, political and social issues. Feminist anthropology is strongly advocated as a force that will prompt, for example, better enquiry into 'how broader political, economic, and social changes impact social reproduction and household organization' (p. 25). In six chapters P. systemically deals with settlement patterns, faunal remains, artefact distributions and activity patterning, iconography, texts and burials. This reviewer found ch. 4, 'Making a living; tributary economies of the fifth and fourth millennia', and ch. 5, 'A changing millennium', particularly interesting. The use of the terms 'human women' and 'human men' in the section on Religion (ch. 7, p. 192) is really unnecessary. The book will be useful for students and meet the aims of the series very well.

K.J. CATHCART

POMEROY, ARTHUR J. (ed.), *Arius Didymus: Epitome of Stoic Ethics* (SBLTT, 44; Graeco-Roman Series, 14; Atlanta: Scholars Press, 1999), pp. ix + 160. $35.00. ISBN 0-88414-001-6.

Around AD 400 Stobaeus wrote an anthology which included an outline of Stoic philosophy. Many scholars are now convinced that this section is an epitome of Arius Didymus, an Alexandrian philosopher who personally advised Augustus. This gives the text and translation of that section of Stobaeus, along with notes and a glossary. It seems to represent one person's view of Stoic philosophy around the turn of the era.

ED.

PRICE, SIMON, *Religion of the Ancient Greeks* (Cambridge: Cambridge University Press, 1999), pp. xii + 217. £35.00/$59.95; paper £12.95/$19.95. ISBN 0-521-38201-7; (paper) 0-521-38867-8.

This introduction to the religions of the Greeks up to the Hellenistic age recognizes the interconnections of religion with other aspects of society. It thus discusses the subject in relation to the teachings of Socrates, the tragic playwrights, and other aspects of Greek culture. There are chapters on the basic pan-Hellenic religious heritage of gods, myths and festivals; religious places; authority and control; girls/boys and men/women; elective cults; Greek thinkers; and finally the Roman, Jewish and Christian reaction to Greek religion. Socrates is treated in a section on 'responses to religious threats'.

ED.

RADNER, KAREN (ed.), using the electronic database of the Neo-Assyrian Text Corpus Project and with the collaboration of numerous colleagues, *The Prosopography of the Neo-Assyrian Empire: Volume 1, Part I: A* (Helsinki: Neo-Assyrian Text Corpus Project, 1998), pp. xxix + 240. $44.00. ISBN 951-45-8163-6.

RADNER, KAREN (ed.), using the electronic database of the Neo-Assyrian Text Corpus Project and with the collaboration of numerous colleagues, *The Prosopography of the Neo-Assyrian Empire: Volume 1, Part II: B-G* (Helsinki: Neo-Assyrian Text Corpus Project, 1999), pp. ix + 241-433 + B-34. $50.00. ISBN 951-45-8645-X.

These volumes offer far more than a listing of Neo-Assyrian personal names in cuneiform records of the Assyrian Empire, but the entries offer as complete a record as possible of the biographies of each of the persons listed. Some of the briefer entries may record that the person was simply mentioned in a text or acted as a witness, but entries on royal courtiers or kings extend over several pages. Meanings of names are provided whenever possible. Particularly useful for biblical scholars is the treatment of all West Semitic personal names, with alphabetic writings of the name given where attested. Although intended as reference works, the books are an interesting read because of the great amount of detailed historical data. The introduction to Part I includes a provisional eponym list which is the basis for dating of documents between 648–609 BCE, at the end of the Assyrian Empire following the reign of Assurbanipal. The Addenda of Part II includes an entry on Atalia, the queen of Sargon II whose tomb was recently discovered. One might speculate whether Sargon married an Israelite princess Atalia, descendant from the ninth-century queen Atalia of the house of Omri.

M.J. GELLER

SANMARTÍN, JOAQUÍN, *Códigos legales de tradición babilónica* (Pliegos de Oriente: Serie Próximo oriente; Barcelona: Trotta/Edicions de la Universitat de Barcelona, 1999), pp. 303. N.P. ISBN (Trotta) 84-8164-316-7; (EUB) 84-8338-105-2.

The core of the introductory section (pp. 9-51) is an analysis of 'law' in Babylonian cultural tradition, illustrated by examples from the legal texts. These texts are then given in translation: The Laws of Eshnunna, The Code of Hammurapi, The Edict of Ammiṣaduqa and the Middle Assyrian and Neo-Babylonian Laws. Each has an introduction and explanatory endnotes. Three appendices list the proper names used, the many technical terms, and the tariffs and prices (with explanations). Although intended for the general public, this paperback can be consulted with profit by scholars. There are extensive endnotes and the system for reference to the laws within each code (a combination of paragraph numbering and line numbers in the margins) is very clear.

W.G.E. WATSON

SANMARTÍN, JOAQUÍN and SERRANO, JOSÉ MIGUEL, *Historia antigua del Próximo Oriente: Mesopotamia y Egipto* (Akal Textos, 22, Madrid: Ediciones Akal, 1998), pp. 381. N.P. ISBN 84-460-1032-1.

The volume comprises 'Libro I', by Sanmartín, on Mesopotamia ('El próximo oriente asiático. Mesopotamia y sus áreas de influencia'), and 'Libro II', by Serrano, on Pharaonic Egypt, each running to about 180 pages. Throughout, sample texts are given in translation. The work is richly supplied with 29 illustrations and maps and 19 tables. Also included are an overall chronological outline, a glossary of technical terms and a general bibliography. The work is very attractive and user-friendly for both teachers and students with, for example, basic or classic bibliographical items marked by an asterisk. It also has the advantages of being up to date and fairly concise.

W.G.E. WATSON

SIEBERT, ANNE VIOLA, *Instrumenta Sacra: Untersuchungen zu römischen Opfer-, Kult- und Priestergeräten* (Religionsgeschichtliche Versuche und Vorarbeiten, 44; Berlin and New York: de Gruyter, 1999), pp. xi + 365. DM 218.00. ISBN 3-11-016126-5; ISSN 0934-2575

Cult and religion were at the heart of the Roman state. To understand it requires a combination of methods, not only of text and philology but of the control offered by archaeological data. This surveys the various aspects of the Roman cult, including a systematic examination of the archaeological remains of sacrificial instruments and priestly clothing. There is also a catalogue of monumental remains and coins that picture the cult in operation. Many points of similarity with the attempts to reconstruct the ancient Israelite and Jewish cult arise, where the data available are often of a similar nature.

ED

TURCAN, ROBERT, *The Cults of the Roman Empire* (trans. A. Nevill; The Ancient World; Oxford: Basil Blackwell, 1999 [1996]), pp. xiii + 399+ 34 plates, 5 figures, 2 maps. £65.00/$76.95; paper £16.99/$26.95. ISBN 0-631-20046-0; (paper) 0-631-20047-9.

In the pre-Constantine period of the Roman empire, a large number of gods and religions were worshipped, many imported from Greece, Egypt and the ancient Near East. This book focuses on these imported (and 'popular') religions. It was with these groups that nascent Christianity had to compete, and its eventual triumph was partially due to adopting some elements of these competitors. Logically, Judaism should have been included here, but it is missing except for the occasional reference. Sadly, the printer has decided to use endnotes, and there is no bibliography, though a 'suggestions for further reading' section focuses on English-language studies.

ED.

VAN DE MIEROOP, MARC, *The Ancient Mesopotamian City* (Oxford: Oxford University Press, 1999), pp. xv + 269. £14.99. ISBN 0-19-815286-8.

Mesopotamia was one of the most urbanized areas of antiquity. It is, therefore, fitting to have a study devoted to the question of the city there. The book traces the origins of the city and urbanism and their subsequent developments. There are chapters on social organization, the urban government, food supply of the citizens, crafts and commerce, credit and management, and religion and learning. Each chapter has a useful biographical guide at the end. M. is well aware of the limits to knowledge, such as the question of population density in ancient Sumer. Those interested in similar sociological questions in ancient Israel would benefit from this knowledgeable and cautious study.

ED.

WATANABE, KAZUKO (ed.), *Priests and Officials in the Ancient Near East: Papers of the Second Colloquium on the Ancient Near East—The City and its Life held at the Middle Eastern Culture Center in Japan (Mitaka, Tokyo) March 22–24, 1996* (Heidelberg: Universitätsverlag C. Winter, 1999), pp. 366, including 135 figures. DM 98.00/AS 715/SwF 87.00. ISBN 3-8253-0533-3.

The results of this Tokyo colloquium on the ancient Near East has much of interest for biblical scholars. Illustrations on cylinder seals of priests and priestesses depict the king and his family as priests (Collon). Two articles describe the extensive personnel in Sumerian temples (Maekawa) and fundamental changes in temple architecture in the Old Babylonian period (Okada). Assyrian political power is discussed by both Grayson and Maul, and Ikeda re-studies the Assyrian conquest of the Aramaean state of Bit-Adini in 856 BCE. A consensus emerges from Sumerian and Ugaritic sources that the king's role in the sacred marriage rite for fertility was purely ritualistic rather than participatory (Steinkeller and Tsumura). Yoshida shows that music accompanied Hittite rituals. Most stimulating is Deller's review of the evidence on Assyrian eunuchs. He not only proves that eunuchs really existed, but

Deller shows that the Akkadian *ša rēši*, from which the Hebrew term *sarīs* 'eunuch' derives, probably refers to the testicles rather than 'of the head', and he explains the functions of eunuchs at the Assyrian court. The edition of an Emar medical text includes some errors (Tsukimoto), while van de Mieroop's discussion of the government of a Mesopotamian city is useful if one does not wish to read his monograph on the same topic (reviwed above).

M.J. GELLER

WATSON, WILFRED G.E. and NICOLAS WYATT (eds.), *Handbook of Ugaritic Studies* (Handbuch der Orientalistik: Erste Abteilung, Der Nahe und Mittlere Osten: 39. Band; Leiden–Boston–Cologne: E.J. Brill, 1999), pp. xiv + 892 + 20 illustrations. Nlg 396.00/$233.00. ISBN 90-04-10988-9; ISSN 0169-9423.

This magnificent work draws on the knowledge and expertise of some of the main Ugaritic specialists in the world today and gives a comprehensive coverage of the state of Ugaritic studies. Four chapters cover the main texts: literary, cultic, correspondence and legal (including the main material at Ugarit in languages other than Ugaritic). Then come chapters on the economy, society, onomastics, religion, iconography and political history. The final chapter is a very modern one: on Ugaritic study and the use of the computer. There are more than 25 named contributors. A large bibliography and full indexes (though not, unfortunately, of modern authors) complete the volume. Although this is a very large volume, it can only skate over the surface, and important topics will necessarily receive only summary treatment. For example, the brief section on the use of comparative philology for Ugaritic lexicography (pp. 125-26) does not mention the studies of either James Barr or myself, even though these make relevant methodological points. This will be a useful handbook and is recommended to all who make any use of Ugaritic in their research.

L.L. GRABBE

WEST, M.L., *The East Face of Helicon: West Asiatic Elements in Greek Poetry and Myth* (Clarendon Paperbacks; Oxford: Clarendon Press, 1999 [1997]), pp. xxvi + 662. Paper £35.00. ISBN (paper) 0-19-815221-3.

The hardback edition of this book was published in 1997 (not noticed in the *B.L.*). It is an impressive and substantial volume, described by its author as a 'little book dealing with the whole subject of the Near Eastern element in early Greek poetry' (p. vii). Some OT scholars dread the presentation of parallels from other Near Eastern literatures and regard the exercise with the same suspicion that some politicians and economists have concerning entry into a single European currency. In this book there is a selection of biblical texts which in the author's view have affinities with Greek poetry. Many more parallels are drawn from Anatolian, Ugaritic and Mesopotamian literatures. W. is 'well aware that some of the parallels are more compelling than others' (p. viii). The book is very readable and OT scholars can learn much from it. The reviewer recommends particularly ch. 1, 'Aegean and Orient', ch. 2, 'Ancient Literatures of Western Asia', ch. 3, 'Of Heaven and Earth', ch. 4, 'Ars Poetica', ch. 5, 'A Form of Words' and ch. 12, 'The Question of Trans-mission'. It is surprising to find only one reference to W.G.E. Watson's *Classical Hebrew Poetry*, and no references to the relevant volumes of *Ras Shamra Parallels*, edited by L. Fisher and S. Rummel.

K.J. CATHCART

9. APOCRYPHA AND POST-BIBLICAL STUDIES

ALEXANDRE, MANUEL, JR, *Rhetorical Argumentation in Philo of Alexandria* (with a foreword by B.L. Mack; BJS, 322; Studia Philonica Monographs, 2; Atlanta: Scholars Press, 1999), pp. xx + 302. $34.95. ISBN 0-7885-0582-3.

This has essentially two parts. The first studies the rhetorical tradition in the Graeco-Roman world, as found in such writers as Aristotle, Cicero and Quintillian. It then asks whether and how Philo might have known about this tradition (he had a good formal education in the subject). The second part investigates how Philo makes use of rhetoric in his writings. The author does this by looking at discourses (including those found in complete treatises, such as *De Vita Mosis*), at the structures of arguments as found in theses and elaborative developments of a theme, and finally rhythmic and periodic structures. The book is a major piece of work and to be commended. However, it was completed in its original Portuguese form in 1990, and this translation has only partially updated it. For example, in his somewhat brief discussion on Philo's use of etymologies (pp. 198-99), he does not know my full study of the subject (*B.L.* 1990, p. 134).

L.L. GRABBE

ANDERSON, GARY A. and MICHAEL E. STONE (eds.), *A Synopsis of the Books of Adam and Eve* (SBL Early Judaism and Its Literature, 17; Atlanta: Scholars Press, 2nd revised edn, 1999), pp. xx + 98. $45.00. ISBN 1-7885-0566-1.

Whereas the first edition of this work (*B.L.* 1995, p. 141) presented the synopsis in Greek, Latin, English (for the Armenian), French (for the Georgian) and German (for the Slavonic), this second edition presents the texts of the five versions (with several variants) in their original languages and appropriate scripts on the left hand page and five columns of English translations on the right. The translations of the Greek and Latin were completed by Anderson, that of the Armenian by Stone (with minor alterations from that in the first edition), that of the Georgian by J.-P. Mahé, but the translator of the Slavonic is not identified. The new Introduction contains details of the manuscript evidence for each version and a set of notes on some of the principal variants in the Georgian tradition. The editors acknowledge that this revision does not represent a detailed analytical edition, but is a further step towards a comprehensive presentation of the evidence. The revision still contains at least one error which I pointed out in 1995: Lechner-Schimidt on p. xix.

G.J. BROOKE

AVERY-PECK, ALAN J., WILLIAM SCOTT GREEN and JACOB NEUSNER (eds.), *The Annual of Rabbinic Judaism: Ancient, Medieval and Modern*, vol. 2 (Leiden–Boston–Cologne: E.J. Brill, 1999), pp. vi + 176. Nlg 136.63/$76.00. ISBN 90-04-11523-4; ISSN 1388-0365.

The second issue of this new annual has a number of articles of potential interest to *B.L.* readers: halakha and the study of rituals (I. Gruenwald), one-dimensional Jew, zero-dimensional Judaism (J. Faur), central authority in Second Temple Judaism: from *synedrion* to Sanhedrin (H.C. Kee), the religious meaning of the halakha (Neusner), merkavah narrative (H.W. Basser), G.F. Moore and E.E. Urbach revisited (J.R. Strange). Of the reviews one should especially note Neusner's review of I.M. Gafni, *Land, Center and Diaspora* (cf. *B.L.* 1998, p. 186). It is good to see the sustained quality of contributions; not all new periodicals manage to keep up their initial promise.

ED.

BAUMGARTEN, ALBERT I., *The Flourishing of Jewish Sects in the Maccabean Era: An Interpretation* (Supplements to Journal for the Study of Judaism, 55; Leiden: E.J. Brill, 1997), pp. xiii + 240. Nlg 151.50/$89.00. ISBN 90-04-10751-7; ISSN 1384-1261.

This monograph is concerned primarily with the causes and origins of a phenomenon which is often seen as the defining feature of the Judaism of this period. What is new is the author's spotlight on the 'why' before the 'how', his desire to follow the generic growth of the sects from genesis to 'full maturity' and his consistent application of sociological concepts and historical analogies, especially that of seventeenth-century English Puritanism. He is widely read in this literature, in addition to his familiarity with the ancient sources, and his interpretations make rewarding, if occasionally laborious, reading. A number of interesting conclusions about the disagreements between groups are derived from a close reading of 4QMMT. B.'s principal arguments are that the sects are an elite, not a mass phenomenon, and that they are the product of the Hasmonaean victory rather than of deprivation. Connections are made with the rise of the 'newly literate', with urbanism in the period and, in a chapter preoccupied with fine distinctions, with messianic phenomena. It is suggested that the new groups which emerged in the first century AD were something qualitatively different. At the same time, a brief attempt is made in a final chapter to show how post-70 conditions were no longer conducive to the earlier kind of fragmentation. There is some struggle in the writing, especially over whether the initial definition of a 'sect' needs to have universal applicability, and again over the role and limits of logic and rationality in explaining human action. The methodology tends to statements of the obvious or to inappropriate expression. 'Social indigestion' may not be a helpful diagnosis of the ills of Second-Temple Palestine, nor 'slogan' for the themes in 1 Enoch. Nonetheless, this is an original contribution which deserves attention.

T. RAJAK

BAUMGARTEN, JOSEPH M., ESTHER G. CHAZON and AVITAL PINNICK (eds.), *The Damascus Document: A Centennial of Discovery: Proceedings of the Third International Symposium of the Orion Center for the Study of the Dead Sea Scrolls and Associated Literature, 4–8 February, 1998* (STDJ, 34; Leiden–Boston–Cologne: E.J. Brill, 2000), pp. ix + 227. Nlg 140.00/$82.50. ISBN 90-04-11462-9; ISSN 0169-9962.

The articles in this volume are as follows: the perception of the past in the *Damascus Document* (= DD) (A.I. Baumgarten), the laws of DD (J.M. Baumgarten), the Judaism(s) of DD (P.R. Davies), CD 12.15-17 and the stone vessels found at Qumran (H. Eshel), the linguistic study of DD (S.E. Fassberg), the laws of DD and 4QMMT (C. Hempel), the relationship between DD and the *Community Rule* (S. Metso), Yose ben Yoezer and the Qumran sectarians on the purity laws (E. Regev), DD from the Cairo Genizah—discovery, early study and historical significance (S.C. Reif), relationship of the Zadokite fragments to the *Temple Scroll* (L.H. Schiffman), Qumran polemic on marital law—CD 4.20–5.11 and its social background (A. Schremer), scriptural interpretations in DD and parallels in rabbinic midrash (A. Shemesh), towards physical reconstructions of the Qumran DD scrolls (H. Stegemann), CD 11.17 (C. Werman).

ED.

BECKER, HANS-JÜRGEN, *Die großen rabbinischen Sammelwerke Palästinas: Zur literarischen Genese von Talmud Yerushalmi und Midrash Bereshit Rabba* (Texte und Studien zum Antiken Judentum, 70; Tübingen: J.C.B. Mohr [Paul Siebeck], 1999), pp. x + 218. DM 168.00. ISBN 3-16-146867-8; ISSN 0721-8753.

This important monograph raises once again the question of the relationship between *Bereshit Rabba* and the *Talmud Yerushalmi*. It is based on a synoptic comparison of three different types of material found in parallel transmission in both these works: (1) exegesis of the Account of Creation (*y. Hag.* 2.1//*Ber. R.* 1.12); (2) halakhah, particularly the parallels between *Ber. R* and the *Bavot*-tractates; and (3) stories, especially the various versions of the tale of the death of Rabbi Shemu'el bar Rav Yizhaq (*y. AZ.* 3.1; *y. Peah* 1.1; *Ber. R.* 59.4 in mss Vatican 30 and 60 and ms London). Earlier researchers, such as Zunz, Frankel, Albeck, Epstein, Goldman and Lerner, tended to take a rather static view of the tradition and to treat *Ber. R.* and the *Yerushalmi* essentially as fixed and bounded texts. B., working from the manuscripts and not from the standard printed editions, emphasizes the fluidity of the texts and demonstrates how problematic it is to try and identify within this textual flux an *Urtext* or an *Endredaktion* for either 'work'. His analysis strongly suggests that the problem is actually insoluble in traditional, static terms: the model which we should have in mind is of these two great *Sammelwerke* growing side by side (probably within the school of Tiberias) and constantly interacting with each other at all stages of their evolution. It is probably not the case that one was finished first and then used by the other. B. could, perhaps, have spent a little more time discussing the problems of synoptic comparison. There is an immense theoretical literature on this method, which shows that it is a highly tricky business, essentially a way of demonstrating inter-textuality, rather than of definitively proving the priority of one form of a pericope over another. And his detailed analysis is sometimes disappointingly thin (a considerable part of the book consists simply of setting out the parallels synoptically). However he has cleared the ground and laid firm foundations on which historians can build. The work is generally competent and well presented, though it does contain one odd misprint. Thanks, perhaps, to computer error, the references to Alexander the Great on pp. 117f. appear in the index under the name of the present reviewer!

P.S. ALEXANDER

BETZ, HANS DIETER, *Antike und Christentum: Gesammelte Aufsätze IV* (Tübingen: J.C.B. Mohr [Paul Siebeck], 1998), pp. ix + 309. DM 168.00. ISBN 3-16-147008-7.

B. is well known as a NT scholar. He begins this collection with an essay on Wellhausen, though in this case it is the latter's statement that 'Jesus was not a Christian but a Jew'. An essay on Jews and the purity of the temple in Mk 11.15-18 has many OT references. 'Jewish Magic in the Greek Magical Papyri' will be of interest to a number of readers. The two essays relating Christianity to Hellenism have implications for the relationship of Judaism to Hellenization.

ED.

BETZ, OTTO, *Was wissen wir von Jesus? Der Messias im Licht von Qumran* (Wuppertal: Brockhaus, 3rd edn, 1999), pp. 159. DM 19.80. ISBN 3-417-24151-0.

The author's short, essentially popular book of 1965 had two principal aims. It reviewed the main Jewish (as well as Roman) sources for our knowledge of Jesus, drawing on the Qumran material as then known. B. was also at pains to point out the inadequacy of the then fashionable minimizing of the extent of that knowledge. His decision, at the age of 83 and in a much changed climate, to reissue the 1965 book with, for the most part, only minor expansions was not without risks: largely without contributions of his own, he revives battles that have long been history. The principal expansions are grouped into an appendix. Four pages report very selectively on the present state of research into Jesus' 'messianic consciousness', and five short studies investigate 'Jesus in the light of the recently edited Qumran fragments'. The most interesting of these are devoted to material from Cave 4, under the heading 'reconciliation through the priestly cult'. This is the main enduringly useful contribution of a book whose appearance forms, nevertheless, a welcome tribute to the life's work of this distinguished octogenarian.

C.J.A. HICKLING

BOCCACCINI, GABRIELE, *Beyond the Essene Hypothesis: The Parting of the Ways between Qumran and Enochic Judaism* (Grand Rapids, MI: Eerdmans, 1998), pp. xxii + 230. $25.00. ISBN 0-8028-4360-3.

B. argues that the Qumran community is part of 'Enochic Judaism' which he equates with Essenism, apparently one of several Judaisms in the Second Temple

Period. The Essene hypothesis, therefore, is not rejected but developed, and the Qumran community is viewed as one branch of this 'common' tradition. There is superficial similarity to the Groningen Hypothesis. B. builds his Enochic/Essene theory on the basis of the assumption that what is in the Qumran 'library' represents the ideology of the Community, since the scrolls were consciously selected and 'represented their past and formative age' (p. 58). Thus the preponderance of Enochic texts and related literature shows how important this form of Judaism and its theology of the angelic origin of evil were for the Qumran community (especially the Two Spirits passage in *Serekh Ha-yahad*). He does not, however, account for the absence of cols. I-IV in 4QS^d. Moreover, given his assumption that the library collection represents sectarian ideology, it seems odd to marginalize biblical tradition as attested by some one quarter of the 800 or so scrolls in favour of the putative Enochic Judaism.

T. LIM

BOCK, DARRELL L., *Blasphemy and Exaltation in Judaism and the Final Examination of Jesus: A Philological-Historical Study of the Key Jewish Themes Impacting Mark 14:61-64* (WUNT, 2 Reihe 106; Tübingen: J.C.B. Mohr [Paul Siebeck], 1998), pp. xiv + 285. DM 98.00. ISBN 3-16-147052-4; ISSN 0340-9570.

Much of this book is devoted to examining how blasphemy was viewed in early Judaism, through a survey of the various Jewish sources (all literary) given in ch. 2. Unfortunately, although the author recognizes that the rabbinic literature is post-first century, he discusses no methodological principles about using it and seems to make no distinction between sources when creating his synthesis. His citation of Jacob Neusner is only incidental, sometimes to his translations of various rabbinic writings. Chapter 3 surveys 'exalted figures' in Judaism, both human and angelic. His final appeal for the 'need for careful work in the socio-cultural environment' of the NT texts (p. 233) is well taken; however, one would have liked to see him address more clearly the issue of how we determine this 'socio-cultural environment' from the problematic sources available to us.

ED.

BORGEN, PEDER, *Early Christianity and Hellenistic Judaism* (Edinburgh: T. & T. Clark, 1998 [1996]), pp. xi + 376. Paper £17.50. ISBN 0-567-08626-7.

This is a paperback version of the book reviewed in *B.L.* 1998 (pp. 177-78).

ED.

BORGEN, PEDER, KÅRE FUGLSETH and ROALD SKARSTEN, *The Philo Index: A Complete Greek Word Index to the Writings of Philo of Alexandria* (Leiden–Boston–Cologne: E.J. Brill; Grand Rapids, MI, and Cambridge: Eerdmans, 2000), pp. xi + 371. Nlg 110.00/$55.00. ISBN (Brill) 90-04-11477-7; (Eerdmans) 0-8028-3883-9.

At first appearance this looks very similar to the *Index Philoneus* of G. Mayer

(1974), and for most purposes it is. However, it is based on an electronic database that includes some texts not available to Mayer, such as F. Petit's edition of the Greek fragments to the *Quaestiones in Genesim et in Exodum* (1978). Also, the database can be corrected and updated for future editions of the index. Another helpful feature is the use of the tractate names (in abbreviated form), whereas Mayer used numbers. Not presently included are those passages and fragments of Philo available only in Latin or Armenian, though one hopes that these will be made available in time. Many will welcome the reasonable price of this volume.

L.L. GRABBE

BRADSHAW, PAUL F. and LAWRENCE A. HOFFMAN (eds.), *Passover and Easter: Origins and History to Modern Times* (Two Liturgical Traditions, 5; Notre Dame, IN: University of Notre Dame, 1999), pp. vii + 252. $25.00. ISBN 0-268-03859-7.

BRADSHAW, PAUL F. and LAWRENCE A. HOFFMAN (eds.), *Passover and Easter: The Symbolic Structuring of Sacred Seasons* (Two Liturgical Traditions, 6; Notre Dame, IN: University of Notre Dame, 1999), pp. vii + 224. $25.00. ISBN 0-268-03860-0.

Essays on Passover include the Passover meal in Jewish tradition, towards a history of the paschal meal, Passover in the Middle Ages, the modern transformation of the ancient Passover haggadah, the possible Jewish origins of Lent, from Passover to Shavuot, a symbol of salvation in the Seder, and haggadah art. A number of the other essays make comparisons between Passover and Easter or discuss Jewish themes in the Christian celebrations.

ED.

BRIGGS, ROBERT A., *Jewish Temple Imagery in the Book of Revelation* (Frankfurt–Bern–New York: Lang, 1999), pp. xvi + 275. £32.00. ISBN 0-8204-3999-1.

To attempt any short survey of temple imagery in the book of Revelation is no easy task. B. surveys the OT, the Pseudepigrapha, the Qumran literature, and then 'the Apocrypha, Philo and Josephus'. There are full footnotes with good bibliographical detail, but the usefulness of the work is diminished by his decision to consider no texts written after 70 CE and to concentrate on temple furniture rather than the priesthood and cult. He defines 'temple' narrowly, for example, finding nothing of significance in Ben Sira (p. 198), and saying that 'the Jerusalem sanctuary makes only one (relatively) unambiguous appearance in the Apocalypse' (p. 53). He is very unwilling to concede temple themes in the first part of *1 Enoch* (p. 119), and there is confusion over the altars (p. 80). There are also mistakes, for example, 'The ark and mercy seat are never referred to separately in the prose texts of the OT' (p. 86). What about Shiloh?

M. BARKER

BUTLER, ELIZABETH M., *Ritual Magic* (Magic in History Series; University Park, PA: Pennsylvania State University Press, 1998 [1949]), pp. viii + 329. £19.95. ISBN 0-271-01846-1.

It says something for an author's staying power to be republished half a century down the line. Those who enjoyed B.'s *The Myth of the Magus* (*B.L.* 1995, pp. 124-25) are in for another treat. This tome, ranging from ancient Mesopotamia to Alistair Crowley, covers in a lively and engaging manner the whole gamut of beliefs about magic and its implementation, which appear on examination to be remarkably narrow in scope, but equally persistent on the fringes of society. Magic as treated here is not Frazer's pre-religion phenomenon, but is an essentially sublunary when not subterranean genre, as so aptly put by Lucan (p. 27):

> That which excites the hate of gods above;
> Magicians' lore, the savage creed of Dis
> And all the shades…

N. WYATT

CALDUCH-BENAGES, N. and J. VERMEYLEN (eds.), *Treasures of Wisdom: Studies in Ben Sira and the Book of Wisdom: Festschrift M. Gilbert* (BETL, 143; Leuven: Peeters/University Press, 1999), pp. xxvii + 463. BEF 3000. ISBN (Leuven University) 90-6186-956-0; (Peeters) 90-429-0754-1.

This *Festschrift* contains 32 articles, 17 on Ben Sira, 12 on the book of Wisdom and 3 linking Ben Sira, Qohelet and Qumran. Contributors are from all over Europe and America, including one from South Korea and two from Jerusalem. Articles are written mostly in English, French and German with some in Italian and Spanish. Articles on Ben Sira cover some uncommon words in the Hebrew text, use of proverbial sayings, a discussion of aromas and fragrances in the book, rabbinic knowledge of Sira shown in the Babylonian Talmud, thoughts on the book's thematic structure, autobiographical references by the author, antithetical thought of good and evil in Ben Sira and the New Testament. One article discusses the Praise of the Fathers as against the canon of the Old Testament and another Ben Sira's view of history. Some particular passages are discussed: 16.26–17.14, 22.5-15, 35.11-24 and 50.26.

Articles on the Wisdom of Solomon include the use of Proverbs as a source, universalism and justice, eschatology, the sacred name and reflections on particular texts: 1.1-15, 3.6, 6.26, 9.9-10, 10.1-2, 14.21 and 18.7. An appendix contains one article linking Qoheleth and Ben Sira on 'women as snares'(!) as a metaphor of warning, and one comparing Qoh. 12.9 and Sira 37.23. Finally an article discusses the present (up-to-date) situation of Sira manuscripts from Qumran. The book contains excellent indexes of authors and ancient texts cited and will prove useful to any interested in the later wisdom books.

J.G. SNAITH

COLLINS, JOHN J., *The Apocalyptic Imagination: An Introduction to Jewish Apocalyptic Literature* (The Biblical Resource Series: Grand Rapids, MI: Eerdmans, 2nd edn, 1999; distributed in the UK by Alban Books, Bristol), pp. xiii + 337. $30.00. ISBN 0-8028-4371-9.

The text of the first edition has been revised at a number of points, and the notes and bibliography have been updated to 1997. The chapter on Qumran has been completely rewritten, and a chapter on early Christianity has been added. This new edition of such a useful introduction to the subject will be widely welcomed.

ED.

COLLINS, JOHN J. (ed.), *The Encyclopedia of Apocalypticism*. I. *The Origins of Apocalypticism in Judaism and Christianity* (New York: Continuum, 1999), pp. xvii + 498. £175.00/$285.00 (set). ISBN (set) 0-8264-1087-1; (vol. 1) 0-8264-1071-5.

MCGINN, BERNARD (ed.), *The Encyclopedia of Apocalypticism*. II. *Apocalypticism in Western History and Culture* (New York: Continuum, 1999), pp. xix + 524. £175.00/$285.00 (set). ISBN (set) 0-8624-1087-1; (vol. 2) 0-8264-1072-3.

STEIN, STEPHEN J. (ed.), *The Encyclopedia of Apocalypticism*. III. *Apocalypticism in the Modern Period and the Contemporary Age* (New York: Continuum, 1999), pp. xxii + 498. £175.00/$285.00 (set). ISBN (set) 0-8624-1087-1; (vol. 3) 0-8264-1073-1.

This magnificent set covers apocalyptic in all its aspects and gives a fitting end-of-the-millennium perspective on the end of the world. Volume 1 has essays on the roots of apocalypticism in Near Eastern myth (R.J. Clifford), Persian apocalypticism (A. Hultgård), end of the world and the individual in Greek and Roman antiquity (H. Cancik), from prophecy to apocalypticism (Collins), apocalypticism in the Dead Sea Scrolls (F. García Martínez), messianism and apocalypticism (J.C. VanderKam), from apocalypticism to early Jewish mysticism (M. Mach). There is also a section on apocalypticism in early Christianity, including Jesus, the synoptic Gospels, Paul, the book of Revelation, and the subject from a sociological perspective. The anthropologist Bruce Lincoln gives a concluding perspective on apocalyptic temporality and politics in the ancient world.

Most readers will be interested primarily in vol. 1; however, the interpretation of apocalyptic literature and the continuation of the apocalyptic tradition and mentality to the present are traced in fascinating detail in vols. 2–3. Volume 2 has sections on the historical development of apocalypticism (including Byzantine apocalypses and Jewish and Islamic apocalyptic) and themes and applications (including antichrist, millennialism, otherworldly journeys, and art and imagery—mainly Christian). Volume 3 also has a section on historical development, looking at how apocalyptic, messianism and millennialism were present during the colonial period and continue into the contemporary world (Judaism and Islam, as well as the dominant Christian culture). A section on secularization studies the influence on literature, popular culture, politics, and so on, even in a scientific age. There is a great deal here, though it would have been interesting to have some discussion of the subject in some of the Far Easter traditions. The set is marred by the annoying habit of putting notes at the end of each chapter.

L.L. GRABBE

CONWAY, COLLEEN M., *Men and Women in the Fourth Gospel: Gender and Johannine Characterization* (SBLDS, 167; Atlanta: Scholars Press, 1999), pp. 230. $35.00. ISBN 0-88414-002-4.

The aim of this literary critical study is to understand the significance of gender identity in Johannine characterization. C. finds that the women are without exception presented positively while the men are unevenly portrayed—Nicodemus, Peter and Pilate being presented negatively and the man born blind and the Beloved Disciple given positive roles. C. concludes that this evidence tells against the view that the point of Johannine characterization was to present women as equal disciples to men: rather, it is possible that the attraction for John of positive characters of both sexes has been their non-participation in recognized structures of authority. Well written and well researched, this book offers an informative and balanced survey of contemporary scholarship together with a detailed analysis of the gospel text which has clearly benefited from careful observation. Unfortunately, the same carefulness has not extended to the bibliographical detail. Nevertheless, there is much of value here, especially C.'s focus on the characters in relation to one another. Indeed, had the conclusion been extended to deal further with issues raised in the study, especially in relation to feminist approaches to the gospel, this would have properly enhanced an already attractive piece of work.

W.E. SPROSTON NORTH

COTTER, WENDY, *Miracles in Greco-Roman Antiquity: A Sourcebook for the Study of New Testament Miracle Stories* (The Context of Early Christianity; London: Routledge, 1999), pp. x + 274. Paper £14.99/$20.99. ISBN 0-415-11863-8; (paper) 0-415-11864-6.

As the sub-title makes clear, this source book has as its focus the NT miracles, for which it provides a literary and topical context; drawing from literary sources as well as from inscriptions and the magical papyri, it gives a wide selection of 'miracle'—an act of rescue or salvation which overturns 'the canons of the ordinary'— narratives from antiquity. The four parts cover (i) healings by Gods and heroes; (ii) exorcisms, prefaced by texts illustrating the understanding of demons/daimons; (iii) nature miracles; (iv) the use of magic. One appendix comprises texts illustrating diseases and doctors, a second, 'Jesus, Torah, and miracles' is the sort of collection of mishnaic passages 'illustrating' ('negative' attitudes to those helped by) Jesus' healings—leprosy, Gentiles, deaf-mutes, and so on—that shows little awareness of recent study and debate about the sources and about Judaism. Also from the Jewish perspective, despite the first-century nodal point, although the 'biblical' miracles of Moses, Elijah and Elisha are given, those of the rewriting of scriptural traditions in Hellenistic Judaism or of 'charismatic Judaism' such as Honi and Hanina ben Dosa are not. 1 Enoch, Jubilees, Philo and Josephus illustrate ideas about 'demons' and refute an exclusively apocalyptic framework, but a wider range of illustrative material from Qumran than the Genesis Apocryphon might be expected. Although the intention of the volume is not to be prescriptive as to its implications—despite an implicit christological focus—the limited contextualization of the texts, for example the lack of discussion about world-views, about the dating, background and sources of the magical papyri, about literary genres, together with occasional simplistic statements, makes what could be a very valuable resource somewhat disappointing.

J. LIEU

DAN, JOSEPH, *The 'Unique Cherub' Circle: A School of Mystics and Esoterics in Medieval Germany* (Texts and Studies in Medieval and Early Modern Judaism, 15; Tübingen: J.C.B. Mohr [Paul Siebeck], 1999), pp. x + 297. DM 168.00. ISBN 3-16-146798-1; ISSN 0179-7891.

D. has been at the forefront of the study of mediaeval Rhineland Jewish mysticism ever since the publication in 1968 of his monograph *The Esoteric Theology of Ashkenazi Hasidism.* Our understanding of Ashkenazi Hasidism has moved on somewhat since then. It has become increasingly clear that Ashkenazi Hasidism in fact embraced a number of different schools, which emerged independently of each other, but whose traditions were later confusingly intertwined in a variety of ways. D. concentrates here on one of these schools—the Unique Cherub circle. He defines it successfully both in terms of a corpus of literature (within which the Baraita de-Yosef ben 'Uzzi'el played a central role), and in terms of a distinctive theology. The circle held a complex view of the Godhead, postulating three levels within the pleroma: God, the Divine Glory (Kavod/Shekhinah) and the Unique Cherub (*ha-keruv ha-meyuhad*), a divine agency which mediated revelation to the prophets. He surveys the literature of the group, text by text, offering a detailed commentary on each, with copious translations. Central to the circle's literature was the Sefer Yet-zira. They were among the first to treat this Talmudic period text as a mystical rather than as a scientific, cosmological and cosmogonical treatise. D.'s study of the circle's literature is rounded off by a couple of essays which trace the influence of Unique Cherub theology both on the main body of the Hasidei Ashkenaz and more widely on the Qabbalah. With characteristic caution he notes that it is impossible to fix with certainty the geographic location of the school and opts for northern France or western Germany. It still makes sense, however, to see it as part of a broader Rhenish Jewish mystical movement: its ideas were certainly perceived of later as being close to those of the Kalonymus school and in some cases they were passed down under the names of the Kalonymides. This is difficult, esoteric material by any standards. In D.'s lucid and masterful account it becomes accessible to all—students both of Jewish mysticism and mysticism in general. It will be welcomed not least by those who are trying to understand in an integrated way the spirituality of the middle Rhine in the age of Hildegard of Bingen.

P.S. ALEXANDER

DAVIES, W.D., *Christian Engagements with Judaism* (with a foreword by D.C. Allison, Jr; Harrisburg, PA: Trinity Press International, 1999), pp. xxx + 321. $29.00. ISBN 1-56338-268-7.

'This collection of essays', says D. in his preface, 'is a swan song in an almost lifelong endeavour for a deeper understanding of Judaism among Christians and of Christianity among Jews'. As with many swan songs, there is a considerable element of reprise: we have heard these melodies before, to our great profit. Three of the essays—one of them from 1997—show this author reflecting yet again on Paul and the Law; while five, of which two were published during the last decade, address more closely the subject announced by the collection's title. One study (1996) shows him in less predictable territory: he argues that not only 'the Jewish background of the Gospel of John' but also its 'foreground'—the vigorously active Jewish groups with which this gospel was contemporary—must be given due attention. We should be grateful to this distinguished near-nonagenarian for his determination to 'gather up [these] fragments', dispersed mainly in publications which are not easily accessible, 'that nothing be lost'.

C.J.A. HICKLING

DEUTSCH, NATHANIEL, *Guardians of the Gate: Angelic Vice Regency in Late Antiquity* (Brill's Series in Jewish Studies, 22; Leiden–Boston–Cologne: E.J. Brill, 1999), pp. xi + 182. Nlg 119.00/$67.00. ISBN 90-04-10909-9.

The angelic vice regent is defined as the figure who mediates between God and the world, with functions of judge, governor, guardian, priest and sometimes hypostatic or demiurgical figure. Mediation in late antiquity is discussed in the first chapter. After that the Jewish figures of Metatron and Akatriel, the Mandean figure of Abathur, and the Gnostic Sabaoth are looked at in detail. One of the concerns is the relationship between Merkavah Mysticism, Ghosticism and Mandeism. Surprisingly, Philo's Logos and the various Jewish traditions about the figure of wisdom are ignored.

ED.

DONFRIED, KARL P. and PETER RICHARDSON (eds.), *Judaism and Christianity in First-Century Rome* (Grand Rapids, MI: Eerdmans, 1998; distributed in the UK by Alban Books, Bristol), pp. xiv + 329. $24.00/£15.99. IBSN 0-8028-4265-8.

The essays collected here arose out of an SNTS seminar on NT Texts and their Environment. D. gives an introductory essay which summarizes and relates the papers to one another. Part 1 on Archaeological and Epigraphic Studies has two articles on synagogues (in Rome and Ostia) and one on the interaction of Jews with non-Jews in Rome. Part 2 on Social-Historical Studies: Roman policy towards the Jews and first-century expulsions, Jewish and Christian families, and two articles on early Christianity. Part 3 on Development Studies: an article on the impact of the Romans on Jewish–Christian relations and two articles on Christianity.

ED.

EBER, IRENE, *The Jewish Bishop and the Chinese Bible: S.I.J. Schereschewsky (1831–1906)* (Studies in Christian Mission, 22; Leiden–New York–Cologne: E.J. Brill, 1999), pp. xvi + 287 + 8 plates. Nlg 184.00/$108.25. ISBN 90-04-11266-9; ISSN 0924-9389.

This historical biography of Samuel Shereschewsky is a fascinating account of the life of an orthodox Jewish convert from Lithuania who became the translator of the Hebrew Bible into Mandarin (1875), the Episcopalian bishop of Shanghai and founder of St John's University. E. traces this transcultural story from Taurage to Zhitomir, Breslau, New York, Allegheny City, Shanghai, Beijing, Tokyo and Cambridge, MA. Distinctive in Schereschewsky's life is his translation of the Old Testament into Mandarin (*guoyu*) from the original Hebrew, rather than via the Vulgate, Septuagint or English. In both his translation and accompanying notes, he clearly drew on his rabbinical training, citing Rashi, Ibn Ezra and the midrashim. For example, he followed Onqelos and Rashi in rendering נְבִיאֶךָ of Exod. 7.1 not as Aaron 'your prophet' but as נִיב שְׂפָתִים 'utterance of the lips'. E. provides a selective, but representative set of examples to illustrate how Schereschewsky translated *ut orator*. Her discussion is insightful, although one might wonder whether there are alternative exegetical explanations for some of them. E. has written a masterful account of one of Schereschewsky's great achievements. One wonders, however, whether the founding of St John's University, dubbed by some as 'the Eton of the East', would not rank alongside his translation of the OT into Mandarin.

T.H. LIM

FARMER, WILLIAM R. (ed.), *Anti-Judaism and the Gospels* (Harrisburg, PA: Trinity Press International, 1999), pp. viii + 311. $24.00. ISBN 1-56338-270-9.

To evaluate the question of anti-Judaism in the NT is a difficult task. This collection attempts to do so by five papers (on Matthew, Luke, John, 'something greater than the temple', and critical study of the Gospels), each accompanied by two responses. The editor gives an introduction, and E.P. Sanders adds concluding reflections on the subject in the NT and Christianity.

ED.

FINE, STEVEN, *This Holy Place: On the Sanctity of the Synagogue during the Greco-Roman Period* (Christianity and Judaism in Antiquity, 11; Notre Dame, IN: University of Notre Dame Press, 1997), pp. ix + 280. £24.00. ISBN 0-268-04206-3.

This interestingly written book presents a vast collection of literary, epigraphic and archaeological evidence charting the process by which the synagogue institution acquired its sanctity. Each concluding with a useful summary, F.'s five chapters present the evidence of vital developments in verbal descriptions and iconographic decorations taking place, in stages, through the first five centuries CE and show how the meeting houses and study houses of Jews became designated as 'holy places' through the application of a mounting corpus of symbolic codes, including what F. characterizes as *imitatio templi*. The material presented is massive, yet thoroughly discussed in clear language but, perhaps because he is researching the process of development of attributed sanctity, F. tends to remain within the perspective of the writers who supply his evidence—though he does from time to time identify idealizing tendencies and haggadic strands. Similarly, perhaps also as a consequence of the wealth of detail in the text, F. presents the abundant notes at the end of the book, rather than more easily accessibly at the foot of each page. Disappointingly too, there is no index of modern authors which makes searching for F.'s response to a particular scholar's work difficult.

H.A. McKay

FINE, STEVEN (ed.), *Jews, Christians, and Polytheists in the Ancient Synagogue: Cultural Interaction during the Greco-Roman Period* (Baltimore Studies in the History of Judaism; London and New York: Routledge, 1999), pp. xviii + 253. £50.00. ISBN 0-415-18247.

F.'s collection 'brings together an international team of historians of ancient Judaism, Christianity, and Samaritan religion' and 'explores the ways in which divergent ethnic, national and religious communities interacted with one another within the context of the synagogue'. The contents comprise: Common Judaism and the synagogue in the first century (E.P. Sanders), was the synagogue a place of sabbath worship before 70 CE? (Pieter W. van der Horst), the early history of public reading of the Torah (Lawrence H. Schiffman), the Rabbis and the non-existent monolithic synagogue (Stuart S. Miller), art in the synagogue: some Talmudic views (Joseph M. Baumgarten), the patriarchate and the ancient synagogue (Lee I. Levine), sage, priest, and poet: typologies of religious leadership in the ancient synagogue (Michael D. Schwartz), Samaritan synagogues and Jewish synagogues: similarities and differences (Reinhard Pummer), the synagogue within the Graeco-Roman city (Tessa Rajak), the Dura Europos synagogue, early Christian art, and religious life in Dura Europos (Robin M. Jensen), Jews, Christians and polytheists in late-antique Sardis (John S. Crawford), the Torah shrine in the ancient synagogue: another look at the evidence (Eric M. Meyers) and non-Jews in the synagogues of late-antique Palestine: rabbinic and archaeological evidence (Steven Fine). The textual descriptions are supported by relevant maps, illustrations and by notes at the end of each chapter; there is a subject index, but no bibliography.

H.A. McKay

FLINT, PETER W. and JAMES C. VANDERKAM (eds.), with the assistance of ANDREA E. ALVAREZ, *The Dead Sea Scrolls after Fifty Years: A Comprehensive Assessment*, II (Leiden–Boston–Cologne: E.J. Brill, 1999), pp. xxii + 816. Nlg 175.00/$98.00. ISBN (vol 2) 90-04-11061-5; (set) 90-04-10858-0.

Volume 1 was reviewed in *B.L.* 1999 (pp. 170-71). To avoid repetition, please note that unless otherwise indicated, the articles all relate to the Scrolls/Qumran. Part 1: Canon, Apocrypha, Pseudepigrapha: the canonical process (J.A. Sanders), Apocrypha and Pseudepigrapha (Flint). Part 2: Selected Topics in the Texts: com-

munity structures (C. Hempel), priesthood (R.A. Kugler), women (E. Schuller), repentance (B. Nitzan), holiness (J.A. Naudé), the purification liturgies (J.M. Baumgarten), calendars (U. Glessmer), horoscopes (M. Albani), demonology (P.S. Alexan-
der), prophets and prophecy (J.E. Bowley), eschatology and messianism (M.A.
Knibb), apocalypticism and literary genre (J.J. Collins), the *Temple Scroll* and the
New Jerusalem (F. García Martínez), heavenly ascents (J.R. Davila). Part 3: The
Scrolls and Judasim: identity and history of the community (VanderKam), others
and intra-Jewish polemic as reflected in the Scolls (S. Goranson), rabbinic Judaism
(L.H. Schiffman). Part 4: The Scrolls and Early Christianity: Jesus (C.A. Evans),
Paul (J.A. Fitzmyer), Book of Revelation (D.E. Aune). Appendix 1 gives an updated
index to biblical passages in the Scrolls (E. Ulrich); appendix 2, an index of Apocrypha and (previously known) Pseudepigrapha passages (Flint); appendix 3, a list of
texts from the Judaean Desert, along with the *editio princeps* in each case (E. Tov).

ED.

FRICK, PETER, *Divine Providence in Philo of Alexandria* (Texte und Studien zum
Antiken Judentum, 77; Tübingen: J.C.B. Mohr [Paul Siebeck], 1999), pp. xiii + 220.
DM 148.00. ISBN 3-16-147141-5; ISSN 0721-8753.

Divine providence is an important concept to Philo: the word *pronoia* is used 66
times in his writings (though not the only word to express the concept). F. begins
with *De Opificio Mundi* 170-72 as a pivotal passage. He relates it to Philo's theory
of creation (ch. 3) and also examines the question of 'astral fatalism', i.e., the view
that fate was determined by the stars, concluding that Philo did not accept the belief
(ch. 4). The next chapter is on the question of theodicy (in which God's causation
of evil is firmly rejected) and the final chapter on 'providence and history'. In his
Legatio ad Gaium Philo had cause to be thankful for God's providence from his
own traumatic experience.

ED.

FRIEDLANDER, ALBERT H. and JONATHAN MAGONET (eds.), *European Judaism: A
Journal for the New Europe*, vol. 32/1 = issue 62 (New York and Oxford: Berghahn,
1999), pp. 1-162. £60.00/$90.00 p.a. ISSN 0014-3006.

This particular issue is on the theme, Recovering the Hebrew Bible. A number of
the essays have arisen out of a Jewish-Christian Bible week held in Germany in
1999. The articles are divided into sections: Politics: Esther Revisited (two articles
on Esther), Psychology: Prophets on the Couch (Isaiah 53; a psychoanalysis of
Jeremiah; Jer. 20.7-18; Hos. 1–3), Spirituality: Visions of Ezekiel (Ezek. 37; Ezek. 1
and its role in mysticism), Literature: Other Stages (1 Kgs 1; translating Ezekiel
into English; Jeremiah as a literary source for twentieth-century Germany), Scholarship: In Pursuit of History (Ezekiel and his times; God, Israel, covenant in Deuteronomy).

ED.

Die Geschichten des Rabbi Nachman, retold by MARTIN BUBER (with an afterword by Paul Mendes-Flohr; Gütersloh: Gütersloher Verlagshaus, 1999), pp. 160. DM 24.80/AS 181/SwF 23.50. ISBN 3-579-02235-0.

This beautifully produced and delightfully illustrated book presents six tales told by one of the most famous of early Hasidic leaders, Rabbi Nachman of Bratzlav (1772–1810). His short stories have long been regarded as classics of their kind, and those presented here include some of the best known: The Ox and the Ram; The Rabbi and his Son; The King's Son and the Maiden's Son; The Master of Prayer; and The Seven Beggars. A preface introduces R. Nachman and briefly expounds the kind of mystical tradition which he represents; and a *Nachwort* by Paul Mendes-Flohr traces the transmission of and interest in these stories by later Jewish scholars, and their place in Martin Buber's representation of the Hasidic masters and their stories.

C.T.R. HAYWARD

GIENIUSZ, ANDRZEJ, CR, *Romans 8:18-30: 'Suffering does not Thwart the Future Glory'* (University of South Florida International Studies in Formative Christianity and Judaism, 9; Atlanta: Scholars Press, 1999), pp. xiv + 339. $39.95. ISBN 0-7885-0546-7.

This book explores the difficulties of understanding Rom. 8.19-30. The author takes a literary-rhetorical approach to the text, offering (he says) a method that is sensitive to philological, literary, epistemological, rhetorical and theological aspects of the text. He argues that Paul's reasoning in Rom. 8.18-30 belongs to a major unit of the argument which begins at 8.1, which is itself a sub-point of the main *propositio* which is Rom. 5.20-21. He also argues that Rom. 8.18 is pivotal in both the immediate passage (Rom. 8.1ff.) and in the wider unit (Rom. 5–8). The author comes up with a novel interpretation of v. 18 (which is quoted in the title to the book) from classical and Hellenistic Greek and shows how Rom. 8.18-30 fits into a coherent and identifiable rhetorical structure to this part of Paul's letter. This book is unlikely to be of immediate interest to OT scholars.

A. BASH

GOLDBERG, ARNOLD, *Mystik und Theologie des rabbinischen Judentums: Gesammelte Studien I* (ed. M. Schlüter and P. Schäfer; Texte und Studien zum Antiken Judentum, 61; Tübingen: J.C.B. Mohr [Paul Siebeck] 1998), pp. xxiii + 457. DM 278.00. IBSN 3-16-146633-0; ISSN 0721-8753.

GOLDBERG, ARNOLD, *Rabbinische Texte als Gegenstand der Auslegung: Gesammelte Studien II* (ed. M. Schlüter and P. Schäfer; Texte und Studien zum Antiken Judentum, 73; Tübingen: J.C.B. Mohr [Paul Siebeck], 1999), pp. viii + 463. DM 278.00. ISBN 3-16-147042-7; ISSN 0721-8753.

The late Arnold Goldberg was a major influence on the revival of Jewish Studies in Germany in the post-war era. His most original contribution, represented here by the essays in the second volume, was in the field of midrash, where he developed a

highly formal and precise method of analysis, which has been carried on with notable success by younger researchers such as Alexander Samely and Lieve Teugels.
He also did some excellent work on early Jewish mysticism (the Heikhalot literature and related texts) and on early rabbinic theology, which is represented here by
the essays in the first volume. That G. is not as well known as he should be is due to
a number of factors. He writes, particularly on midrash, in highly technical, even id-
iosyncratic German, which is not easy to follow even for German speakers (only
one piece by him has ever appeared in English). Most of his articles were published
in the *Frankfurter Judaistische Beiträge* and in *Judaica*, hardly the most widely circulated of Jewish studies periodicals. And his thinking is always rigorous and
uncompromising and demands the closest of attention from the reader. The editors
provide an excellent overview of his work in the introduction to vol. 1. They are to
be congratulated for producing this fine collection, which includes a hitherto unpublished major study of *Re'uyot Yehezqe'el* (vol. 1, pp. 93-147). These volumes are a
fitting tribute to a scholar of stature. It would be worth selecting from them a number of representative articles and translating them, together with the editors' introduction, into English.

P.S. ALEXANDER

GOODMAN, LENN E., *Judaism, Human Rights and Human Values* (Oxford: Oxford
University Press, 1998), pp. xxi + 202. £32.00. ISBN 0-19-511834-0.

This is the second appearance in the *B.L.* of a work by the well-known American
philosopher Lenn Goodman, perhaps even less justified than the first (*B.L.* 1997, pp.
92-93), but nonetheless one that will interest and inform anyone concerned with the
role of Scripture in the contemporary world. Described on the cover as 'an incisive
contemporary dialogue between reason and revelation', it is rooted both in the traditional biblical, rabbinic and mediaeval Jewish (and Arabic) sources, and in the
metaphysical idea of deserts which G. has developed in *On Justice* (1991) and *God
of Abraham* (1996). He focuses on four broad topics 'Judaism and Human rights',
'Abortion and the Emergence of Life', 'Liberty' and 'The Rights and Wrongs of
Nations', and illustrates how it is possible for a philosopher, no less than a halakhist,
to take Scripture seriously in its application to contemporary ethical and political
issues.

J.F.A. SAWYER

GÖRG, MANFRED, *In Abraham's Bosom: Christianity without the New Testament*
(trans. Linda M. Maloney; Collegeville, MN: Liturgical Press, 1999), pp. xiii + 146.
$14.95. ISBN 0-8146-2886-9.

This booklet collects some loosely related *disjecta membra* presented on what
was evidently some very informal university-sponsored occasion in Munich. The
eye-catching subtitle is misleading: 'the New Testament' features in the caption of
only a short second of two parts of the book, and offers brief and unexciting observations on the name 'Jesus', Messiahship, and the Son of Man title. The first part is
more explicitly a contribution to the conversation between Jews and Christians: the

Old Testament (*sic*, even though G. confines himself exclusively to the Hebrew canon) is asserted to belong to Jews, and the appropriation of it by Christians is traced in broad overview and with disapproval. A long section deals with the history of his own subject during the Nazi period; it is uncomfortable to be reminded how many household names were working, if not publishing, during that time. In all, this is a curious contribution, in both form and substance, from the occupant of a chair in OT theology.

C.J.A. HICKLING

GRADWOHL, ROLAND, *Was ist der Talmud? Einführung in die 'Mündliche Tradition' Israels* (Calwer Taschenbibliothek, 2; Stuttgart: Calwer, 1999), pp. 80. DM 15.80/SwF 15.20/AS 115. ISBN 3-7668-3615-3.

With the aim of introducing non-Jews to the 'Talmud', the late G. gives a simplified overview that shows little engagement with methodological developments in the past several decades. His historical survey, for example, makes no distinction between data from the Babylonian Talmud, Josephus or the NT, and the picture that emerges reminds one of G.F. Moore or more especially his successors of lesser stature. With the still common misunderstandings about rabbinic literature among ordinary Christians, one can sympathize with G.'s somewhat apologetic concerns, and he probably succeeds in correcting some biased views about Judaism. This is not the introduction to recommend to students or enquirers, however.

ED.

HALLAMISH, MOSHE, *An Introduction to the Kabbalah* (trans. R. Bar-Ilan and O. Wiskind-Elper; SUNY Series in Judaica: Hermeneutics, Mysticism, and Religion; Albany: State University of New York, 1999), pp. viii + 379. $27.95. ISBN 0-7914-4012-5.

Ever since Gershom Scholem demonstrated in *Major Trends in Jewish Mysticism* that mysticism played a leading role in the historical development of Judaism there has been a growing stream of introductions to the Qabbalah. This new one by H. has much to commend it. The author, who has a comprehensive knowledge of the primary literature, has chosen a broadly synchronic approach and illustrates certain central themes of the Qabbalah from texts which range from the Bahir to the writings of Moshe Hayyim Luzzato and the modern Hasidic masters. He divides the work into two parts. In Part 1 he deals with how one becomes a Qabbalist, the prerequisites which one needs, the preparations which one must undertake, the techniques for exploring the mysteries and the dangers which the adepts face. In Part 2 he surveys the differing views of leading Qabbalists on some of the basic concepts of the Qabbalah: the Sefirot, good and evil, creation, the Torah, the soul and transmigration. His synchronic approach will create some problems for the tyro, who may find it difficult to get a clear sense of the historical evolution of the Qabbalah. However, it has the undoubted advantage of allowing the reader to explore in depth the dynamic richness and inner logic of the Qabbalistic tradition. The subjects treated are somewhat selective. More should, perhaps, have been said about prayer and the performance of the *mitzvot,* and the references to messianism and escha-tolgy are decidedly thin. The work will be hard going for the beginner, who will not be helped by a rather inelegant translation from the Hebrew. However, those inter-ested in this fascinating and important tradition, which for some five centuries em-bodied Judaism's profoundest theological thinking, should rest assured that it is worth persevering and that close study will in the end pay handsome dividends.

P.S. ALEXANDER

HALPERN-AMARU, BETSY, *The Empowerment of Women in the Book of Jubilees* (Supplements to Journal for the Study of Judaism, 60; Leiden–Boston–Cologne: E.J. Brill, 1999), pp. x + 182. Nlg 115.00/$64.00. ISBN 90-04-11414-9; ISSN 1384-2161.

The main concern of this book is the *Book of Jubilees* and the sort of biblical in-terpretation found within it. Yet in its paraphrase and re-interpretation of Genesis, *Jubilees* gives women a more prominent role than in the original text. One impor-tant theme is the message that the 'moral quality of each generation is ultimately determined by the females who bear and wive its leaders' (p. 147). Women are also added to the Genesis genealogies because they are determiners of male character: the offspring of forbidden unions are the characters prone to go astray. The penulti-mate chapter outlines the interpretative techniques used in *Jubilees* to illucidate the Bible.

ED.

HAMILTON, ALASTAIR, *The Apocryphal Apocalypse: The Reception of the Second Book of Esdras (4 Ezra) from the Renaissance to the Enlightenment* (Oxford-War-burg Studies; Oxford: Clarendon Press, 1999), pp. xii + 393 + frontispiece. £50.00. ISBN 0-19-817521-3.

This is a fascinating account of the reception history of *2 Esdras*, which high-lights the complex relationship between texts and their interpreters. After a brief introduction and overview of the book, H. discusses its status and use in the period from the Renaissance to the Enlightenment. At first, a new sensitivity to questions of authenticity and a veneration of Jerome, led to *2 Esdras* being regarded as 'apoc-ryphal' and treated with contempt. However, the new biblical scholarship also re-sulted ultimately in criticism of the Vulgate and of Jerome, and in this new context some (e.g. Giovanni Pico della Mirandola) made out a case for its canonicity and consulted it as a source of prophecy. H. argues that these debates were then skewed in the first phase of the Reformation by larger questions of authority and intercon-fessional polemics. However, H. finds that *2 Esdras* did not become so much a coun-tersign between Protestants and Catholics, as 'an emblem', both for the many Protestants prepared to disagree with Luther on certain points (p. 299) and for mys-tics and pietists caught in the crossfire between Protestants and Catholics (e.g. Antoinette Bourignon, pp. 198, 299-300). In the climate of new criticism of the late seventeenth century, scholars studied *2 Esdras* as an interesting first-century doc-ument. In contrast, a dissenting minority, mostly anti-deists, were fascinated by its

claims to revelation and used it, not surprisingly, as a source of millenarian speculation. Spain is highlighted as a country where the book was influential. I therefore
found it fascinating to read of Columbus referring to it in his request for sponsor-
ship from Ferdinand and Isabella. H. also highlights the much more sinister use of
the text in the sixteenth- to eighteenth-century Spanish debates. Some said, in the
light of *2 Esd.* 13.39-47, that the American Indians were descendents of the lost
tribes of ancient Israel and should be treated accordingly (pp. 206-17)!

D.J. BRYAN

HAYES, CHRISTINE ELIZABETH, *Between the Babylonian and Palestinian Talmuds:
Accounting for Halakhic Difference in Selected Sugyot from Tractate Avodah
Zarah* (Oxford: Oxford University Press, 1997), pp. xvii + 270. £42.50. ISBN 0-19-
509884-6.

H. uses a detailed analysis of several *sugyot* from *Avodah Zarah* to investigate
the question of how much can be inferred from the halakhic differences between the
two Talmuds about the distinctive history of the two communities which produced
them. She criticizes previous researchers such as Ginzberg and Alon for assuming
that legal differences must reflect external social and cultural influences and for
ignoring the possibility that they may be the outcome of internal exegetical processes. She does not deny that history can be derived from these sources, but suggests that only texts in which 'the rabbis violate their own interpretive canons and
strategies' should be used for historical reconstruction. In other words, differences
between the Talmuds which involve different, but predictable, interpretations of the
Mishnah tell us nothing about the Palestinian and Babylonian Jewish communities
in late antiquity. There are problems with this analysis. All early Jewish literature,
both rabbinic and non-rabbinic, is broadly exegetical in character (as was much
philosophical, scientific and legal literature in late antiquity), so the issue which H.
addresses is by no means confined to the Talmuds. Are we to assume that we cannot derive any history from any of these texts, whenever they are following their
own hermeneutical codes? This is surely to misunderstand the nature of hermeneutics and of the act of reading, which are always influenced by external factors. The
whole thrust of modern textual analysis has been to problematize the concept of
pure exegesis. All exegesis involves choices and those choices are, arguably, always
influenced by external factors. The possibility therefore remains of identifying external influences even where the differing choices of the Yerushalmi and the Bavli
fall within the parameters of the Talmudic hermeneutical code. This said, H.'s
analysis is generally thorough and judicious. This volume is a welcome and valuable addition to a growing body of literature which treats Talmudic subjects in
English in a serious but accessible way. It is a 'must' for any student reading list.

P.S. ALEXANDER

HEDRICK, CHARLES W., *When History and Faith Collide: Studying Jesus* (Peabody,
MA: Hendrickson, 1999), pp. xix + 179. $16.95. ISBN 1-56563-235-4.

H. explores the tension between faith and critical study. He focuses specifically on the example of Jesus, but many of his principles—and indeed a number of his examples—relate to the OT as well. His first chapter, 'History and Faith', covers the subject generally and should be recommended to all students of the Bible.

ED.

HENGEL, MARTIN, *Judaica et Hellenistica: Kleine Schrift II* (with the assistance of Jörg Frey and Dorothea Betz, and appendices by Hanswulf Bloedhorn and Max Küchler; WUNT, 109; Tübingen: J.C.B. Mohr [Paul Siebeck], 1998), pp. x + 466. DM 278.00. ISBN 3-16-146847-3; ISSN 0340-9570.

Volume I was reviewed in *B.L.* 1998 (p. 188). The essays (all in German) include scriptural interpretation and scriptural development in the Second Temple period, on the history of the influence of Isaiah 53 in pre-Christian times, Jerusalem as a Jewish and Hellenistic city, the old and the new 'Schürer', earliest Christianity as Jewish messianic and universalistic movement, Matthew's sermon on the mount and its Jewish background, the Gospel of John as a source for the history of early Judaism, the LXX as a collection of writings claimed by Christians according to Justin and the pre-Origenic fathers. There is also an article by Max Küchler on Jn 5.2 in the light of archaeology, and an addenda to H.'s bibliography (1996–98).

ED.

HENGEL, MARTIN and C.K. BARRETT, *Conflicts and Challenges in Early Christianity* (ed. Donald A. Hagner; Harrisburg, PA: Trinity Press International, 1999), pp. viii + 103. $14.00. ISBN 1-56338-291-1.

This book arose out of lectures sponsored by Fuller Theological Seminary in Pasadena, California. H. discusses the relationship of Judaism to early Christianity, Christian writings as a source for early Judaism, and when Judaism and Christianity finally separated. B. addresses the questions of the council(s) in Galatians 2 and Acts 15. In the final chapter, members of the Fuller department of NT put questions to the two speakers, and their responses are recorded.

ED.

HEUSER, MANFRED and HANS-JOACHIM KLIMKEIT, *Studies in Manichaean Literature and Art* (Nag Hammadi and Manichaean Studies, 46; Leiden–Boston–Cologne: E.J. Brill, 1998), pp. xi + 331 + 32 figures. Nlg 222.50/$131.00. ISBN 90-04-10716-9; ISSN 0929-2470.

LIEU, SAMUEL N.C., *Manichaeism in Central Asia and China* (Nag Hammadi and Manichaean Studies, 45; Leiden–Boston–Cologne: E.J. Brill, 1998), pp. xiii + 258. Nlg 175.00/$103.00. ISBN 90-04-10405-4; ISSN 0929-2470.

MIRECKI, PAUL and JASON BEDUHN (eds.), *Emerging from Darkness: Studies in the Recovery of Manichaean Sources* (Nag Hammadi and Manichaean Studies, 43; Leiden–Boston–Cologne: E.J. Brill, 1997), pp. x + 294 + 10 plates. Nlg 209.00/$123.00. ISBN 90-04-10760-6; ISSN 0929-2470.

The relationship of Manicheism to early Judaism is a subject still needing a good deal of investigation, but that there is some connection is widely accepted (e.g., the *Book of Giants* and other Enoch literature). These studies focus on various aspects of Manicheism. The volume of Heuser and Klimkeit collects together the doctoral thesis of Heuser on the Manichaean myth (including eschatology) and a series of studies by Klimkeit (including use of Scripture). Lieu, who has established a significant reputation in the subject area (*B.L.* 1994, p. 144; 1995, p. 155), adds a collection of essays. The volume of Mirecki and BeDuhn is a collection of essays, one of which is on a Manichaean treatise on biblical exegesis. Unfortunately, only Lieu's volume has proper indexes which could guide the reader to discrete topics.

L.L. GRABBE

HIRSCHBERG, PETER, *Das eschatologische Israel: Untersuchungen zum Gottesvolkverständnis der Johannesoffenbarung* (WMANT, 84; Neukirchen-Vluyn: Neukirchener Verlag, 1999), pp. x + 340. DM 98.00/AS 715/SwF 89.00. ISBN 3-7887-1750-5.

The driving concern behind this study, based on a Tübingen doctoral dissertation, is whether the use of language and imagery of 'the people of God' implies fulfilment of, continuity with, or the displacement of Israel. While these questions are inspired by the modern concerns of Jewish–Christian dialogue and of Jewish-Christian identity, in which the author is involved, the book is careful not to project theological conceptions provoked by later historical developments back into this period and text. The careful and clear analysis focuses first on the epithet 'synagogue of Satan' in the letters to Smyrna and Philadelphia, then on the imagery of ch. 7, and thirdly on the 'new Jerusalem' of 21.1–22.5. The first section leads to a detailed study of the position of the Jews and of Christians in Asia Minor, as well as of the possible causes of conflict between them; this largely draws from recent work on the subject and follows a familiar 'safe' path. The other sections are based on careful exegesis which emphasizes the passages as reinterpreting earlier biblical texts and subsequent Jewish tradition, which themselves are treated to thorough analysis. While the study affirms the positive implications of the themes of continuity and fulfilment, it also acknowledges that the seer effectually excludes unbelieving Israel, and in the Conclusion evaluates the significance of this for subsequent and contemporary theological reflection. While not all will be persuaded by all the argument, the presentation and the attention to exegetical detail are models of clarity.

J. LIEU

HOLMGREN, FREDRICK C., *The Old Testament and the Significance of Jesus* (Foreword by W. Brueggemann; Grand Rapids, MI: Eerdmans, 1999; distributed in the UK by Alban Books, Bristol), pp. xviii + 204. $16.00/£9.99. ISBN 0-8028-4453-7.

In this rather bland contribution to Jewish–Christian dialogue, H. offers ten mostly unrelated chapters, consisting in turn of short and often only loosely connected sections, to convince us that Jewish readings of various passages in the OT are as fruitful as Christian equivalents have been. Familiar ground is retrodden in somewhat broad reflections on the promise-fulfilment schema, and adjacent to them are some thoughts on 'creative' or 'depth' exegesis; but the author takes us little further than what in a Qumran context would be called 'pesher' application of texts. Closing chapters on the emergence of high christological assessment of Jesus make predictable but unexplored statements about the figure of wisdom in the OT as an important Jewish contribution. There is no bibliography, though the footnotes allude to a wide range of both Christian and Jewish writing related to the debate.

C.J.A. HICKLING

HÜBNER, HANS, *Die Weisheit Salomons: Liber Sapientiae Salomonis* (Das Alte Testament Deutsch, Apokryphen, 4; Göttingen: Vandenhoeck & Ruprecht, 1999), pp. 227. DM 42.00. ISBN 3-525-51404-2.

The author claims this book as the first evangelical commentary on the book of Wisdom in German from a Protestant hand since 1938. H. therefore tries to cater for specialist and non-specialist alike. In fact he seems to 'round up' the work of the last 60 years adequately, referring to Spanish, French and, particularly, Scarpat's work in Italian, much of which is scattered in articles in various journals. For H. the place of origin is deeply significant—Alexandria—because Alexandria around the time of Christ was an important meeting place for Greek and Oriental ideas. That would also account for the attack on Egyptian idolatry in the second part of the book (though the lack of more supporting geographical or historical evidence in the book is strange). The date is discussed in some detail, and Paul's presumed use of it is mentioned. As the book seeks to serve technical and non-technical readers alike, Greek script is kept to the footnotes. H. finds the book of Wisdom to be 'the most theological book in the Apocrypha'. He draws out many comparisons with Stoic and Platonic thought, tracing the technical terms. A useful book, and one would like to see such a discussion of Wisdom's philosophical thought in English.

J.G. SNAITH

KRASSEN, MILES (ed.), *Isaiah Horowitz, the Generations of Adam* (preface by Elliot R. Wolfson; The Classics of Western Spirituality; New York and Mahwah, NJ: Paulist Press, 1996), pp. xiv + 449. $24.95. ISBN 0-8091-3590-6.

Isaiah Horowitz (d. 1626) is remembered as the author of the encyclopaedic *Two Tablets of the Covenant (Sheney Luhot ha-Berit)*, one of the masterworks of Jewish writing of its day, and a text which combines to a remarkable degree the Ashkenazic intellectual tradition in which he was brought up (and notably the dialectical form of Talmudic study known as *pilpul*) with the Lurianic Kabbalah which developed in Safed during the sixteenth century. *The Generations of Adam (Toledot Adam)* forms the introduction to the *Two Tablets*, but it can be read in its own right as an introduction to the main topics of Jewish theology. Despite its heavy and somewhat repetitious style (well conveyed in this English translation by K.) and the extensive quotations from earlier authorities, this work, very influential in its time, is not without a certain interest today.

N.R.M. DE LANGE

KUGLER, ROBERT A., and EILEEN M. SCHULLER (eds.), *The Dead Sea Scrolls at Fifty: Proceedings of the 1997 Society of Biblical Literature Qumran Section Meetings* (SBL Early Judaism and Its Literature, 15; Atlanta: Scholars Press, 1999), pp. viii + 227 + 7 plates. $49.95. ISBN 0-7885-0543-2.

This mis-titled (*The Dead Sea Scrolls Research at Fifty* instead?) volume publishes the papers that were given at the SBL annual meeting in 1997 to mark the jubilee of the discovery of the Qumran scrolls. The papers and responses are published basically in the form in which they were presented: the plenary papers are popular and entertaining; the history of Qumran scholarship contributions consist of a statement and responses (misreadings and all); and the sessional discussions on the *editio princeps* of the *Damascus Document* are narrowly defined. As presented by Qumran specialists primarily of the 'second generation', the scholarly value of these contributions vary widely from the quaint to the insightful. There is also quite a bit of repetition and overlap as would be expected from a collected but lightly edited volume. From the cis-Atlantic perspective, the contributions by García Martínez and Trebolle Barrera on European scholarship and Tov on Israeli scholarship are useful overviews, although there are notable omissions on the British and Scandinavian scene and the French school in Jerusalem. Also, there is no specific paper devoted to American (and Canadian) scholarship. I would highlight the responses by Newsom and especially Collins to Nickelsburg's discussion of currents in Qumran scholarship as particularly stimulating, even if both are constrained by time and format to be little more than extended sound bites.

T.H. LIM

LAMBRECHT, JAN, *Second Corinthians* (Sacra Pagina, 8; Collegeville, MN: Liturgical Press, 1999), pp. xiii + 250. $29.95. ISBN 0-8146-5810-5.

This commentary is a useful general commentary serving as an introduction to 2 Corinthians. The commentary is suitable for the student with no knowledge of Greek or Hebrew. There is little strikingly new in the commentary. The brief introduction (pp. 1-16) sets the context for the rest of the commentary. There are enough leads in the bibliographies for the serious student to find out more. The author's exploration of the Jewish background of Paul's thought and its influence on 2 Corinthians is minimal (e.g. p. 108 n. 2: 'Paul considers Scripture as relevant to his own day.'). The consideration of Isa. 49.8 (pp. 111-12) is basic; basic also are the sections on the Jewish background to the idea of reconciliation (2 Cor. 5.18-20), on Moses, on the new covenant and on *doxa* (glory). Nevertheless, this commentary is a good basic introduction to 2 Corinthians with a bibliography that is international in its scope.

A. BASH

LANGE, NICHOLAS DE, *An Introduction to Judaism* (Cambridge: Cambridge University Press, 2000), pp. xxii (including 7 maps) + 247. £37.50/$54.95; paper £13.95/$19.95. ISBN 0-521-46073-5; (paper) 0-521-46624-5

L. wrote a widely used introduction, entitled *Judaism*, in 1986. The present book seems to be intended as a replacement for it (though the other book does not appear to be referred to here), and is a more substantial volume. One useful feature is a detailed glossary of terms. Those who teach introductory courses in Judaism will welcome this inexpensive volume which can be easily used as a text.

ED.

LESSES, REBECCA MACY, *Ritual Practices to Gain Power: Angels, Incantations, and Revelation in Early Jewish Mysticism* (Harvard Theological Studies, 44; Harrisburg, PA: Trinity Press International, 1998), pp. xvii + 429. $22.00. ISBN 1-56338-219-9.

The Heikhalot literature remains one of the most puzzling products of late antique Judaism. Debate still rages as to whether we should regard these texts as purely imaginative literary creations, or as the remains of a geniunely mystical movement of adepts who tried to put their ideas into practice. L. comes down firmly in favour of seeing real mystical and magical praxis behind the texts. She argues this from a close analysis of the adjurations of angels which are scattered liberally throughout the Heikhalot corpus, claiming that these should be read as instructions for the performance of rituals aimed at acquiring power of various kinds. Central to her case is a comparison of Heikhalot adjurations and their associated ascetic practices with ritual practices attested in the Greek magical papyri and in the Aramaic incantation bowls. The similarities are striking, though there are also differences: the Greek texts are fuller and more precise about the rituals (and therefore more practically useful); the Heikhalot texts seem to display more literary artifice. L.'s analysis of the adjurations is full and persuasive and advances our understanding of these difficult texts. However, her analysis of the social setting of these adjurations of the circles which used them could, perhaps, have been a little fuller and more incisive. To categorize the adjurations as 'ritual practices to gain power' raises obvious sociological and political questions. Were the practitioners of this ritual in any way challenging the religious or political establishment of the societies to which they belonged? What exactly is the relationship of these circles to the rabbinic movement? L. discusses at some length Gruenwald's comparison of the Heikhalot texts with the practices of the Elchasaites and other Mesopotamian baptist sects, but decides that the parallels are not all that significant. In the end she leaves the Heikhalot mystics rather sociologically hanging in the air. However, overall this is a sterling piece of work, a major contribution to the study of Judaism in late antiquity.

P.S. ALEXANDER

LEVINE, LEE I., *The Ancient Synagogue: The First Thousand Years* (New Haven and London: Yale University Press, 2000), pp. xvi + 748. $60.00/£45.00. ISBN 0-300-07475-1.

KEE, HOWARD CLARK and LYNN H. COHICK (eds.), *Evolution of the Synagogue: Problems and Progress* (Harrisburg, PA: Trinity Press International, 1999), pp. viii + 183. $17.00. ISBN 1-56338-296-2.

An explosion of books about the synagogue has occurred in the past few years (e.g. pp. 138 and 182-83 above). The two books here continue the debate and confirm a number of recent trends, especially the late origin of the synagogue in Palestine. Levine has wrestled with the problem for many years and here synthesizes his vast knowledge into one of the largest studies of the subject available. It demonstrates his judicious conclusions with regard to various aspects of the debate, but other points of view are catalogued and acknowledged. The set of essays edited by Kee and Cohick has some very interesting studies. Kee continues his assault on the Theodotus inscription. It must be said that not many are so far convinced, and he seems to feel the need to attack those who actually provide support for his more general position. James Strange finds archaeological evidence of four synagogues in pre-70 Palestine. Richard Horsley discusses the synagogue in Galilee and the gospels, arguing that the synagogue was primarily a local assembly for local self-government. In an important study Shaye Cohen investigates seven ancient passages with the questions of whether Pharisees and rabbis were leaders of communal prayer and Torah study, concluding in the negative. A number of the other essays focus on later data about the synagogue in antiquity.

L.L. GRABBE

LIESEN, JAN, *Full of Praise: An Exegetical Study of Sir. 39,12-35* (Supplements to Journal for the Study of Judaism, 64; Leiden–Boston–Cologne: E.J. Brill, 2000), pp. xii + 341. Nlg 165.00/$97.50. ISBN 90-04-11359-2; ISSN 1384-2161.

This study of a hymnic passage immediately following the famous passage on the 'sage' (39.1-11) was originally done as a doctoral thesis under M. Gilbert at the Pontifical Biblical Institute in 1997. The first chapter covers introductory matters of textual criticism, method, and the like. Chapter 2 looks at the immediate context, the structure of the passage, and the relationship of the passage to the wider context. Chapter 3 is on the 'protagonists', since the various verbs in 39.12-15 and 39.32-35 are taken to refer to the activities of different persons, namely, the sage and his disciples; there is therefore an autobiographical element in the passage. Chapter 4 is on the concept of fullness (*ml'*), which explains the relationship between wisdom, the law, and Ben Sira himself. The wisdom hymn of 39.16-31 is treated in ch. 5. The textual variations suggest that the Hebrew text was created by some editing which showed a particular concern for eschatology. The educational strategy that emerges includes the practice of praise. Two concepts of the 'work of God' occur: a double creation (which includes both blessings and punishments) and the saving acts of God in history.

ED.

LOHSE, EDUARD and GÜNTER MAYER (eds.), *Die Tosefta, Seder I: Zeraim 1.1 Berakot–Pea* (Rabbinische Texte: Reihe 1; Stuttgart–Berlin–Cologne: Kohlhammer, 1999), pp. vii + 198. DM 368.00/AS 2686/SwF 328.00/Eur 188.16. ISBN 3-17-013610-0.

This volume offers an accurate translation with notes of the Erfurt manuscript of the Tosefta to the tractates *Berakhot* and *Pea*. The notes, though extensive, helpful and well informed, are in the nature of discrete glosses which deal with philological and linguistic matters, with realia, with theological points of interest and with significant parallels in rabbinic and other early Jewish texts. Little is said about the literary structure of the tractates and of their relationship to the Mishnah. When this long-running translation first began in the 1950s, glossing was the standard form of commentating on rabbinic texts, but fashions have changed and scholarship, thanks largely to the work of Jacob Neusner, is now more sensitive to literary questions. It seems a little perverse to retain the old outdated format for the series when at least a gesture to contemporary concerns could be made by expanding the general introduction to each tractate. The volume concludes with an excellent series of indices which include biblical references, rabbinic and geographical proper-names, a highly useful *Sachregister*, a register of Hebrew terms and phases, and lists of Greek and Latin loanwords.

P.S. ALEXANDER

LONGENECKER, RICHARD N., *Biblical Exegesis in the Apostolic Period* (Grand Rapids, MI, and Cambridge: Eerdmans; Vancouver: Regent College Publishing, 2nd edn, 1999), pp. xli + 238. $20.00. ISBN (Eerdmans) 0-8028-4301-8; (Regent) 1-57383-074-7.

This is a straightforward reprint of the 1975 edition with a 30-page introduction to bring it up to date. The main concern is NT exegesis, but the chapter on Jewish exegesis in the original edition was rather simplistic, and the new introduction does little to correct this situation. Although some of the more recent bibliography on rabbinic midrash and on the Dead Sea Scrolls is noted, there is no indication of the significant work being done on biblical interpretation in other areas, such as on the LXX and Philo. There is a strong indication that the author is not very *au fait* with what has been happening in Jewish studies in the past three decades.

ED.

MCDONOUGH, SEAN M., *YHWH at Patmos: Rev. 1:4 in its Hellenistic and Early Jewish Setting* (WUNT, 2, Reihe 107; Tübingen: J.C.B. Mohr [Paul Siebeck], 1999), pp. x + 276. DM 98.00. ISBN 3-16-147055-9; ISSN 0340-9570.

The greater part of this revised St Andrews thesis is concerned with exploring the background of the divine name in the greeting of Rev. 1.4, taken as a reflection on the divine name as revealed in Exod. 3.14, and so will be of considerable interest to readers of the *B.L.* The first chapter focuses on Greek philosophical discussion of 'Being' and on uses of the threefold formula particularly in connection with the worship of Aion and with Isis in Plutarch. Next M. discusses the evidence for a developing avoidance of the divine name, arguing for a greater knowledge than sometimes assumed, particularly with the (mis-) pronunciation *Yao*; he then explores the way the term was interpreted, both in association with themes of redemption and creation in contrast to the idols, and in addressing more Greek concepts of 'Being'. The analysis ranges widely through biblical texts, Qumran, Apocrypha and Pseudepigrapha, Josephus, Philo, magical texts, rabbinical literature, and the NT;

inevitably there is an unevenness in treatment, some passages being discussed in considerable detail, while at other times sweeping or incautious statements are made, suggesting the author is not always in total control of his material—which is understandable in view of its breadth. The last part of the book analyses Rev. 1.4 and its meaning against this background and within its literary context. In its systematic and industrious approach the book retains the hall-marks of a thesis committed more to a thorough coverage of the material and questions than to a radical reading or fluent narrative; as such it serves its purpose well and will be much consulted.

J. LIEU

MCKNIGHT, SCOT, *A New Vision for Israel: The Teachings of Jesus in National Context* (Studying the Historical Jesus Series; Grand Rapids, MI: Eerdmans, 1999; distributed in the UK by Alban Books, Bristol), pp. xiv + 263. $21.00/£12.99. ISBN 0-8028-4212-7.

This is another American attempt to see Jesus in his original cultural context. After a general introduction, M. devotes his first main chapter to God, correctly seen as central to Jesus' whole life. Two chapters on the kingdom now present and the kingdom yet to come show a good grasp of the broad overarching nature of this term. Two final chapters lay out Jesus' ethical teaching in a Jewish context. The whole book displays detailed acquaintance with selected secondary literature, and genuine familiarity with the synoptic Gospels in Greek. The author does not, however, seem fully familiar with Jewish sources in their original languages. Traditional mistakes include Jesus avoiding *Elohim* (p. 27), and 'nests' at Lk. 9.58 (p. 32). Selected Christian secondary literature is used to interpret Mt. 10.23, Mk 9.1 and Mk 13.24-27 as predictions of the fall of Jerusalem (pp. 133-43), seen as God's just judgment on Israel in accordance with the teaching of Jesus. What ethics! The achievement of the author's stated aims will require greater learning, with less absorption in Christian traditions. In the meantime, scholars interested in the relationship between Jesus and Judaism will find some steps forward in some parts of this book.

P.M. CASEY

MEYNET, ROLAND, *Jésus passe: Testament, jugement, exécution et résurrection du Seigneur Jésus dans les évangiles synoptiques* (Rhétorique biblique, 3; Paris: Cerf; Rome: PUG Editrice, 1999), pp. 489. FF 270/Lire 75,000. ISBN (Cerf) 2-204-06315-0; (PUG) 88-7652-816-4.

This is a rhetorical—with an exegetical and theological emphasis—reading of the Synoptic Passion narratives, starting with Matthew despite a nominal nod in the direction of Markan priority, and is part of a series of such readings by the same author. The generous font size, frequent tables, and use of a variety of fonts and type forms to demonstrate parallels and internal structure promise much, but few conclusions or significant insights are drawn in the accompanying commentary. There is no historical analysis, and the exegesis is almost entirely an internal explication of the narrative; the minimal references to setting say only the obvious. Thus this volume will not be of immediate interest to most readers of the *B.L.*

J. LIEU

MOESSNER, DAVID P. (ed.), *Jesus and the Heritage of Israel: Luke's Narrative Claim upon Israel's Legacy* (Luke the Interpreter of Israel, 1; Harrisburg, PA: Trinity Press International, 1999), pp. xii + 395. $40.00. ISBN 1-56338-293-8.

This includes essays on Israel's heritage and claims upon the genre(s) of Luke and Acts, promise and fulfilment in Hellenistic Jewish narratives, Acts and the fragments of Hellenistic Jewish historians, the legitimation of the Jewish Diaspora and early Christian mission, Israel's future and the delay of the parousia according to Luke, the story of Israel in the Lukan narrative, 'Israel' and the story of salvation.

ED.

MORALDI, LUIGI (trans.), *Antichità Giudaiche di Giuseppe Flavio: II Libri XI–XX* (Classici delle religioni: La religione ebraica; Torin: Unione Tipografico-Editrice Torinese, 1998), pp. 650-1328. N.P. ISBN 88-02-05252-2.

This second and final volume of a modern, very readable and nicely produced Italian translation of Josephus's *Antiquities* is lightly annotated. The notes are mainly explanatory or concerned with parallels from the Hebrew Bible or Josephus's other works. There are useful indices and a convenient analytical list of the contents of *Antiquities* XI–XX book by book.

T. RAJAK

MUSSNER, FRANZ, *Jesus von Nazareth im Umfeld Israels und der Urkirche: Gesammelte Aufsätze* (ed. Michael Theobald; WUNT, 111; Tübingen: J.C.B. Mohr [Paul Siebeck], 1999), pp. viii + 368. DM 138.00. ISBN 3-16-146973-9; ISSN 0340-9570.

This collection of essays (all in German) shows a particular focus on issues relating to Jewish–Christian dialogue. There is a section of three essays on the question of 'Jesus the Jew'. Other essays are on Israel and the origin of the gospel, the question of what the Jews have to do with Christian ecumenism, and Jesus the Jew and the Shoah. One essay is on 'JHWH the *sub contrario* acting God of Israel' (with reference to a statement of Martin Luther's that God hides himself by doing the opposite of human expectations).

ED.

NEUBRAND, MARIA, *Abraham—Vater von Juden und Nichtjuden: Ein exegetische Studie zu Röm 4* (FzB, 85; Würzburg: Echter Verlag, 1997), pp. xiii + 329. DM 48.00/AS 350/SwF 46.00. ISBN 3-429-01978-8; ISSN 0935-0764.

This monograph, based on a 1996–97 dissertation at the Catholic Theological Faculty of the Ludwig-Maximilians University at Munich, fulfils precisely the task set by its title. The main part of the book is a detailed exegesis of Romans 4 set within a context both of the preceding chapters of the letter, and of current scholarly debate. The wider context is current Jewish–Christian dialogue and the responsibility 'after Auschwitz' to avoid any form of 'anti-Judaism'. Those who share this context will regret the epistolary setting as being only the preceding and not the subsequent chapters of Romans; readers of the *B.L.* will note the absence of almost any reference to relevant Jewish traditions of practice and exegesis—the few potential exceptions, the discussion of Gen. 15.6 in the context of Genesis 15, of Paul's argument in the light of rabbinic midrash, and of circumcision as a mark of Jewish identity, are heavily dependent on secondary literature. This approach obviously has its value in encouraging an exegetical theological engagement with the implications of Pauline theology, but its limitations in encouraging dialogue and understanding are evident.

J. LIEU

NEUSNER, JACOB, *The Mishnah: Religious Perspectives* (Handbuch der Orientalistik: Erste Abteilung, Der Nahe und Mittlere Osten: 45. Band; Leiden–Boston–Cologne: E.J. Brill, 1999), pp. xii + 249. Nlg 165.28/$92.00. ISBN 90-04-11492-0; ISSN 0169-9423.

NEUSNER, JACOB, *The Mishnah: Social Perspectives* (Handbuch der Orientalistik: Erste Abteilung, Der Nahe und Mittlere Osten: 46. Band; Leiden–Boston–Cologne: E.J. Brill, 1999), pp. xviii + 267. Nlg 176.30/$98.00. ISBN 90-04-11491-2; ISSN 0169-9423.

These two volumes form a unit in which N. brings together in compact form the results of a great deal of his systematic programme investigating the Mishnah, the work of many years. The first volume asks three basic questions, with a chapter devoted to each: (1) What is the relationship of the Mishnah ('oral Torah') to the Hebrew Bible ('written Torah')? (2) How are the developing religious ideas to be related to the events of the times in which they were being generated? (3) How does the formal language of the Mishnah express its religious views in the context of that society? He describes the origins of many of the mishnaic laws in the Second Temple period and the possible context in which they arose (though the development of the mishnaic *system* of law was not earlier than the second century CE), as well as how language in the Mishnah takes the place of ritual, with style being as important in expressing the message as the substance. The writings of Clifford Geertz are seen as particularly helpful. The second volume involves the three intellectual tasks of politics, economics and science. Aristotle is found to provide a surprising parallel to these topics as outlined in the Mishnah, drawing attention to the fact that the Mishnah was written by philosophers who expressed themselves in the form of law. It is stressed that the Mishnah is a systematic document, mapping a particular thought world, and not just a traditional document.

ED.

NEUSNER, JACOB, ALAN J. AVERY-PECK and WILLIAM SCOTT GREEN (eds.), *The Encyclopaedia of Judaism* (Leiden–Boston–Cologne: E.J. Brill, 2000), pp. xxxvi + 1592 (3 vols.). Nlg 495.00/$300.00. ISBN (set) 90-04-10583-2; (vol. 1) 90-04-11004-6; (vol. 2) 90-04-11005-4; (vol. 3) 90-04-11377-0.

Neusner, Avery-Peck and Green, who teach, respectively, at the University of South Florida, the College of the Holy Cross in Worcester, Massachusetts, and the University of Rochester, New York, have set out, with the collaboration of the Museum of Jewish Heritage in New York, to construct a reliable and readable guide to Jewish religious theory and practice from ancient to modern times, with broad coverage of social, economic and political factors as well as theological themes. They have proceeded on the assumption that Judaism is a living religion, to be respected as such (page xiv), but have employed a broadly based team of scholars (some of them the leading experts in their fields) to cover the 120 topics and have ensured that due attention has been paid to the interchange with Christianity and Islam. The volume is attractively designed, with some 200 figures, illustrations and maps, and there are 38 pages of indexes, as well as an editorial preface and an epilogue by the late Chaim Bermant. Of particular interest to biblical scholars will be the entries on circumcision (L.A. Hoffman), covenant (Avery-Peck), Dead Sea writings (J. Maier) and their Judaisms (P.R. Davies), exegesis of Scripture (H.W. Basser), idolatry (Avery-Peck), Israelite religion (Sara Mandell), Jesus (Bruce Chilton), Josephus (Steve Mason), ancient Israel (Mandell), Second Temple times (Lester Grabbe), mythology (S. Daniel Breslauer), pagan philosophers and historians (Robert Berchman and Stephen Stertz), translations of Scripture (Paul Flesher), sin (Avery-Peck) and biblical theology (K.-J. Illman).

The treatment is generally balanced and informative although there are occasional trends towards a more dogmatic approach as, for instance, in Mandell's first essay. The choice of contributors and topics must inevitably be subjective in such projects but the overall result here is satisfactory. The reviewer should perhaps also mention that Neusner has contributed almost a third of the entries, leaving little room for alternative interpretations in subjects of special interest to him; that insufficient account is sometimes taken of the fact that rabbinic Judaism was not always totally innovative and may have had some precedents in the pre-Christian period; that there is some inconsistency in the matters of bibliography, annotation, spelling and indexing; and that among leading Jewish scholars listed in the index there is not even one mention of such names as Saul Lieberman and E.E. Urbach. In sum, however, these three very full volumes will undoubtedly be found useful as a rich source of information about the Jewish religion.

S.C. REIF

ORTON, DAVID E. (ed.), *The Composition of Mark's Gospel: Selected Studies from Novum Testamentum* (Brill's Readers in Biblical Studies, 3; Leiden–Boston–Cologne: E.J. Brill, 1999), pp. ix + 272. Nlg 59.50/$34.00. ISBN 90-04-11340-1; ISSN 1389-1170.

This is primarily of interest to NT scholars, though there are occasional references to the OT. These mainly fall in the essays 'The Literary Structure of Mark 11.1–12.40' (Stephen H. Smith) and 'Markan Sandwiches: The Significance of Interpolations in Markan Narratives' (James R. Edwards).

ED.

PAPER, HERBERT H. (ed.), *Hebrew Union College Annual*, vol. 68 (Cincinnati: Hebrew Union College, 1997 [1998]), pp. (Eng.) 140 + (Heb.) 61. $20.00. ISSN 360-9049.

The current issue of the *Annual* contains its usual crop of items relating to the Hebrew Bible. Expanding on a view expressed by E.Y. Kutscher some 35 years ago, John Makujina undogmatically argues that the formula *sim ṭeʿem* of Daniel, Ezra and contemporary Aramaic letters is a calque from some such Old Persian phrase as *frāmānamaiy ništāyati* which was easily assimilated because of an existing Semitic construction. Some of the data in the Masorah to Onqelos are carefully analysed by Michael Klein in order to demonstrate how the translators made use of techniques of 'translational divergence' and how their choice of vocabulary took account of the original context, rabbinic interpretation and the synagogal setting. JoAnn Scurlock's folkloristic study compares attitudes to ghosts in the Hebrew Bible with those of ancient Mesopotamian, European and Chinese literature and concludes that many of the sources acknowledge the pitiable side of ghostly existence. Their assistance was nevertheless sought and their wrath feared so that even Israelites may have practised a form of ancestral cult to keep them under control. Joseph Fleishman suggests (in Hebrew and on mainly internal grounds) that the Book of Esther reflects a popular and widespread hatred of Jews in the Persian Empire and an assumption that support could easily be found for anti-Semitic aggression, both of which possibly arose as a response to the growing influence of monotheistic ideas and feelings about Jewish separatism. The remaining articles deal with talmudic, halakhic and Karaite themes (in English), and Ibn Ezra's grammatical terminology and Babylonian *piyyuṭ* (in Hebrew).

S.C. REIF

RENGSTORF, KARL HEINRICH (ed.), with the assistance of P. Freimark, W.E. Gerber, W.F. Krämer, G. Lisowsky, E. Lohse, G. Mayer and G. Schlichting, *Die Tosefta. Seder I: Zeraim, Text* (Rabbinische Texte: Reihe, 1; Stuttgart-Berlin-Cologne: Kohlhammer, 1994 [1983]), pp. xxiii + 341 (Heb.). DM 550.00/SwF 550.00/AS 4290. ISBN 3-17-002868-5.

This further instalment in the long-running *Rabbinische Texte* series publishes the Hebrew text of the first order of the Tosefta on the basis of the Erfurt manuscript with an apparatus of variants drawn from the Vienna and Zurich manuscripts, the Cairo Geniza fragments and the first printed edition of the Tosefta which appeared in the Venice 1521–22 printing of Alfasi. It offers a valuable alternative to the editions of Saul Lieberman (1955–88), who uses the Vienna manuscript as his base-text for this order, and of M.S. Zuckermandel (1880), who rather inaccurately transcribes and muddles up Erfurt and Vienna, but who still offers the only complete text of the Tosefta. The Rengstorf edition's use of the Zurich manuscript, in an Italian cursive of the seventeenth century, is noteworthy (see the description on p. xxi n. 43). However, the status of this manuscript is highly problematic (it may be copied from a printed text), and the sparse references to it in the *apparatus criticus* suggest that textually it is not very interesting. It is a pity that the apparatus does not list the divergent mediaeval quotations of the Tosefta which are of primary importance for the history of the text. This edition of *Tosefta Zer'im* follows an earlier edition of *Toharot* in the same series which appeared in 1967.

P.S. ALEXANDER

RUNIA, DAVID T. and GREGORY E. STERLING (ed.), *The Studia Philonica Annual: Studies in Hellenistic Judaism*, XI (BJS, 323; Atlanta: Scholars Press, 1999), pp. viii + 194. $34.95. ISBN 0-7885-0596-3.

This annual publication, with its now familiar format, retains its high standard and usefulness. This year there are four principal studies, all of them important not only to Philonists but to all concerned with Greek-speaking Judaism. Sterling examines the importance of Philo to his contemporaries and successors, Jewish and pagan, attempts to judge whether he was a real influence on neo-Platonic thought, and concludes that he received more attention than has been believed. Marin Niehoff explores the Jewish mother in Philo as a contribution to a significant but surprisingly neglected element in the construction of Jewish identity. Hindy Naiman looks at Philo's understanding of the authority of Torah against a background of Stoic ideas on the Law of Nature. Bernard Besnier offers a close reading in French of the allegory in *de Migratione Abrahami*. Of historical interest, and perhaps more, is Adam Kamesar's edition and translation from notes of an old attempt to emend a still-obscure phrase in Philo's narration of day one of the creation of the world. This is preceded with remarks on the author's role in the development of epigraphic studies at the Hebrew University. In the 'Instrumenta' section, Runia exploits a synoptic survey published by Françoise Petit on the back of her monumental edition of the *Catena in Genesim* to tabulate and analyse the direct or indirect citations to Philo that he finds in 73 of its lemmata. There is an annotated bibliography for 1996, with a supplement covering 1997–99 provisionally. Six book reviews include David Hay on Bruce Winter's *Philo and Paul among the Sophists* and Adele Reinhartz on Francesca Calabi's *Language and the Law of God*.

T. RAJAK

SCHÄFER, PETER (ed.), *The Talmud Yerushalmi and Graeco-Roman Culture I* (Texte und Studien zum Antiken Judentum, 71; Tübingen: J.C.B. Mohr [Paul Siebeck], 1998), pp. viii + 690. DM 178.00. ISBN 3-16-146857-0; ISSN 0721-8753.

This volume contains essays by members of the *Yerushalmi* project of the Institut für Judaistik of the Freie Universität Berlin (which is publishing the magnificent *Synopse zum Talmud Yerushalmi*), supplemented by papers delivered by experts from a number of different countries at a Conference held in Berlin in 1996 under the title, 'Text and Context: The Talmud Yerushalmi in its Graeco-Roman Environment'. The diverse contents, grouped under the headings Literature, History, Everyday Life, and Philosophy and Law, are all aimed at contextualizing the *Yerushalmi* in the world of late antiquity and showing that it broadly conforms to the cultural patterns of its time. In a thoughtful introduction S. notes that previous research in this subject has tended to define the problem in terms of the relationship between 'Judaism' and 'Hellenism'. Though he questions and probes this binary opposition he seems content in the end to define the culture in which he would contextualize the *Yerushalmi* as 'Hellenistic'. It is a pity he did not follow through the thrust of his analysis and abandon altogether the notion of Hellenism, which really does very little for the historiography of the fourth or fifth-century CE Levant. And, although the wide range of the volume's contents and its lack of methodological dogmatism are to be welcomed, some key topics are conspicuous by their absence. More, for example, could surely have been said about rabbinic schools. The distinctive literary features of the *Yerushalmi* are arguably all to be explained by the fact that it is a 'school' text of a type well attested in the schools of medicine, law, philosophy and engineering in late antiquity. The securest way of contextualizing the *Yerushalmi* in its world is through comparing and contrasting the organization, curriculum, methods of teaching and values of the rabbinic *Batei Midrash* with comparable institutations of higher learning in the Graeco-Roman world. Perhaps this topic will be addressed in the subsequent volume. Though there are many good things in this volume and it is somewhat invidious to single out particular contributions, the present reviewer found especially interesting the articles by Martin Jafee on 'The Oral-Cultural Context of the Talmud Yerushalmi', Leib Moscovitz on 'Double Readings in the Yerushlami', Tessa Rajak on 'The Rabbinic Dead and the Diaspora Dead at Beth She'arim', and Catherine Hezser on '"Privat" und "offentlich" im Talmud Yerushalmi und in der griechisch-römischen Antike' and 'The Codification of Legal Knowledge in Late Antiquity: The Talmud Yerushalmi and Roman Law Codes'.

P.S. ALEXANDER

SCHRECKENBERG, HEINZ, *Die christlichen Adversus-Judaeos-Texte und ihr literarisches und historisches Umfeld (1.-11. Jh.)* (Europäische Hochschulschriften, Reihe 23: Theologie, 172; Frankfurt–Bern–New York: Lang, 4th revised and enlarged edn, 1999), pp. 795. SwF 65.00. ISBN 3-631-33945-3; ISSN 0721-3409.

This first appeared in 1982 (not noticed in the *B.L.*) and presents an ambitious attempt to survey all the texts (Jewish included) relating to Christian 'adversus Judaeos' positions up to the Middle Ages. For this edition, a supplementary section adds bibliography to about 1997. One can add O. Limor and G. Stroumsa, *Contra Judaeos* (*B.L.* 1997, p. 147). There are good indexes, though these do not include the supplementary section.

ED.

SIEGERT, FOLKER and JACQUES DE ROULET (eds.), *Pseudo-Philon, Prédications synagogales: Traduction, notes et commentaire* (with the collaboration of Jean-Jacques Aubert and Nicholas Cochand; Sources Chrétiennes, 435; Paris: Cerf, 1999), pp. 220. FF 177.00. ISBN 2-204-06262-6; ISSN 0750-1978.

In a volume of 1980 S. published a German translation of three homilies attributed to Philo that survive only in Armenian, of which two, the homilies on Jonah and on Samson, are clearly not by Philo, but are anonymous Hellenistic-Jewish synagogue homilies; they probably were composed in Alexandria and date approximately from the time of Philo. In a subsequent volume in 1992, Siegert has also provided a valuable commentary on these texts (*B.L.* 1981, p. 128; *B.L.* 1993, pp. 149-50). The present work, in which Siegert has collaborated with French colleagues, now offers a French translation of the German version of the two homilies and an abridgement of the German commentary. But he has checked the translation and revised the commentary in some respects, so that the whole constitutes a kind of *editio minor correctior*. The volume also contains a very helpful introduction to the two texts. In commenting on the two German volumes (in *B.L.*) Sebastian Brock drew attention both to the importance of the homilies on Jonah and on Samson for the study of subsequent Jewish and Christian homiletical literature and to the neglect they had suffered at the hands of scholars. The publication of the present volume provides a welcome indication of a new interest in the homilies.

M.A. KNIBB

STEGEMANN, EKKEHARD W. and WOLFGANG STEGEMANN, *The Jesus Movement: A Social History of Its First Century* (trans. O.C. Dean, Jr; Edinburgh: T. & T. Clark; Minneapolis: Fortress Press, 1999), pp. xx + 532 + 2 maps, 8 tables, 6 figures. £29.95/$45.00. ISBN (Clark) 0-567-08688-7; (Fortress) 0-8006-2795-4.

This is an excellent book but of interest primarily to NT scholars. The book is a social history of the early Christian communities in the first century AD offering information on the economy and society (Part 1) and describing the social world of Jesus (Part 2) and the social history of the post-Jesus Christian communities in the urban Roman empire (Part 3). Part 4 explores the social roles and social situation of women in both the Mediterranean world (a term popularized by Bruce Malina) and in early Christianity. The focus of the book is on Jesus and the resulting Christian communities and touches on matters of concern to OT scholars only obliquely. For those interested in the subject of this book, I know of nothing as comprehensive or accessible in such compact form.

A. BUSH

STENSCHEKE, CHRISTOPH W., *Luke's Portrait of Gentiles Prior to their Coming to Faith* (WUNT, 2, Reihe 108; Tübingen: J.C.B. Mohr [Paul Siebeck], 1999), pp. xx + 458. DM 128.00. ISBN 3-16-147139-3; ISSN 0340-9570.

A number of recent studies address the issue of Jewish–Christian relations in the writings of Luke. This Aberdeen PhD thesis (under I.H. Marshall) wants to give balance by focusing on the Gentiles. Although S. attempts to address the subject in the context of our knowledge of Judaism of the time, and there are occasional references to the OT, most of this is dealt with in passing. This study will be primarily of interest to NT scholars. However, he does deal with the question of Luke's alleged anti-Jewish stance.

ED.

STERN, JOSEF, *Problems and Parables of Law: Maimonides and Nahmanides on Reasons for the Commandments* (Ta'amei Ha-Mitzvot) (SUNY Series in Judaica: Hermeneutics, Mysticism and Religion; Albany: State University of New York, 1998), pp. xiv + 201. $16.95. ISBN 0-7914-3824-4.

Though this book is not concerned with the original character of biblical law, but rather with the debate regarding its rationality among leading mediaeval Jewish philosophers, it contains much material from mediaeval Jewish Bible exegesis which can still prompt valuable hypotheses for the student of the original texts. Its six chapters, some revised from earlier publications, address *Ta'ame Hamitsvot* and the Philosophical Foundations of Judaism; Maimonides on the *Huqqim* and Antinomianism; Maimonides on Decrees of Scripture; Maimonides and Nahmanides on the Interpretation of Parables and Explanation of Commandments; Maimonides on the Parable of Circumcision; Maimonides and Nahmanides on the *Huqqim*, astrology and idolatry.

B.S. JACKSON

STOOPS, ROBERT F., JR and DENNIS R. MACDONALD, JR (eds.), *The Apocryphal Acts of the Apostles in Intertextual Perspectives* (Semeia, 80; Atlanta: Scholars Press, 1997), pp. v + 303. $40.00 (members $25.00) for 4 issues; $19.95 for a single issue. ISSN 0095-571X.

This has little to do with the OT, except for occasional references, but is an example of the application of intertextual study presently so popular. The relationship of the various non-canonical acts to the canonical NT literature is not a new subject, but some of the writers in this volume are willing to see some of the non-canonical literature as primary rather than secondary. H.W. Attridge argues that the Greek version of the *Acts of Thomas* shows mainly NT allusions but the Syriac recension shows more references to the OT, reflecting two different milieus for their development.

ED.

STROUMSA, GUY G., *Barbarian Philosophy: The Religious Revolution of Early Christianity* (WUNT, 112; Tübingen: J.C.B. Mohr [Paul Siebeck], 1999), pp. xii + 345. DM 178.00. ISBN 3-16-147105-9; ISSN 0512-1604.

As the title indicates, most of the essays in this volume relate to Christianity of the NT and the early patristic period. Several of the essays address themes in a Jewish context, however. An essay on Celsus, Origen and the nature of religion includes the subjects of the Jews and OT interpretation. Another addresses the question, 'From Anti-Judaism to Anti-Semitism in Early Christianity'. An essay on dreams and visions in early Christian discourse mentions the subject in relation to the Jews and the OT. There is also an essay on the early Christian group known as the Audians, including Jewish traditions known to them.

ED.

TARGARONA BORRÁS, JUDIT and ANGEL SÁENZ-BADILLOS (eds.), *Jewish Studies at the Turn of the Twentieth Century: Proceedings of the 6th EAJS Congress, Toledo, July 1998*. I. *Biblical, Rabbinical, and Medieval Studies* (Leiden–Boston–Cologne: E.J. Brill, 1999), pp. xiii + 635. Nlg 275.00/$162.00 (set). ISBN (set) 90-04-11559-5; (vol. 1) 90-04-11554-4.

TARGARONA BORRÁS, JUDIT and ANGEL SÁENZ-BADILLOS (eds.), *Jewish Studies at the Turn of the Twentieth Century: Proceedings of the 6th EAJS Congress, Toledo, July 1998*. II. *Judaism from the Renaissance to Modern Times* (Leiden–Boston–Cologne: E.J. Brill, 1999), pp. xv + 701. Nlg 275.00/$162.00 (set). ISBN (set) 90-04-11559-5; (vol. 2) 90-04-11558-7.

This set publishes almost 170 articles under the headings of (1) Hebrew and Jewish Languages, (2) Bible, Biblical Versions and Exegesis, (3) Rabbinic Period: History and Literature, (4) Middle Ages: Jewish History, Literature and Thought, (5) The Study of Judaism: Manuscripts, Books, and Media in vol. 1. In vol. 2 are (1) Jewish Mysticism and Philosophy, (2) Jewish Art, (3) Jewish Literature, (4) History and Sociology, (5) Sephardic Studies. Articles of interest include lexical analysis of the Copper Scroll, rabbinic Greek and Judaeo-Greek, Joshua and genocide (S.C. Ehrlich), Jeremiah's concept of the convenantal relationship, 50 years of research on the Dead Sea Scrolls and its impact on Jewish studies (F. García Martínez), the terminology of the law in the Second Temple period, Hezekiah as King Messiah in the Tannaitic tradition, the mythical background of the Wisdom of Solomon (A.P. Hayman) *aiōn* in Philo of Alexandria, the impact on Jewish studies of a century of Geniza research (S.C. Reif), resources in Jewish studies on your home computer, Hebrew manuscript fragments in the European archives, Jewish mysticism in the twentieth century (P. Schäfer), a survey of studies in Jewish art in the past 50 years (G. Sed-Rajna). Many of the contributions are in Spanish, reflecting the thriving work in Jewish studies in Spain at the present. The volumes are dedicated to the late Shelomo Morag who contributed the first essay of the collection: some observations on the revival and the oral legacy of Hebrew.

ED.

TYSON, JOSEPH B., *Luke, Judaism and the Scholars: Critical Approaches to Luke–Acts* (Columbia, SC: University of South Carolina Press, 1999), pp. xi + 196. $29.95. ISBN 1-57003-334-X.

This is primarily a survey of scholarship from F.C. Baur to the present, focusing on how scholars have interpeted Luke's treatment of Jews and Judaism. T. shows how the events of 1933–45 have had a major influence on how scholars have approached the subject.

ED.

VALLER, SHULAMIT, *Women and Womanhood in the Talmud* (trans. B.S. Rozen; foreword by J. Hauptman; BJS, 321; Atlanta: Scholars Press, 1999), pp. xx + 139. $29.95. ISBN 0-7885-0597-1.

V.'s aim in this short and fascinating volume is to analyse the editing process in some passages concerning women contained in the Babylonian Talmud (such as those dealing with dancing before brides, the procedures to be followed when a bride is not a virgin, women and wine, and so on). This analysis provides V. with clues to the attitudes of those doing the editing. While there can be no denying the overt patriarchal nature of the Jewish writings of the time or the society that produced them. V. demonstrates that the Sages sometimes show a sensitivity towards women and their feelings that forms a direct contrast to their public pronouncements. Interestingly, V. finds that there is a gap 'between the letter of the law and actual practice in matters connected with the status of women' (p. 122). The value of this clearly written and very scholarly book lies not just in its conclusions, important though these are, but in the methods of analysis used in examining the texts. Such methods could well be applied in other contexts. In addition, for those who are less familiar with the Talmudic literature, there is a useful introduction to it at the beginning of the book.

C. SMITH

VERMES, GEZA, *An Introduction to the Complete Dead Sea Scrolls* (London: SCM Press, 1999), pp. xxii + 256, including 2 maps. £14.95. ISBN 0-334-02784-5.

This is a new edition of the work that was originally published in 1977 under the title *The Dead Sea Scrolls: Qumran in Perspective* and has subsequently been republished more than once in slightly revised editions in England and America; see *B.L.* 1978 (p. 135) and (most recently) *B.L.* 1995 (p. 172). The most significant change made in the new edition is that the number of texts listed in the chapter on the contents of the Qumran library has been almost doubled, from 66 to 117. The selection of texts treated in this chapter is geared to the texts contained in *The Complete Dead Sea Scrolls in English*, although there are some slight differences between the two volumes in the way the texts are arranged in order. Apart from this, the text has been lightly revised for this new edition, and references to more recent publications have been added: but essentially this work retains its character as an introduction to scroll studies as they were at the time of its original publication in 1977.

M.A. KNIBB

VOS, CRAIG STEVEN DE, *Church and Community Conflicts: The Relationships of the Thessalonian, Corinthian, and Philippian Churches with their Wider Civic Communities* (SBLDS, 168; Atlanta: Scholars Press, 1999), pp. x + 332. $39.95. ISBN 0-7885-0563-7.

This book considers relations between Paul's churches and the wider civic communities in which those churches found themselves. The author explores in particular the Thessalonian, Corinthian and Philippian churches and how those churches 'interacted' with outsiders. In particular, the author wants to explore '*why some of Paul's churches experienced conflict with the wider civic communities and others did not*' (p. 5—author's italics). The author constructs a social-scientific model for explaining differences of incidence of conflict within different societies and cultures. His argument is that 'differences in...incidence of conflict...[are] the result of different attitudes, beliefs, social structures and other socio-cultural factors' (p. 8). One of the most interesting features of the book is the descriptions of church and civic community relations in Part 2. This will not be of significant interest to OT scholars as its primary focus is on three NT Pauline communities and the wider social world in which they were situated. The social-scientific model the author develops (and which he regards as needing further testing) does not immediately have relevance to the OT.

A. BASH

WEISS HALIVNI, DAVID, *Peshat and Derash: Plain and Applied Meaning in Rabbinic Exegesis* (Oxford Paperbacks; Oxford: Oxford University Press, 1998 [1991]), pp. xx + 249. £11.99. ISBN 0-19-511571-6.

Standing at the conservative extreme of Conservative Judaism, W. addresses in this book the tricky question why the Rabbis in their interpretation of Scripture (*derash*) sometimes deny the plain meaning (*peshat*) of the text. The answer, reduced to its essentials, is that they were not departing from the revealed truth but rather restoring it. After Moses, the sinful Israelites corrupted the revealed text. Ezra, after the Exile, restored the true meaning through the *derash* (cf. Ezra 7.10), so laying the foundations of the Oral Torah later developed by the Rabbis. By this device the author distances himself simultaneously from Orthodoxy, which rejects the principle of historical analysis of the tradition, and from the liberal wing of Conservative Judaism, which would adapt Halakhah to changing circumstances.

N.R.M. DE LANGE

WILLIAMS, DAVID S., *The Structure of 1 Maccabees* (CBQMS, 31; Washington, DC: The Catholic Biblical Association of America, 1999), pp. vi + 152. $7.00. ISBN 0-915170-30-2.

In this literary study W. uses the techniques of rhetorical criticism to provide an analysis of the structure of 1 Maccabees and in so doing offers an interesting follow-up to the 1984 study by N. Martola, which hitherto has been almost the only work to deal in any detail with the literary structure of the book. W. draws attention to repetition of words and, more importantly, of phrases in more than one literary unit as an important indication of structure, and in the light of his analysis of instances of repetition argues that 1 Maccabees consists of three main sections—1.1–6.17; 6.18–14.14; 14.16–16.24—the first two of which have a chiastic structure. Formal symmetries between the paired literary units within sections one and two are held to confirm the existence of the chiastic structures. W.'s analysis cuts across the common view that a major break in the book occurs at 9.22 (the death of Judas), but he claims that his analysis of 1.1–14.15 makes it possible to take account both of the traditional view that 1 Maccabees was written to glorify the Hasmonaean dynasty and of the view of Martola that its theme is the liberation of the temple and Jerusalem. W. also identifies 'double causality'—the interaction of divine aid and human initiative—as a third major theme in the book. In a final chapter, he argues in support of the view that 1 Maccabees originally ended at 14.15 and is perhaps to be dated about 130. The final section continues the themes of 1.1–14.15, but is also concerned to underline the role of Simon as the legitimate leader and of John as his worthy successor. The second edition, in which this final section was added, is perhaps to be dated about 100.

M.A. KNIBB

WILLIAMS, MARGARET H., *The Jews among the Greeks and Romans: A Diaspora Handbook* (London: Duckworth, 1998), pp. xv + 236, including 2 maps. £40.00; paper £14.99. ISBN 0-7156-2811-9; (paper) 0-7156-2812-7.

Specialists in Judaism in the Greek and Roman periods will be well aware of M. Stern's *Greek and Latin Authors on Jews and Judaism* (1974–84). W. has now produced a work designed primarily for students but a useful supplement to Stern. It is a collection of sources in English translation, drawing on Jewish literary works, Greek and Roman writers, Christian writings, and especially inscriptions, papyri and coins. The material is organized by topic under a number of subject headings, though the logic of the arrangement is far from clear. There is a concordance of the sources used and five indexes. This will be a useful handy reference for any student of Judaism in this period.

ED.

WINEMAN, ARYEH (ed.), *Mystic Tales from the Zohar* (Mythos; Princeton, NJ: Princeton University Press, 1998 [1997]), pp. ix + 161. $12.95. ISBN 0-691-05833-4.

The late thirteenth-century *Book of Splendour* (*Sefer ha-Zohar*) is the 'Bible' of the Spanish Qabbalah and arguably the single most influential text in the history of Jewish mysticism. In the past this sprawling work has tended to be mined for its theological and mystical ideas. It is, however, a work of immense literary power, 'a kind of expansive prose poem, the fruit of an almost unbounded imagination that draws from layer upon layer of earlier Jewish lore, adding to them [its] own mythic nuances and themes'. W.'s attractive little volume is part of a recent trend to stress the literary aspects of the Zohar and to see its numerous and often elaborate tales as being as central to its message as are Plato's myths to his Dialogues. W. selects a number of these stories, translates them and provides them with detailed notes and commentary which elucidate their content, set them within the context of the Zoharic *derush*, and explain their relationship to earlier tradition and to the wider Qabbalistic literature. The author or authors of the Zohar had an encyclopaedic knowledge of earlier Jewish tradition and have preserved and reinterpreted some very ancient motifs. For example, as W. shows, the exposition of *zeh sefer toledot adam* in Gen. 5.1 contains allusions to the idea of heavenly books which can be traced back through the Midrash, Second Temple Apocalyptic and the Bible to Babylonia. This is a work of real quality, an excellent introduction to the world of the Zohar.

P.S. ALEXANDER

YINGER, KENT L., *Paul, Judaism, and Judgment According to Deeds* (SNTSMS, 105; Cambridge: Cambridge University Press, 1999), pp. xiv + 318. £40.00/$64.95. ISBN 0-521-63243-9.

This is an excellent book and well worth reading. The question Y. asks is 'Why does the apostle [Paul] appear to sense no serious tension between judgment according to deeds and justification by faith?' (p. 15). The answer is that Paul demonstrates 'fundamental continuity with second temple Jewish sources' (pp. 15-16). In Part 1, Y. explores judgment according to deeds in Jewish literature (the Jewish Scriptures, the OT Pseudepigrapha and Qumran literature); Part 2 is an exploration of judgment according to deeds in Paul's letters (including Colossians). The conclusion is that the motif of judgment according to deeds is surprisingly widespread in Judaism and that NT writers are drawing upon an axiomatic theological conviction. The motif is, according to Y., set in the framework of covenantal nomism and he concludes: 'Within this framework of covenantal nomism, divine judgment according to works functions to confirm or reveal one's fundamental loyalty to God and his covenant. One does not *become* righteous at this judgment, but one's righteousness is revealed or confirmed' (pp. 285-86). This is a first-rate book and is highly recommended for those interested in the question.

A. BASH

10. PHILOLOGY AND GRAMMAR

BENNETT, PATRICK R., *Comparative Semitic Linguistics: A Manual* (Winona Lake, IN: Eisenbrauns, 1999), pp. xii + 269, including many maps. $29.50. ISBN 1-57506-021-3.

'This modest book is not a source for comparative Semitic grammar and lexicon; it is a collection of tools for Semitic reconstruction' (p. 1). It is intended for readers with at least one year's study of a Semitic language. The seven parts, or chapters, deal with (1) descriptive linguistics, (2) the Semitic family of languages, (3) an outline of comparative linguistics, (4) lexicostatistics, (5) linguistic reconstruction, (6) less-common techniques, (7) 'Onward and Beyond'. The rest (more than half) of the book consists of paradigms of phonology and morphology, a bibliography, nine word lists (one of them containing many maps illustrating isoglosses), an appendix by P.T. Daniels on classical Semitic scripts, and indexes of languages of glosses, and of glosses. There are 25 exercises. The bibliography does not claim to be complete, but there are some surprising omissions. For example, the first edition of the Hebrew lexicon by L. Koehler and W. Baumgartner is listed, but not the more useful third. The list of periodicals fails to mention *Vetus Testamentum*. Amid much that is accurate, it is strange to find the Hebrew numeral for 'one' printed as *'eḥad* with the second vowel as *pathaḥ* (in both transliteration and Hebrew type), and the Hebrew noun *laylâ* 'night' described as feminine (p. 31). This book can serve a useful purpose, preferably with the help of a teacher (if the reader is not to fail to see the wood for the trees).

J.A. EMERTON

BLACK, MATTHEW, *An Aramaic Approach to the Gospels and Acts* (with an introduction by Craig Evans; Peabody, MA: Hendrickson, 3rd, edn, 1998 [1967]), pp. xxxii + 359. $24.95/£14.99. ISBN 1-56563-086-6.

This is a reprint of the third edition of Matthew Black's classic study, which includes the well-known appendix by Geza Vermes on the expression *bar nāsh/bar nāshā'*, reviewed in *B.L.* 1968, pp. 67-68. Both the introduction (pp. v-xvii) and bibliography (pp. xvii-xxv) are surprisingly brief and limited in scope, and offer only a somewhat partial account of some developments in Aramaic scholarship over the last 30 years or so.

C.T.R. HAYWARD

CHISHOLM, ROBERT B., JR, *From Exegesis to Exposition: A Practical Guide to Using Biblical Hebrew* (Grand Rapids, MI: Baker Book House, 1998), pp. 304. $19.99. ISBN 0-8010-2171-5.

The concept is a bold one: to show seminarians and seminary-trained pastors how to 'preach accurate, informative, and even exciting sermons that are solidly rooted in the Hebrew text and do not require an inordinate amount of time to pre-pare'. Since few seminarians in Britain and Ireland study any Hebrew at all, the book might be thought irrelevant to all but those few, but it also makes a valiant effort to prove that Hebrew is worth the time and the effort. The focus is on the prin-ciples and methods of exegesis of the Hebrew Bible, introducing language tools (books and computer-based tools), discussing the evaluation of readings in textual criticism, illustrating the potential and the pitfalls of biblical Hebrew semantics, giving an account of Hebrew syntax and its importance for exegesis, describing biblical stylistics, and so on. Sections are accompanied by suggested exercises (e.g. on the lexical analysis of Gen. 6.5-13) and bibliographies. Although aimed at trainee pastors the book is thought-provoking and entertaining at the same time as being didactic. It could be used profitably by theology students in general, indeed by all intermediate students of biblical Hebrew.

J.F. HEALEY

CLINES, DAVID J.A. (ed.), *The Dictionary of Classical Hebrew.* IV.ל–י (Sheffield: Sheffield Academic Press, 1998), pp. 642. £50.00/$75.00. ISBN 1-85075-681-3.

With the publication, right on schedule, of Volume IV, the immense task under-taken by the Sheffield lexicography team is half done. This will probably turn out to be the longest of the eight volumes, because it covers a disproportionately large number of words occurring more than 1000 times (כל, ידע, יד, יום, ישראל, יהוה, כי, ל, לא, etc.). Except in the case of the very frequently occurring prepositions כ (3200×) and ל (26,000×), and the negative particles לא (6500×), every occurrence of every word is recorded in the dictionary, and the editor wishes it to be known that every single one of these occurrences has actually been looked up by hand. Despite the ready accessibility of electronic concordances and modern resources, everything written in the *Dictionary* has 'passed through the mind of a living Hebraist'. This applies even to a word like יהוה which occurs over 7000 times. On the other hand, readers who were confident that, for the authors of the new Sheffield *Dictionary*, gratuitious 'etymologizing' was a thing of the past, will be intrigued to find two separate entries for יום, three for יד and no less then thirteen for ידע.

J.F.A. SAWYER

HANSACK, ERNST, *Die altrussische Version des 'Jüdischen Krieges': Unter-suchungen zur Integration der Namen* (Slavica, 1; Heidelberg: Universitätsverlag C. Winter, 1999), pp. 560. DM 128.00/AS 934/SwF 114.00. ISBN 3-8253-0888-X.

This has two main aims: to investigate how the names of Josephus's *Bellum*

Judaicum were taken over in the Old Russian translation (as a first stage in compiling a dictionary of names for Old Slavonic translation literature) and to investigate the character of the translation's *Vorlage*. The answer to the latter: a Greek original was used, one similar to the standard Greek text of today. Robert Eisler's theory that a Jewish translator worked from a Hebrew-Aramaic *Vorlage* is to be rejected. The present Old Russian version is probably a reworking (in the latter half of the eleventh century) of an Old Church Slavonic version dating from the tenth century. This is a dense textual study and forms a welcome addition to a neglected area of Josephan scholarship.

ED.

HORBURY, WILLIAM (ed.), *Hebrew Study from Ezra to Ben-Yehuda* (Edinburgh: T. & T. Clark, 1999), pp. xiv + 337. £39.95. ISBN 0-567-08602-X.

These 22 essays, among which Cambridge scholarship is especially well represented, form a useful complement to A. Sáenz-Badillos's *History of the Hebrew Language* (*B.L.* 1994, p. 162). A cheaper edition is a desideratum, as this is a volume which could profit many scholars, not just linguists, in the areas of postexilic and post-biblical Judaism, Christian Hebraism and Modern Hebrew language and literature. From a purely linguistic viewpoint, the contributions by Philip S. Alexander ('How Did the Rabbis Learn Hebrew?') and Edward Ullendorff ('Hebrew in Mandatary Palestine') are outstanding. The papers by Joachim Schaper ('Hebrew and its Study in the Persian Period') and Jonathan Campbell ('Hebrew and its Study at Qumran') are valuable surveys that contribute particularly to our understanding of the role of the *sōpēr māhīr* and the importance of Aramaic vis-à-vis Hebrew in the Dead Sea Scrolls. Also of interest to students of the Second Temple period are James Atken's study of Ben Sira's use of the Hebrew Bible and Jan Willem van Henten on 'The Ancestral Language of the Jews in 2 Maccabees'. Robert Hayward provides a detailed analysis of Jerome's transcription and interpretation of the names of the high-priestly vestments (comparing and contrasting with Philo and Josephus), and Graham Davies examines sixteenth-century renderings of elements from Exod. 15 (*zèh, zū, yām, sūp*, tenses in vv. 13-18). Nicholas de Lange's ground-breaking survey of 'A Thousand Years of Hebrew in Byzantium' and the papers by Judith Olszowy-Schlanger and Geoffrey Khan on Hebrew in the Karaite tradition are outstanding representatives of the rest of this excellent volume.

J.F. ELWOLDE

KHAN, GEOFFREY, *A Grammar of Neo-Aramaic: The Dialect of the Jews of Arbel* (Handbuch der Orientalistik: Erste Abteilung, Der Nahe und Mittlere Osten: 47. Band; Leiden–Boston–Cologne: E.J. Brill, 1999), pp. xxi + 586. Nlg 220.00/$129.50. ISBN 90-04-11510-2; ISSN 0169-9423.

A number of studies of neo-Aramaic have appeared recently (*B.L.* 1994, p. 158; 1995, p. 177; 1998, p. 216), and this is a welcome addition. Some such dialects continue in use and can be studied *in situ*, but others are rapidly dying out, such as the one here. This particular dialect was spoken by Jewish groups in Iraq until they migrated to Israel about 1951, where the dialect is nearing extinction. It is part of the North-Eastern Neo-Aramaic sub-family. The grammatical description is based mainly on the stories collected in field work by the author and printed in transcription and translation at the end of the book. All vocabulary known to the author (whether part of the texts or not) is collected into a glossary, though a considerable portion of it is Kurdish or Arabic in origin (or came via Kurdish). All students of Aramaic will be grateful not only for this detailed descriptive study but also for the work of the author in saving these valuable date from irretrievable loss.

L.L. GRABBE

KOEHLER, LUDWIG and WALTER BAUMGARTNER (eds.), subsequently revised by Walter Baumgartner and Johann Jakob Stamm, with assistance from B. Hartmann, Z. Ben-Hayyim, E.Y. Kutscher and P. Reymond, *The Hebrew and Aramaic Lexicon of the Old Testament*. IV. שׂ–ת (trans. and ed. under the supervision of M.E.J. Richardson; Leiden–Boston–Cologne: E.J. Brill, 1999), pp. vi + 1365-1803. Nlg 259.00/$144.00. ISBN (vol. 4) 90-04-10076-8; (set) 90-04-09700-8.

This completes the Hebrew section of *HAL*, previous parts being reviewed in *B.L.* 1995 (p. 178), 1996 (p. 164), 1998 (p. 217). Although illness has caused a slight hiatus, the way that M.E.J. Richardson and his team have pushed this translation forward is a model of industry. It is hoped and expected that the final volume, with Aramaic and indexes will appear shortly and bring this most worthwhile project to a rapid close.

ED.

MERWE, CHRISTO H.J. VAN DER, JACKIE A. NAUDÉ and JAN H. KROEZE, *A Biblical Hebrew Reference Grammar* (Biblical Languages: Hebrew, 3; Sheffield: Sheffield Academic Press, 1999), pp. 404. £50.00/$85.00; paper £18.95/$29.95. ISBN 1-85075-861-1; (paper) 1-85075-856-5.

The purpose of this useful grammar is to provide a tool for moving an 'ordinary interpreter' (p. 10) of biblical Hebrew from a basic to an intermediate stage. Thus, its guiding principles have much to do with didactic issues: there are copious English examples, translations mainly follow the RSV, charts and tables are plentiful and appear at the appropriate point in the text, discussions with recent studies of biblical Hebrew are scarce. In fact, it 'avoids discussing problems regarding the description of B[iblical] H[ebrew]' (!). This is a competent work which may serve its intended audience well. I wonder, however, if the limitations outweigh the benefits. A 'reference grammar' in classical Hebrew studies usually refers to something like the venerable GKC: a comprehensive description of the language, raising problems, discussing anomalies, and offering possible solutions. This work runs the risk of confusing students by its very brevity. One small example: the awkward overlap between determination in biblical Hebrew and modern English is well known, and there are some 'textbook' problem examples; here, however none is noted and a bare notice that 'BH differs from English' is offered with no further guidance other than to be careful! The majority of space is taken up with morphology; I would have thought the balance for this readership should tip towards syntax. Likewise, its highly select bibliography (collected at the end of the volume: perhaps better styled a 'reference list'?) offers little further guidance. In sum, this will be a useful book for reinforcing a basic course in biblical Hebrew, but there are probably better options for significantly advancing students beyond the elementary level.

D.J. REIMER

MILLER, CYNTHIA L. (ed.), *The Verbless Clause in Biblical Hebrew: Linguistic Approaches* (Linguistic Studies in Ancient West Semitic, 1; Winona Lake, IN: Eisenbrauns, 1999), pp. xi + 368. $39.50. ISBN 1-57506-036-1.

These twelve papers, written in a lucid and explanatory style, could perhaps form the basis of an advanced class in Hebrew syntax, as most of them do not require too great a struggle with modern linguistic theory: the editor's introductory survey; Walter Groß's arguments against the concept of the 'compound nominal clause' (i.e. noun-verb as against verb-noun [verbal] or noun-noun [nominal]) in biblical Hebrew; Cameron Sinclair on deriving nominal clauses from ellipsis of clauses with *hāyāh*; Randall Buth on word-order (an example of how to present linguistic theory in an unfrightening way); Takamitsu Muraoka on tripartite nominal clauses (which include a 'copulative' pronoun); Alviero Niccacci on 'Types and Functions of the Nominal Sentence'; Kirk E. Lowery's preliminary attempts to distinguish subject and predicate in nominal clauses on the basis of the varying 'definiteness' of the parts of speech that fill these slots; Lénart J. de Regt on the textual function of nominal clauses in Genesis, Deuteronomy, Joshua, Judges, Esther, Ruth, Ezra and Nehemiah; and E.J. Revell on nominal clause word order in Judges, Samuel and Kings (contextually rather than grammatically determined). The remaining contributions are by Vincent DeCaen, Janet W. Dyk and Eep Talstra, and Ellen van Wolde.

J.F. ELWOLDE

MUCHIKI, YOSHIYUKI, *Egyptian Proper Names and Loanwords in North-West Semitic* (SBLDS, 173; Atlanta: Scholars Press, 1999), pp. xxv + 357. $48.00. ISBN 0-88414-004-0.

From Burchardt (1911) via Albright and Edel (among others) down to Hoch (*B.L.* 1995, p. 176), several invaluable reference-works have documented Semitic terms found in ancient Egyptian texts. In contrast, no equivalent work had listed and studied Egyptian words found in Semitic languages, beyond a few incomplete papers. Hence, M.'s book very neatly fills the gap. It systematically lists Egyptian words and names attested in Phoenician/Punic, Aramaic (mainly 'imperial'), biblical and epigraphic Hebrew, Ugaritic and Amarna 'Canaanite', establishing reliable overall equivalences between Egyptian and Northwest Semitic consonantal phonemes for the first time. These sometimes differ from one Northwest Semitic language to another—and as between words passing from Egyptian into Semitic and vice-versa, it should be noted; a new result is that spirantization can be seen to have originated with Phoenician (not Aramaic). There is a sprinkling of English misprints, but none affect the sense. This book provides a convenient, reliable and comprehensive reference-work.

K.A. KITCHEN

MURAOKA, T. and J.F. ELWOLDE (eds.), *Sirach, Scrolls, and Sages: Proceedings of a Second International Symposium on the Hebrew of the Dead Sea Scrolls, Ben Sira, and the Mishnah, held at Leiden University, 15–17 December 1997* (STDJ, 33; Leiden–Boston–Cologne: E.J. Brill, 1999), pp. vii + 364. Nlg 190.00/$106.00. ISBN 90-04-11553-6; ISSN 0169-9962.

The articles in this volume include the semantics of 'glory' in Ben Sira (J.K. Aitken), nominal clauses with locative and possessive predicates in Qumran Hebrew (M.F.J. Baasten), the Hebrew text of Ben Sira 32(35).16–33(36).2 (P.C. Beentjes), an unusual use of the definite article in biblical and post-biblical Hebrew (M. Ehrensvärd), some lexical structures in 1QH (Elwolde), word order in Ben Sira (S.E. Fassberg), the linguistic profile of Ben Sira (A. Hurvitz), pseudo-classicisms in Late Hebrew (J. Joosten), notes on biblical expressions and allusions and the lexicography of Ben Sira (M. Kister), the participle in Qumran Hebrew (Muraoka), linguistic analysis of 4QMMT (M. Pérez Fernández), negation in Ben Sira (W.T. van Peursen), derivation of the noun תשבוחת in Qumran Hebrew (E. Qimron), Ben Sira's use of כרת (F.V. Reiterer), the participle as main verb in direct discourse and narrative in pre-Mishnaic Hebrew (M.S. Smith), a comparison of prescriptive text types—Qumran and Mishnah (N.A. van Uchelen), the language of the Hebrew Bible contrasted with Ben Sira and the Scrolls (J.W. Wesselius).

ED.

RABIN, CHAIM, *The Development of the Syntax of Post-Biblical Hebrew* (foreword by Lewis Glinert; Studies in Semitic Languages and Linguistics, 29; Leiden–Boston–Cologne: E.J. Brill, 2000), pp. xv + 205. Nlg 175.00/$103.00. ISBN 90-04-11433-5; ISSN 0081-8461.

The late R. submitted a DPhil thesis to Oxford in 1943, but it has remained unpublished and largely unknown until now. It was a study of syntax in the Hebrew writings of Jews in Southern France and Spain from the twelfth to the fifteenth centuries. The thesis is printed unrevised, with only an index of passages added.

ED.

SMITH, RICHARD, *A Concise Coptic–English Lexicon* (SBLRBS, 35; Atlanta: Scholars Press, 2nd edn, 1999 [1983]), pp. xvii + 59. $36.00. ISBN 0-7885-0561-0.

Intended as a basic tool for classroom use, '[t]his lexicon is fundamentally a Sahidic lexicon' (p. xiii) and was largely compiled as an aid to reading the Nag Hammadi codices, discovered in 1954. A brief introduction and a bibliography are supplied. The first edition (1983) of this very handy concise lexicon has now been corrected and revised.

W.G.E. WATSON

TAKÁCS, GÁBOR, *Etymological Dictionary of Egyptian*. I. *A Phonological Introduction* (Handbuch der Orientalistik: Erste Abteilung, Der Nahe und Mittlere Osten: 48/1. Band; Leiden–Boston–Cologne: E.J. Brill, 1999), pp. xix + 471. Nlg 240.00/ $141.50. ISBN 90-04-11538-1; ISSN 0169-9423.

During the last century, the relationship of ancient Egyptian to early Semitic languages (in terms of cognates) has been well studied. Both ancient Egyptian and the early Semitic languages reach back in parallel through the last three millennia BC in first-hand written documents. By contrast, the relations of ancient Egyptian with neighbouring African languages have been much less studied, usually on too narrow a basis, and such work must contend with the fact that (apart from Meroitic, not fully deciphered!) we have no written ancient African corpus contemporary with early Egyptian and Semitic. The present work is an introductory volume to a forthcoming full dictionary of Egyptian with its cognates both in Semitic and in African languages from the Red Sea to Morocco. It presents the consonantal equivalents between Egyptian and its neighbours with back-up examples. These seem to be sound; only the full data will confirm this. If so, this is a massive and major contribution to its field.

K.A. KITCHEN

VAN VOORST, ROBERT E., *Building Your New Testament Greek Vocabulary* (SBLRBS, 40; Atlanta: Scholars Press, 2nd edn, 1999 [1990]), pp. xii + 107. $7.50. ISBN 0-7885-0552-1.

As indicated by the title, this is a learning aid for students of New Testament Greek wishing to build a vocabulary base sufficient for fluent reading of the New Testament. It is based on the 'frequency' principle with the added advantage of grouping words by 'families', and also includes an introduction to the way Greek words are formed, and lists of prepositions, conjunctions etc. and principal parts. While the provision of one meaning per word can mislead, any aid and encouragement for students to learn vocabulary is to be welcomed, and this is well laid out and probably as user-friendly as possible.

J. LIEU

XELLA, PAOLO (ed.), *Studi epigrafici e linguistici sul Vicino Oriente antico, vol. 15* (Verona: Essedue edizioni, 1998), pp. 131. Lire 50,000. ISBN 88-85697-49-6.

The issue for 1998 is on the theme of 'Magic in the Ancient Near East'. The opening survey and bibliography (S. Ribichini) includes a section on magic in ancient Israel for research on which the studies comprising this issue provide rich comparative material. They are on the following topics: magic and divination in Ebla (A. Catagnoti and M. Bonechi), Sumerian incantations (G. Cunningham), the way 'in which an Akkadian prayer treats or presents the experience of illness, suffering and death brought on by an attack of witchcraft' (T. Abusch), magic in Assyrian hemerologies and menologies (A. Livingstone), magic in a Hittite ritual

(G. Torri) and Late Egyptian magic (J.F. Quack). The closing study, on the iconography of incantation bowls (E.C.D. Hunter), has illustrations and in an appendix the text and annotated translation of a bowl from the Iraq Museum. Finally, there are book reviews.

W.G.E. WATSON

BOOKS RECEIVED TOO LATE FOR NOTICE IN 2000

The books in the following list came after copy went to press for the 2000 issue and will be reviewed in the *Book List* for 2001.

AUWERS, JEAN-MARIE, *La composition littéraire du Psautier: un état de la question* (Cahiers de la Revue Biblique, 46; Paris: Gabalda, 2000), pp. 230. FF 250.00. ISBN 2-85021-119-2; ISSN 0575-0741.

BALLARD, HAROLD WAYNE, JR, *The Divine Warrior Motif in the Psalms* (Bibal Dissertation Series, 6; N. Richland Hills, TX: BIBAL Press, 1999), pp. xi + 155. $15.95. ISBN 0-94103748-7.

BAUMANN, GERLINDE, *Liebe und Gewalt: Die Ehe also Metapher für das Verhältniss JHWH—Israel in den Prophetenbüchern* (Stuttgarter Bibelstudien, 185; Stuttgart: Katholisches Bibelwerk, 2000), pp. 261. DM 49.80/AS364/SwF 47.00/ EUR 25.46. ISBN 3-460-04851-4.

BEN ZVI, EHUD, *Micah* (FOTL, 21B; Grand Rapids, MI: Eerdmans, 2000; distributed in the UK by Alban Books, Bristol), pp. xvi + 189. $35.00/£23.99. ISBN 0-8028-4599-1.

BEUKEN, WILLEM A.M., *Isaiah II, Volume 2: Isaiah 28-39* (Historical Commentary on the Old Testament; Leuven: Peeters, 2000), pp. xxxi + 420. BEF 1800. ISBN 90-429-0813-0.

BOTTERWECK, G. JOHANNES, HELMER RINGGREN and HEINZ-JOSEF FABRY (eds.), *Theological Dictionary of the Old Testament*. X. נקם־עזב *nāqam–'āzaḇ* (trans. Douglas W. Stott; Grand Rapids, MI: Eerdmans, 1999; distributed in the UK by Alban Books, Bristol), pp. xxiv + 592. $48.00/£29.99. ISBN 0-8028-2334-3.

BRIGHT, PAMELA (ed. and trans.), *Augustine and the Bible* (The Bible through the Ages, 2; Notre Dame, IN: University of Notre Dame, 1999), pp. xvi + 352. $30.00. ISBN 0-268-00655-5.

BRODIE, THOMAS L., OP, *The Crucial Bridge: The Elijah-Elisha Narrative as an Interpretive Synthesis of Genesis–Kings and a Literary Model for the Gospels* (Collegeville, MN: Michael Glazier [Liturgical Press], 2000), pp. xiii + 114. $11.95. ISBN 0-8146-5942-X.

BROYLES, CRAIG C., *Psalms* (NICOT, 11; Peabody, MA: Hendrickson; Carlisle: Paternoster, 1999), pp. xvi + 539. ISBN (Henrickson) 1-56563-220-6; (Paternoster) 0-85364-732-1.

BRUEGGEMANN, WALTER, *Texts that Linger, Words that Explode: Listening to Prophetic Voices* (ed. Patrick D. Miller; Minneapolis: Fortress Press, 1999), pp. xi + 140. $16.00. ISBN 0-8006-3231-1.

COLLINS, JOHN J., *Between Athens and Jerusalem: Jewish Identity in the Hellenistic Diaspora* (The Biblical Resource Series; Grand Rapids, MI: Eerdmans; Livonia, MI: Dove Booksellers, 2nd edn, 2000; distributed in the UK by Alban Books, Bristol), pp. xvi + 327. $32.00/£19.99. ISBN 0-8028-4372-7.

EGO, BEATE, ARMIN LANGE and PETER PILHOFER (eds.), in conjunction with Kathrin Ehlers, *Gemeinde ohne Tempel/Community without Temple: Zur Substituierung und Transformation des Jerusalem Tempels und seines Kults im Alten Testament, antiken Judentum und frühen Christentum* (WUNT, 118; Tübingen: J.C.B. Mohr [Paul Siebeck], 1999), pp. x + 519. DM 218.00. ISBN 3-16-147050-8; ISSN 0512-1604.

FLOYD, MICHAEL H., *Minor Prophets*, part 2 (FOTL, 22; Grand Rapids, MI: Eerdmans, 2000; distributed in the UK by Alban Books, Bristol), pp. xviii + 651. $49.00/£30.00. ISBN 0-8028-4452-9.

FOWL, STEPHEN E., *Engaging Scripture: A Model for Theological Interpretation* (Oxford: Basil Blackwell, 1998), pp. vii + 219. £55.00/$62.95; paper £16.99/$28.95. ISBN 0-631-20863-1; (paper) 0-631-20864-X.

FREEDMAN, DAVID NOEL, *Psalm 119: The Exaltation of Torah* (with Jeffrey C. Geoghegan and Andrew Welch; Biblical and Judaic Studies from the University of California, San Diego, 6; Winona Lake, IN: Eisenbrauns, 1999), pp. vii + 94. $19.50. ISBN 1-57506-038-8.

GERTZ, JAN CHRISTIAN, *Tradition und Redaktion in der Exoduserzählung: Untersuchungen zur Endredaktion des Pentateuch* (FRLANT, 186; Göttingen: Vandenhoeck & Ruprecht, 2000), pp. 438. DM 144.00. ISBN 3-525-53870-7.

JASPER, DAVID and STEPHEN PRICKETT (eds.), assisted by Andrew Hass, *The Bible and Literature: A Reader* (Oxford: Basil Blackwell, 1999), pp. xv + 333. £55.00/$62.95; paper £15.99/$29.95. ISBN 0-631-20856-9; (paper) 0-631-20857-7.

KNIBB, MICHAEL A., *Translating the Bible: The Ethiopic Version of the Old Testament* (Schweich Lectures of the British Academy 1995; published for the British Academy by Oxford University Press, 1999), pp. xii + 145. £20.00. ISBN 0-19-726194-9.

KUTSKO, JOHN F., *Between Heaven and Earth: Divine Presence and Absence in the Book of Ezekiel* (Biblical and Judaic Studies from the University of California, San Diego, 7; Winona Lake, IN: Eisenbrauns, 2000), pp. xiv + 185. $29.50. ISBN 1-57506-041-8.

LOHFINK, NORBERT, SJ, and ERICH ZENGER, *The God of Israel and the Nations: Studies in Isaiah and the Psalms* (trans. Everett R. Kalin; Collegeville, MN: Michael Glazier [Liturgical Press], 2000), pp. vii + 234. $39.95. ISBN 0-8146-5925-X.

MINETTE DE TILLESSE, CAETANO (ed.), *Revista Bíblica Brasileira*, Ano 17, Número especial 1-3: C. Minette de Tillesse (trans.), *Apócrifos do Antigo Testamento*, vol. II (Fortaleza, Brazil: Nova Jerusalém, 2000), pp. 591. $50.00 (US) p. a.

OEMING, MANFRED, *Das Buch der Psalmen: Psalm 1-41* (Neuer Stuttgarter Kommentar: Altes Testament, 13/1; Stuttgart: Katholisches Bibelwerk, 2000), pp. 232. DM 44.00/AS 321/SwF 42.00/EUR 20.25. ISBN 3-460-07131-1.

PETERSON, EUGENE H., *First and Second Samuel* (Westminster Bible Companion; Louisville, KY: Westminster/John Knox Press, 1999), pp. xii + 270. £9.99. ISBN 0-664-25523-X.

REIF, STEFAN C., *A Jewish Archive from Old Cairo: The History of Cambridge University's Genizah Collection* (Culture and Civilisation in the Middle East, 3; Richmond, Surrey: Curzon, 2000), pp. xx + 277. £35.00; paper £14.99 ISBN 0-7007-1276-3; (paper) 0-7007-1312-3.

ROSSING, BARBARA R., *The Choice between Two Cities: Whore, Bride, and Empire in the Apocalypse* (Harvard Theological Studies, 48; Harrisburg, PA: Trinity Press International, 1999), pp. xv + 180. ISBN 1-56338-294-6.

SCHNEIDER, TAMMI J., *Judges* (Berit Olam, Studies in Hebrew Narrative and Poetry; Collegeville, MN: Liturgical Press, 2000), pp. xxi + 317. $34.95. ISBN 0-8146-5050-3.

SLAVITT, DAVID R., *The Book of the Twelve Prophets* (New York and Oxford: Oxford University Press, 2000), pp. xv + 133. £13.95. ISBN 0-19-513214-9.

TURNER, LAURENCE A., *Genesis* (Readings: A New Biblical Commentary; Sheffield Academic Press, 2000), pp. 229. £35.00/$57.50; paper £13.95/$23.75. ISBN 1-84127-033-4; (paper) 1-84127-034-2. ISSN 0952-7656.

INDEX OF PUBLISHERS

The Society for Old Testament Study is a British Society for Old Testament Scholars. Candidates for membership, which is not confined to British subjects, must be nominated by two members of the Society. All correspondence concerning membership and domestic affairs of the Society should be sent to:

Dr John Jarick
Department of Theology and Religious Studies
University of Surrey Roehampton
Southlands College
80 Roehampton Lane
London SW15 5SL
England